ILOKANO DICTIONARY

PALI LANGUAGE TEXTS: PHILIPPINES

Social Sciences and Linguistics Institute
University of Hawaii

Howard P. McKaughan
Editor

ILOKANO DICTIONARY

ERNESTO CONSTANTINO

The University Press of Hawaii
Honolulu

The work reported herein was performed pursuant to a contract with the Peace Corps, Washington, D.C. 20525. The opinions expressed herein are those of the author and should not be construed as representing the opinions or policies of any agency of the United States government.

First printing 1971
Second printing 1976

Library of Congress Catalog Card Number 78-152462
ISBN 0-87022-152-3
Manufactured in the United States of America

INTRODUCTION

This *Ilokano Dictionary* has been prepared by Ernesto Constantino, professor of linguistics at the University of the Philippines. Professor Constantino was on a research leave, appointed as the associate director of this project under which materials for seven Philippine languages have been developed. The project was supported by a contract with the Peace Corps (PC25-1507), and Dr. Constantino with the other developers worked through the Pacific and Asian Linguistics Institute of the University of Hawaii under the general direction of the undersigned, editor of the materials.

The dictionary is a part of a series including *Ilokano Lessons* by Emma Bernabe and Virginia Lapid and an *Ilokano Reference Grammar* by Dr. Constantino. These in turn are part of a larger series which contains similar materials for six other Philippine languages (Bikol, Cebuano, Hiligaynon, Kapampangan, Pangasinan, and Tagalog).

The Ilokano dictionary includes basically lexical entries of word length, but also has some affixes and idioms used in the language. Entries are followed by an indication of the word class if pertinent (designated by the usual abbreviations) and then the major affixes that occur with the particular entry.

Since many words may occur in more than one part of speech class (e.g., as nouns, verbs, or adjectives), explanations include information for such differences. Further, affixes for verbal entries are grouped together between solidi to indicate similar meanings. Further information about the affixes can be found in the reference grammar referred to above.

Many of the entries are illustrated by Ilokano sentences. Usage is thereby clarified. Related meanings of the same entry are numbered in the explanations for ease in following examples of the information given. Homophonous forms are indicated by raised numbers before the entries.

This dictionary contains some 7,000 Ilokano entries. The information given is the most comprehensive available to date for Ilokano. The work has been prepared as a part of a set of materials to teach Ilokano to Peace Corps Volunteers. The author of the dictionary and the editor of the series believe that the dictionary will be found useful both to learners of Ilokano and to native speakers of the language. The English definitions are comprehensive and carefully thought out.

The work of dictionary making never ends. No dictionary is complete. Thus it is our hope that users will send us their comments so that another edition, when possible, can be fuller and of even more value.

Howard P. McKaughan
Editor

ILOKANO DICTIONARY

[1]A, adv. indeed, of course; then: a confirmatory particle
that is used at the end of a word, phrase or sentence.
Wen a. Yes, indeed.

[2]A, var. of NGA.

AAK, n. dirt, anything dirty - usually in child's talk.

AANAKAN, see under ANAK.

AANGSAN, see under ANGES.

ABA, n. taro.

AB-AB, v. /MANG-:-AN/ to drink from a fountain or faucet
with the lips touching the source of the water. Saan
mo nga ab-aban dayta gripo ta narugit. Don't drink
from the faucet with your lips for it is dirty.

SANGKAAB-AB, n. one draught or draft.

ABABA, adj. /(NA-)/ short in extent or duration. Ababa
ti dila na. His tongue is short.
v. /-UM-/.   --ant. ATIDDOG.

ABABAW, adj. /(NA-)/ shallow, not deep; superficial,
not profound. Ababaw dayta waig. That brook is
shallow.
v. /-UM-/.   --ant. ADALEM.

ABAGA, n. shoulder.
v. /MANGI:I-/ to place (something) on the shoulder.

ABAGAT, n. south wind.

ABAGATAN, n. south, the southern region.

[1]ABAK, v. /AG-, MANG-/ to win (in gambling, a contest,
etc.). Nangabak diay balasang. The young woman won.
/MANG-:PANG--AN/ to win (in gambling, a contest, etc.).
Nangabakak ti pisos. I won one peso. Pisos ti
pinangabakak. I won one peso.   /-UM-:-EN/ to defeat
or win over (someone) (in gambling, a contest, etc.).
Siak ti immabak kanyana. It was I who defeated him.
Isu ti inabak ko. It was he whom I defeated.

[2]ABAK, v. /MA-/ 1. to lose money (in gambling, a contest,
etc.). Naabakak idiay swipstik. I lost money in the

sweepstakes. 2. to lose or be defeated (in a contest,
etc.). Naabak diay baro. The young man lost. /MA-/
to lose (money) (in gambling, a contest, etc.).
Naabakak ti pisos idiay swipstik. I lost one peso in
the sweepstakes.

ABAKA, n. Manila hemp.

ABAL-ABAL, n. a kind of brown, burrowing June beetle
or June bug.

ABALAYAN, n. 1. the relationship between the parents
of a married couple. 2. the father or mother of the
spouse of one's child--a 'co-parent'. Abalayan ko ni
Ana. Ann is the mother of my child's spouse. 3. a
title of address or reference for one's co-parent
(sometimes with the co-parent's name following it).
Umulika, Abalayan Juan. Come upstairs, Co-father
John.
  AGABALAYAN [pl. AGAABALAYAN], the term used to
  designate two parents whose children are married
  to each other, or the mutual relationship between
  such parents. Agabalayan kami ken Ana. Ann's child
  and my child are married to each other.

ABALBALAY, n. toy, plaything.
  v. /AG-, MANG-:-EN/ 1. to play with as with a toy;
to trifle with. Saan mo nga abalbalayen dayta. Don't
play with that. 2. to handle or finger (one's genitals, especially of the male).

ABALEN, n. a kind of white larva that lives in the
earth and kills plants by gnawing at their roots.

ABANIKO [f. Sp.], n. fan. --syn. PAYPAY.

ABANG, n. rent.
  v. /-UM-, MANG-:-AN/ to rent. Kayat ko nga abangan
ta kariton mo. I want to rent your cart.

[1]ABANG, v. /AG-:-AN/ to wait for (a person, a bus, etc.)
in the way. Agabang kayo iti transit. You wait for a
transit.

[2]ABANG, v. /-UM-:-AN/ to ambush, waylay; to lie in wait
for and attack. Apay nga abangan yo ida? Why are you
going to ambush them? --syn. TAMBANG.

[1]ABAY, n. side (of). Mapan ka idiay abay ni manong mo.
Go to the side of your older brother.
    v. /-UM-:-EN/ to stay or stand by the side of.
Umabay ka ken ni tatang mo. Stand by the side of
your father.   /MAKI-:KA-/ to stay or stand by the
side of. Kinaabay na diay tatang na. He stood by the
side of his father.   /AG-/ [with pl. subject] to
stand side by side. Nagabay diay lakay ken baket.
The old man and the old woman stood side by side.
/MANGI-:I-/ to put or place by, or take (someone or
something) to the side of. Iyabay mo dayta kanyana.
Put that by his side.

[2]ABAY, n. best man in a wedding.

ABBAT, v. /MANG-:-AN/ to let the water or liquid (of
what one is cooking) evaporate, to allow to dry up
by steaming. Saan mo nga abbatan dayta lutlutoem.
Don't let the liquid of what you are cooking
evaporate.

ABBONG, n. cover, lid.
    v. /AG-, MANG-:-AN/ to cover (face, pot, hole,
etc.). Saan mo nga abbongan ta rupam. Don't cover
your face.   /MANGI-:I-/ to cover with, use to cover.
Iyabbong mo daytoy dita rupam. Cover your face with
this.   /MA--AN/ to be covered with, be screened off
by. Narigat nga makita daydiay bunga ti abokado ta
naabbongan ti bulong. It is difficult to see the
fruit of the avocado because it is covered with
leaves.

ABEL, n. textile, specifically cloth woven in the
native loom (PAGABLAN).
    v. /AG-/ to weave cloth, especially in the native
loom. Nalaing nga agabel diay balasang. The young
woman weaves cloth well.   /MANG-:-EN/ [=ABLEN] to
weave (a blanket, a curtain, etc.), especially in
the native loom. Isu ti nangabel ti daytoy kurtina
mi. She was the one who wove this curtain of ours.

    PAGABLAN, n. native loom.

ABENTURERO [abɛnturéro; f. Sp.], n. adventurer,
explorer.

ABER, n. a kind of fish about the size and shape of
a sardine whose meat is esteemed.

ABI, v. /MANG-:-EN/ to mock, insult, affront, villify; to belittle. Ab-abien da ta napanglaw. They are belittling him because he is poor.

ABIDAY, v. /AG-/ to throw a wrap over one's shoulder, to wrap oneself around the shoulder. /MANG-:-AN/ to cover or wrap with a drape, a curtain, etc. /MANGI-:I-/ to wrap oneself (or someone) around the shoulder with; to use a drape, curtain, etc. to cover or wrap (someone or something). Iyabiday mo daytoy ta nalam-ek. Wrap this around your shoulder for it is cold. /MA--AN/ to be wrapped or covered with a drape, a curtain, etc. Saan ko nga nakita diay uneg ti balay da ta naabidayan diay ruagan da. I was not able to see the inside of their house for their entrance was covered with a drape (or curtain).

ABIG, v. /MAKI-/ to have adulterous relations with someone; to commit adultery. Saan ka nga makiabig. Don't commit adultery. /MAKI-:KA-/ to have adulterous relations with, to commit adultery with. Sino ti kinaabig mo? With whom did you have adulterous relations?

ABILIDAD [f. Sp.], n. ability, competence, skill, power. --syn. KABAELAN.

ABIRAT, n. 1. the relationship between two persons whose spouses are brothers or sisters, or brother and sister. 2. a brother- or sister-in-law whose wife or husband is the sister or brother of one's spouse. 3. a title of reference or address for such brother- or sister-in-law.

ABLAT, v. /MANG-:-AN/ to whip in a slashing manner. /MANGI-:I-/ to whip with in a slashing manner.

ABLEN, = ABEL + -EN.

ABOGADO [f. Sp.], n. lawyer.

ABOGASIA [f. Sp.], n. law course, law degree.

ABOKADO [f. Sp.], n. avocado.

ABOOS, var. of BOOS.

ABRAW, v. /AG-/ to cook a vegetable dish (INABRAW).
/MANG-:-EN/ to cook (vegetables) into a vegetable
dish. Abrawem man daydiay tarong ken parya. Cook
the eggplant and bitter melon into a vegetable dish
please.

INABRAW, n. vegetable dish. --syn. DINENGDENG.

ABRIL [f. Sp.], n. April.

ABRILATA or ABRILLATA [f. Sp.], n. can-opener.

ABRISIETE [abrisiéte; f. Sp.], v. /MANG-:-EN/ to hold
(someone) around the waist. /AG-/ [with pl. subject]
to hold (each other) around the waist.

ABROT, v. /MANG-:-EN/ to recover, redeem, win back.
Abrotem ti abak mo idi kalman. Recover your losses
yesterday.

ABUG, v. /MANG-:-EN/ to drive off, drive away. Abugem
dayta aso. Drive away that dog. /MANGI-:I-/ to drive
away toward (a place, a person, etc.). Iyabug mo
dayta aso idiay ruar. Drive the dog to the outside.

ABULOG, n. fence enclosing the space under a house
built on stilts. Adda abulog na nga kawayan diay
balay mi. The space under our house is fenced with
bamboo.
    v. /MANG-:-AN/ to fence the space under (a house).

ABULOY, v. /MANG-:-AN/ to acquiesce to, consent to,
agree with, approve. Saan mo nga abuloyan ta kaykayat
na. Don't acquiesce to what he wants.

ABUNG, n. hut; a temporary shelter.

    ABUNG-ABUNG, n. a small hut; a small hut-like
    structure used in religious processions as a
    repository for the Blessed Sacrament.

ABUNGOT, v. /AG-/ to cover one's head or eyes (with a
handkerchief, a bandana, etc.). Agabungot ka ket
agar-arbis. Cover your head (with a bandana or any
piece of cloth) for it is drizzling. /MANG-:-AN/
to cover (one's eyes or of someone); to blindfold
(oneself or someone). Abungotan mi dagiti mata na
iti panyo. We cover his eyes with a handkerchief.

/MANGI-:I-/ to use to cover the head with. Iyabungot mo daytoy lupot ta napudot. Use this cloth to cover your head for it is hot.

ABUROY, n. a female who gave birth to twins, triplets, etc. of the same sex.

ABUS; ABUS TA, ABUS MAN PAY TA, conj. while, whereas, although, in spite of the fact that. Abus ta isu ti nakabasol, isu pay ti nagunget. In spite of the fact that it was he who sinned, it was also he who got angry.

ABUSO, v. /AG-/ to pester, bother, irritate someone. /MANG-:-EN/ to pester, bother, irritate.

ABUT, v. /-UM-/ to reach, arrive in. Immabutak idiay Manila. I reached Manila. /MAKA-:MA-AN/ to (be able to) overtake or reach. Isu ti nakaabut kanyak. He was the one who overtook me.

ABUT, n. hole, opening, leak, puncture, crevice.
    v. /MANG-:-AN/ to put or make a hole on, to puncture. Abutam ta niog ta alaem ta digo na. Make a hole on the coconut and get its water. /MANGI-:I-/ to put or drop in a hole or opening; to put or drop inside (something) through a hole or opening. Iyabut mo dayta kuartam idiay alkansiam. Put your money inside your piggy bank. /MAI-/ to fall into a hole or opening; to go through a hole or opening accidentally. Naiyabut ti saka na. His leg went through a hole accidentally.

ABUYO, n. wild jungle or mountain chicken.

AD-ADDA, see under ADDA.

ADAL, v. /AG-/ to study one's lesson or course. Agadal ka nga naimbag tapno makaruar ka. You study your lesson well so that you will pass it. /MANG-:EN/ to study, examine, investigate. Adalem nga nalaing dayta leksion mo. Study your lesson well.

ADALEM, adj. /(NA-)/ deep; profound.
    v. /-UM-/.

ADANI, v. /-UM-/ to approach, come near. Umadanin ti
    paskua. Christmas is approaching.   --syn. ASIDEG.
    --var. ADDANI.

ADAT, n. bad or unpleasant taste, as the aftertaste of
    oysters or mangoes. Ngem ti adat na, awan ti ladawan
    nga irapit maipanggep iti salaysay. The bad taste
    lies in that there is no picture enclosed pertaining
    to the story.
        adj. /NA-/ having bad or unpleasant taste.

[1]ADAW, v. /-UM-, MANG-/ to borrow fire or light. Umadawak
    man. May I borrow fire (from you). Inka mangadaw dita
    karruba ta awan ti apoy tayo. Go borrow fire from the
    neighbor for we have no fire.

[2]ADAW, v. /MANG-:-EN/ to remove (a pot or something that
    is being cooked) from the fire or stove. Adawem ta
    banga. Remove that pot from the fire.

[3]ADAW, v. /MANG-:-EN/ to copy, quote, draw or extract
    from. Inadaw da daytoy nga istoria idiay biblia.
    They extracted this story from the Bible.

ADAYO, adj. /(NA-)/ far, distant, remote (in space or
    probability); far from (someone or something). Adayo
    ti Amerika ditoy Pilipinas. America (or the U.S.A.)
    is far from the Philippines. /NA-/ distant; i.e. not
    close or intimate (toward someone). Naadayo diay
    gayyem ko kaniak. My friend is distant toward me.
        v. /-UM-/ to go far from (in space). Immadayo da
    kadakami. They went far from us. /MANGI-:I-/ to put,
    transfer or take away from. Iyadayom ta asom kanyak.
    Take your dog away from me.   --ant. ASIDEG.

    ADDAYO, v. /AG-/ [with pl. subject] to be far or
        distant from each other. Agaddayo da. They are far
        from each other.   --ant. ASSIDEG.

ADDA, as a particle it indicates: 1. the existence or
    presence of someone or something. Adda tao idiay
    balay. There is someone in the house. 2. the
    possession of something by someone. Adda kuartam?
    Do you have money?
        v. /MA--AN/ to have, to be in possession of.
    Naaddaan kami ti katulong. We had a helper.   --ant.
    AWAN.

ADDAAN, adj. having, possessing, endowed with. Isuda
ti addaan ti nalawa nga daga. There are the ones
who have extensive lands.

AD-ADDA, adj. more probable or plausible - followed
by a sentence introduced by NGA. Ad-adda nga
sumangpet da inton bigat. It is more probable
that they will arrive tomorrow.
     v. /-UM-/ to increase, grow further. Umad-adda
ti loko na tatta ta dakkelen. His foolishness has
increased now that he is grown up. /MANGI-:I-/ to
increase, add more to. Iyad-addam ti lutoem nga
sida ta adu tayo. Add more to the sidedishes that
you are going to cook for there will be many of us.

ADDADDIAY, var. of ADDAYDIAY.

ADDADTA, var. of ADDAYTA.

ADDADTOY, var. of ADDAYTOY.

ADDAG, v. /MANG-:-AN/ to put weight on so as to press
(it) down, to lie on. Saan mo nga addagan dagita
kallaba nga lupot. Don't lie on those newly-washed
clothes. /MANGI-:I-/ to lay on, to put or place on
so as to press (it) down. --syn. PANDAG.

ADDAGIDIAY, pl. of ADDAYDIAY.

ADDAGITA, pl. of ADDAYTA. --var. DAGITA.

ADDAGITOY, pl. of ADDAYTOY. --var. DAGITOY.

ADDANI, var. of ADANI.

ADDANG, v. /AG-/ to move the legs so as to walk; to
make a step; to pace, walk. Damo na pay la ti
agaddang. He is still beginning to walk. /MANG-:-EN/
to make it in one step; to go over or across by one
step; to step over. Mabalin mo nga addangen dayta?
Can you step over that?

ADDA-ADDANG, v. /AG-/ to walk with regular, measured
steps; to walk step by step. Saan ka nga makadanon
idiay papanam no mangadda-addang ka. You cannot
reach where you are going if you walk step by step.

ADDAYDIAY [pl. ADDAGIDIAY], there yonder (it) is, there
yonder (they) are. --var. ADDADDIAY, ARIDDIAY, ARDIAY.

ADDAYO, see under ADAYO.

ADDAYTA [pl. ADDAGITA], there near you (it) is, there
near you (they) are. --var. ADDADTA, ADTA, ARIDTA,
ARTA.

ADDAYTOY [pl. ADDAGITOY], here is, here are. --var.
ADDADTOY, ADTOY, ARIDTOY, ARTOY. Adtoy kami nga
agkakabbalay. Here we are, the whole household.

ADDI, pl. of [1]ADI.

[1]ADI, n. [pl. ADDI] younger brother or sister; anyone,
especially a relative, younger than oneself.
v. /AG-/ to have a younger brother or sister.
Agadi daytoyen. This one has now a younger brother
or sister. /AG-/ to treat a younger brother or
sister or anyone younger than oneself as such. Ammo
na ti agadi. He knows how to treat a younger brother
or sister.

ADING, n. affectionate or endearing form of ADI.
This is also used as term of reference or address
(sometimes with the name of the person following
it). Umaykan, Ading. Come now, younger brother
(or sister).

[2]ADI, var. of MADI, usually used with AG- or NAG-.

ADIAY, var. (dial.) of DAYDIAY.

ADIGI, n. post, pillar.
v. /MANG-:-AN/ to put a post or posts to; to
provide with posts. /MANGI-:I-/ to use as post,
to put or place as post. Daytoy ti iyadigim dita.
Put this there as post.

ADIN, ADINO, var. of SADINO.

ADING, see under ADING.

ADIPEN, n. slave; servant.
v. /MANG-:-EN/ to enslave; to force (someone) to
serve free. Isu ti nangadipen kanyak. He was the one
who forced me to serve free. --syn. TAGABU.

ADIWARA, v. /AG-/ to spread, diffuse. Agadiwara ti
banglo dayta sampagita. The fragrance of that
sampaguita flower spreads.

ADMINISTRASION [f. Sp.], n. administration.

ADOBO [f. Sp.], n. a meat dish consisting usually of
pork, beef or chicken cooked with vinegar, salt,
garlic and bay leaves.
v. /AG-/ to cook this dish. /MANG-:-EN/ to cook
as such.

ADTA, var. of ADDAYTA.

ADTOY, var. of ADDAYTOY.

ADU, adj. /NAG-/ many, much, plenty, numerous. Immay
ti adu nga tao. Many people came.

[1]AG- [pt. NAG-, prp. AG- + R1, ptp. NAG- + R1], active
verbalizing prefix with diverse meanings, such as:
1. to do the action (usually intransitive) expressed
by the stem. Agsangitak. I shall cry. 2. to use the
object denoted by the stem as instrument, clothing,
ornament, etc. Agaradoak. I shall use a plow. or: I
shall plow. 3. to play the game or sport denoted by
the stem. Agmadyong tayo. Let's play Mah-Jongg. 4.
be affected by the ailment or disease denoted by the
stem. Aggurigor diay ubing. The child has a fever.
5. to pursue the profession or career denoted by the
stem. Agmaestra ni Pilar. Pilar will study to be a
teacher. 6. to reach approximately the number
indicated by the stem. Agtallopulo a tawen nan. He
is about thirty years old.

AG- may occur with one or more (rarely more than two)
other affixes with a single stem, such as the
following:

AG--INN-, same as AG--INN--AN 1.

AG--INN-AN, 1. to do the action denoted by the stem
to each other. Nagpinnakawan da. They forgave each
other. 2. to compete as to the quality expressed by
the stem. Agpinnapintasan da. They will compete
with each other in beauty.

AGKA--AN, to cause or allow oneself to undergo or
suffer the effect of the action denoted by the
stem. Nagkatudoan diay mannalon. The farmer stood
in the rain.

AGKAI-, to suffer or show the state or condition
expressed by the stem. Agkaiwara ti lupot idiay

salas. Clothes are scattered all around in the living room.

AGKARA-, to suffer or do repeatedly the action indicated by the stem. Agkarasakit diay kabayo mi. Our horse always gets sick.

AGKARAI-, same as AGKARA-. Agkaraibelleng ti bagas. The rice is always spilling out.

AGPA-, active causative: to cause the action indicated by the stem to be done (by someone). Agpaalaak iti asin. I will ask (someone) to get salt.

AGPAKA-, to cause (someone) to suffer the effect of the action expressed by the stem. Usually used in negative constructions. Saan nga agpakaturog dagiti lamok no awan ti moskitero. The mosquitoes won't allow (us) to sleep if (we) have no mosquito net.

AGTAGI-, see under TAGI-.

[2]AG-, a plural noun prefix which has at least two meanings: 1. with a noun indicating a relation or similarity: to bear the relation or similarity indicated by the noun stem. Agkabsat diay asawa da. Their wives are sisters. 2. with a family name: to belong to the family or clan bearing that family name, or to have the same family name. Nabaknang dagiti ag-Lopez. The Lopezes are rich.

[3]AG- + R2, a noun prefix with the meaning: one who sells or deals in the thing indicated by the noun stem. Agnanateng diay manang na. Her older sister is a vegetable vendor.

[4]AG- [pt. NAG-, prp. AG- + R1, ptp. NAG- + R1], a prefix which forms adverbs of time with temporal nouns. Nagpatnag nga nagbasa diay baro. The young man studied the whole night.

[1]AGA- [agá?], a noun prefix which means: to smell like the thing named by the stem. Aga-bawang ta balasang. That young woman smells of garlic.

[2]AGA- [aga?], var. of PAGA-.

AGAABALAYAN, pl. of AGABALAYAN.

AGAAL, var. of AGAL.

AGAAMA, pl. of AGAMA.

AGABALAYAN, see under ABALAYAN.

AGABIRAT, see under ABIRAT.

AGADDAYO, see under ADAYO.

AGAL, v. /AG-/ to moan, wail, whine (because of pain or hardship); to complain. Agagal maipanggep ti kangina ti magatgatang. He complained about the expensiveness of commodities.

AGAMA, see under AMA.

AGAP, v. /AG-/ to cut something into thin slices, to slice something thinly. /MANG-:-EN/ to cut into thin slices, to cut thinly. Agapem diay kamotit ta agaramid ta ti kankanen. Slice the sweet potato thinly and we shall bake a cake.

AGARUP, adv. 1. seemingly, apparently; to seem or appear. Agarup mayat. He seems to be willing. 2. almost, nearly. Nagpaut ti uram iti agarup uppat nga oras. The fire lasted for almost four hours.

AGAS, n. medicine, remedy, cure.
   v. /AG-, MANG-:-AN/ to treat with medicine, medicate on, cure (a wound, a disease, a sick person or animal, etc.). Isu ti nangagas kaniak. He was he who treated me.

   MANGNGAGAS, n. physician, doctor.   --syn. DOKTOR, SIRUHANO; see also ERBULARIO.

AGASEN; AGASEM [with singular actor], AGASEN YO [with plural actor], just imagine. Agasem, agsueldo ti dua nga gasut. Just imagine, he earns two hundred (pesos).

AGASSAWA, see under ASAWA.

AGASSIDEG, see under ASIDEG.

AGATOL, n. an edible, fresh water crab living mostly in a hole that it digs in rice fields or brooks.

AGAW, v. /-UM-, MANG-:-EN/ to snatch off or away, take or carry away by force or violence; to get or obtain by robbing. Saan mo nga agawen dayta abalbalay na. Don't snatch off his toy.

AGAWA, adj. /NA-/ diligent, assiduous, industrious, eager.
    v. /AG-, -UM-/ to be diligent, assiduous, industrious, eager. Umagawa ka tapno maturpos mo ti adal mo. Be diligent so that you can finish your studies. /-UM-:-AN/ to hasten, hurry up, be fast. Agawaam nga ileppas ta trabahom. Hurry up and finish your work.

AGAY-AYAM, see under AYAM.

AGDAMA, see under DAMA.

AGDAN, n. ladder; flight of steps; stairs; staircase.
    v. /MANG-:-AN/ to provide with a ladder or stairs; to put or add a ladder or stairs to; to make a ladder or stairs for. Isu ti nangagdan diay balay mi. It was he who provided our house with a ladder.

AGEK, n. kiss.
    v. /MANG-:-AN/ [= AGKAN] to kiss. Inagkan nak. He kissed me.   --syn. UNGNGO, BISUNG, ANGGO.

AGEP, v. /-UM-, MANG-:-EN/ to kiss. Mapanak umagep ken ni Apo Nazareno. I'll go kiss (the hand or raiment of) St. Nazarene.

AGI-, active transitive verbalizing prefix. Agibilag kayo ti pagay. Dry some unhusked rice under the sun. --see MANGI-.
    AGIPA-, causative of AGI-.   --see AGPA under [1]AG-.

AGIINA, pl. of AGINA.

AGIING, v. /-UM-/ to be timid, shy, bashful. Saan ka nga umagiing. Don't be shy.

AGIN- + R2, a verbalizing prefix with the meaning: to pretend to do or be what the stem indicates. Aginbubuteng diay pulis. The policeman pretends to be afraid.

AGINA, see under INA.

AGING, n. remote or isolated and unfrequented place; hidden place.

AGINGGA, AGINGGANA, see under INGGA.

AGIS, v. /AG-, MANG-:-AN/ to make narrower or less wide, to remove part of along lengthwise edge(s). Agisam ta tabla ta akaba unay. Make that board narrower for it is very wide. /MANG-:-EN/ to cut or remove part of along lengthwise edge(s). Dua nga porgada ti agisem dita tabla. Remove two inches from the lengthwise edge(s) of that table.

AGIWARWARNAK, see under WARNAK.

AGKA-, a verbalizing prefix used with numerals to form fractional (cardinal) numbers. Agkapito daytoy. This will be divided into seven parts.

AGKAN, = AGEK + -AN.

AGLALO, see under LALO.

AGLIKMOT, see under LIKMOT.

AGLIPAY, n. a Church founded in the Philippines by Gregorio Aglipay officially known as the Philippine Independent Church (Iglesia Filipina Independiente).

AGLIPAYANO, n. a member of the AGLIPAYAN Church.

AGNANAYON, adv. always, eternally; eternal, perpetual. --syn. KANAYON.

AGNEB, adj. /NA-/ damp, moist, humid, slightly wet. Naagneb ditoy kuartom. It is damp in your room.
   v. /AG-/ to become damp, moist, humid, slightly wet. No agtudtudo agagneb dagitoy tugtugaw. When it is raining these seats become moist.

AGOO, n. a kind of tree resembling the pine tree.

AGOSTO [f. Sp.], n. August.

AGPALPALAMA, n. beggar, pauper, indigent. --syn. AGPALPALIMOS, MAKILIMLIMOS, MAKILKILIMOS, MAKIPALPALAMA. --see PALAMA.

AGPALPALIMOS, see under LIMOS.

AGPAPAN, see under PAPAN.

AGPAYSO, see under PAYSO.

AGRAMAN, see under RAMAN.

AGRIKULTURA [f. Sp.], n. agriculture.

AGSAW, v. /MANG-:-EN/ to collect, gather, glean, scoop
  whatever is left. Agsawem amin nga mabalin nga
  pagtungo. Gather all those that can be used as
  firewood.

AGSIPUD, prep. because of, on account of, due to.
  --syn. GAPU.
    AGSIPUD TA, conj. because, since, for the reason or
    cause that.   --syn. GAPU TA.

AGSIT, n. layer of nipa leaves or cogon grass used for
  thatching.

AGTURAY, see under TURAY.

AGTUTUBO, see under TUBO.

AGUB, adj. /NA-/ to smell like rotten rice.   --syn.
  BAOG.

AGUM, v. /MANG-:-AN/ to covet, desire, crave, long for.
  Saan mo nga aguman ti saan mo nga kukua. Don't covet
  what is not yours.
    adj. /NA-/ covetous, greedy. Bimmallaet ti tao nga
  naagum. The greedy person interfered.

AGUNG, n. nose.
    adj. /-AN/ having a big nose.

AGUS, n. current.   --see AYOS.

AHENSIA [ahɛnsia; f. Sp.], n. agency; shop.

AHENTE [ahɛntɛ; f. Sp.], n. agent, representative.

-AK, pron. I, me: the enclitic nominative case form of
  SIAK.

AKABA, adj. /(NA-)/ wide, broad. Atiddog ken naakaba ti lamisaan yo. Your table is long and wide.
  v. /AG-/ [with pl. subject] to have the same length, to fit each other along the longer side. Agakaba dagitoy dua nga tabla. These two boards have the same length. --ant. AKIKID.

AKAK, n. double chin.
  v. /AG-/ to have or develop a double chin.

[1]**AKAR**, v. /-UM-/ to move, transfer oneself (to or from); to change one's residence. Immakar kami idiay Manila. We transferred to Manila. /MANGI-:I-/ to move, transfer (to or from); to change someone's residence or place. Iyakar mo dayta tugaw ditoy. Transfer that chair here.

[2]**AKAR**, v. /MANGI-:I-/ to transfer, to infect with (a disease or sickness). Inyakar na kanyak ti panateng na. He infected me with (or transferred to me) his cold. /MAKA-:MA--AN/ to infect (with a disease or sickness). Isu ti nakaakar kanyak. He was the one who infected me. /MA--AN/ to be infected by (a disease or sickness). Naakaranak ti panateng mo. I was infected by your cold. --syn. ALIS.

AKAS, v. /AG-, MANG-:-EN/ to take, collect or gather inside (usually clothes) (from where they have been placed to dry). Akasem dagita bilag mo ket malemen. Gather what you are drying for it is already late (in the afternoon).

AKASIA [f. Eng.?], n. acacia, monkey pod tree. --syn. ALGARRUBO.

AKAY, v. /MANG-:-EN/ to guide, lead especially by holding the hand; to herd, to drive as a herd, a group, etc. Sino daydiay nangakay kenka? Who guided you? Akayem dagita kaldingen. Drive the goats now.

AKEM, v. /AG-:-EN/ to take charge of, be in charge of, be responsible for, take the obligation of. Isu ti nagakem ti daytoy nga pabuya. He took charge of this show. Saan mo nga akmen no dimo kabaelan. Don't take charge of (it) if you cannot do (it).

AKIKID, adj. /(NA-)/ narrow, of little breadth. --ant. AKABA, LAWA.

AKILIS, v. /MANG-:-EN/ to weave (yarn, thread, fiber).
Isu ti nangakilis diay sagut. It was he who wove the
fiber. Narigat nga akilisen daytoy nakulkul nga sagut.
It's hard to weave this entangled fiber.
n. strip of bamboo or rattan used for tying together
laths, etc.

[1]AKIN-, a noun prefix indicating ownership. Sino ti
akin-balay dayta? Whose house is that? --var. MAKIN-.

[2]AKIN-, a prefix used with place nouns in forming adverbs
which indicate relative position. --var. MAKIN-.

AKKANG, var. of PAKKANG.

AKKOB, var. of AKOB.

AKKUB, n. cover (of a box, a magazine, etc.).
v. /MANG-:-AN/ to cover. Sino ti nangakkub diay
banga? Who covered the pot? /MANGI-:I-/ to use to
cover with. Inyakkub na daytoy idiay banga. He
covered the pot with this.

AKLILI, v. /MANG-:-EN/ or /MANGI-:I-/ to carry under
the armpit or arm. Saan mo nga iyaklili dayta ubing.
Don't carry that child under your arm.

AKLO, n. ladle.
v. /MANG-:-EN/ to ladle out; to hit, strike or
beat with a ladle.

AKLON, v. /MANG-:-EN/ to receive or accept under one's
responsibility or charge, to receive or accept and
keep in trust. Inaklon na ti ayat ko. She accepted
my love to keep in trust.

AKO, v. /MANG-:-EN/ to admit or confess (one's fault
or mistake). Isu ti nangako nga basol na. He was
the one who admitted that it was his fault. Apay
nga inakom nga basol mo? Why did you confess that
it was your fault?

AKOB, v. /AG-/ [with pl. subject] to be joined or
placed together facing each other (e.g. hands, plates,
shells), to be clasped as hands. Nagakob ti ima na.
His hands are clasped. /MANG-:(PAG-)-EN [with pl. go
goal] to join or place together the inner side facing
each other, to clasp as hands. Sino ti madi mangakob

ti ima na? Who does not want to clasp his hands?
--var. AKKOB.

AKSIDENTE [aksidɛntɛ; f. Sp.], n. accident, mishap.
v. /MAKA-:MA-/ to injure (a person or an animal)
in an accident. /MA-/ to have an accident, to
figure or be injured in an accident.

AKUP, v. /MANG-:-EN/ to take up or out with both hands,
two brooms, a scoop, etc.; to scoop. Ibagam nga
akupen na diay rugit. Tell him to scoop the dirt.

AKUP-AKUP, n. a kind of hymenopterous insect resembling
a bumblebee but more slender and very thin at the
junction of the abdomen and the thorax. --var.
AKUT-AKUT.

AKUT-AKUT, var. of AKUP-AKUP.

AKUY, v. /MANG-:-EN/ to gather or collect with the
hands toward oneself. Inakuy na amin nga kuarta
idiay rabaw ti lamisaan. He gathered toward himself
with his hands all the money on the table.
/MANGI-:I-/ to gather or collect by pushing with the
hands toward (someone). Inyakuy na diay rugit kanyak.
He pushed the dirt to me with his hands.

[1]ALA, v. /MANG-:-EN/ to get, obtain, acquire. Apay nga
innalam dayta abanikok? Why did you get my fan?

[2]ALA, v. /-UM-:-AN/ to take after, to be like, to
resemble. Immala dagiti annak mo kenka met laeng.
You took after no one but you.

[1]ALA, interj. an exclamation used: 1. to urge or request
someone to continue. Ngem, ala, ituloy mo. But, go
on, continue. 2. to wish some previously mentioned
event to happen. Ala kuma. I hope so.

[2]ALA [f. Sp.], o'clock - used exclusively before UNA.
Ala unan. It is now one o'clock. --var. ALAS.

ALAD, n. fence or hedge around a house, a yard, a
garden, etc.
v. /AG-/ to make a fence. /AG-, MANG-:-AN/ to
fence, put a fence at or around. Inaladak diay
paraangan mi. I put a fence at our front yard.

/MANGI-:I-/ to use to fence with. Daytoy ti iyalad mo idiay paraangan tayo. Use this in fencing our front yard.

ALAGADEN, n. rule, regulation. Dagitoy ti alagaden ti nasayaat nga umili. These are the rules of good townspeople.

ALAHAS [f. Sp.], n. jewels, gems; jewelry.

AL-AL, v. /AG-/ to pant. Agal-al-al diay asok. My dog is panting.

AL-ALIA, n. ghost, specter, apparition; spirit.
v. /MANG-:-EN/ to haunt or visit, as a ghost; to play ghost on. Sino ti nangal-alia kenka? Whose ghost visited you? or: Who played ghost on you? /MA-, -EN/ to be visited by a ghost.

AL-ALUTIIT, see under ALUTIIT.

AL-ALYA, see AL-ALIA.

ALAN [= ALA + -EN], go on, continue, proceed; see [1]ALA.

ALAN-AN, v. /MANG-:-EN/ to pull or spin toward oneself (a string, rope, etc.). Alan-anem dayta lubid mo. You spin your rope. --syn. KUNIKON.

ALANG-ANG, var. of ANANG-ANG.

ALANGON, v. /MANG-:-EN/ to mend, repair, restore; to compensate, make up for; to make good again. Isu ti nangalangon ti dayaw ko. He was the one who restored my honor.

[1]ALAS, adj. /NA-/ ugly, not pretty; improper, indecent. --var. (dial.) GALAS.

[2]ALAS [f. Sp.], n. ace of playing cards.

[3]ALAS [f. Sp.], o'clock - used only before numerals of Spanish origin except $_2$UNA. Alas dosen. It is two o'clock now. --var. [2]ALA.

ALAS-AS, v. /MANG-:-EN/ to remove, strip, detach, tear off. Alas-asem amin nga lasag dayta pityo ti manok.

Remove all the meat of that chicken breast.

ALAT, n. a kind of basket made of closewoven bamboo.

ALAT-AT, v. /MANG-:-EN/ to pull or tear off forcibly.
Alat-atem amin nga kumalkalatkat iti dayta kayo.
Pull off all those (vines) climbing on that tree.

ALAW, v. /MANG-:-EN/ to save, rescue, deliver from
distress; to help, succor; to give aid to; to take,
get. Inka alawen daydiay ubing nga umaw-awag ti
tulong. Go give aid to the child who is calling for
help.

ALAWIG, n. whirlwind, cyclone; sometimes, hurricane.
     v. /AG-/ to have a whirlwind, cyclone or hurricane.
Nagalawig idi kalman. There was a whirlwind yesterday.
/MA-, -EN/ to be hit, blown or destroyed by a
whirlwind, cyclone or hurricane. Naalawig diay balay
mi. Our house was hit by a whirlwind. Inalawig kami.
We were hit by a whirlwind.

ALAY-AY, v. /MANG-:-AN/ to cook slowly over low heat
or small fire. Alay-ayam laeng dayta karne tapno
lumukneng. Cook that meat over low fire so that it
will become tender.
     adj. /NA-/ soft and tender, soft and gentle, soft
and slow. Naalay-ay ti panagsao na. He speaks softly
and slowly. Nalay-ay ti pannagna na. He walks softly
and slowly.

ALDAW, n. 1. day, daylight, daytime. 2. day of
reckoning. Addanto met la aldaw mo. You will have
your day of reckoning.

ALDAWEN, it's already late (as said between about
    7 and 12 a.m.).

INALDAN-ALDAW, adv. everyday, day after day, daily.

KAALDAWAN, n. day of.

KASANGAALDAW, SANGAALDAW, the day before last.

BIGAT KASANGAALDAW, any time now.

KANIKADUA NGA ALDAW, two days ago. KANIKATLO NGA
    ALDAW, three days ago.

KADA SUMUNO NGA ALDAW, every other day.

ALDAW RABII, ALDAW KEN RABII, day and night.

ALENG-ALENG, v. /-EN, I-/ not to do seriously, to do carelessly, haphazardly or absent-mindedly. Inyaleng-aleng na ti agbasa. He read haphazardly.

ALEP-EP, n. plaster, bandage; poultice, anodyne; also, a piece of banana leaf placed over a pot of rice under the cover when the rice is not cooking properly.
    v. /MANG-:-AN/ to place a bandage, plaster or poultice on (wounds, etc.); to place a banana leaf over (rice being cooked in a pot). Alep-epam dayta sugat mo. Put a bandage on your wound.

ALGARRUBO, n. monkey pod tree. --syn. AKASIA.

ALI, v. /MANG-:-AN/ to stain, discolor. Daytoy nga lupot ti nangali kadagitoy puraw nga ules. This cloth was the one that stained these white blankets. /MA--AN/ to be stained, discolored. Naalian dagita ules. Those blankets were stained.
    adj. /MAKA-/ capable of staining, discoloring. Makaali daytoy nga lupot. This cloth is capable of staining. or: This cloth stains.

ALIAW, v. /MA-/ to be frightened, scared, alarmed, startled. Saan ka nga kumita ti baba ta dika maaliaw. Don't look down so that you won't get scared.
    adj. /MAKA-/ causing fright. Makaaliaw ti kumita ti baba. Looking down causes fright.

ALIBANGBANG, n. a kind of tree whose young leaves are used in preparing some kind of meat dish.

ALIBONGOBONG, n. vapor, steam.

ALIBTAK, adj. /NA-/ fast, clever; shrewd.

ALIBUT, n. a lizard much larger than the common house lizard that lives outdoors.

ALIBUYONG, adj. /NA-/ cloudy, overcast.

ALIDUNGET, n. boredom, restlessness, sullenness, gloominess.
    adj. /NA-/ bored, restless, gloomy, sullen.
    v. /AG-/ to be bored, restless, sullen, gloomy.

ALIGUSGUS, var. of ALIPUSPUS.

ALIKAKA, adj. /NA-/ careful, solicitous.
v. /AG-/ to be careful or solicitous of, to cherish someone or something. /AGI-, MANGI-:I-/ to be careful or solicitous of, to cherish. Iyalikakam dagita alikamem. Be careful of your personal belongings.

ALIKAMEN, n. tools, implements; furniture; personal belongings.

ALIKUBKUB, v. /MANG-:-AN/ to fence around, encircle, surround. Alikubkubam dayta pagay tapno saan nga kaldingen. Put a fence around the rice so that it won't be eaten by goats

ALIKUMKUM, v. /AG-, MANG-:-EN/ to gather, put together. Darasem nga alikumkumen dagita pinggan tapno makapan tayon. Gather the plates fast so that we can go.

ALIKUTEG, adj. /NA-/ restless, turbulent, mischievous; adept in pilfering.
v. /-UM-/.

ALILIS, v. /MANGI-:I-/ to postpone, delay. Iyalilis yo koma ti ponsion tapno makaumay kami. I hope you will delay the party so that we can come.

ALIMADAMAD, v. /MAKA-:MA-/ to hear or remember (something) indistinctly or vaguely. Ania ti naalimadamad mo idiay tiendaan? What did you hear indistinctly at the store?

ALIMATEK, n. leech.

ALIMBADAW, v. /AG-/ to turn about while sleeping, to be restless while sleeping.

ALIMBASAG, v. /-EN/ to have insomnia, be sleepless or wakeful.

ALIMBUBUYOG, n. bumblebee.

ALIMBUYOGEN, n. a cock with dark red plumage.

ALIMON, v. /MANG-:-EN/ to swallow, engulf.

ALIMONOMON, n. track, trail, path.

ALIMPATOK, n. top, peak, summit, topmost point; pinnacle.   --syn. TOKTOK.

ALIMUKENG, n. a variety of thin-skinned, small, greenish banana.

ALIMUTENG, v. /MANG-:-EN/ to bother, pester, irritate. Saan mo nga alimutengen ta ubing. Don't pester that child.   /MA-, -EN/ to be irritated. Alimutengenak. I am irritated.
     adj. /MAKA-/ to be irritating, causing irritation. Makaalimutengka. You are irritating.

ALINAAY, adj. /NA-/ smooth, calm, placid, peaceful.
     v. /-UM-/ to become smooth, calm or peaceful: said of the weather. Umay kaminto no umalinaay ti tiempo. We'll come when the weather is calm.

ALINAMNAM, v. /MANG-:-EN/ to enjoy with much pleasure; to relish.

ALINDADAY, v. /MANG-:-EN/ to carry on the head without holding with the hands. Saan mo nga alindadayen dayta karamba. Don't carry that jar on your head without holding it.

ALINDAW, v. /MA-/ to become dizzy, giddy; to have vertigo. Maalindawak nga kumita ti baba. I get dizzy looking down.

ALINO, v. /MA-/ to have one's teeth sensitive, to feel a tingling pain in the teeth when biting hard food, drinking cold water, etc.   /MAKA-:MA-/ to cause one's teeth to become sensitive or feel painful when biting hard food, drinking cold water, etc. Mangga ti nakaalino kaniak. My teeth were made sensitive by (eating) mangoes.

ALINONO, n. whirlpool, eddy of water.
     v. /AG-/ to produce whirlpools, to eddy. Agalinono diay karayan. The river eddies.

ALINSAWAD, v. /MANG-:-EN/ to grope for, look for by feeling. Inalinsawad na diay buneng na nga natinnag diay waig. He groped for his big knife which fell into the brook.

ALINTA, n. earthworm.

ALINGAAS, n. a kind of ghost or specter.

ALINGASAW, n. exhalation in the form of vapor, steam, etc.
v. /-UM-/ to effuse strong and offensive odor.

ALINGGAGET, v. /AG-/ to be scared, frightened, shocked.
--see ALINGGET.

ALINGGET, NAKAAL-ALINGGET, adj. frightening, scary, horrible, dreadful, terrible, hideous. Nakaal-alingget daytay dalan. The road was scary.   --syn. NAKAAM-AMAK, NAKAAM-AMES, NAKABUTBUTENG.   --see ALINGGAGET.

ALINGO, n. wild boar.

ALIPAGA, n. flake of fire, ember.   --syn. DALIPATO.

ALIPUGPUG, n. whirlwind.
v. /AG-/ to have a whirlwind. Nagalipugpug ditoy idi kalman. There was a whirlwind here yesterday.

ALIPUNGET, adj. /NA-/ quick-tempered, hot-tempered, irascible, irritable, choleric.
v. /AG-/.

ALIPUSPUS, n. whorl in the hair, cowlick.   --var. ALIGUSGUS.

[1]ALIS, v. /-UM-/ to transfer, move, go away (to or from). Umalis ka dita. Go away from there.   /MANGI-:I-/ to transfer, move (to or from). Iyalis mo man dayta anak mo ditoy sangwanak. Will you please move your child from my front.

[2]ALIS, v. /MAKA-:MA--AN/ to infect with a disease or sickness. Isu ti nakaalis kanyak. He was the one who infected me with a disease.   /MA--AN/ to be infected with a disease or sickness. Dika umasideg tapno saan ka nga maalisan. Don't come near so that you won't be infected with a disease.
adj. /MAKA-/ to be infectious or contagious. Makaalis ti sakit na. His sickness is contagious.
--syn. AKAR.

ALIS, v. /MA--AN/ to have an abortion or miscarriage;
   to give birth prematurely. Naalisan ni nanang na.
   His mother had a miscarriage.
      n. product of abortion.

ALISON, v. /MANGI-:I-/ to pour out or transfer (to).
   Iyalison mo dayta naggian ta labba. Pour out the
   contents of that basket.

ALISTO, adj. /(NA-)/ fast, clever, smart. --syn.
   PARTAK, PARDAS.

ALISU, n. a kind of fish whose meat is very much
   esteemed.

ALISUASO, n. steam, vapor.
      v. /AG-/ to produce or exude steam or vapor.
   Kalpasan ti tudo nagalisuaso ti daga. After the rain,
   the earth exuded vapor.

ALIT, v. /MANG-:-AN/ to patch or mend. Alitam dayta
   banga ta adda rata na. Mend that pot for it has a
   crack. /MANGI-:I-/ to patch or mend with. Daytoy ti
   iyalit mo iti dayta banga. Patch that pot with this.
   /MA--AN/ to be patched or mended. Saan mo nga
   gatangen dayta nga banga ta naalitan. Don't buy that
   pot for it is patched.

ALIWAKSAY, v. /AG-/ to entertain or amuse oneself; to
   keep oneself occupied, active, busy. Agaliwaksay ka
   tapno dika madukutan. Keep yourself busy so that you
   won't become restless.

ALIWEGWEG, adj. /NA-/ restless, active, turbulent,
   fidgety, uneasy.

ALKALDE [alkáldε; f. Sp.], n. mayor, city or mayor.
   mayor.. --syn. MAYOR.

ALLA, interj. an exclamation used to threaten or to
   express wonder. Alla ka Marya. Beware Mary.

ALLA-ALLA, v. /AG-/ to be undecided, wavering,
   vacillating, perplexed, unsettled, unresolved.
   Agalla-alla ti panunot ko. My mind is unresolved.

ALLAGAT, a shrub or vine with long, soft leaves and
   red flowers and edible fruits.

ALLATIW, v. /-UM-/ to go (to a place) without any definite purpose or reason, to go and see (a place). Saanak nga umallatiw pay dita balay yo ta adu ti trabahok. I am not going to your house yet because I have much work to do. /MANGI-:-/ to take (to a place) without any definite purpose or reason.

ALLAWA, var. (dial.) of ULLAW.

ALLAWAGI, n. carpenter.   --syn. KARPINTERO.

[1]ALLAWAT, v. /MANG-:-EN/ to meet and carry, to fetch. Allawaten na kaminto ti sabali nga trak no makadanon kami idiay ballasiw ti karayan. Another truck will fetch us when we reach the other side of the river.

[2]ALLAWAT, v. /MANG-:-EN/ to understand. Allawatem diay sarita na. Understand his speech.   --syn. [2]AWAT.

ALLEG, v. /AG-:-AN/ to do quickly, fast, or in a hurry. Allegam ti mangan ket aldawen. Make haste in eating for it's getting late.   /AG-:-AN/ to hurry up, make haste. Allegam ket aldawen. Hurry up for it is getting late. Agalleg ka tapno dika nga maudi. Hurry up so that you won't be late.

ALLID, n. paste, beeswax.   --syn. PIGKET.

ALLILAW, v. /MANG-:-EN/ to confuse, deceive, cause to make a mistake. Saan nak nga allilawen. Don't deceive me.   /MA-/ to be confused or deceived, to be mistaken. Narigat ti maallilaw. It is bad to be deceived.

ALLINGAG, v. /MANG-:-EN/ often /MAKA-:MA-/ to hear indistinctly or confusedly. Adu ti maallingag ko no addaak diay tiendaan. I can hear many things when I am in the store.

ALLON, n. wave, ripple.

ALLUDOY, v. /AG-/ to move or walk slowly so as not to be noticed. Nagal-alludoy nga nagawid diay balasang. The young woman walked slowly home.

ALLUKUD, v. /MANG-:-EN/ to lead, guide, conduct by holding or supporting by the hand. Allukudem ni lelang mo ket nakapsut. Hold your grandmother by the hand and guide her for she is weak.

ALLUP, v. /MANG-:-EN/ to invite (someone) to be one's
partner in dancing; to invite (someone) to dance with
oneself. Inka allupen daydiay balasang. Go invite
that girl to dance with you.

ALMIDOR [f. Sp.], n. starch (for clothes).
    v. /AG-/ 1. to make starch for clothes. 2. to
starch clothes. /MANG-:-AN/ to starch (clothes),
put starch on (clothes). Dimo nga almidoran daytoy
pantalon ko. Don't starch my pants.

ALMIRES [f. Sp.], n. small stone mortar.

ALMORANAS [f. Sp.], n. hemorrhoids, piles.

ALMUSAR [f. Sp.], n. breakfast.
    v. /AG-/ to eat breakfast, to have (something for)
breakfast. Agalmusarak iti itlog. I'll have an egg
(or eggs) for breakfast. Itlog ti pagalmusar ko.
My breakfast will consist of eggs.

ALNAAB, adj. /NA-/ damp, humid, moist.
    v. /AG-/. Agalnaab dagitoy tugtugaw no agtudtudo.
These seats become damp when it rains.

AL-O, n. pestle.

ALOG, n. lowland, low field.   --syn. LUNGOG, TANGKIG;
see also SALOG.

ALOMIIM, v. /MA-:KA-/ to feel queasy, qualmish, timid,
afraid, wary (to do something). Maalomiimak nga mapan
idiay. I feel queasy to go there.

ALSA [f. Sp.], v. /-UM-/ to rise up (as dough); to rise
up in arms, revolt. Immalsa ti adu nga tao. Many
people revolted. /MANG-:-EN/ to raise up, lift up,
heave.

ALSEM, adj. /NA-/ sour, tart, acidic; not sweet.
    v. /-UM-/.
    PAGALSEM, n. fruit, vegetable or leaves used in
    making a dish sour.

ALSONG, n. mortar.

ALTAPRESION [altapresión; f. Sp.], n. high-blood
pressure.

ALUAD, v. /AG-/ to be careful, watchful, cautious, wary; to beware, watch out. Agaluad ka, barok. Watch out, my son. /MANG-:-AN/ to care for, take care of, pay attention to. Dina nga inaluadan dagiti alikamen na. He did not take care of his personal belongings.

(TI) DIOS TI ALUAD NA (NGA), (the) late or deceased. Nasingpet daydi Dios ti aluad na nga uliteg mo. Your late uncle was kind.

ALUBUG, v. /-UM-/ to be proper, appropriate, suitable, equitable. Saan nga umalubug dayta nga aramid mo. That act of yours is not proper. /AG-/ [with pl. subject] to be suited to each other. Agalubug dagitoy dua nga itoy. These two are suited to each other.

ALUD, n. 1. embryo or fetus of animals. 2. small compartment inside a trunk, chest or locker.

ALUDAID, v. /AG-/ to sidle, shuffle; to move by dragging the feet in a sitting position. Agal-aludaid nga dimmanon ditoy. He reached this place by shuffling. /MANGI-:I-/ to do by sidling, shuffling or dragging the feet in a sitting position. Inyal-aludaid na ti nagawid. He shuffled his way home.

ALUDIG, n. a kind of tree with small scabrous leaves.

ALUD-UD, v. /AG-/ to glide or slide down. Nagalud-ud nga immulog. He slid coming down. --syn. ALUS-US.

ALUKON, n. a kind of tree whose flowers are eaten.

ALUMAMAY, adj. /NA-/ soft, kind, gentle, tender; mild, sweet. --var. ALUMANAY, ALUMAYMAY.

ALUMANAY, var. of ALUMAMAY.

ALUMAYMAY, var. of ALUMAMAY.

ALUMPIPINIG, n. small stinging bee.

ALUN-UN, v. /MANG-:-EN/ to gobble up, gorge; to gulp, swallow hurriedly and greedily. Saan mo nga alun-unen amin pati tulang. Don't swallow everything including the bones.

ALUNUS, v. /AG-/ to eat the sidedish(es) only, i.e.
without eating rice. Saan ka nga agalunus. Don't eat
sidedishes only. /MANG-:-EN/ to eat (sidedish)
without eating rice. Naimas nga alunusen dayta sida.
It's nice to eat that sidedish without eating rice.

ALUPASI, n. dry sheath of the banana leaf. --syn. see
UBBAK.

ALUS, v. /AG-, MANG-:-EN/ to receive or inherit (used
clothes, shoes, etc.). Adunto ti mabalin mo nga
alusen kenkuana. There will be many (used) things
that you will inherit from him.

ALUS-US, v. /AG-/ to slide down. Kitaem dayta ubing ta
saan nga agalus-us. Watch that child that he won't
slide down. /MANGI-:I-/ to slide down with. Saan mo
nga iyalus-us dayta ubing. Don't slide down with that
child. --syn. ALUD-UD.

ALUTEN, n. firebrand, a piece of burning wood, a piece
of half-burned wood with or without fire.

[1]ALUTIIT, n. house lizard. --syn. SALTEK; also see
ALIBUT.

[2]ALUTIIT, v. /AG-/ to protrude or rise up angrily and
temporarily, as the muscle of the arm when pinched
or struck sharply.

AL-ALUTIIT, n. the result of this action.

ALUT-UT, v. /MANG-:-EN/ to pull in order to loosen.
Narigat nga alut-uten daytoy lansa. It's hard to
loosen this nail.

ALWAD, see ALUAD.

AMA, n. father. --syn. TATANG, DADI.

AMA TI BUNYAG, TATANG (TI) BUNYAG, godfather.

AMA TI KASAR, TATANG (TI) KASAR, sponsor at one's
wedding.

AGAMA, n. pl.father and a child of his. AGAAMA, n.
pl. father and two or more of his children.

KAAMAAN, n. relatives on the father's side.

PANNAKAAMA, n. foster father, one who acts as father of.

AMAD, n. essence, sense, meaning; content, gist, topic, theme. Ania ti amad na diay sermon? What is the theme of the sermon?
v. /MANG-:-EN/ to determine, understand, perceive or analyze the sense or meaning of, to construe. Amadem nga nalaing no ania ti kayat na nga saw-en. Construe well what he wants to say.

AMAK, v. /MA-:KA-/ to be afraid or scared of, to fear, to be apprehensive about. Maamakak nga agtalaytay ti daytoy nga rangtay. I am scared to walk on this bridge.
adj. /NA-/ alleged or supposed with apprehension, to be feared. Naamak nga nalmes diay ubing. It is feared that the child drowned.

NAKAAM-AMAK, adj. frightening, scary. --syn. NAKAAL-ALINGGET, NAKAAM-AMES, NAKABUTBUTENG.

AM-AMANGAW, v. /AG-/ to be delirious, rave; to have one's mind wandering. Nadanaganak ta agam-amangaw met diay ubingen. I became worried because the child became delirious.

AM-AMMO, see under AMMO.

[1]AMANG, n. refuge, shelter, protection; protector.
v. /-UM-/ to take refuge or shelter, to seek protection. Mapan ka umamang iti adayo nga lugar. Go take refuge in a far place. /MANGI-:I-/ to take to (a place or someone) for refuge, shelter or protection. --var. KAMANG.

[2]AMANG, adv. by far. Napatpateg nga amang ngem sika daytoy anak ko. My child is more precious by far than you.

AMANGAN, interj. an exclamation expressing wonder - followed by a sentence introduced by NGA. Amangan nga nagadu ti tao. Oh, there were so many people.

AMANGAN NO, conj. lest, for fear that. Agawid kan amangan no agtudo. Go home lest it rains.

AMBING, v. /AG-, -UM-/ to envy or desire to have or eat something which some other person has. Apay nga umam-ambing ka dita? Why are you there envying what somebody has? /-UM-:-AN/ to envy or desire to have. Ti badok ti inambingan na. My dress is the one which she envied. --syn. APAL.

AMBUG [f. Sp.?], adj. /(NA-)/ proud, haughty, arrogant, insolent; vain, conceited; presumptuous, supercilious.

AMBULANSIA [f. Sp.], n. ambulance.

AMBULIGAN, n. corncob.

AMENG, adj. /NA-/ covetous, grasping, avaricious, greedy. v. /AG-, MANG-:-EN/ to covet. Dika agameng ti dimo kukua. Don't covet what is not yours.

AMERIKA [amérika; f. Sp.], n. America, the United States of America. --syn. ESTADOS UNIDOS.

AMERIKANA, n. 1. a female American, usually a citizen of the U.S.A. 2. a coat of the American or European style.
v. /AG-/ to wear a coat.

AMERIKANO, n. a male American, usually a citizen of the U.S.A. --var. KANO.

AMES; NAKAAM-AMES, adj. frightening, scary, dreadful, horrible. --syn. NAKAAL-ALINGGET, NAKAAM-AMAK, NAKABUTBUTENG, NAKAAP-APRANG.

AMIAN, n. north wind.

AMIANAN, n. north; northern region.

[1]AMIN, pron. all, whole; everyone, each one, everybody.

[2]AMIN, v. /MANG-:-EN/ to admit or confess (one's guilt, mistake, wrongdoing, etc.). /-UM-/ to admit or confess one's guilt or mistake. Immamin met laeng dayti kriminal. The criminal finally confessed his guilt.

AMIRIS, v. /-UM-, MANG-:-EN/ to determine, sense, perceive; to tell, construe. Narigat nga amirisen ti kayat na. It is hard to tell what he wants.

AMISIG, v. /-UM-, MANG-:-EN/ to observe or notice carefully, to pay careful attention to. Amisigem

nga nalaing ti kababalin mo. Pay very careful
attention to your capabilities.

AMITAW, n. an animal with only one testis in the
scrotal sac.

AMLID, v. /AG-/ to wipe the nose with the arm. Saan
ka nga agamlid. Don't wipe your nose with your arm.
/MANGI-:I-/ to wipe or rub on. Daytoy biks ti iyamlid
mo idiay agung na. Rub this Vicks ointment on his
nose.

AMMA, pl. of AMA.

AMMINGAW, v. /-UM-/ to make a brief appearance or visit,
to pass by, drop in briefly. Dika pay umammingaw ditoy.
You don't even show yourself here.

AMMO, n. knowledge, information; volition. Adu ti ammo
na. He knows many things.
    v. know(s), knew, (it is) known (by someone). Ammok
ti nagan mo. I know your name. /MANG-:-EN/ to know,
recognize, acknowledge. Ammoem nga awan ti basol ko.
Let it be known by you that I am not to be blamed.
/MAKA-/ to be responsible for. Sika ti makaammo ti
pagluganan. You be responsible for the transportation.
  AMMOK PAY?, AMMOK KADI?, How do I know?, or: I don't
  know.
  PAKAAMMO, v. /AG-:I-/ to make known, give notice of,
  inform. Ipakaammom kanyada nga agponsion tayo no
  bigat. Inform them that we are going to have a feast
  tomorrow.
  AM-AMMO, n. acquaintance (of), one who is known (to
  someone). Am-ammok ni baket mo. I know your wife.
      v. /MAKI-:KA-, -EN/ to make the acquaintance of,
  to introduce oneself to, to meet formally. Mabalin
  kadi ti makiam-ammo diay nobiam? May I make the
  acquaintance of your fiancee? /MANGI-:I-/ to
  introduce (someone) to, to make or let (someone)
  meet or make the acquaintance of. Diak kayat nga
  iyam-ammo kaniana daiy nobiak. I don't want to
  introduce my sweetheart to him.

AMMOL, v. /AG-, MANG-:-AN/ to hold in the mouth without
biting or sucking with the lips folded in over the
teeth. Saan mo ammolan ta lapis ta narugit. Don't

hold that pencil in your mouth because it is dirty.
/AG-/ to hold something in the mouth. --syn. MOLMOL.

AMMUYO, v. /MANG-:-EN/ to request to work with oneself
gratuitously, to ask the help of. --syn. BATARIS.

AMNAW, adj. /NA-/ weak, flat (wine, liquor, food, etc.).

AMNESIA [amnísia; f. Eng.], n. amnesia.

AMNOT, adj. /NA-/ strong, tough, solid; robust, hardy,
vigorous.
    v. /-UM-/.

[1]AMO, n. master, lord; leader, protector. --var. AMONG.

[2]AMO, adj. /NA-/ tame, domesticated; meek, gentle, mild;
kind.
    v. /-UM-/. --ant. ATAP.

AMONG, var. of AMO.

AMPANG, adj. /NAG-/ silly, foolish, wanton: said of
women.
    v. /AG-/.

[1]AMPAW, n. a kind of native sweet made of glutinous rice
powder which is cooked in lard until it swells and
forms a hollow ball after which it is rolled on
popped glutinous rice steeped in melted sugar.

[2]AMPAW, adj. /NAG-/ foolish, silly, nit-wit.
    v. /AG-/.

AMPAYAG, var. of AMPAYOG.

AMPAYOG, v. /AG-/ to glide, float, hover. Agam-ampayog
diay eroplano. The airplane is gliding. --var.
AMPAYAG.

AMPIR, v. /-UM-/ to stay or go close to. Umampir ka
dita diding tapno saan ka nga mabasa. Stay close to
the wall so that you won't get wet. /MANGI-:I-/ to
put or place close to. Iyampir mo dayta banko dita
diding. Put that bench close to the wall.

AMPO, n. a kind of small, blackish fish whose meat is
esteemed.

AMUY, v. /MANG-:-EN/ or /MANGI-:I-/ 1. to gather at the edge of table, floor, etc., e.g. dust. 2. to push back and put in place, e.g. hair. Amuyem ta book mo. Push your hair back in place.

[1]-AN [pt. -IN--AN, prp. R1 + -AN, ptp. -IN- + R1 + -AN], a passive verbalizing prefix which focuses the location, goal, or cause of the action expressed by the verb. Its principal meanings are the following: 1. to do the action at a certain place, or to someone or something. Punasan na ta lamisaan. He will wipe that table. Pukisan na diay ubing. He will give the child a haircut. 2. to do the action at, from, toward or away from someone or something. Kinatawaan nak. He laughed at me. 3. to give or get (something) from (someone). Siak man ti gatangan yo ti asin. Please buy salt from me. 4. to put or add the thing identified or implied by the stem to something. Dinanuman na dayta ap-apoyem. He added water to what you are cooking. 5. to earn (something) by doing the action expressed by the stem. Salapi ti dinaitan na. He earned fifty centavos by sewing. 6. to pay for (something) with the amount indicated by the stem. Pisosan da daytoy bagas. They will pay one peso for this husked rice. 7. to do the action expressed by the verb because of something. Ania ti sangitan diay balasang? What is the young woman crying for? 8. to do (something) in the manner described by the stem. Pinartakan da ti nagtaray. They ran fast.

-AN forms locative-focus verbs with the following verbalizing affixes: MAKA-, MAKI-, PAG-, PANG-, PANGI-, -UM-; see also MA--AN.

[2]-AN, a nominalizing suffix meaning: that which is used to do the action expressed by the stem; e.g. gilingan, grinder. The first consonant and first vowel of some stems is reduplicated; e.g. sasakayan, that which is used as conveyance.

ANA, var. (dial.) of ANIA.

ANAAW, n. a tall and slender palm tree (Livistona rotundifolia. Bart.) whose leaves are used to make native raincoats (ANNANGA) and hats. --syn. LABID.

ANABAAB, n. the sound or echo of speech that is not heard distinctly. Matmaturog da ngata ta awan ti

anabaab da. Maybe they are sleeping for they don't
make any noise.
v. /-UM-/ to be noisy. Umanabaab kay la dita.
You are very noisy.

ANAG, n. meaning, essence; flavor, characteristic
property. Daytoy ti anag ti biag ko. This is the
meaning of my life.

[1]ANAK, n. [pl. ANNAK; AN-ANAK for fishes] offspring,
young; son, daughter.
v. /AG-/ to give birth, to bear or deliver an
offspring or offsprings. Naganak diay aso yon? Has
your dog given birth? /MANGI-:I-/ to give birth to,
to bear or deliver. Singin ti inyanak na. She gave
birth to twins.

INANAK, n. child, offspring, son, daughter.

AANAKAN, n. uterus, womb. --syn. MATRIS.

ANAK TI BUNYAG, godchild.

ANAK TI RUAR, illegitimate child.

ANAK TI SAL-IT, an expression used in cursing.

[2]ANAK, v. /MANG-:-EN/ to be the godparent of. Sino ti
nanganak kenka? Who was your godparent?

[3]ANAK, n. interest on money loaned or deposited.
v. /AG-:-EN/ to earn as interest: said of money
loaned or deposited. Naganak ti lima nga pisos diay
kuartak idiay banko. My money in the bank earned
four pesos as interest.

ANAMONG, v. /-UM-:-AN/ to agree, concur, consent. Saan
ka nga umanamong no saan nga nasayaat dagiti kondision
da. Don't agree if their terms are not good.
/AG-:PAG--AN/ [with pl. subject] Nagaanamong da nga
mapan idiay Manila. They agreed to go to Manila.

AN-ANAK, pl. of [1]ANAK n.

ANANAY, interj. an exclamation expressing sudden pain,
ouch. --see ANNAY.

AN-ANAY, see under [1]ANAY.

AN-ANNONG, v. /MANG-:-AN/ to make (someone) ill
  through the influence of the spirit of one's dead
  relative. Saannak nga an-annongan. Don't make me
  sick through the influence of the spirit of your
  dead relative. /MA-AN/ to be made ill or sick by
  the spirit of someone's dead relative.
    adj. /MAKA-/ able to make someone sick through
  the spirit of his dead relative.

AN-ANO, v. /AG-/ to do, to happen, to be the matter
  with (usually in questions). Agan-ano ta sakam?
  What is the matter with your foot? /MANG-:-EN/ to
  do something with, to use for (usually in questions).
  An-anoem dagitoy nakaad-adu nga karne? What are you
  going to do with this so much meat? /PAG-/ to do
  with, to use for (usually in questions); to do
  something with. Saan ko nga pagan-ano dayta nga
  bado. I have no use for that dress. /MA-/ to happen
  (usually in questions). Naan-ano dayta ulom? What
  happened to your head?

  AN-ANO is a substitute for the stem of a verb used
    interrogatively.

ANANSA; ANANSA TA, ANANSA TA NGARUD: hence, wherefore,
  therefore - used in formal or religious situations.
  Anansa ta inkan. Hence go now.

ANANG-ANG, v. /AG-/ to whine, howl as a dog. --var.
  ALANG-ANG.

ANAT, adj. /NA-/ calm, tranquil, serene, placid,
  peaceful; slow.

ANATUP, v. /-UM-/ to be enough or sufficient; to be
  suited or appropriate. Saan nga umanatup dayta. That
  is not appropriate. /MANGI-:I-/ to make enough or
  sufficient or appropriate; to compensate for. Saan
  nga maiyanatup dayta nga aramid mo kadagiti adu nga
  rigrigat na kenka. That behavior of yours cannot
  compensate for all the hardships she suffered for
  you.

  KAANATUP, n. that which corresponds.
    v. /AG-/ [with plural subject] to correspond to
  each other.

  KAANATUPAN, n. that which has the same value, the
    equivalent. Ti ited mo, dayta kaanatupan ti

kuartak. Give the one that is the equivalent of my money.

ANAWA, v. /MANG-:-EN/ to stop from making noise or from quarreling; to make quiet, to silence. Anawaem man dagidiay ubbing ta matmaturog ni tatang da. Will you please tell the children to keep quiet for their father is sleeping. /MA-/ to be stopped from making noise or from quarreling, to be made quiet, to be silenced. Apay nga saan kay nga maanawa? Why can't you be stopped (from making noise)?

ANAY, n. termite, white ant.
v. /-EN/ to be eaten or attacked by termites. Inanay diay adigi ti balay da. The post of their house was attacked by termites.

[1]ANAY, v. /-UM-/ to be enough or sufficient. Saan nga umanay dayta nga kanen ti lima nga tao. That won't be enough for five persons to eat. /MANG-:-AN, -EN/ to increase to a certain quantity. Anayam nga sanga salup daytoy bagas. Increase this rice to one 'salup'. /MANGI:I-/ to add to especially in order to make sufficient. Iyanay mo daytoy dita kuartam. Add this to your money.

AN-ANAY, adj. /NA-/ sufficient, enough. Pagarupek a daytoy panagkalap no maipaayan iti naan-anay a panawen, mabalin a taudan ti rang-ay. I think that if fishing is given sufficient time, it will bring about progress.

[2]ANAY, n. silt.

ANDADASI, n. a leguminous, erect, suffrutescent herb with moderately large yellow flowers. Its leaves are used to cure skin diseases.

ANDAP, n. opalescence, luminescence, phosphorescence.
v. /AG-/ to be luminous.

ANDAS [f. Sp.], n. a frame on which a religious image is carried; bier.

ANDIDIT, n. cicada. --syn. KUNDIDIT.

ANDINGAY, v. /MANG-:-EN/ to keep company, to entertain. Saan ka pay nga agawid ta andingayen na kam pay ditoy. Don't go home yet and entertain us here.

ANDUR, n. perseverance, endurance.
      v. /MAKA-:MA--AN/ to be able to suffer or endure. Diak nga maanduran ti sakit daytoy ulok. I cannot endure my headache.

ANEM-EM, adj. /APAG-/ just beginning to get hot. Apag-anem-em daytoy danum. This water is just beginning to get hot.
      v. /MANG-:-EN/ to make hot (but not boiling hot). Anem-emem ta danum. Make the water hot (but not boiling hot).

ANENG-ENG, v. /AG-/ to whine, whimper, moan. Agan-aneng-eng diay masakit. The sick person is moaning.   --syn. ARENG-ENG.

ANEP, adj. /NA-/ fond of, eager, diligent. Naanep nga mapan ditoy diay aso yo. Your dog is fond of coming here.

ANI, v. /AG-/ to harvest crops, reap crops. Mapan kami agani. We're going to harvest the crops. /MANG-:-EN/ Saan mo pay nga anien dagita ta saan da pay nga natangkenan. Don't harvest those yet for they are not yet mature.

ANIA, inter. what?, which? Ania ti kayat mo? What do you want?

   ANIAMAN, anything, whatever, whatsoever. Aniaman ti kayat mo gatangek. Whatever you want I will buy. Awan ti ania man. You're welcome.

   ANIA NGARUD? So what can be done?

   ANIA KAN?, ANIA KA LA KETDIN?, You're too much. You're impossible.

   ANIA TA, ANIA KETDI TA, why is that, what is the reason that. Ania ketdi ta adda ka man ditoyen? Why is it that you're here again?

ANIATAY, short for ANIA DAYTAY, what is it?, what do you call it? Siguro, umay mangipatakder iti aniatayen, Lakay? Maybe, he came to build, what is it now, my husband?

ANIB, n. protective talisman for house or person,
defensive weapon, amulet, charm.   --syn.
ANTING-ANTING.

ANIMAL [f. Sp.], n. animal, beast.   --syn. AYOP.

ANIMAL! or: ANIMAL KA! You beast!

ANINAW, n. reflection, outline.
    v. /MAKA-:MA--AN/ to be able to perceive or see
vaguely. Narigat nga maaninawan ti sumungsungad
nga awto. It is hard to see clearly the approaching
car.

ANINIWAN, n. shadow, shade; image.   --see ANINAW.

ANIS [f. Sp.], n. anise.

ANITO, n. spirit, ghost of ancestor; superstition.
    v. /AG-/ to worship the ancestral spirits. Saan
mo nga patien dagiti aganito. Don't believe those
who worship the ancestral spirits.

ANNAD, v. /AG-/ to be careful, cautious, wary; to
beware. Agannad ka ta nagalis ta dalan. Be careful
for the road is slippery. /MANG-:-AN/ to take care
of, be careful, cautious, or wary about. Annadam
nga bagkaten dayta banga ta dinto ket mabuong. Be
careful about carrying that pot for it might get
broken.
    adj. /NA-/ careful, cautious, wary; meticulous.
Naannad ni nana Rosa nga agtagibalay. Mother Rose
is meticulous about keeping the house.

ANNAK, pl. of [1]ANAK n.

ANNANGA, n. a kind of raincoat made of palm leaves
usually of the ANAAW or LABID.

ANNAWID, see KAANNAWIDAN.

ANNAWIL, var. of ANNAWIR.

ANNAWIR, v. /AG-/ to speak or pronounce words badly,
imperfectly or incorrectly; to have a speech defect.
Saan mo nga katawaan no agannawir. Don't laugh at
him if he pronounces some words incorrectly.   --var.
ANNAWIL.

ANNAY, v. /AG-/ to moan or cry because of pain, to express pain, to say ouch. Nalaing ka la unay nga agannay. You are good in expressing pain. --see ANANAY.

ANNAYASAN, see PAGANNAYSAN.

[1]ANNONG, v. /MAKA-:-MA-AN/ to be able, competent or qualified to do or carry. Saan ko nga maannongan dayta ta nadagsen. I cannot carry that because it is heavy.

[2]ANNONG, see AN-ANNONG.

ANNUGOT, v. /-UM-, MANG-:-EN/ to obey; to consent to, to acquiesce, permit. Saan mo nga annuguten nga basol mo. Don't acquiesce that it is your fault.
  adj. /NA-/ obedient, meek, submissive, dutiful; willing. Naannugot ni Pepe nga agidulin. Pepe is willing to do the dishes. --syn. ANNUROT, TULOK.

ANNUROT, v. /-UM-/ to acquiesce, consent, agree; to comply, obey. Umannurot kan tapno awan ti riri. Acquiesce so that there will be no trouble. /MANG-:-EN/ to follow, obey, do obediently. Annurotem dagiti bilin ko kenka. Follow my instructions to you. --syn. ANNUGOT, TULOK.

ANO, n. pus, purulent matter. --syn. (dial.) NANA.

ANO, see AN-ANO, INTONANO, KANNO, KAPIN-ANO, KASANO, MAMIN-ANO, PAANO, TAGAANO.

ANONANG, var. of ANONAS.

ANONAS [f. Sp.], n. custard apple (Anona reticulata). --var. ANONANG.

ANSISIT, n. dwarf, elf. --syn. KIBAAN, KATAWTAW-AN.

[1]ANTA, v. /MANGI-:I-/ to soak, immerse. Iyantam dayta dita danum tapno nadardaras nga maikkat ta rugit na. Soak that in that water so that it would be easier to remove its dirt.

[2]ANTA, var. of YANTA.

ANTIGO [f. Sp.], adj. /(NA-)/ of good quality, genuine, not an imitation.

ANTING-ANTING, n. amulet, charm, talisman. --syn. ANIB.

ANTIMANO [f. Sp.], adv. right away, immediately, straightaway. --syn. DARAS, SIGUD.

ANUD, v. /MANGI-:I-/ to carry away: said of water currents. Saan mo nga ibbatan dayta swekos mo ta dinto iyanud toy karayan. Don't drop your shoes for it might be carried away by the currents of this river. /MAI-/ to be carried away by water currents. Naiyanud diay malo. The clothes beater was carried away by the currents. --syn. AYOS.

ANUG-UG, v. /AG-/ to weep, wail, sob. --syn. IBIT, SANGIT.

ANUNSIO [f. Sp.], n. advertisement, announcement.

ANUP, v. /AG-/ to hunt wild animals usually with dogs and guns or bows and arrows and spears. /MANG-:-EN/ to hunt usually with dogs and guns, or bows and arrows and spears. Inkami manganup ti alingo. We'll go and hunt a wild pig.

MANGNGANUP, n. hunter.

ANUS, adj. /NA-/ patient, kind, gentle, considerate, lenient, indulgent, forbearing.
   v. /AG-/ to be patient, kind, gentle, etc.
/AG-, MANG-:-AN/ to be patient with, to be kind to, to endure, suffer (someone or something). An-anusam ta nanang ken tatang mo ta nakapsut dan. Be kind to your mother and father for they are already weak. Anusam ti agtrabaho tapno makaurnong ka ti pagadal mo. Be patient with your work so that you can save money for your schooling.

ANG-ANG, adj. /NAG-/ stupid, dumb.

ANGAT, v. /MAKI-:-EN, KA-/ to fight or quarrel with (someone). /AG-/ [with pl. subject] to fight or quarrel with each other. Saan mo nga pagtipunen dagita aso ken pusa tapno saan da nga agangat. Don't put together that dog and cat so that they won't quarrel with each other. --syn. 2APA.

ANGAW, v. /AG-/ to joke, tease; to make jokes.
Agang-angaw kansa. You seem to be joking. /MANG-:-EN/
to joke with, tease; to make fun of. Saan mo nga
angawen ta ubing ta dinto agsangit. Don't make fun of
that child lest he cries.
    adj. /NA-/ fond of joking with or teasing someone.
--syn. ARTYUK.

ANGAY, v. /MANG-:-EN/ to invite. Angayem amin nga
gagayyem mo. Invite all your friends.   --syn. IMBITAR.

ANGDOD, adj. /NA-/ having offensive odor: said of
animals, men, milk, etc.

ANGED, n. nasal discharge, mucus.
    v. /AG-/ to have a running nose, to have much nasal
discharge.

ANGEP, n. mist, fog.
    adj. /NA-/ misty, foggy.

ANGER, v. /AG-, MANG-:-EN/ to cook by boiling, to boil.
Angrem dayta karne inggana ti lumukneng. Boil that
meat until it gets soft.

ANGES, v. /-UM-, AG-/ to breathe, to respire.

    ANGSEN, adj. asthmatic.   --syn. ANGKITEN.

    AANGSAN, n. windpipe, region of the windpipe.

ANGGO, v. /-UM-, MANG-:-EN/ to kiss.   --syn. AGEK,
UNGNGO, BISUNG.

ANGHEL [aŋhέl; f. Sp.], n. angel.

ANGIN, n. wind, draft, current of air.
    v. /AG-/ to have a wind, to produce a wind.   /MAI-/
to be blown or carried away by the wind, to be blown
down by the wind.   /-EN/ to be filled with gas: said
of the stomach. Agules ka ta dinto anginen ta tian mo.
Cover yourself with a blanket lest your stomach will
be filled with gas.   /MA-/ to be caught in a draft,
to be hit by a wind.
    adj. /NA-/ windy, drafty. Naangin ita nga aldaw. It
is windy today.

ANGKAT, v. /-UM-:-EN/ to borrow, take on credit
(merchandise). Mapanak umangkat ti alahas nga ilakok.
I'm going to take on credit jewels to sell. --syn.
UTANG.

ANGKIT, n. asthma.
      v. /AG-/ to have asthma, to contract asthma, to
have an attack of asthma.
      adj. /-EN/ asthmatic.

ANGLEM, n. smoke or smell of smoke of burning cloth,
paper, etc.
      v. /AG-/ to burn cotton, cloth, etc. in order to
drive away evil spirits that cause sickness.

ANGLIT, adj. /NA-/ having repulsive odor coming mostly
from the armpit, having strong odor like that of a
goat.
      v. /AG-/ to be afflicted with a disease of the
armpit, to diffuse a strong odor from the armpit,
to have halitosis.

ANGNGAB, v. /MANG-:-AN/ to take or hold with the lips
or teeth without biting. Saan mo nga angngaban dayta
lapis. Don't hold that pencil with your teeth. --syn.
AMMOL.

ANGNGUYOB, var. of ANGUYOB.

ANGOL, n. epidemic, pest.
      v. /AG-, MA-, -EN/ to be attacked by pest or
epidemic: usually said of chickens. Agangol dagiti
manok. The chickens are attacked by pest. --syn.
PESTE.

ANGOT, v. /-UM-:-EN/ to smell.
      adj. /NA-/ having a strong, offensive smell, ill-
smelling, stinking.

ANGREN, = ANGER + -EN.

ANGRI, adj. /NA-/ having a smell like that of fish,
bats, etc.

ANGSAB, v. /AG-/ to pant.

ANGSEG, adj. /NA-/ having a smell like that of putrid
urine.

ANGSEN, see under ANGES.

ANGSET, adj. /NA-/ having the smell of burned rice, meat, etc.

ANGTEM, adj. /NA-/ having the smell of burning resin, pitch, burning flesh, etc.

ANGTIT, n. stench of fermenting fish, meat, etc. adj. /NA-/ having the stench of this.

ANGUYOB, n. blowpipe. --var. ANGNGUYOB.

AON, v. /-UM-/ to come up, climb up, as from a hole, a canal, etc. Adu ti alinta nga immaon idiay kanal. Many earthworms climbed up from the canal. /MANGI-:I-/ or /MANG-:-EN/ to pull up from, to push out from, to take out from, to scoop from. Inda iyaon diay ubing nga natnag idiay adalem nga abut. They are going to pull up the child who fell into the deep hole.

[1]APA, n. thin rolled wafer made of rice starch and brown sugar.

[2]APA, v. /MANG-:-EN/, /Maki-:-EN/, /AG-/ [with pl. subject] to quarrel, fight, wrangle or argue with one another. --syn. ANGAT.

APAG, n. share. --syn. BINGAY, BAGI.

APAG-, a prefix meaning 1. as soon as. Apagsangpet na, naturog. As soon as he arrived, he went to sleep. 2. just, no more than, in just. Apagbiit ka laeng. Be away in just a little while.

APAL, v. /-UM-:-AN/ to envy or be envious of (someone or something). Umapal ken ni Rosa ta adu ti bado na. She is envious of Rose because she has many clothes. --syn. AMBING.

APAMAN, adv. scarcely, barely, hardly. Apaman nga nagtaul ta asom. Your dog hardly barked. conj. as soon as. Apaman nga malpas ti misa, agawid tayon. As soon as the mass is finished, let's go home.

APAGAPAMAN, hardly enough, scarcely sufficient. Apagapaman ti balon tayo. Our provisions are hardly enough.

APAN, n. bait.
    v. /MANG-:-AN/ to put a bait on. Apanam dayta
banniit mo. Put a bait on your fish hook.
/MANGI-:I-/ to put as bait, to use as bait. --syn.
AR-ARAK. --var. APPAN.

AP-AP, n. a piece of cloth, paper, leaf, etc. that is
    spread on the floor, ground, table, bed, etc.
    v. /MANG-:-AN/ to spread a piece of cloth, paper,
leaf, etc. on (the floor, the ground, a table, a
bed, etc.). Ap-apam ta pagtugawan na. Spread
something on the place where he is going to sit.
    v. /MANGI-:I-/ to spread on, to use as spread.
--syn. APLI, APIN.

APAS, v. /MA-/ to be irritated, to be a poor sport.
    Saan ka nga makiangaw no nalaka ka nga maapas. Don't
joke with others if you get irritated easily. /KA-/
to be irritated with. Kinaapas nak. He was irritated
with me.

[1]APAY, v. /-UM-/ to feel strongly, be affected or
    attacked by (illness, emotional distress, etc.).
No malagip ko ni nanang ko, umapay ti iliw ko.
Whenever I remember my mother, I am attacked by
homesickness.

[2]APAY, inter. why?, what is the reason? Apay nga
    agsangsangit ka? Why are you crying? --var. (dial.)
SAPAY.

    APAYA, same as APAY.

APELYIDO [apɛlyido; f. Sp.], family name, surname, last
    name. Ania ti apelyidom? What is your family name?

APGAD, adj. /NA-/ salty.
    v. /-UM-/.

APGES, adj. /NA-/ sharp, acute, smarting: said of pain.
    v. /-UM-/.

APIG, v. /MANG-:-EN/ to part: said of the hair, grasses,
    underbrush, etc. Apigem ta buok mo. Part your hair.

APIN, n. any leaf or pieces of leaf, usually of the
    banana, spread at the bottom of an earthen pot before

the rice that has to be cooked is poured into it.
v. /AG-/ to place this at the bottom of a pot.
/MANG-:-AN/ to place this at the bottom of. Apinam
nga umuna ta banga sa mo ipisok diay bagas. Spread
a leaf at the bottom of the pot first then pour in
the rice.   --syn. AP-AP, APLI.   --var. PALUNAPIN.

APIRAS, v. /-UM-, MANG-:-EN/ to grope, search by
feeling; to feel with the hand. Apirasem dayta
rabaw ti lamisaan. Feel with your hand the surface
of the table.   --syn. ARIKAP.

APIRING, v. /-UM-/ to stay or stand close or adjacent
to, to cling to. Umapiring ka dita alad. Stay close
to the fence.   /AG-/ [with pl. subject] to be close
to each other almost or actually touching one
another. Iyasideg mo dayta tugaw dita pader inggana
ti agapiring da. Put that seat near the wall until
they are close to each other.   /MANGI-:I-/ to put,
place or take close to.

APIT, v. /AG-, MANG-:-EN/ to harvest, reap.   --syn.
ANI; see also BURAS.

APLAG, v. /MANGI-:I-/ to spread, roll out, unfurl.
Iyaplag mo dayta ikamen ditoy. Spread the mat here.

APLAT, n. a kind of aphid or plant louse.

APLI, syn. of AP-AP and APIN.

APLIT, v. /MA NG-:-AN/ to whip in a slashing way. Saan
mo nga aplitan dayta asok. Don't whip my dog.
/MANGI-:I-/ to whip (someone or something) in a
slashing way. Saan ka nga umasideg ti dayta buaya
ta dinanto ket iyaplit ta ipus na kenka. Don't go
near that crocodile lest he slashes his tail on you.

APNUT, v. /MANG-:-AN/ to wax: said of strings, threads,
etc. Apnutam dayta panait tapno lumagda. Wax the
sewing thread so that it will become strong.
adj. /NA-/ strong, resilient.

APO, n. a respectful term of address used to an older
man or woman, or a person of authority; (sir, ma'am)
may be followed by the surname of the person or the
title of his or her position. Wen, apo. Yes, sir.

APO, n. 1. grandparent, grandfather, grandmother. --
--see APONG. 2. grandchild. grandson, granddaughter.
--see APOKO.

APO TI TUMENG, great-grandparent, great-grandchild.

APO TI DAPAN, great-great-grandparent, great-great-
grandchild.

APOKO, n. grandchild, grandson, granddaughter. --see
APO 2.

APON, n. dwelling place, abode.
v. /AG-/ to roost: said especially of fowls.
/MANGI-:I-/ to put in a roost, to roost.

APONG, n. grandparent, grandfather, grandmother; may
be used as a term of address. --see APO 1.

APONG (NGA) LAKAY, grandfather. --syn. LELONG, LOLO.

APONG (NGA) BAKET, grandmother. --syn. LELANG, LOLA.

APOY, n. fire, light. Awan ti apoy mi. We have no fire
(or light).
v. /-UM-/ to produce or give off sparks, to spark
or sparkle. Immapoy diay buneng nga intagbat na idiay
bato. The big knife which he hit that big stone with
gave off sparks. /AG-/ to cook rice, to cook a meal.
Agapoy kan ta mabisinakon. Cook the meal now for I am
already hungry. /AG-, MANG-:-EN/ to cook (rice or
the food for a meal). Agapoy ka ti adu nga bagas.
Cook plenty of rice.

APPO, pl. of APO 1, 2.

APPOEN, n. pl. descendants.

APPOPO, v. /AG-/ to become or be shaped like a cup: said
of the hands. Nagappopo ti imana. His hands were
shaped like a cup. /MANG-:-EN/ to hold in the cup of
one's hands. Appopoen na dagitoy. He will hold these
in the cup of his hands.

APPUT, v. /AG-/ to cover one's external genitals with
one's hands. /MANG-:-EN/ to cover, screen off with
one's hands. Apputem ta matam. Cover your eyes with
your hands.

APRAD, v. /MAKA-:MA--AN/ to cause (someone) to become
hoarse. Daytoy ti nakaaprad kanyak. This is the one

which causes me to become hoarse.
adj. /MAKA-,′ causing hoarseness. Diak kayat dayta
ta makaaprad. I don't like that for it causes
hoarseness.

APRANG; NAKAAP-APRANG, adj. horrible, horrid, dreadful,
terrible, shocking, ghastly.   --syn. NAKAAM-AMES.

APRAS, v. /MANG-:-EN/ to beat, to strike with a stick,
pole, etc. so as to drop down. Aprasem dagita bunga
ti mangga tapno matnag da. Strike the fruits of the
mango with a stick so that they will drop down.

APRO, n. bile, gall.

APROS, v. /MANG-:-EN/ to touch, rub or stroke softly
and gently with the hand. Aprosem daytoy takkiag ko.
Touch my arm.

APSAY, v. /AG-/ to sit down with the legs stretched out.

APUG, n. lime.

APUNGOL, v. /MANG-:-EN/ to embrace, hug; to clasp in
one's arms. Apungolem ni nanang mo. Embrance your
mother.

ARAB, v. /AG-/ to graze, to eat grass. Saan mo nga
ipalubos nga agarab dagita kalding ditoy inaladan
tayo. Don't allow those goats to graze in our yard.
/AG-:-EN/ to eat, graze on. Inarab dagitay kalding
ta mulam. The goats ate your plants.

ARADAS, v. /AG-/ to go stealthily and rape a sleeping
woman.   /MANG-:-EN/ to go to (a woman) stealthily and
rape. Saan mo nga aradasen diay balasang ko. Don't
rape my young daughter.

ARADO [f. Sp.], n. plow.
v. /AG-/ to plow, to use a plow. Dina pay ammo ti
agarado. He still does not know how to use a plow.
/MANG-:-EN/ to plow, to use a plow on. Inka man
aradoen diay talon ko. Will you please go plow my
field.

ARAGAAG, adj. /NA-/ old, such as utensils, tools, etc.

[1]ARAGAN, n. an edible, brown seaweed or alga with flat thallus.

[2]ARAGAN; IMMARAGAN, adj. undulate, wavy, e.g. the hair.

ARAK, n. wine, liquor; any fermented drink.

ARAKIAK, v. /AG-/ to cackle, to cry: said of hens and roosters. Apay nga agarakiak dagidiay manok? Why do the chickens cackle?

ARAKUP, v. /-UM-, MANG-:-EN/ to embrace, hug, clasp with both hands. --syn. APUNGOL, RAKEP.

ARAMANG, n. a kind of small, edible, marine shrimp. --var. ARMANG.

ARAMAT, v. /AG-, MANG-:-EN/ to use. Daytoy ti aramatem. Use this. /MAKA-:MA-/ to need. Maaramat ko daytoy. I need this. --syn. USAR, ARWAT.

ARAMID, v. /AG-, MANG-:-EN/ to make, manufacture, construct, build. Ammok ti agaramid iti allawa. I know how to make a kite.

ARAN, n. witch, sorcerer, sorceress, conjurer, magician.

ARANG, v. /AG-, MANG-:-EN/ to block, blockade; to obstruct; to ambush. Isuda ti nangarang kaniak. They were the ones who ambushed me.

ARAPAAP, n. dreams, ambition, aspirations.
    v. /MANG-:-EN/ to dream of, imagine, aspire for. Adu la unay ti ar-arapaapem. You imagine so much. --syn. TAGAINEP.

AR-ARAK, n. bait, anything used as a lure, enticement.
    v. /MANG-:-AN/ to entice or lure to do something. Ar-arakam dayta manok tapno adu ti iyitlogna. Entice that hen so that it will lay many eggs. --syn. APAN.

ARARASAN, n. a very large black ant.

ARARAW, v. /-UM-:-EN/ to beg, plead, implore for. Adu ti umararaw kenkuana iti trabaho. There are many who beg him for work.

ARARAWAN, n. an edible, soft-winged insect that lives in wet places.

ARAS, n. a disease of the mouth of children and occasionally of adults characterized by pearl-colored flakes. --syn. MANGMANG.

ARASAAS, v. /AG-/ to whisper, mumble, mutter. /MANGI-:I-/ to whisper, to say or tell in a whisper. Iyarasaas mo kaniak ti nagan na. Whisper to me his name.

ARASAW, n. water used in washing or rinsing rice. v. /AG-/ to wash or rinse husked rice. /AG-, MANG-:-EN/ to wash or rinse in water. Arasawem ti mamitlo ta bagas. Rinse that rice three times.

ARAYAT, v. /-UM-:-EN/ to go and help, to give aid. Arayaten dak man ta matayakon. Please come help me for I am going to die. --syn. SARUNGKAR, TULONG.

ARAY-AY, v. /MANG-:-EN/ to tear, e.g. clothes. adj. /(NA-)/ torn, rent. --syn. PIGIS.

ARBAAKA, n. an aromatic plant used as a diuretic and to facilitate menstruation.

ARBAN, n. flock, herd, drove.

ARBAS, v. /AG-, MANG-:-AN/ to prune. Saan mo pay nga arbasan dayta nga kayo. Don't prune that tree yet.

ARBIS, n. drizzle, light rain, light shower. v. /AG-/ to drizzle, to rain lightly. /MA--AN/ to be caught in a drizzle or light rain. --syn. ARIMUKAMOK.

ARDIAY, var. of ADDAYDIAY.

AREB-EB, v. /AG-, -EN/ to gurgle, burp. Nagareb-eb diay ubing. The child burped. --syn. MULUMOG.

AREM, v. /AG-/ to court or woo a girl. Mapanak agarem dita ili. I'll go woo a girl in town. /AG-:-EN/ [= ARMEN] to court, woo, desire, covet. Saan mo nga armen dayta kasinsin mo. Don't woo your cousin.

ARENG-ENG, v. /AG-/ to neigh, whinny; to whine, moan.
Kasla ka la al-alia nga agar-areng-eng dita suli.
You are like a ghost moaning in that corner. --syn.
ANENG-ENG.

ARGAAY, see REGGAAY.

ARI, n. king, emperor, ruler.
   v. /AG-/ to become supreme, to be king.

ARIBASAY, v. /AG-/ to ooze, leak, trickle, flow out.
Agaribasay ti ling-et na. Perspiration oozed from his
body.

ARIBUDBUD, n. sediment, settling, lees, dregs.

ARIBUNGBUNG, v. /MANG-:-AN/ to surround, encircle,
gather around, throng around. Saan yo nga
aribungbungan dayta masakit. Don't gather around
that sick person.

ARIDAKDAK, v. /-UM-/ to walk heavily on floor, to stamp
the floor. Sann kay nga umaridakdak dita ta adda
matmaturog. Don't stamp the floor there for someone
is sleeping. --syn. ARIMPADEK.

ARIDTA, var. (dial.) of ADDAYTA.

ARIDTOY, var. (dial.) of ADDAYTOY.

[1]ARIEK, n. intestinal worm.

[2]ARIEK, v. /MA-/ [= MAARIEK or MARIEK] to be tickled,
excited or stirred up agreeably. Saan mo nga iggaman
ta siket ko ket mariekak. Don't hold my waist for
I'll get tickled.
   n. /KA-/ that which causes repulsion, revulsion,
withdrawal or a strong reaction, that which is
repulsive or revolting. Kaariek ko nga iggaman ta
igges. It is revolting for me to hold that worm.
   adj. /MAKA-/ [= MAKAARIEK or MAKARIEK] causing
someone to get tickled.

ARIG, v. /MANGI-:I-/ to compare, liken; treat like.
Inyarig nak as kas maysa nga kabsat na. He treated
me like a brother of his.

KAYARIGAN, PAGARIGAN, n. example, model.

KAS PAGARIGAN, for example.

ARIGENGEN, v. /AG-/ to shake, tremble, quiver, shiver.
Nagarigengen toy balay. This house shook.

ARIKAP, v. /MANG-:-EN/ to grope for, frisk for, feel
with the hand. Arikapem tay tulbek ko dita tuktok ti
aparador. Grope for my key on top of the cupboard.
--syn. APIRAS.

ARIMASAMAS, adj. /NA-/ coarse.

ARIMBANGAW, adj. /NA-/ noisy, boisterous, tumultous.
v. /-UM-, AG-/. --syn. ARIWAWA, ARIMEKMEK, TAGARI.

ARIMBUKENG, n. a species of crab.

ARIMEKMEK, n. noise, sound.
v. /AG-/ to make a noise or sound, to be noisy.
--syn. ARIWAWA, ARIMBANGAW, TAGARI.

ARIMPADEK, v. /AG-/ to walk heavily or noisily, to
stamp the feet. Saan ka nga agarimpadek ket adda
matmaturog. Don't stamp your feet because someone
is sleeping. --syn. ARIDAKDAK.

ARIMUKAMOK, v. /AG-/ to drizzle lightly, to rain
lightly. --syn. ARBIS.

ARIN-; ARIN--EN, AR-ARIN--EN + R2, adjectivizing affixes
meaning: to seem what the stem implies. Arintudoen
ita. It seems about to rain today.

ARINA [f. Sp.], n. flour, especially wheat four.

ARINSAED, var. of RINSAED.

ARINSAYAD, v. /AG-/ to trail, as a skirt or a pole
carried on the shoulder. Ingatom dayta pandiling mo
tapno saan nga agarinsayad. Pull up your skirt so
that it won't trail.

ARINUNOS, n. the latter period (of), the terminal period
(of), the period toward the end (of). Arinunos ti

Disiembre idi naawat ko diay surat mo. It was toward
the end of December when I received your letter.

ARINGGAWIS, n. top, peak, summit. --syn. TOKTOK.

ARIPAPA, v. /-UM-/ to calm down, to tone down, to pipe
down. Sa met la umaripapa idi makita na nga
agpudotakon. He then piped down when he saw that I
was getting angry.

ARIPIT, n. hairpin, pliers; vise. --syn. HERPIN.

ARIRING, n. difference, especially a slight one. Kasla
da la agkabaat ta bassit la ti ariring da. They are
like brothers and/or sisters because their difference
is slight.
    v. /AG-/ [with pl. subject] to be similar, to differ
slightly, to look alike. Agariring dagita annak yo.
Those children of yours differ slightly.

ARISANGSANG, n. spark, a flake of fire.

ARUSGA, v, /-UM-:-AN/ to do something beyond the limit
of one's capability, competence or endurance. Umarisga
nga agbasa diay ubing. The child tries to read (though
he still cannot read, etc.). Arisgaan na ti agmaneho.
He tries to drive a car (though he can hardly drive).

ARISIT, v. /MANG-:-EN/ to rid of sediments or dregs by
pouring off gently: said of oil and other liquids.
Arisitem dayta manteka. Remove the sediments of that
cooking oil by pouring it off gently (into a container).
/MANGI-:I-/ to pour off gently into a container in
order to remove the sediments or dregs of.

ARIT, v. /-UM-, MANG-:-EN/ to provoke, incite, goad,
stir up; to irritate; to challenge. Saan mo ar-ariten
dayta ub-ubing ngem sika. Don't challenge one who is
younger than you.

ARITOS [f. Sp.], n. earring.
    v. /AG-/ to wear earrings. Saan na kayat ti agaritos.
She does not like to wear earrings. /MANGI-:I-:-AN/
to put on (someone) or wear as earrings, to use as
earrings. Saan mo nga iyaritos ta aritos ko. Don't
wear my earrings.

ARIWAWA, adj. /NA-/ noisy, boisterous, tumultous.
--syn. ARIMBANGAW, ARIMEKMEK, TAGARI.
v. /-UM-/.

ARIWEKWEK, v. /-UM-/ to abound, teem; to be abundant,
plentiful, numerous. --var. ATIWEKWEK.

ARIWENG, var. of RIWENG.

ARKO [f. Sp.], n. arch.

ARKOS [f. Sp.], n. decoration, ornament.
v. /MANG-:-AN/ to decorate, adorn, ornament, deck.
Kasayaaten yo nga arkosan dayta altar. Decorate the
altar well. /MANGI-:I-/ to decorate with, to use
to decorate. /MA--AN/ to be decorated with. --syn.
DIKORASION.

ARMADA [f. Sp.], n. the armed forces.

ARMANG, var. of ARAMANG.

ARMAS [f. Sp.], n. arms, weapons. --syn. IGAM.

ARMEN, = AREM + -EN.

ARNAS, v. /MANG-:-EN/ to glean, to pick up bit by bit.
Arnasem amin nga rutruting. Pick up all the small bits
of wood.

ARNIS, v. /MAKI-:KA-/ to fence with. /AG-/ [with pl.
subject] to fence with each other. /MANGI-:I-/ to
use to fence with.

AROO, n. a leafless, dioecious tree with oblong cones.
Its roots and bark are used for medicinal purposes.

ARPA [f. Sp.], n. harp.

ARPAD, n. side (of).
v. /-UM-/ to go to the side of. Umarpad ka dita
tawa da. Go to the side of their window. --syn. ABAY.

ARPAW, v. /MANG-:-AN/ to cover (a sleeping child, a
flower bed, etc.). Arpawam ta ubing ti ules. Cover
that child with a blanket. /MANGI-:I-/ to cover with,

to use to cover. Iyarpaw mo dayta ules idiay ubing nga matmaturog. Use that blanket to cover the child who is sleeping.

ARRAP, adj. one who cannot see at night like a chicken. --syn. KORARAP.

ARSAB, adj. /NA-/ gluttonous, voracious, greedy. --syn. RAWET, SARABUSAB.

ARSADANAN, n. threshhold; base of ladder; foot of mountain.

ARSAGID, adj. /NAG-/ sensitive, touchy; one whose feelings get hurt easily.

ARSANG, v. /MANG-:-AN/ to snuff (e.g. a candle), to remove the ash of (e.g. a cigarette). Arsangam dayta sigarilyom. Remove the ash of your cigarette.

ARTA, var. (dial.) of ADDAYTA.

ARTAP, v. /MAKA-:MA--AN/ to surpass, outdo. Saan na nga maartapan ti kinabaknang ti karruba na. He cannot surpass the wealth of his neighbor. --syn. ^{2}ABAK.

ARTE [f. Sp.], n. art, style, manner of doing. adj. /NA-/ stylish, showy.

ARTEK, n. drunkard. --syn. BARTEKERO.

ARTEM, v. /MANG-:-EN/ to pickle, to preserve in vinegar and salt. Mangartem ka iti mangga. Pickle some mangoes.

ARTESIANO [artɛsiano; f. Sp.], n. pump well. Also called POSÓ or POSO ARTESIANO.

ARTIPISIAL [f. Sp.], adj. /NAG-/ artificial, fake, imitation.

ARTIUK, see ARTYUK.

ARTISTA [f. Sp.], n. actor or actress.

ARTOY, var. (dial.) of ADDAYTOY.

ARTYUK, v. /MANG-:-EN/ to tease, provoke, incite; to
humor. Ar-artyukem ni nanang mo tapno igatangan na
ka ti badom. Humor your mother so that she will buy
you a dress of yours.   --syn. ANGAW.

ARUB, v. /MANG-:-EN/ to make over, repair, redo, remake.
Arubem daytoy bado na. Remake this dress of hers.

ARUBAYAN, n. yard, surroundings (of a house or building),
premises.   --syn. INALADAN, SOLAR.
   v. /MANG-/ 1. to loiter around especially in the
premises of a house or building. 2. to flow to the
edge as almost to overflow, e.g. tears.

ARUBOS, v. /AG-/ to flow, trickle. Nalaka nga agarubos
ti lua na. His tears flow easily.

ARUBUOB, v. /MANG-:-AM/ to fumigate, smoke. Arubuobam
dayta kayo ta barbareng no agbunga. Fumigate that
tree so that it may bear fruit.   --syn. SUOB.

ARUDOK, v. /AG-/ to move crouching, cowering or
squatting, so as to escape observation. Nagar-arudok
nga pimmanaw. He left crouching.   /MANG-:-EN/ to
reach or go (to someone or a place) by crouching,
cowering or squatting.

[1]ARUG, v. /-UM-, MANG-:-EN/ to challenge, defy, dare.
Mapan mi arugen ida ti basketbol. We are going to
challenge them in basketball.

[2]ARUG, syn. (dial) of AREM.

ARUKONG, v. /AG-/ to stoop, bend as when entering a cave
or a low door.

ARUN, n. burning firewood.
   v. /AG-, MANG-:-AN/ to feed fire with firewood or
any inflammable material, to build a fire with firewood
in the stove. Inka arunan diay dalikan ta rugian ta ti
agluton. Go build a fire in the stove so that we can
start cooking.

ARURUB, v. /MANG-:-EN/ to gulp, swallow, drink in big
gulps. Saan mo nga aruruben amin dayta gatas. Don't
gulp all that milk.

ARUTANG, n. bundle of rice straws from which the grains have been removed. This is burned and its ashes used in making native shampoo.

ARUYOT, v. /AG-/ to gush out, flow out copiously and freely. Agar-aruyot ti dara idiay sugat na. Blood is gushing out from his wound.

    PAARUYOT, v. /MANG-:-AN/ to drain. Paaruyutan na na kano dagiti pinggan. He said he will drain the plates.

ARWAT, v. /NAG-, MANG-:-EN/ to use, especially personal things; to wear. Ania ti arwatem nga mapan idiay eskuela? What will you wear to go to school? --syn. ARAMAT, USAR.

ARYEK, see ARIEK.

ASA, v. /AG-, MANG-:-EN/ to whet, sharpen. Asaem ta labaham. Sharpen your razor.

ASAAS, v. /MANG-:-EN/ to learn or study well. Asaasem dayta leksion mo nga para intono bigat. Learn well your lesson for tomorrow.

ASAK, v. /MANG-:-EN/ to pass or step through, to trample on. Mapan na ketdi inasak diay mulak. He went to trample on my plant. --syn. PAYAT.

ASANG, n. gill.

ASAR, v. /MANG-:-EN/ to roast. Sapaen na nga asaren diay baboy. He will roast the pig early. --syn. TUNO.

[1]AS-AS, n. dry leaf (of sugarcane, corn, etc.).

[2]AS-AS, v. /MANG-:-EN/ to pound a second time thoroughly: said of rice. As-asem nga nalaing dayta bagas. Pound that rice for the second time thoroughly. --syn. KIR-OS.

ASAWA, n. [pl. ASSAWA] spouse, husband, wife; mate, member of a pair.
    v. /AG-/ to get married, to marry someone. Agasawakan ta lakay kan. Get married now for you are already an old man. /-UM-:-EN/ to sexually assault,

to have sexual relations with.   /MANG-:-EN/ to marry,
wed. Awan ti mayat nga mangasawa kenkan. No one wants
to marry now anymore.   /MAKI-:KA/ to get married to,
to marry with. Kayat na kano ti makiasawa kaniak.
They say he wants to get married to me.   /AG-/
(plural actor) to marry each other, get married to
each other. Agasawa kayon. Get married.   /MANGI-:I-/
to marry off, to cause to be married, to mate, pair.
Mapan ko iyasawa daytoy balasang ko idiay Manila. I
am going to marry off my daughter in Manila.

ASSAWA, n. pl. /AG-/ husband and wife, a married
   couple.

ASEMBLEA [asɛmblɛa; f. Sp.], n. assembly.

ASI, n. pity, mercy, compassion.
   v. /MA--AN:KA--AN/ to pity, have mercy on. Kaasian
nak. Have mercy on me.
   adj. /NA-/ merciful, compassionate, charitable.
ASI PAY, woe to.

KAASI, n. pity, mercy, compassion.

KAKAASI, adj. having great difficulties or hardships
   (in doing something), to be pitiful (while doing
   something). Kakaasi nga nagna diay doktor. The
   doctor walked pitifully.
      adj. /NAKA-/ pitiful.
      v. /MANGI-:I-/ to do something (for someone) as
   an act of mercy.

ASIDEG, n. vicinity, neighborhood (of), near (someone
   or something). Urayen nak idiay asideg ti simbaan.
   Wait for me near the church.
      adj. /NAG-/ near, close (in time and space);
   approaching. Asideg ti pannakayanak kon. My birthday
   is now near.   /NA-/ close, intimate. Naasideg la unay
   diay kasinsin ko kenka. My cousin is too close to you.
      v. /-UM-/ to go near or close to; to approach, draw
   near. Umasideg ka ken ni Apo Padi. Go near the priest.
   /MANGI-:I-/ to put, place or take near or close to.
   Iyasideg mo dayta inapuy idiay baket. Put that rice
   near the old woman.   --ant. ADAYO.

ASSIDEG, v. /AG-/ [with pl. subject] to be close or
   near one another. Agassideg ni Juan ken ni Juana.
   John and Joan are close to each other.   --ant.
   ADDAYO.

ASIDO [f. Sp.], n. acid.

ASIMBUYOK, v. /AG-/ to produce smoke, fume. Puroram dagita bulong dita sirok ti kayo tapno agasimbuyok. Burn those leaves there under the tree so that they will produce smoke. --syn. ASOK.

ASIN, n. salt.
    v. /MANG-:-AN/ to put or add salt to. /AG-/ to use salt with food.

ASITGAN, = ASIDEG + -AN.

ASIN, ASINO, var. of SIASINO.

ASKAW, v. /AG-/ to stride, straddle, to walk with legs far apart, to make long steps. Narigat ti agaskaw. It is hard to walk with legs wide apart. /MANG-:-EN/ to go over in one big step, to step over. Saan mo nga askawen ta kabsat mo nga matmaturog. Don't step over your brother (or sister) who is sleeping.

ASKUL, v. /MATA-:MA-/ to come across; to meet, find or see by accident or by chance. Naaskulak nga agtaktakaw ti bunga ti mangga mi. I came across him stealing our mango fruits.

ASMANG, v. /MAKI-:KA-/ to team with, group with. /AG-/ [with pl. subject] to team together. Agasmang kayo. You team together.

    KAASMANG, v. [with pl. subject] to be partners, to be members of the same team or group. Nagkakaasmang dagiti babbai. The girls formed a team.

ASO, n. dog.
    v. /-EN/ to be attacked by dogs.

ASO, v. /MANGI-:I-/ to set on, urge on, to offer or suggest as wife or husband, partner, etc. Isuda ti mangiyas-aso ken ni Rosa kaniana. They are the ones who are suggesting Rose as wife to him.

ASOK, n. smoke, fume, steam, vapor.
    v. /AG-/ to produce smoke, steam or vapor.
    adj. /NA-/ smoky, steamy. --syn. ASIMBUYOK.

ASOSASION [f. Sp.], n. association.

ASPALTO [f. Sp.], n. asphalt.

ASPILI, n. pin, straight pin.

ASPING, v. /-UM-/ to be similar to, to resemble.
Umasping dayta badom ti daytoy badok. Your dress is
similar to mine. /MANGI-:I-/ to compare with, liken
to. Iyasping na ka iti maysa nga sabong. He compares
you with a flower.
   n. /KA-/ likeness, that which is similar or equal
to. Kaasping na ti anghel. She is like an angel.

ASSAWA, see under ASAWA.

ASSIBAY, v. /-UM-/ to stay around, to be within sight.
Umassibay ka laeng amangan no masapul da ka. Stay
around in case they need you. /MANG-:-AN/ to be or
stay by the side of. Assibayam ni nanang mo ta
nakapsut. Stay by the side of your mother because
she is weak.

ASSIDEG, see under ASIDEG.

ASSIW, n. a pole for carrying weight across the
shoulders of two persons.

ASSUETE, see ATSUETE.

ASUG, v. /AG-/ to moan, complain. /MANGI-:I-/ to
complain about. Dagitoy ti iyasug tayo ken ni Apo
Senador. These are the things we will complain about
to our honorable senator.

ASUKAR [f. Sp.], n. refined sugar, white sugar, sugar.
--syn. REPINADO, TAGAPULOT.

ASUL [f. Sp.], adj. blue.

ASUT, v. /AG-, MANG-:-EN/ to pull or draw out (from
scabbard, case, etc.); to unsheathe. Inasut na ti
paltog na. He drew out his gun.

[1]ATA, adj. /NA-/ 1. green, immature, not ripe. --syn.
LOOM. 2. not thoroughly cooked, especially rice.

[2]ATA, var. (dial.) of DAYTA.

ATAAT, v. /MANG-:-AN/ to slacken, relax on; diminish, lessen; to slow down. Saan mo nga ataatan dayta trabahom inggana ti di malpas. Don't slow down your work until it is finished.

ATAB, v. /-UM-/ to rise, swell: said of a body of water. Sipsiputam nga umatab dayta waig. Watch the river swell. /AG-/ to rise: said of the water or the tide. Agatab manen. The water (or tide) is rising again.

ATAG, v. /MANG-:-EN/ to lie by the side of. Isu ti nangatag iti ubing. It was he who lay by the side of the child. /MANGI-:I-/ [with pl. goal] to lay alongside each other, to lay parallel to one another. Iyatag mo dagita unas ditoy. Lay those sugar canes parallel to each other here.

ATAKE [atakɛ; f. Sp.], v. /-UM-, MANG-:-EN/ 1. to go on the attack, to attack. 2. to develop or recur suddenly: said of diseases or emotions. Inataki nak ti sakit ti puso. I had a heart attack.

ATAL, v. /MAKA-:MA--AN/ to run over especially with a vehicle. Isu ti nakaatal diay manok. It was he who ran over the chicken.

ATANUD, n. 1. the relationship between godparents (i.e. the sponsors at a baptism or wedding) and the parents of their godchild. 2. the term used to refer to or address either parent of one's child or either parent of one's godchild.

ATANG, v. /AG-/ to offer something to the spirits, to give offerings to the spirits. /AGI-, MANGI-:I-/ to offer to the spirits. Dagitoy ti iyatang yo. Offer these.

[1]ATAP, n. suspicion, doubt, misgivings. --syn. DUDA, SUSPETSA.

[2]ATAP, adj. /NA-/ 1. wild, savage, untamed, undomesticated. Naatap daydiay pusam. That cat of yours is wild. 2. shy, suspicious, aloof. Naatap diay balasang kaniak. That young woman is aloof toward me.
   v. /-UM-/ to be wild, savage, untamed or

undomesticated.   /MANG-:-EN/ to suspect. Saan mo
nga atapen nga agliblibakak. Don't suspect that I
am telling a lie.

ATAY, v. /MANG-:-EN/ to divide, apportion, share.
--syn. BINGAY.

ATEP, n. roof.
   v. /AG-/ to roof a house.   /MANG-:-AN/ to roof,
to put a roof on. Kayat mo nga atepak ta balay mo?
Do you want me to roof your house?   /MANGI-:I-/ to
roof with, to use to roof. Pan-aw ti inayatep na
idiay kusina da. He roofed their kitchen with
'cogon' grass.

ATIAN, v. /MANG-:-AN/ to dry out, to remove the water
of by letting it flow out or by evaporation, to
empty of water or other liquid contents. Saan mo
nga atianan ta bubon mi. Don't dry out our well.
/MA--AN/ [= MAATIANAN or MATIANAN] to be dried out
or emptied of all liquid contents. Aronam dayta
banga inggana ti maatianan. Leave that pot over
the fire until its liquid content is dried out.
--var. PATIAN or PAATIAN.

ATIBANGRAW, v. /-UM-/ to hum, drone, buzz. Umatibangraw
dagitoy ngilaw. These flies are humming.

ATIBUOR, adj. /NA-/ smelly, having strong and offensive
odor. Naatibuor ken nalibeg ta isbo ti nuang mo. The
urine of your water buffalo is smelly and turbid.
   v. /AG-/ to spread, diffuse. Agatibuor ti banglo
ditoy. Some fragrance is spreading here.

ATIDDAG, var. of ATIDDOG.

ATIDDOG, adj. /(NA-)/ long, lengthy.
   v. /-UM-/.   --var. ATIDDAG.   --ant. ABABA.

ATINGAW, v. /AG-/ to walk or run without looking, to
walk or run wildly. Saan ka nga agat-atingaw ta
dikanto ket maatalan. Don't walk or run without
looking for you might be run over by a vehicle.

ATIPA, v. /MANG-:-EN/ to stop, block, obstruct, impede,
hinder. Atipaem ida nga makiringgor. Stop them from
quarreling.

ATIPOKPOK, v. /AG-/ to fly, float, to be blown (e.g.
papers, dust, etc.). Saan mo nga ilukat dayta tawa
tapno saan nga agatipokpok dagitoy papel. Don't open
that window so that these papers won't fly.

ATIR, v. /MANG-:-EN/ [with pl. goal] to arrange side
by side, e.g. pieces of wood.
   adj. /NA-/ [with pl. subject] arranged side by
side.

ATIS, n. sweetsop (Anona squamosa).

ATIW, v. /MANG-:-EN/ to defeat, outdo, surpass.
--syn. 1ABAK.

ATIWEKWEK, var. of ARIWEKWEK.

ATOLE [atolɛ; f. Sp.], n. clothes starch.
   v. /MANG-:-EN/ to starch especially clothes.
--syn. ALMIDOR.

ATONG, n. firebrand, a log that burns the whole day,
or the whole night.

ATOR, v. /MANG-:-EN/ 1. to straighten, make erect.
Atorem dayta likud mo. Straighten your back. 2. to
correct, rectify, amend. Isu ti nangator ti
kinasukir na. He was the one who rectified his
stubbornness.

ATOY, var. (dial.) of DAYTOY.

ATROS, n. a kind of ghost that is supposed to be blown
about by the wind bringing sickness or death to
anyone that it touches.

ATSUETE [atsuɛ́tɛ; f. Sp.], n. a shrub with burry fruit
whose red seeds are used for coloring.   --var.
ASSUETE.

AWA, v. /MANGI-:I-/ to preserve or protect against, to
keep away from (injury, illness, misfortune, etc.).
Iyawam ta bagim ti sakit. Protect yourself against
sickness. Isu ti nangiyawa kadakami ti disgrasia. It
was he who kept us away from misfortunes.

AWAG, v. /-UM-:-EN/ to call, summon. Umawag ka ti
doktor. Call a doctor. --syn. AYAB. /MANG-:-AN/ to
invoke. /MANGI-:I-/ to proclaim, publish,
disseminate. Inyawag ni mayor ti baro nga linteg.
The mayor proclaimed the new law.

AWAN, as a particle it indicates: 1. the non-existence
or absence of someone or something. Awan ti tao idiay
balay. There is nobody in the house. 2. the non-
possession of something by someone. Awan latta ti gasat
ko. I simply don't have any luck. --ant. ADDA.
v. /MA-/ to vanish, disappear. Maawan to dayta ulep.
That cloud will disappear. /MA--AN/ to be deprived
of, to be lacking or wanting of, to run out. Naawanan
da ti kuarta. They ran out of money.

  AWANAN, adj. deprived of, bereft of, dispossessed of;
  lacking or wanting for, in need of. Adda da manen
  dagiti awanan ti bain. They are here again, those
  bereft of shame.

  AW-AWAN, v. /MANGI-:I-/ to baffle, deceive, confuse;
  to mislead; to cause to be lost, go astray or be
  misled; to cause (worry, problems, etc.) to
  disappear. /MAI-/ to be lost, confused, misled;
  to disappear (such as worries, problems, etc.).

[1]AWAT, v. /-UM-:-EN/ to accept, receive, admit. Awatem
daytoy supplim. Receive your change. /MANGI-:I-/ to
deliver, hand over, give. Iyawat mo kaniana diay
suppli na. Hand over to him his change.

[2]AWAT, v. /-UM-:-EN/ often /MAKA-:MA--AN/ to understand,
comprehend, follow. Indiak nga maawatan ti ibagbagam.
I don't understand what you are saying.
    adj. /MAKA-/ able to understand or comprehend
things. --syn. ALLAWAT.

AW-AW, v. /AG-/ to spill out. Nagaw-aw diay danum diay
karamba. The water in the jar spilled out.

AW-AWAN, see under AWAN.

AWAY, n. any place outside the town proper; field,
barrio, sitio.
    v. /-UM-/ to go to this place. Umaway kami intono
bigat. We are going to the field tomorrow.
/MANGI-:I-/ to take (something) to this place. --ant.
UDONG.

AWENG, v. /AG-/ to resound, reverberate, to produce a sonorous or echoing sound. Napigsa nga agaweng dagiti kampana. The bells reverberate loudly.
adj. /NA-/ sonorous, resonant.

AWER, v. /AG-/ to roar: said of the ocean, river, wind, etc. Mangngegko nga agawer ti baybay. I hear the sea roaring.

[1]AWID, v. /AG-/ to go home. Madi na kayat ti agawiden. He does not want to go home anymore. /MANGI-:I-/ to bring or take or carry home. Mangiyawid ka ti nateng nga dengdengen tayo. Bring home some vegetables which we will cook into a vegetable dish.

[2]AWID, v. /MANG-:-EN/ to pull back or toward oneself. Awidem dayta tugaw ditoy. Pull that chair back here.

[3]AWID; SANGKAAWID, n. one twenty-fifth of a skein of a hand of cotton yarn.

AWIR, v. /AG-, MANG-:-EN/ to take care of, look after (a child or a baby). Awirem daytoy ubing ta adda papanak. Take care of this child for I have to go somewhere.

AWIS, v. /-UM-, MANG-:-EN/ to invite, urge to go; to attract, allure, move, entice. Awisem nga mangan dayta sangailim. Invite your guest to eat.
adj. /MAKA-/ inviting, alluring, enticing. Makaawis ti ayamoom ti kape nga itoy. The aroma of this coffee is inviting.

AWIT, v. /AG-, MANG-:-EN/ to carry. Awitem man daytoy maletak? Will you please carry my suitcase?   --syn. BAEL.

AWTOR [f. Eng.], n. author.

AWTORIDAD [f. Sp.], n. authority.

[1]AY, v. /-UM-/ auxiliary and intransitive verb: to come. Umay ka mangan. Come eat. Umay ditoy uneg. Come here inside.

IYAAY, nominalized form: (his) coming.

[2]AY, interj. ah, oh; alas.

> AY SIAY, interj. an exclamation expressing disgust mixed with wonder.

AYA, adv. an interrogative word with the added notion of wonder. Napanak aya? Did I go?

AYAB, v. /AG-, MANG-:-AN/ to call, summon. Ay-ayaban na ka diay maestra. The lady teacher is calling you. --syn. AWAG.

AYAM, v. /MANG-:-EN/ to play with, toy with, amuse oneself with.

> AY-AYAM, n. 1. game, sport, play, recreation, diversion, amusement. Ania nga ay-ayam dayta? What game is that? 2. toy, plaything. Nagadu ti ay-ayam na. He has many playthings.   --syn. ABALBALAY.
>
> v. /AG-/ to play, amuse oneself. /MAKI-:KA-/ to play with. Saan da nga makiay-ayam kanyak. They won't play with me.

[1]AYAM, n. chicken tick.

[2]AYAM, v. /AG-/ to crawl, creep. Saan mo nga lukatan dayta kuribot ta dinto agayam dagita kappi. Don't open that basket lest the crabs crawl out. Nagayam digiti mula ditoy. The plants crept here.   --syn. KARAYAM.

> AGAY-AYAM, n. reptile or any creeping creature.

AYAMOOM, n. fragrance, pleasant odor, aroma.

AYAN, n. place, location, site. Napannayag ti ayan ti balay da. Their house is in a clear place.

AYAT, n. love, affection, desire. Awaten na ngata ti ayat ko? Do you think she will accept my love?
   v. /AG-/ to like, love, want to; to take delight or pleasure in (doing something). Isu ti agayat nga mapan kami. It is he who wants us to go. 2. to love, like, want, desire. Sino met ti mangayat kenka? Who is going to love you? Ay-ayaten ka. I love you. --see KAYAT, MAYAT.
   adj. /NA-/ fond of. Naayat diay baket nga balasang kenka. The spinster is fond of you.

AY-AY, adj. /NA-/ pitiful, sad.

AY-AYAM, see under AYAM.

AYEK-EK, v. /-UM-/ to laugh in a suppressed manner, to
titter, to giggle. /-EN/ to giggle uncontrollably.

AYNA, interj. an exclamation expressing wonder and
admiration. Ayna, dayta a ti babai. That's indeed
a woman.

AYO; AY-AYO, v. /MANG-:-EN/ to comfort, soothe, pacify,
cheer up. Ay-ayoen na daydiay balasang nga
agsangsangit. He is comforting the lady who is
crying.
    adj. /NAKA-/ comforting, soothing, pacifying,
cheering. Nakaay-ayo ti saom. Your words are
comforting.
    n. /KA-/ object or cause of one's comfort or
pleasure, what one is fond of. Kaay-ayo ti aso ti
karne. Dogs are fond of meat.

AYON, v. /-UM-:-AN/ to agree with, side with, favor,
approve, to incline toward. Saan mo nga ayonan
dayta aramid na. Don't agree with that deed of his.

AYOP, n. animal, beast. --syn. ANIMAL.

AYOS, n. current, flow.
    v. /AG-/ to flow. Agayos ti dara. Blood will flow.
/MANGI-:I-/ to be carried by the current, to be
flown away. /MAI-/ to be carried by the current,
to be flown away. Naiyayos diay sapatos ko idiay
waig. My shoes were carried away by the current in
the brook. --syn. ANUD.

AYUG, n. accent, manner of speaking or pronouncing;
intonation; tempo.
    v. /MANGI-:I-/ to prolong, stress, enunciate.

AYUNGIN, n. a kind of small, blackish fish which is
edible.

AYUYANG, n. haunt, a place habitually frequented.

AYWAN, v. /AG-, MANG-:-AN/ to watch, look after, attend
to, take care of, guard. Aywanam dayta kabsat mo ta

adda la papanak. Watch over your brother (or sister) for I am going somewhere.

BA, interj. an exclamation used 1. to startle people, or 2. to make a child laugh by pretending to startle him. In sense 2, it follows the exclamation IT.

BAAG, n. a G-string, loincloth, breechclout.
   v. /AG-/ to wear this.

BAAK, adj. /NAG-/ old, aged: said of rice, tobacco, wine, etc.
   v. /MANG-:-EN/ to age, to keep (rice, tobacco, wine, etc.) for a period of time. Baakem nga nalaing dayta basi tapno naim-imas. Keep that wine for some period of time so that it will improve in taste. --syn. DAAN; also, see BAKET, LAKAY. --ant. BARO.

BAAR, n. ten bundles (ABTEK) of rice, tenth part of an UYON.

BAAW, adj. /NA-/ not hot (nor cold), lukewarm. Nabaaw ta inapuyen. The rice is not hot anymore.
   v. /AG-, -UM-/ 1. to lose heat; to cool off. 2. abate, decrease, go down (as fever, anger, etc.). Bimmaaw met la ti gurigor na. His fever finally went down. --syn. LAMIIS. --ant. PUDOT, BARA.
   n. leftover rice, cold rice. --syn. KILABBAN.

BABA, n. 1. any place down or under something. 2. downstairs. Maturog ka idiay baba. Sleep downstairs.
   adj. /NA-/ low, not high. Nababa ti tayab diay eroplano. The airplane is flying low.
   v. /-UM-/ 1. to become low or lower, to go down. Bimmaba ti presio ti bagas ita nga bulan. The price of rice went down this month. 2. to go or come down or downstairs, to descend. Bumaba ka dita toktok ti balay. Come down from the top of the house.
   /AGI-, MANGI-:I-/ to take, bring or carry down or downstairs. Mangibaba kayo ti tallo nga baso ti danum. Bring downstairs three glasses of water. --ant. NGATO.

BABAEN, prep. by means of, by the use of, through. Nakapagadalak met laeng iti kolehiyo babaen ti tulong mo. I was able to study in college through your help.

BABAI [pl. BABBAI], n. 1. a female; woman, girl. 2.
mistress, concubine.   --syn. KABBALAY 2, KERIDA.
    v. /AG-/ to have or keep a mistress or concubine.
Dika agbabbabai ta dakes. Don't keep a mistress
because that's bad.   /MANG-:-EN/ to make or keep
(someone) as one's mistress or concubine.

    BINABAI, adj. womanlike, womanish; effeminate.
--syn. BAIEN.
    n. a capon, a castrated rooster, especially one
fattened for eating.   --syn. KAPON.

BABAK, n. sin, moral failure - used only in prayers.
--syn. BASOL, BIDDUT.

BABALAW, v. /MANG-:-EN/ to criticize, correct, reprove,
reprimand, censure. Babalawen da ti kinaladaw mi.
They criticized our tardiness.

BABASA, see under BASA.

BABASIL, n. whitlow or felon; an inflammation at the
end of a finger near or under the nail.
    v. /AG-/ to have this inflammation: said of a
finger.

BABAWI, see under BAWI.

BABUY, n. 1. pig, hog, swine. 2. a person regarded as
acting or looking like a pig; dirty or filthy
person.

BABUMBABUY, v. /AG-/ to move or walk on the hands and
knees. Saan ka nga agbabumbabuy ta marugitan ta
imam. Don't walk on your hands and knees for your
hands will get dirty.

BABUYBABUY, n. pill bug.

[1]BADANG, v. /MANG-:-AN/ to help, aid, assist, succor.
Badangan yo dagiti marigrigat. Help the poor.   --syn.
TULONG, SARUNGKAR.

[2]BADANG, n. a kind of large knife (BUNENG) or bolo with
a pointless blade, and shorter and much broader than
the common knife.
    v. /MANG-:-EN/ to hit or threaten with this.

BADDEK, v. /-UM-/ to step in or be present at (a place).
Saan ka nga bumaddek ditoy balay mi. Don't step in our
house. /MANG-:-EN/ to step or trample on. Saan mo nga
baddeken ta mula. Don't trample on that plant.   --syn.
ASAK, PAYAT.

BADIGARD [f. Eng.], n. bodyguard, guard.   --syn. BANTAY,
GUARDIA.

BADO, n. clothes, garment, attire, raiment, dress.
--syn. KAWES.
    v. /AG-/ to put on one's clothes or dress, to
clothe or dress oneself. Agbado kan ta mapan tayon.
Put on your clothes for we are going. /MANG-:-AN/
to clothe or dress (someone). Baduam ta kabsat mo.
Dress your brother (or sister). /PAG-/ to wear.
Daytoy ti pagbadom. Wear this one. /MANGI-:I-/ to
dress (someone) with, to cause (someone) to wear.
Daytoy ti ibado na idiay kabsat na. This is what he
will dress his brother (or sister) with.

BADUYA, n. a kind of native rice cake which is flat and
round.

BAED, adj. /NAG-/ talking through the nose, as one with
a harelip.
    v. /AG-/ to talk through the nose.

BAEL, v. /MANGI-:I-/ to carry. Isu ti nangibael kadagiti
karga mi. It was he who carried our load.   --syn.
BAGKAT, KARGA.

BAELAN, v. /MAKA-:MA-/ to be able, competent or fit (to
do something). Makabaelan ka nga agmanehon? Are you
able to drive a motor vehicle now?
    adj. /MAKA-/ able, competent, capable; powerful,
almighty. Makabaelan ni Apo Dios. God is almighty.

    KABAELAN, n. power, capability, competence, ability.
    Saan na pay nga kabaelan ti agmaneho. It is not
    yet within his capability to drive a motor vehicle.

BAEN, v. /AG-/ to sneeze.

BAET, n. interval (in space or time).
    v. /-UM-/ 1. to put, place or go between. Saan ka
nga bumaet kadakami nga dua. Don't place yourself
between the two of us. 2. to intervene, interpose.

Saan ka nga bumabaet ka dimo ammo daytoy. Don't
intervene for you don't know this. /MANGI-:I-/
1. to put or place between. 2. to intercede or
intervene for (someone). Ibabaet na kami. Intercede
for us.

BAETAN, n. main road. Adayo ti kasilyas iti igid ti
baetan. The toilet is far from the side of the main
road.

¹BAG [f. Eng.], n. bag, handbag.

²BAG, short of IMBAG, as in BAG NO, it's good if.

BAGA, v. /AGI-, MANGI-:I-/ 1. to tell, say, declare,
utter. Ania ti imbaga na? What did he say? --syn.
KUNA. 2. to tell on, inform against. No dika nga
agsardeng, ibaga ka ken ni tatang ko. If you don't
stop, I'll tell on you to my father. --syn. PULONG.

BAGBAGA, v. /MANG-:-AN/ [= MAMAGBAGA] to advise,
counsel. Bagbagaam dayta adim iti nasayaat nga
aramid. Advise your younger brother (or sister)
about good deeds. --syn. BALAKAD.

BAGAMUNDO [f. Sp.], n. vagabond.

BAGAS, n. 1. husked or polished rice. Awan ti bagas
mi. We have no (polished) rice. --syn. MAKAN. 2.
substance or content (of fruits); seed or kernel
(of rice, corn, etc.); tuber or tuberous root (of
potatoes, taro, etc.). Awan pay ti bagas na dayta
kamotit yo. Your sweet potatoes have no tuberous
roots yet. 3. substance, content, essence, meaning.
Ania ti bagas daydiay sinao na? What was the content
of what he said?
    adj. /NA-/ pithy, full of substance.
    v. /AG-/ to have substance or content; to develop
seeds or kernels, or tuberous roots. Agbagas daytoy
maisen. This corn is now developing seeds.

BAGAS LING-ET, n. prickly heat. Nagadu ti bagas
ling-et na. His prickly heat papules are so many.

BAGAT, adj, /(MAI-)/ befitting, becoming; suitable,
agreeable; appropriate. Maibagay kenka dayta pukis
mo. Your haircut becomes you.
    v. /MANGI-:I-/ to adjust, fit; to make suitable,

agreeable or appropriate. Ibagay mo ti bagim iti biag ditoy barrio. You adjust yourself to life in this barrio.

BAGBAG, n. a leguminous tree with large, bright-red flowers whose leaves are supposed to cure headaches.

BAGBAGA, see under BAGA.

BAGBAGUTOT, n. a shrub which bears black, fleshy fruits which are edible.

BAGGAK, n. morning star, daystar, Lucifer, Venus.

BAGGIING, n. porous stone, pumice.

[1]BAGI, n. 1. share, portion, part, lot. Ited mo kanyak ta bagik. Give me my share. 2. child or children, offspring. Adu ti bagikon. I have already many children. 3. genitals. --var. MABAGBAGI.

[2]BAGI, n. 1. body. Dakkel ti bagi na. His body is big. 2. self. Annadam ta bagim. Be careful of your self. v. /MANGI-:I-/ to represent, stand for. Isu ti nangibagi kadakami. He was the one who represented us.

KABAGIAN, n. relative, relation, kinsman, kinswoman.

BAGINGET, n. big pincers.

BAGIO, var. of BAGYO.

BAGIS, n. intestine, bowel, entrail, gut. --see SILET.

BAGKAT, v. /AG-, MANG-:-EN/ to lift up, carry, heave, raise up. Kayat mo, bagkaten ka? Would you like me to lift you up? --syn. BAEL, KARGA.

BAGKONG, v. /MANG-:-EN/ to stab, as with a dagger.

BAGNAW, v. /MANG-:-AN/ or /MANGI-:I-/, to rinse. --var. (dial.) BUGNAW. --syn. BELNAS.

[1]BAGNET, v. /MANG-:-EN/ to dry, to cause to become dry. Bagnetem nga nasayaat dagita kayo. Dry those pieces of wood well.

[2]BAGNET, n. pieces of fat from which lard has been extracted.

BAGNOS, n. guide, leader.
v. /MANGI-:I-/ to guide, lead, conduct. Ibagnos mo ida nga mapan idiay plasa. Lead them in going to the plaza.

BAGON [f. Sp.], n. wagon.

BAGSANG, n. a kind of small, fat fish living either in the sea or at the mouth of rivers.

BAGSOL, v. /MANG-:-EN/ to stab or pierce. --syn. BAGKONG, DUGSOL.

BAGTIN, v. /MANG-:-EN/ to lift up so as to estimate the weight. Bagtinem dayta maletak. Lift up and estimate the weight of my suitcase.

BAGTIT, adj. /NAG-/ crazy, lunatic, demented.
v. /AG-/ to become crazy or demented. --syn. BALLA, MURYOT, BULAN-BULANEN.

BAGUTOT, see BAGBAGUTOT.

BAG-UT, v. /MANG-:-EN/ to pull out, uproot. Bag-utem dagita bikal. Pull out those bikal. Uproot those climbing bamboos. --var. PAG-UT. --syn. PARUT.

BAGYO, n. typhoon, storm, hurricane; strong, violent wind.
v. /AG-/ to have a typhoon, storm or hurricane. Agbagyo man siguron intono maysa nga bulan. Perhaps there will be a typhoon again next month. /-EN/ to be hit by a typhoon, storm or hurricane. Binagyo ti piesta mi. Our festival was hit by a typhoon. /MA-/ to be destroyed or demolished, felled, blown down, or carried away by a typhoon, storm or hurricane. Nabagyo ti balay mi. Our house was destroyed by a typhoon. --var. BAGIO.

BAHO [f. Sp.], n. bass horn, a tuba.

BAIEN [ba?ien], adj. effeminate, womanly, womanish. --syn. BINABAI.

BAILITA, n. the part of the rice plant with the grains
that are cut and laid out on the rice field on top
of the stubble to dry.

BAIN, n. shame. Awan ti bain mo. You are shameless.
   v. /MA-:KA-/ to be ashamed or feel embarrassed (to
do something; to see or talk to someone). Mabainak
kenka. I am ashamed to see you.

   BABAIN, v. /MANGI-:I-/ to shame, disgrace or embarrass.
   Saan nak nga ibabain kadagiti gagayyem mo. Don't
   shame me before your friends. /MAI-/ to be shamed,
   disgraced or embarrassed.
      adj. /(NA)KA-/ shameful, disgraceful, embarrassing.
   Nakababain ti inaramid mo. What you did was shameful.

   PABAIN, v. /MANG-:-AN/ to refuse to do or give what
   one has requested; hence, to disgrace or embarrass
   (someone). Saan nak nga pabainan. Don't refuse to
   do or give what I shall request of you. /MA--AN/
   to be refused; hence, to be disgraced.

BAINA, n. scabbard, sheath (of knives, swords, etc.).

BAIN-BAIN, n. Mimosa pudica. A thorny, creeping weed
whose leaves are sensitive to touch.

BAIS, v. /MANGI-:I-/ to charge against what one owes.
Ibais mo dagitoy innalak ti utang mo kanyak. Charge
these that I took against what you owe me.

BAKA [f. Sp.], n. cow, bull, ox; cattle; beef.

BAKABAKA, v. /AG-/ to be hesitant, troubled, perplexed.
Saan tayo nga mapan no agbakabaka ka. We won't go if
you are hesitant.

BAKAL, v. /MANGI-:I-/ to throw, toss. Saan mo nga
ibakal dayta pungan. Don't throw that pillow.   --syn.
PURWAK.

BAKAL, n. war, fight, battle. Gumilgilang pay laeng ti
apoy ti bakal. The flames of war are still burning.
--syn. GERRA, GUBAT.
   v. /MAKI-:KA-/ to engage in a war, a fight or
battle. Narigat ti makibakal. It is hard to engage
in a war. /MANG-:-EN/ 1. to wage a war at. 2. to
throw stones at. Bakalem dagidiay baboy. Throw stones
at the pigs.

BAKANTE [f. Sp.], adj. vacant, unoccupied, empty.

BAKARA, n. a kind of small fish found at the mouths of rivers.

BAKAS, v. /MANG-:-AN/ to strip off some part of (a wall, roof, window, etc.). Daytay napalabas a bagyo ti nangbakas iti balay mi. The past typhoon stripped off some parts of our house. /MA--AN/ to be unroofed. Nabakasan daydiay tienda ni Rosa. The store of Rose was unroofed.

BAKASYON [f. Sp.], n. vacation. Bakasyon manen. It's vacation time again.
v. /AG-/ to have a vacation, spend a vacation. Agbakasyon ta idiay Baguio. Let's spend our vacation in Baguio. /MANGI-:I-/ to take on a vacation, to take to a place for a vacation. Ibakasyon ko daytoy baket ko idiay Amerika. I'll take my wife to the United States for a vacation. --var. BAKASYON.

BAKAT, v. /AG-/ to leave a trace, mark or impression. Uray la nga nagbakat diay plantsa ti pudot na. The iron left a mark because of its heat.

BAKED, adj. /NA-/ 1. stocky, heavily built, sturdy, muscular. 2. nice, pleasing, exquisite. Nabaked ti agsakay ti eroplano. It is nice to ride in an airplane.

BAKES, n. monkey, ape. --syn. SUNGGO.

BAKET, adj. /NAG-/ old in years: said of the female, especially women.
n. 1. old woman. 2. wife.
v. /-UM-/ to grow old or older: said of the female. Bumaket ni Maryan. Mary is growing older.

BAKBAKETAN, adj. very old, extremely old: said of the female. Bakbaketan daydiay naasawa na. The one he married was extremely old.

AGBABAKET, adj. fond of old women - used derisively.

BAKI, n. nest made by man for hens in which to lay and hatch their eggs.

BAKIG; SANGABAKIG, n. ten units or heads (of cows, coconuts, etc., except persons, rice bundles, etc.).

BAKIR, n. forest, woods.
    v. /AG-, MANG-/ [= MAMAKIR] to cut trees in the
forest. Intay mamakir. Let's go cut trees in the
forest.

BAKKA, n. 1. a large, shallow earthen basin, used
    especially for washing and cleaning rice, fish,
    vegetables, etc. 2. figuratively, a very large
    vulva.
    BIMMAKKA, adj. of the size and shape of a BAKKA:
    said especially of the vulva.

BAKKUAR, v. /AG-/ to vomit, throw up. Narigat ti
    agbakkuar. It is hard to vomit. /AG-:I-/ to vomit,
    throw up, spew. Adu ti imbakkuar na. He vomitted
    much. --var. BAKWAR. --syn. SARWA, BEL-A.

BAKLAY, v. /MANGI-:I-/ or /MANG-:-EN/ to carry on
    one's shoulder. Ibaklay mo dayta maleta. Carry
    that suitcase on your shoulder.

BAKNAD, n. shoal, reef.

BAKNANG, n. [pl. BABAKNANG] the rich, wealthy or
    affluent.
        adj. /NA-/ rich, wealthy, affluent.
        v. /-UM-/ to become like this.

BAKRANG, n. side of man's body extending from the
    armpit to the waist.
        v. /-EN/ to feel pain or have pains at the side
    of one's body. Saan ka nga agbagkat iti nadagsen
    tapno saan ka nga bakrangen. Don't lift heavy
    things so that you won't have pains at the side of
    your body.

BAKTAW, v. /AG-:-AN/ to skip, omit. Saan ka nga
    agbaktaw. Don't skip (something). /MANG-:-EN/ to
    jump over, step over. Isu ti nangbaktaw kanyak.
    It was he who jumped over me. --syn. LAGTO.

BAKUL; BINAKUL, adj. twilled.

BAKWAR, var. of BAKKUAR.

BAKYA, n. wooden shoes. --syn. KAMMADANG, SUEKOS.

BALA, n. bullet; missile; ammunition. Naibusan kami
ti bala. We ran out of ammunition.
v. /MANG-:-AN/ to put bullets in, to load: said
of weapons. /MANGI-:I-/ to load with or in (as
bullets), to use as bullet. Daytoy ti ibalam dita
paltog mo. Load your gun with this.

BALABAG, v. /MANG-:-EN/ to hit with something, to
throw or hurl something at. Isu ti nangbalabag
kanyak. It was he who threw something at me.
/MANGI-:I-/ to throw, cast, hurl. Saan mo nga
ibalabag dayta. Don't throw that. --syn. PALAPAL.

BALABAL, v. /MANG-:-AN/ to wrap (something) around.
Balabalan yo dayta ubing ti ules ket nalam-ek.
Wrap a blanket around that child for it is cold.
/MANGI-:I-/ to wrap with, to use to wrap. Dayta
ules ti ibalabal yo kanyana. Wrap him with that
blanket.

BALABALA, n. thought, idea; guess, conjecture, surmise;
apprehension, misgiving. Nagbunga ti balabala na.
His idea came to fruition.
v. /MANG-:-EN/ to guess, suppose, surmise; to be
apprehensive that. Balabalaen na nga napukaw da.
He is apprehensive that they got lost.

BALAGTONG, v. /-UM-/ to jump, leap, bound. Saan ka
nga agbalagtong ta adda matmaturog. Don't jump for
someone is sleeping.

BALAKAD, v. /MANG-:-AN/ to advise, counsel. Balakadam
ida ta nasukir da unay. Give them some advice for
they are very disobedient. /MANGI-:I-/ to give us
advice. Denggem dagiti ibalakad da kenka. Listen to
the pieces of advice that they will give you. --syn.
BAGBAGA.

BALAKI, v. /AG-/ to turn to the opposite direction, as
joy to sorrow. Saan kay nga katawa nga katawa ta
dinto agbalaki dagita katkatawa yo. Don't laugh and
laugh lest your laugh turn to sorrow.

BALANGAT, n. crown, diadem; wreath, garland.

BALANGEG, n. a widely spreading water vine whose young
leaves are eaten. --syn. KANGKONG.

BALANGGOT, n. hat.   --syn. KALLUGONG.

BALANGKANTIS, adj. /NAG-/ 1. (one who) bargains hard all the time. 2. deceitful.

BALASANG, n. [pl. BABBALASANG] 1. adult or mature female; woman. Balasang dayta anak mon. Your daughter is already an adult. 2. single or unmarried woman; spinster; maiden, virgin. Balasang ka pay laeng wenno saanen? Are you still single or not anymore?   --ant. BARO.   --see BUMALASANG.
   v. /MANG-:-EN/ to court, woo. Adda balbalsangen mi dita sumuno nga ili. There is someone whom we are wooing in the next town.

[1]BALASBAS, v. /MANG-:-AN/ to trim, e.g. a log, bamboo, etc. Binalasbasan na daydiay pinukan mo nga kawayan. He trimmed the bamboo that you felled.

[2] BALASBAS, v. /MANG-:-AN/ to whip, beat, hit with a stick, a branch of a tree, etc. Saan mo nga balasbasan ta kabayo. Don't whip that horse.

BALASITANG, n. [BABBALASITANG] syn. of BUMALASANG 1.

BALAT, n. birthmark, skin blemish.

[1]BALAT, v. /MANGI-:I-/ to throw down, as in judo or wrestling. Dinak nga maibalat. He cannot throw me down. [MAI- is the potential of I-.]

[2]BALAT; NAKABALBALAT, adj. haughty, arrogant, supercilious. Nakabalbalat ta kaduam. Your companion is arrogant.

BALAW, v. /AG-/ to wonder or take notice of something or a situation. Agbalaw ka ngem naladawen. You may wonder about the situation but it is too late. /MANG-:-EN/ to take notice of, to wonder about. Isu ti nangbabalaw ti kaawan mo. It was he who took notice of your absence.

BALAWBAW, n. awning, canopy, covering, especially of a cart.
   v. /AG-/ to use this. /MANG-:-AN/ to provide (especially a cart) with this.

¹BALAY, n. [pl. BALBALAY or BABBALAY] house, home;
abode, residence, habitation, dwelling.
    v. /AG-/ to build one's house; to establish one's
home, residence or dwelling place; to reside.
Agbalay tayo idiay ili dagiti appo tayo. Let's
reside in the town of our ancestors. --see KABBALAY.

²BALAY, v. /AG-/ to curdle, coagulate, solidify (as
lard or cooking in cold weather). Nagbalay ti
manteka. The cooking oil solidified.

BALAYANG, n. a variety of banana with thick skin and
numerous seeds.

BALAYBAY, v. /MANGI-:I-/ to hang (usually articles of
clothing) in order to dry, air or screen off
something. Inka man ibalaybay daytoy nagsukatak
idiay pagsalapayan ta nabasa ti ling-et. Will you
please hang my clothes which I just changed on the
clothesline for they are wet with perspiration.
--syn. SALAPAY.

BALBAL, v. /MANG-:-AN/ to rinse or wash lightly,
clean with water. Balbalam nga nasayaat ta kusina.
Clean the kitchen very well with water. --syn. UGAS.

BALBALLUSA, n. a spreading, spiny herb with white
flowers and whitish-gray fruits; it resembles the
eggplant.

BALBALSIG, see under BALSIG.

BALDADO [f. Sp.], adj. seriously wounded or injured.

BALDI [f. Sp.], n. a large can, either rectangular or
cylindrical; a kerosene can. --syn. LATA.

BALE [bále; f. Sp.], n. value, account, importance,
significance, import. Awan ti bale na dayta. That
is of no account.
    v. /-UM-:-EN/ to buy on credit. Kayat na kano ti
bumale iti dua nga kaha ti sigarilyo. He says he
wants to buy on credit two packs of cigarettes.

    SAAN NGA BALE, it does not matter, it is of no
importance, never mind.

BALEDIKTORIAN [balɛdiktorian; f. Sp.], n. valedictorian.
v, /AG-/ to become the valedictorian of a class.

BALENGBENG, v. /MANGI-:I-:-AN/ to hang, put or use as
screen or curtain. Isu ti mangibalengbeng ti daytoy
idiay salas. It is he who will hang this (as screen
or curtain) in the living room. Ibalengbeng na daytoy
idiay salas. He will hang this (as screen or curtain)
in the living room. Balengbengan na diay salas da ti
lupot. He will hang a piece of cloth (as screen or
curtain) in their living room.

[1]BALES, v. /-UM-, AGI-/ to take revenge on someone; to
repay someone. Saan ka nga bumales. Don't take
revenge on anyone. /-UM-:-EN/ to take revenge on;
to repay, return the favor to. Apay nga balsen nak?
Why do you take revenge on me? /MANGI-:I-/ to take
revenge for; to repay (someone) for. Isu ti nangibales
kanyak. It was he who took revenge for me.

[2]BALES, v. /MANGI-:I-/ to seam and hem (a dress, etc.).

BALIBAD, v. /MANG-:-EN/ often /MAKA-:MA-/ to pronounce
wrongly, especially by interchanging the sounds; to
mispronounce. Kanayon ko nga mabalibad ti nagan mo.
I always mispronounce your name.

BALIKAS, n. speech, pronunciation, expression.   --syn.
SAO.
v. /MANG-:-EN/ to pronounce, say, utter, express.
Baliksem ti nagan mo. Say your name.

BALIKID, n. the other side, the opposite or reverse
side.
v. /-UM-/ to turn or roll oneself sideways to the
other side, to turn over. Bumalikid ka man bassit.
Please turn over for a moment.   /MANG-:-EN/ to turn
or roll (someone or something in a resting position)
sideways to the other side; to turn over. Saan mo
nga balikiden ta papel mo. Don't turn over your
paper.   --var. BALLIKID.

BALIKONGKONG, adj. /NA-/ twisted, contorted.

BALIKTAD, adj. inside out. Baliktad ti bado na. Her
dress is inside out.   --var. BALITTAD.
v. /MANG-:-EN/ 1. to turn the inside out. 2. to
turn over. Isu ti nangbaliktad ti libro na. It was
he who turned over his book.

BALIKUSKUS, var. of BALIKUTKUT.

BALIKUTSA, n. a coil of string of soft, white-yellowish
sugar.

[1]BALIN, v. /AG-/ to be possible or effective. Saan nga
nagbalin ti luko na kanyak. His foolishness was not
effective on me.   /MA-/ to be possible or probable
(followed by a sentence introduced by NGA). Mabalin
nga sumangpet da ita. It is possible that they will
arrive today. Mabalin ko siguro nga sabten ida. Maybe
it will be possible for me to meet them.   /MA--AN/ to
be able (to do something). Mabalinan nan ti magna.
He is able to walk now.
   adj. /MA-/ possible, probable, effective. Saan nga
mabalin ti luko na kanyak. His foolishness is not
effective on me.   /MANNAKA-/ almighty, all-powerful.

   KABABALIN, n. habit, custom; nature. Nagdakes ti
   kababalin mon. Your habit is very bad.   --syn.
   UGALI, KUSTUMBRE.

   KABALINAN, n. ability, capability, competence.   --syn.
   KABAELAN.

[2]BALIN, v. /AG-/ to become, to grow, develop or turn
into (followed by a noun or adjective introduced by
NGA). Nagbalin nga sadut diay barok. My son turned
into a lazy person.

BALINO, n. water lily.

BALINSUEK, adj. upside down.
   v. /AG-/ to stand upside down.   /MANG-:-EN/ or
/MANGI-:I-/ to put or place upside down. Saan mo
nga balinsueken ta anak mo. Don't put your child
upside down.   /MA-/ to fall head first, upside
down.

BALINSWEK, var. of BALINSUEK.

BALINTUAG, v. /AG-/ to somersault, tumble.   /MANG-:-EN/
or /MANGI-:I-/ to roll over, to cause to somersault,
tumble or rotate.   /MA-/ to roll over. Nabalintuag ti
tugaw ko. My chair rolled over.   --syn. BATTUAG.

BALINTWAG, var. of BALINTUAG.

BALISONGSONG, n. funnel, cone, especially one made of
   paper or a leaf.
      v. /AG-/ to make a funnel or cone, especially using
   a piece of paper or a leaf. Ammom ti agbalisongsong?
   Do you know how to make a funnel? /MANG-:-EN/ to
   make or shape into a funnel or cone.

BALITANG, n. a bamboo seat.

BALITI, n. a tree (Ficus sp.) which gives valuable
   timber.

BALITOK, n. gold.

BALITTAD, var. of BALIKTAD.

BALITUNGEG, v. /-EN/ to be worm-eaten, to become
   affected with blight: said of the sweet potato
   (KAMOTIT). Balitungegen manen ta kamotit yo. Your
   sweet potatoes will become affected with blight
   again.
      adj. /(-IN)/ worm-eaten, affected with blight:
   said of the sweet potato.
      n. any portion of the sweet potato that is affected
   with blight or is worm-eaten. Adu ti balitungeg na
   daytoy inted mo kanyak nga kamotit. This sweet potato
   which you gave me has many worm-eaten parts.

[1]BALIW, v. /-UM-/ to cross, go across, traverse; to
   come over. Bumaliw danto intono bigat. They will come
   over tomorrow. /MANGI-:I-/ to take or carry across.
   Ibaliw mo dayta maletak dita kalsada. Carry my
   suitcase across the street. --syn. BALLASIW, LASAT.

[2]BALIW, v. /AG-/ to change, alter. Nagbaliw ti nakem na.
   He changed his mind. /MANG-:-AN/ to change, alter,
   replace. Balbaliwan tayo ti plano tayo. Let us
   change our plans. --syn. SUKAT.

BALKON [f. Sp.], n. porch, balcony.

BALKUT, n. package, bundle.
      v. /AG-/ to wrap or bundle up things, especially
   one's personal belongings or household effects.
   /MANG-:-EN/ to wrap or bundle up. --syn. BUNGON.

BALLA, adj. crazy, lunatic, demented.
    v. /AG-/ to become crazy, lunatic, demented.
--syn. BAGTIT.

BALLAAG, n. loud argument, loud voice or screams in an
    argument; cry for help.
    v. /AG-/ [with pl. subject] to argue loudly.
/AG-/ to cry or scream for help.

BALLAET, v. /MANGI-:I-/ to insert in regular intervals,
    to intertwine in a regular pattern, to mix with
    according to a pattern. Iballaet mo dagitoy puraw
    kadagita asul. Mix these white ones with those blue
    ones.

BALLAIBA, n. eel grass, tape grass; a common, edible,
    submerged, hydrocharitaceous, fresh water plant.
    Its leaves and roots (GURGURMOT) are eaten.

BALLAIBI, v. /-EN/ to suffer from pains in the region
    of the spleen. Saan ka nga agtaray-taray ta ballaibien
    ka. Don't run back and forth for you will suffer from
    pains in the region of the spleen.

BALLAIGI, var. of BALLIGI.

BALLASIW, n. the opposite side (of), the place across
    (a river, a street, an ocean, etc.).   --syn. BANGIR.
    v. /-UM-/ to cross, go across. /MANG-:-EN/ to
cross, go across. /MANGI-:I-/ to take across or to
the opposite side of, to go across with.   --syn.
BALIW.

BALLATAD, v. /AG-/ to throw a big knife (BUNENG) at
    someone. /MANG-:-EN/ to throw a big knife at, to
    hit with a big knife. No umasideg ka, ballataden ka
    iti daytoy iggem ko nga buneng. If you come near,
    I'll throw this big knife which I am holding at you.

BALLATIK, v. /MAKA-:MA--AN/ to hit: said of a chip, a
    splinter or a sliver. Ania ti nakaballatik kenka?
    What hit you? /MA--AN/ to be hit by a chip,
    splinter or sliver. Naballatikan ta ulom. Your head
    was hit by a chip.

BALLIGI, n. victory, triumph.
    v. /AG-/ to win, be victorious or triumphant. Isu

ti nagballigi idiay lumba. He was the one who was
victorious in the race.   --var. BALLAIGI.   --syn.
[1]ABAK.

BALLIKID, var. of BALIKID.

BALLIKUG, v. /MANG-:-EN/ to modify, distort or pervert
(what someone has said). Binallikug na ti imbagak
kaniana. He modified what I told him.

BALLOLONG, v. /AG-/ to place hands that are joined
around the head.

BALLUKATTIT, v. /AG-/ to hurry up, hasten.
Nagbalballukattit nga nagawid. She hurried up going
home. Agballukattit ka ket rabiin. Hurry up for it
is already late.

BALLUSA, see BALBALLUSA.

BALNAS, v. /AG-, MANG-:-AN/ to rinse in water, especially
dishes that have been soaped. Balnasam dagita pinggan.
Rinse those plates.   --syn. BAGNAW.

BALO, n. widow, widower.
      v. /MANG-:-EN/ to cause (someone) to become a widow
or widower.   /MA-/ to be widowed. Nabalo diay barok
idi napalabas nga tawen. My son was widowed the past
year.

[1]BALO, v. /AG-/ to make or dig holes in the ground with
a stake for posts or plants. Napan da nagbalo. They
went to make holes in the ground with a stake.
/MANGI-:I-/ 1. to cause to step or fall into a hole.
2. to cause to sink deeply in (debt, hardships, etc.).
Sika ti mangibalo kanyak iti utang. You are going to
cause me to sink deeply in debt.   /MAI-/ 1. to step
or fall into a hole. 2. to sink deeply in (debt,
hardships, etc.).

[2]BALO, syn. of [1]SALOG.

BALOG, n. a wild pigeon.

BALON, n. provision, supply; something provided,
prepared or supplied for the future.
      v. /AG-:-EN/ to have or carry as provision, to

provide oneself with. Agbalon ka ti kanen tayo.
Provide yourself with something for us to eat.
/MANG-:-AN/ [= MAMALUN] to carry provisions or
supplies to. Isu ti namalon kadakami. It was he who
carried provisions to us.

BALOR [f. Sp.], price, value.   --syn. PRESIO, PATEG,
    BAYAD.
    adj. /NA-/ gallant.

    PABALOR, v. /MANG-:-AN/ to cause a price or value to
    be put on (by someone), to cause (someone) to
    appraise.

BALOT, n. duck's egg with a developed embryo that is
    cooked and eaten.

BALOTA [f. Sp.], n. ballot, especially one used in an
    election.

BALSA [f. Sp.], n. raft.   --syn. RAKIT.

BALSIG, v. /AG-, MANG-:-EN/ to chop with an axe.
    Mapanak agbalsig ti pagsungrud tayo. I'll go chop
    what we are going to use as firewood.

    BALBALSIG, n. praying mantis.

[1]BALTIK, v. /MANG-:-EN/ to flip, flick or fillip
    something at. Saan mo nga baltiken dagita ubbing.
    Don't fillip something at those children.   /MANGI-I-/
    to flip, flick or fillip (something) at.   --syn.
    PITIK.

[2]BALTIK; BALBALTIK, n. wriggler, larva of the mosquito.

BALUBAL, v. /AG-/ [with pl. subject] to be rivals, to
    be set against each other. Agbalubal ti ili mi ken
    ti ili da. Our town and their town are rivals.
    /MAKI-:KA-/ to compete against (someone), to rival
    (someone). Sino ti nakibalubal kenka? Who competed
    against you?

BALUD, n. prisoner.   --syn. PRESO, PRISONERO.
    v. /MANG-:-EN/ to imprison, confine in prison.
    Apay nga binalud da ka? Why did they confine you
    in prison?   --syn. PRESO, KALABUS.

    PAGBALUDAN, n. prison, jail.   --syn. PRESO, KALABUS.

BALUDBUD, adj. /NA-/ growing vigorously, robust, healthy, as a person or a plant. Nabaludbud ta tagibim. Your baby is robust. --syn. LAPSAT.

BALUKNIT, v. /MANG-:-EN/ to turn inside out. Baluknitem dayta bituka sa mo dalusan. Turn that stomach inside out and then clean it.

BALUNET, n. a door or window bar.

BALUNGYAD, v. /MANG-:-EN/ to move or push backward (a finger, a toe, the head, etc.). Saan mo nga balungyaden ta ramay ko. Don't push backward my finger.

BALUTBUT, v. /MANGI-:I-/ to drive in the ground. Ibalutbut mo dagita bikal dita. Drive the bamboo stakes there.

BAMBAN, n. a strip of young and pliant bamboo used for tying.

BAMBANDI, n. scarecrow.

BANAAL, adj. /NA-/ having the stench of feces or excrement.

BANABA, n. a kind of tree (Lagerstroemia speciosa (L.). Pers.).

BANAG, n. 1. thing, object. Kasta ti aramiden yo no adda mapidut yo a banag, ubbing. That is what you should do when you pick up any object, children. 2. result, outcome, effect. Kas banag na, naurnong dagiti sobra nga tabako kadagiti bodega. As a result of it, the surplus tobacco was stocked in the warehouses.

BANARBAR, n. the sound of broken bells or of a broken voice.
    v. /AG-/ to sound like this.

BANDERA [bandɛra; f. Sp.], n. flag, banner, standard.

BANDIDO [f. Sp.], n. bandit, robber, thief. --syn. MANNANAKAW, TULISAN.

BANDILI, n. the fine-toothed blade of a hack saw or coping saw.

BANDUS, n. comet.

BANEG, adj. /NA-/ broad, strong, muscular. Nabaneg
dagiti ima ti kapitan nga nangtengngel kadagiti
abaga ni Andres. The hands of the captain which
held the shoulders of Andrew were strong.

BANEGBEG, v. /AG-/ to make a regular thumping sound,
to pound or knock on something regularly. Mangngeg
ko nga agbanegbeg dagiti al-o da. I hear their
pestles pounding regularly. /MANG-:-EN/ to pound
or knock on. Isu ti nangbanegbeg diay ruangan. It
was he who pounded on the gate.

BANERBER, n. the sound of a swollen river, a strong
wind or the like.
    v. /-UM-/ to sound like this.

BANESBES, v. /-UM-/ to rush, whish; to move with a
whish especially when moving fast. Apay nga
bumanesbes dagita tao? Why are the people whishing?

BANIAGA, v. /AG-/ to travel to foreign lands.

BANIAS, n. a large lizard, a kind of iguana whose
eggs and meat are eaten by some people. --var.
BANYAS.

BANIIT, adj. /NA-/ having the odor of burned food.

BANINGRUT, v. /AG-, -UM-/ to suck in air through the
nose, to inhale breath as a sign of displeasure,
especially when crying or sulking; to sniff, sniffle.

BANNAWAG, n. the period before sunrise, dawn. --syn.
PARBANGON.
    v. /AG-/ to approach this period, to be at the
beginning of this period. Umay kaminto dita no
agbannawag. We will go there at the approach of
dawn.

BANNAYAT, adj. /NA-/ slow, sluggish, gentle. --syn.
INAYAD.

BANNIEKES, v. /AG-/ to stand with one or both hands
akimbo. Apay nga agbanniekes ka? Why are you standing
with hands akimbo? /MANG-:-AN/ to fall or confront a

person with hands akimbo. Saan nak nga banniekesan.
Do not confront me with your hands akimbo.

BANNIIT, n. fishing tackle.
   v. /AG-/ to catch fish with a fishing tackle.
Mapanak agbanniit. I'll go fishing with a fishing
tackle. /MANG-:-AN/ to catch with a fishing tackle.
Isu ti nangbanniit kadagitoy. He was the one who
caught these with a fishing tackle.

BANNOG, v. /AG-/ to tire oneself. Dika nga agbanbannog,
   barok ko. Don't tire yourself, my son. /MA-/ to be
   tired, weary, fatigued. Nabannogakon. I am already
   tired. /MANG-:-EN/ to tire, to make tired, weary or
   exhausted. Diyo nga banbannogen dayta kabayok. Don't
   tire my horse.
      adj. /MAKA-/ tiresome, tiring, wearisome, fatiguing,
   boring. Makabannog ka nga anak. You are a tiresome
   child.

   BANBANNOG, n. futile, useless or fruitless effort.
      Banbannog monto la dayta. That will be a useless
      effort of yours.

BANNUAG; AGKABANNUAG, adj. in the prime of youth,
   youthful.

BANNUAR, n. hero, idol. Dagiti nabaknang ti nagbalinen
   nga bannuar da. The rich became their heroes.

BANSAG, syn. of BANGSAL.

[1]BANTAY, n. mountain.

[2]BANTAY, n. guard, watch. --syn. GUARDIA.
   v. /AG-/ to be the guard or watch, to guard or
   watch something, to stand as guard or watch. Sika
   ti agbantay ditoy balay mi. You will be the guard
   in our house. /MANG-:-AN/ to guard, watch, protect.
   Dina kayat nga bantayan daytoy lako tayo. He does
   not want to watch our merchandise.

BANTENG, n. line, clothesline; a rope, wire and the
   like stretched between two fixed objects.
      v. /MANGI-:I-/ to tie the ends of to two fixed
   objects in order to make this. Ibanteng mo dayta
   barot. Tie the ends of that wire to two fixed
   objects.

BANTIL, v. /-UM-, MANG-:-EN/ to pinch, slap, squeeze,
etc. (a sick person who is near death) in order to
revive.

[1]BANTOT, adj. /NA-/ heavy, ponderous. --syn. DAGSEN.
--ant. LAG-AN.

[2]BANTOT, adj. /NA-/ having a strong offensive odor.
--syn. BANGSIT.

[3]BANTOT; BABANTOT, v. /AG-/ to feel indisposed, sluggish,
lazy. Saan nga makaumay ta agbabantot. He cannot come
for he is feeling indisposed. /MAMAG-/ to cause to
feel indisposed, sluggish, lazy. Ania ti namagbabantot
kanyana? What caused him to feel indisposed? --syn.
LALADUT.

BANTULAY, adj. /NAG-/ unstable, unbalanced. Bantulay ta
lamisaan. That table is unstable. --syn. BATTUAG.

BANURBUR, /AG-, -UM-/ to make a roaring sound: said of
a strong wind or a swollen river. Saanak nga nakaturog
ta bumanurbur ti angin. I could not sleep because the
wind was roaring.

BANWAR, see BANNUAR.

BANYAGA, see BANIAGA.

BANYAS, var. of BANIAS.

BANGA, n. earthen or clay pot, especially one used to
cook rice in.

BANGABANGA, n. skull.

BANGABANGA, v. /AG-/ to swarm in a heap: said of bugs,
bees, etc. Agbangabanga dagidiay abal-abal. The bugs
are swarming in a heap.

[1]BANGAD, n. back of a knife, a saw, etc.

[2]BANGAD, adj. /(NA-)/ heedless, obstinate, stubborn,
disobedient. Bangad ka nga ubing. You are an
obstinate child. --syn. TULOK.

BANGAG, var. of BANGEG.

BANGAR, a spreading tree with rank-smelling flowers
(Sterculia foetida, L.).

BANG-AR, v. /MA--AN/ to be relieved, comforted, cheered.
Mabang-aranak nga makakita kenka. I am cheered to see
you.
    adj. /MAKA-/ relieving, comforting, cheering,
refreshing. Makabang-ar tin angin ditoy. The wind
here is refreshing.

BANGBANGIR, see ^{2}BANGIR.

BANGBANGLO, see under BANGLO.

BANGBANGSIT, see ^{2}BANGSIT.

BANGDOL, v. /-UM-:-EN/ to collide with. Sino ti
bimmangdol kenka? Who collided with you? /AG-/
[with pl. subject] to collide with each other.
Nagbangdol dagiti kotse. The cars collided.
--syn. ^{1}DUNGPAR, (dial.) BANGGA.

BANGEG, adj. /NAG-/ having a hoarse, low-pitched, bass
or deep voice or sound. Bangeg ta maestra yo. Your
teacher has a low-pitched voice. Nakabangbangeg diay
kampana ti romano nga simbaan. The bell of the Roman
Catholic Church is very low-pitched.   --var. BANGAG.

BANGEN, n. a fence-like device placed at the doorsill
to prevent small children from getting out of the
room.

BANGGA, syn. (dial.) of BANGDOL.

BANGGAL, v. /AG-/ to tie a handkerchief or a similar
piece of material around the crown of one's head,
folding it diagonally and knotting the ends in front
so as to form a kind of a cone. Saan ka nga agbanggal
ta napudot. Don't tie a handkerchief around the crown
of your head for it is warm.   /MANGI-:I-/ to tie
around the crown of one's head. Sino ti nangibanggal
iti panyok? Who tied my handkerchief around the crown
of his head?

BANGGERA, n. place in the kitchen or adjoining the
kitchen where the plates, glasses, silverware, etc.
are washed, drained, and sometimes stacked.   --var.
BANGKERA.

BANG-I, adj. /NA-/ having the smell of toast or broiled fish.

BANGIBANG, v. /AG-/ [with pl. subject] to be adjacent, contiguous, next to each other, close to each other. Agbangibang ti ili mi ken ti ili da. Our town and their town are adjacent.
    n. /KA-/ one that is adjacent or close. Isuda ti kabangibang mi. They are the ones who are adjacent to us.

[1]BANGIR, n. the other side, opposite side. --syn. BALLASIW.
    v. /-UM-/ to go or transfer to the other side. /-EN/ to use the other side for doing something. Bangirem dayta ubing. Nurse that child with your other breast.

    BANGBANGIR, n. one half of anything, e.g. a squash.

[2]BANGIR; BANGBANGIR, adj. having some parts cooked and other parts uncooked: said of boiled or steamed rice.
    v. /AG-/ to be like this: said of boiled or steamed rice. Nagbangbangir daydiay inapoy na. The rice that she cooked has some parts uncooked.

BANGKA, n. a large boat made of boards and without outriggers. --syn. BILOG.

[1]BANGKAG, n. 1. vacant, uncultivated land. 2. a piece of land planted with vegetables; vegetable garden.
    v. /AG-/ to have a vegetable garden. /MANG-:-EN/ to make into a vegetable garden, to plant with vegetables.

[2]BANGKAG, v. /-UM-/ to disembark, go ashore. Bimmangkag da apaman a nakasanglad ti biray da. They went ashore as soon as their boat reached the shore. /MANGI-:I-/ to carry ashore. Ibangkag mo dagita natnateng. Carry ashore the vegetables.

BANGKAY, n. 1. corpse, cadaver. 2. body of a cart, sledge, etc.

BANGKERA, var. of BANGGERA.

BANGKING, adj. 1. odd, uneven, unequal, not correctly matched or paired. 2. unstable. --syn. BANTULAY.

BANGKIRIG, adj. sloping, slanted, tilted.
   v. /MANG-:-EN/ to cause to slope; slant; tip; to
tilt.   /MA-/ to be caused to slope; slant; tip; to
be tilted.

BANGKO [f. Sp.], n. bench, seat, chair.   --syn. TUGAW.

BANGKO [f. Sp.], n. bank, an establishment for the
   custody, loan, exchange, or issue of money, for the
   extension of credit and for facilitating the
   transmission of funds.

BANGLES, adj. /NA-/ spoiled, putrefied; sour, acidic;
   musty, rancid: said of foods. Nabangles daytoy
   inapoyen. This boiled rice is already spoiled.

BANGLIG, adj. /NA-/ having the stench of rancid oil,
   lard, etc.   --syn. BUNGLUG.

BANGLO, adj. /NA-/ fragrant, sweet-smelling,
   sweet-scented, odoriferous, odorous. Nabanglo dayta
   sabong mo. Your flower is fragrant.
   v. /-UM-/.   --ant. BANGSIT.

   BANGBANGLO or PABANGLO, n. perfume, cologne.

BANGON, v. /-UM-/ to rise, get up; to become erect.
   Bumangon ka ta aldawen. Get up for it is already
   late.   /MANG-:-EN/ or /MANGI-:I-/ 1. to erect, build,
   construct. Isuda ti nangbangon toy balay mi. It was
   they who constructed this house of ours. 2. to set
   upright. Bangonem dayta mula nga nabual. Set upright
   that plant which fell down.

BANGOS, n. milkfish.

BANGSAL, n. an annex to the kitchen consisting of a kind
   of platform raised on posts and not covered by any
   kind of roof. It is primarily a place for cleaning and
   washing pots and pans, rice, vegetables and clothes.
   --syn. BANSAG.

[1]BANGSIT, adj. /NA-/ foul-smelling, having offensive or
   unpleasant odor. Adda maangot ko nga nabangsit ditoy.
   I smell something foul-smelling here.
   v. /-UM-/ to be like this.   --ant. BANGLO.   --see
   BANGBANGSIT.

²BANGSIT, n. a coarse, labiate herb (Hyptis suaveolus
(L.) Poir.) with blue flowers.

BAO, n. rat, mouse, rodent. --syn. UTOT.

BAOG, adj. /NA-/ 1. spoiled or rotten due to lack of
air and moisture: said of rice and other seeds. 2.
having the smell of this. --syn. AGUB.

BAON, v. /AG-/ to order someone to do something, to
send someone on an errand, to give orders. Nalaing
nga agbaon dayta baket mo. Your wife is good in
giving orders. /AGI-, MANGI-:I-/ to order, send.
Agibaon ka man ti umay agburas ti mangga. Will you
please send someone to come pick the mangoes.

BABAUNEN, n. servant. --syn. TAGABU, KATULONG,
ADIPEN.

BAOR, v. /MANG-:-AN/ to mix non-glutinous rice (MAKAN)
with, to adulterate with non-glutinous rice: said of
glutinous or sticky rice (DIKET). Baoram dayta diket
tapno saan nga nakilnet unay. Adulterate that
glutinous rice with non-glutinous rice so that it
will not be very sticky. /MANGI-:I-/ to mix with or
to use to adulterate (glutinous rice): said of
non-glutinous rice or any of its substitutes. Daytoy
ti ibaor mo dita diket. Use this to adulterate that
glutinous rice.

BAPOR [f. Sp.], n. ship.
v. /AG-/ to go by or ride on a ship or boat.
Nagbapor da nga napan idiay Manila. They went by
boat to Manila.

¹BARA, adj. /NA-/ hot, warm; feverish. Nabara ti
pingping mo. Your cheek is hot.
v. /-UM-/ to be like this.

BABARA, v. /AG-, -EN/ to be feverish, hot with fever.

²BARA, n. yardstick, a unit of measurement almost
equivalent to a yard.

BARA, n. lung.

BARABAD, n. bandage, wrapping.
v. /MANG-:-AN/ to put a bandage around something,

to swathe.   /MANGI-:I-/ to put or tie as bandage around something, to use to swathe something.

[1]BARAIRONG, v. /AG-/ to rotate, revolve, turn around, pirouette; to whirl about one's body. Saan ka nga agbarairong dita tengga ti kalsada. Don't whirl about your body in the middle of the street.
   adj. /NA-/ restless, roving, rambling.

[2]BARAIRONG, var. of BARRAIRONG.

BARAKS [f. Eng.], n. barracks.

BARAKUBAK, n. a withered leaf.

BARAKUS, v. /MANG-:-AN/ to tie a string, rope and the like around. Barakusam dayta maleta. Tie a string around that suitcase.   /MANGI-:I-/ to tie around, to use to tie around. Ibarakus mo daytoy tali iti dayta maleta. Tie this string around that suitcase.

BARANDIS [f. Sp.], v. /AG-:I-/ to throw or toss. Urayem nga agbarandis da ti kuarta. Wait for them to throw money.   /MANG-:-AN/ to throw or toss money to. Isu ti nangbarandis kanyada ti kuarta. It was he who tossed money to them.   /MANGI-:I-/ to throw or toss (as money) to. Ibarandis mo daytoy kuarta kanyada. Toss this money to them.   --syn. BITOR.

BARANGABANG, /MANGI-:I-/ to put on or cover with hot ashes or live embers or near a fire so as to warm or cook slowly. Ibarangabang mo daytay inapuy tapno pumudot. Put the rice near the fire so that it will get warm. Isu ti nangibarangabang iti tarong. He was the one who put an eggplant in hot ashes near the fire so as to cook it.

BARANGAY, n. a boat smaller than the BIRAY.

BARANGET, v. /AG-/ to provoke a quarrel by arguing noisily and offensively.
   adj. /NA-/ loud-mouthed, argumentative, provocative.

BARAT, adj. /NAG-/ one who bargains hard in order to pay rock-bottom prices.
   v. /MANG-:-EN/ to buy at the lowest possible price.

BARATO [f. Sp.], n. some small portion of one's winnings
in a game of chance given to another. No mangabakak
addanto baratom kanyak. If I win you will have some
portion of my winnings. /-UM-:-EN/ to ask for this.
Bumarato ka ti pisos ken ni Julia ta nangabak manen.
Ask for one peso from Julia inasmuch as she won again.

  PABARATO, v. /AG-:-AN/ to give a small portion of
    one's winnings. Pabaratoan nak met. Give me also
    a small portion of your winnings. /MANGI-:I-/ to
    give (a small portion of one's winnings). Mano ti
    impabarato na kenka? How much of his winnings did
    he give you?

BARAWID, v. /MANG-:-AN/ to put a band around; also, to
  put additional bands around. /MANGI-:I-:-AN/ to tie
  around. Ibarawid daytoy tali ti dayta karton. Tie
  this rope around that box. Barawidam dayta kahon ti
  tali. Tie a rope around that box.

BARAYUBOY, adj. /NAG-/ wasteful, extravagant. --syn.
  BUSLON.
    v. /AG-/ to be this.

BARBAKUA, v. /MANG-:-EN/ or /MANGI-:I-/ to roast,
  broil. Barbakuaem daydiay ikan. or: Ibarbakuam
  daydiay ikan. Broil that fish.

BARBAS [f. Sp.], n. beard. --syn. IMING.

BARBASA, n. interpreter, translator; prompter, one
  who dictates. Ibarbasam dayta kenkuana. Dictate that
  to him. --var. BARUBASA.

BARBERO [f. Sp.], n. barber. --syn. MAMMUKIS.
    v. /AG-/ to become a barber.

BARBURAN, see under BURBUR.

BARENA [f. Sp.], drill, auger, brace and bit.
    v. /MANG-:-EN/ to drill with an auger.

BARENG; BARENG (NO) or BARBARENG (NO), hoping, perchance,
  perhaps, possibly, in the event that. Aguray tayo
  bassit bareng no lumung-aw da met laeng. Let's wait
  for a while hoping that they will eventually appear.

BARENG-BARENG, adj. false, feigned, alleged.
Bareng-bareng diay sakit na. His sickness is
feigned.

PABPABARENG, v. /MANGI-:I-/ to hope, suppose. Saan
mo nga ipabpabareng nga pabulodan ka ti kuarta.
Don't suppose that I will lend you money.

BARESBES, n. brook, creek.   --syn. KULOS, LIPNOK,
WAIG.

BARIBAR, v. /AG-/ to turn around in a half circle.
/MANG-:-EN/ to turn (someone or something) around
in a half circle. Isu ti nangbaribar diay tugaw.
It was he who turned around the chair.

BARIBARI, interj. an exclamation used to drive evil
spirits away from one's way or place.

BARIKES, n. belt, girdle, cincture.
    v. /AG-/ to put a belt or a similar thing around
one's waist, to tie a string, a band and the like
around one's waist. Agbarikes ka. Tie something
around your waist.   /MANG-:-AN/ [= BARIKSAN] to tie
a string and the like around the waist or midsection
of. Bariksam dayta ubing. Tie something around the
waist of that child.   /MANGI-:I-/ to tie around the
waist. Ibarikes mo dayta buneng mo. Tie your big
knife around your waist.   --var. BARRIKES.

BARILES [f. Sp.], n. barrel.

BARINSAWAY, adj. /NA-/ fidgety as when sleeping.
--syn. TIWENG.
    v. /AG-/ to be fidgety, restless. Saan ka nga
agbarinsaway. Don't be fidgety.

BARINGRING, v. /MANG-:-EN/ to invert or reverse the
position of.

BARIW-AS, v. /AG-:-EN/ to go out and gather. Inka
agbariw-as ti pagtungo tayo. Go out and gather
firewood for us. Bariw-asem amin nga bunga ti
mangga nga makitam. Go out and gather all the
mango fruits that you see.

BARIWENGWENG, /AG-/ to whirl, revolve, rotate, gyrate.
Agbariwengweng ti makitak. What I see is whirling.

BARKADA [f. Sp.?], n. gang. /MAKI-:KA-/ to join
(someone) in a gang, to gang up with. Dina kayat
ti makibarkada kadakami. He does not want to gang
up with us.

BARKES, v. /MANG-:-EN/ to tie up into a bundle. Isu
ti nangbarkes kadagiti bungbungon. He was the one
who tied up all the bundles.

BARKO [f. Sp.], n. barge, cargo boat.

BARNIS [f. Eng.], n. varnish, shellac. --syn. SIALAK.
v. /AG-, MANG-:-AN/ to varnish, to apply or brush
varnish or shellac on. Masapul nga barnisam dayta
aparador. It is necessary that you varnish that
cupboard.

BARO, adj. /NAG-/ new, recent, modern, novel; fresh;
virgin. Baro dayta sagaysay mo a. Your comb is new
I see.
n. [pl. BABBARO] 1. adult male, man. Baro dayta
ading mon. Your younger brother is already an adult.
2. single or unmarried man; bachelor. Ania, baro ka
pay laeng wenno adda asawa mon? What, are you still
a bachelor or do you have a wife now? --ant.
BALASANG. --see BUMARO.

BAROKBOK, n. the bubbling sound produced when water
enters an immersed container.

BARRAIRONG, n. a rhinoceros beetle which is very
destructive to coconut palms.

BARRENA, see BARENA.

BARRIKES, var. of BARIKES.

BARRIO [f. Sp.], n. a political subdivision of a town,
outside the POBLACION, a suburb of a town. --var.
BARYO.
BARBARRIO, adj. characteristic of a BARRIO, or of
one coming from a BARRIO: used derisively.

BARRUGA, v. /MANG-:-EN/ to throw a piece of wood or
stick at. Saan nak nga barrugaen no di mo kayat ti
masaktan. Do not throw a piece or stick at me if you
don't want to be injured.

BARSAK, v. /MANGI-:I-/ to drop or let fall, to put
down heavily. Saan mo nga ibarbarsak dayta karamba
ta mabuong. Don't put that jar down heavily for it
will break. /MAI-/ to drop or fall. Naibarsak diay
itlog ngem saan nga nabuong. The egg dropped but it
did not break.

BARSANGA, n. a slender sedge, a kind of grass.

BARTAY, v. /MANGI-:I-/ to stretch a piece of string,
rope or wire by tying each end to two opposite posts,
trunks or branches of trees, etc. Ibartay mo dayta
tali. Tie and stretch that rope.

BARTEK, v. /AG-/ to get oneself drunk, to cause oneself
to become drunk. Panawan ka no agbartek ka. I will
leave you if you get yourself drunk. /MANG-:-EN/ to
cause (someone) to become drunk, to get (someone)
drunk. Saan dak nga barteken ta panawan nak ni baket
ko. Don't cause me to become drunk because my wife
will leave me. /MA-/ to become drunk. Mabartekak
no uminomak ti arak. I will become drunk if I drink
liquor.
ARTEK, BARTIKERO, MAMMARTEK, n. drunkard.

BARTEKERO, see under BARTEK.

BARTILIA [f. Sp.?], n. shuttle of a loom.

BARTIN, n. a venomous snake with variegated skin.

BARUBASA, var. of BARBASA.

BARUKONG, n. chest, breast, bosom.

BARUSBUS, v. /AG-/ 1. to produce new shoots or buds,
to sprout again, to revive. 2. to grow luxuriantly.

BARUT, n. wire, fence wire.

BARYO, var. of BARRIO.

BASA, v. /AG-/ 1. to read. Dina pay ammo ti agbasa.
He does not know how to read yet. 2. to go to school,
attend school. Dina kayat ti agbasa. He does not
want to go to school. /-UM-, MANG-:-EN/ to read

(a letter, a book, a newspaper, etc.). Basbasaen
na daydiay surat ko. He is reading my letter.

BASA, v. /MANG-:-EN/ to wet, to put in water or
other liquid, to put water or other liquid on.
/MA-/ to become wet, to get wet. Nabasa toy
badok. My clothes are wet.

   BABASA, v. /AG-/1. to get oneself wet; to cause
   oneself to get wet, as when playing in or with
   water. Saan ka nga agbabasa. Don't get yourself
   wet. 2. to become wet or moist.

BASABAS, v. /AG-/ to wipe or sponge one's body with a
wet cloth or sponge. Agbasabas ka ti napudot nga
danum. Wipe your body with hot water. /MANG-:-AN/
to wipe or sponge. Basabasam dayta ubing ti napudot
nga danum. Sponge that child's body with hot water.
/MANGI-:I-/ to wipe or sponge with. Napudot nga
danum ti ibasabas mo kenkuana. Sponge him with hot
water.

BASAK; BASAKBASAK, v. /AG-/ to trespass, intrude rudely.

BASISAW, n. urinary bladder or the like.

BASAR, n. floor.   --syn. DATAR.

BASE [f. Sp.], n. base, basis.
   v. /MANGI-:I-/ to base on.

BASI, n. sugarcane wine, fermented sugarcane juice.

BASIBAS, v. /AG-, MANG-:-EN/ to throw a piece of wood
or stick at (someone or something) with force or
violence. Inka man basibasen diay babuy nga simmari
idiay inaladan tayo. Will you please go throw a
piece of wood at the pig which broke into our yard.

BASING, v. /MAI-/ to totter; to buckle at the knees;
to stumble. Uray ka la nga maibasbasing ti bartek
mon. You were even tottering because of your
drunkenness.

BASKAG, v. /AG-/ to bulge, swell outward especially
garments. Apay nga agbaskag dayta badom? Why is
your dress bulging out. /MANGI-:I-/ to stretch
outward, cause to bulge or swell outwards.

BASKET [f. Eng.], n. a basket, especially one with a handle.

BASNUT, v. /AG-/ to beat someone with a cane or a similar instrument. /MANG-:-AN/ to beat with a cane or a similar instrument. Saan mo nga basnutan dayta aso ta kagaten na ka. Don't beat my dog with a cane for he will bite you.

BASO [f. Sp.], n. glass, especially drinking glass or a broken piece of it. --see SARMING.

BASOL, n. sin, error, fault, mistake. Adu ti basol mo. You have many sins.
    v. /AG-/ to sin, err, make a mistake. Saan ka nga agbasol tapno mapan ka sadi langit. Don't sin so that you will go to heaven. --syn. BIDDUT.

PABASOL, v. /AG-:-EN/ to blame, put the blame on.

BASSAWANG, v. /AG-/ to talk presumptuously, arrogantly, haughtily; to blaspheme. Saan ka nga agbassawang. Don't talk arrogantly.

BASSIT, adj. /NAG-/ 1. small, little (in size). Bassit ka pay laeng. You are still small. --ant. DAKKEL. 2. few, little (in number). Bassit laeng ti napan idiay pabuya da. Only a few went to their show. --ant. ADU. --var. BATTIT.
    adv. for a moment, for a while; please; rather. Tulungan nak man bassit. Will you please help me. Umay ka bassit ditoy. Come here for a while. Isu bassit ti mapan. He'd rather be the one to go.

BASSIUSIT, adj. very small, very little, very few; diminutive. Bassiusit la ti tao nga immay. Only very few people came. --var. BATTIT-USIT.

SANGKABASSIT, adj. little, few.

TAGIBASSIT, v. /MANG-:-EN/ to belittle, depreciate, deprecate. Adu ti naipaay na iti distrito na ngem tagibassiten na pay laeng. He has given much to his district but he still belittles this.

BASSIUSIT, see under BASSIT.

¹BASTA, adv. nevertheless, nonetheless, despite anything,
in spite of everything; of necessity; simply, just.
Basta mapanak uray no agunget kayo. Even if you get
angry I am going nevertheless. Basta maturog ka.
Just go to sleep.

²BASTA [f. Sp.], v. /MANG-:-EN/ to baste (a dress).
Bastaem pay nga umuna dayta sakanto daiten dita
makina. Baste that first before you sew it in the
sewing machine. /MANGI-:I-/ to baste (a part of a
dress). Ibastam dayta gayadan ti badok. Baste the
hem of my dress.

BASTARDO [f. Sp.], n. illegitimate child, bastard.
--syn. ANAK TI RUAR.

BASTIPUR, n. a sun helmet made of bamboo frame and
palm leaves.

BASTON [f. Sp.], n. walking cane.

BASTOS [f. Sp.], adj. /NAG-/ rude, impolite, indecent,
obscene.
   v. /MANG-:-EN/ to act toward or treat rudely,
impolitely or indecently.

BASURA [f. Sp.], n. garbage.

BATAD, adj. /NA-/ clear, plain, obvious, evident,
manifest. Nabatad ti nagdalanan ti kuko iti rupa
na. The nail marks on his face are evident.

BATAK, v. /MANG-:-EN/ to give or extend help, aid or
assistance to. Inka bataken daydiay bulsek. Give
assistance to the blind.

BATANG, n. turn; chance or opportunity to do something.
Dimteng met laeng ti batang ko nga agsarita. My turn
to speak finally came.
   v. /MA--AN/ chosen or appointed by chance to do
something. Nabatanganak nga nagdalus iti silid. I
was chosen by chance to clean the bedroom.

BATAY, n. stand, support; perch.
   v. /AG-:-AN/ to step on for support or in order to
raise oneself; to perch on. Agbatay ka ditoy lamisaan

tapno magaw-at mo daydiay lawwalawwa. Step on this
table so that you can reach for that spider.
/MANGI-:I-/ to place or set on for support; to
perch (someone or something) on. Saan monnga ibatay
dayta sakam ditoy alad mi. Don't set your foot on
our fence.

BATBAT, v. /MANG-:-EN/ to beat: said of cotton and
other fibers; to scutch. Batbatam dayta kapas.
Beat that kapok.

BATEK, n. glass bead.

BATENG, n. a large, coarse, rectangular net used in
hunting.
    v. /AG-/ to hunt wild animals with a net. Napan
da nagbateng. They went to hunt wild animals with
a net. /AG-, MANG-:-AN/ often /MAKA-:MA--AN/ to
hunt or catch with a net. Adu ti nabatingan da.
They were able to hunt many with a net.

BATERYA [batérya; f. Sp.], n. battery.

[1]BATI, v. /AG-/ to remain, stay behind. Agbati ka ditoy.
Stay behind here. /AGI-, MANGI-:I-/ to leave behind.
Agibati ka ti gastoen mi. Leave behind some money for
our expenses. /MA-/ to be left behind. No dika
agdardaras mabati ka. If you don't hurry up you'll
be left behind.

[2]BATI, var. of BATIL.

BATIA [f. Sp.], n. a large, shallow basin for washing
clothes; a laundry tub. --var. BATYA.

BATIBAT, v. /-EN/ to have a nightmare. Binatibatak idi
rabii. I had a nightmare last night.

BATIK, n. white spot on leaves.
    BATIKBATIK, adj. spotted.

BATIKULENG, n. gizzard.

BATIL [f. Sp.], v. /AG-, MANG-:-EN/ to beat, stir.
Agbatil ka ti dua nga itlog. Beat two eggs. --var.
BATI.

BATILLOG, n. testicle. --syn. UKEL.

BATINGTING, n. bell. --syn. KAMPANA.

BATIWAWA; SIBABATIWAWA, adj. open all the time, such as doors, windows, jars, etc.

BATO, n. in a game of coins or any similar game, the coin or a similar object that is used to hit the other coins or similar objects used in the game.

BATO, n. stone, pebble, gravel.
    v. /MANG-:-EN/ to throw stones at, lapidate. /MANGI-:I-/ to throw, hurl, toss. Ibatom kanyak dayta sardinas. Throw to me that can of sardines.

BATTALAY, adj. /NA-/ occurring, appearing, coming or set apart at regular distant intervals. Nabattalay ti panagsangpet ti surat na. His letters come at regular distant intervals. --var. BATTAWAY.

BATTAWAY, var. of BATTALAY.

BATTIT, var. of BASSIT.

BATTIT-USIT, var. of BASSIUSIT.

BATTOOG, v. /MANG-:-EN/ to drop or let fall from a high place. Sino ti nangbattoog kenka? Who let you fall from a high place? /MA-/ to drop or fall. Nabattoog diay burnay. The jar fell.

BATTOON, v. /MANG-:-AN/ to put a weight on in order to hold down, to press down. Battoonan yo dayta papel tapno saan nga itayab ti angin. Put a weight on that paper so that it won't be blown away by the wind. /MANGI-:I-/ to put as weight on, to use to hold or press down (something).

BATTUAG, v. /MANG-:-EN/ to tilt or tip backward. Saan mo nga battuagen dayta tugaw. Don't tilt that chair backwards.
    adj. /NAG-/ having the tendency to tilt backward, unstable, unbalanced.

BATTUABATTUAG, syn. (dial.) of KULUMPIO.

BATTUAGAN, n. a lever used for drawing water from a well (BUBON).

BATUBAT, v. /AG-/ to rest briefly.

¹BATUG, n. front, opposite (of). Agsardeng ka idiay batug ti kamposanto. Stop in front of the cemetery.
v. /MANG-:-EN/ to go in front of or opposite to, to face. Batugem dayta poste. Go in front of that post.

KABATUG, n. that which is in front of or opposite to (someone or something).

KAIBATUGAN, n. equivalent, something of equal worth.

²BATUG, n. row, file; line of words.

BINATOG, n. line, passage. Nailanad daytoy nga binatog iti libro. This line was written in the book.

BAT-UG, n. a big-bellied toad that croaks at night. --syn. (dial.) PILAT.

BATUK, v. /-UM-/ to dive into or go under water. /MANG-:-EN/ to dive into the water or go under the water in order to look for and get or reach (someone or something). Batukem man daydiay singsing ko nga natnag idiay karayan. Will you please dive into the water and look for my ring which fell into the river. /MANGI-:I-/ to dive into or go under the water in order to give (something to somebody) or to put (something there); to dive with. Padasem man nga ibatok dayta asom? Will you try to dive into the water with your dog?

BATUMBALANI, n. magnet, lodestone.

BATUNGOL, n. a disease characterized by skin eruptions all over the body - especially common among chickens.
v. /AG-/ to have this disease.

BATYA, var. of BATIA.

BAUD, v. /MANGI-:I-/ to tie to, fasten to, attach to with a string or rope. Ibaud mo dayta babuy idiay poon ti kayo. Tie the pig to the trunk of the tree.
/AG-/ to keep a gamecock.
n. gamecock; a rooster kept in a cage and trained to fight another rooster, especially in a cockpit.
Adu ti baud na nga Texas. He has many Texas gamecocks.

BAUL [f. Sp.], n. chest, trunk, locker, footlocker.
--syn. LAKASA.

BAUT, n. stick used for beating, whip.
v. /AG-/ to beat or whip someone. Dina ammo ti
agbaut daydiay madre. The nun does not know how to
whip anyone.   /-UM-, MANG-:-EN/ Sino ngarud ti
bimmaut kenka? Who then whipped you?   /MANGI-:I-/ to
whip or beat (on someone or something).

BAUTEK, n. a piece of bamboo (rarely of wood) used to
make the frame of a ladder, a door or a window.

BAWANG, n. garlic.

BAWBAW, v. /AG-/ to become flat, insipid, tasteless:
said of liquors and wines. Kalubam dayta botelya
tapno saan nga agbawbaw dayta basi. Cover that bottle
so that that sugarcane wine will not become tasteless.
/MA--AN/ to become insipid, flat, tasteless.
Nabawbawan diay basi. The sugarcane wine has become
tasteless.

BAWI, v. /-UM-/ to win back one's losses in gambling.
/MAKA-/ to be able to win back one's losses in
gambling.   /MAKA-:MA-/ to be able to win back (one's
losses in gambling). Nabawi na diay naabak kanyana
idi kalman. He was able to win back his losses
yesterday.

BABAWI, v. /AG-/ to repent or regret what one has
done. Agbabawi kanto ngem naladawen. You will
repent later but it will be late.   /AG-:-EN/ to
repent or regret. Isu ti nagbabawi ti iyaay na
ditoy. It was he who regretted his having come
here.   /MANGI-:I-/ to take back (what one has
given away).

BAY-A or BAYBAY-AN, v. /MANG-:-AN/ [= (BAY)BAY-AN] 1.
to allow, permit, let. Baybay-an tayo nga maturog
diay doktor. Let's let the doctor sleep. 2. to
leave alone, let alone, leave, abandon, forsake;
hence, also to neglect. Saan mo nga baybay-an
dayta lutlutoem. Don't neglect what you are cooking.

BAYABAS, var. of BAYYABAS.

BAYABAY, v. /MANG-:-EN/ to escort, flank, accompany,
guard, protect. Isu ti nangbayabay kanyak. He was
the one who escorted me.

BAYAD, n. payment, price. --syn. PRESIO.
    v. /AG-:-AN/ to pay (as debt). Agbayad ka ti utang
mo kanyak. Pay your debt to me. /AG-, MANG-:-AN/ to
pay (someone) a wage or salary. Agbayad ka ti tao
nga tumulong kadatayo. Pay a wage to a person who is
going to help us. Bayadan na ti tao nga tumulong
kadatayo. He will pay any person who is going to
help us. /AG-:I-:-AN/ to pay (a wage or salary) to
(someone). Isu ti agbayad ti pisos ti tao nga
tumulong kadatayo. It is he who will pay one peso
to any person who is going to help us. Pisos, to
ibayad na iti tao nga tumulong kadatayo. He will pay
one peso to any person who is going to help us.
Bayadan na ti pisos ti tao nga tumulong kadatayo.
He will pay one peso to the person who is going to
help us.

BAYAG, adj. /MA-/ to be long in duration. Mabayag
kaminto nga agsarita inton malem. We will talk for
a long time this afternoon. /NA-/ long in duration
(in the past). Nabayag kami nga nagsarita idi kalman
ti malem. We talked for a long time yesterday
afternoon. --ant. BIIT.
    v. /AG-/ to stay long, tarry. Saan ka nga agbayag
idiay balay da Ana. Don't stay long in the house of
Ann.
    n. 1. the generic name for late rice. --ant. BIIT.
2. any plant that gives a second harvest.

BAYAKABAK, v. /-UM-/ to pour, splash, spray: said of
rain or water. Bumayakabak ti tudo idi rabii.

BAYANGGUDAW, adj. /NAG-/ idle, lazy, shiftless.

BAYAT, prep. during, while, for the duration of. Awan
ti kinnan na bayat ti dua nga aldaw. He did not eat
anything for two days.

BAYAW, n. brother-in-law, the husband of one's brother
or sister. --syn. KAYONG. --ant. IPAG. --see BILAS.
    AGBAYAW, two brothers-in-law.

BAYBAY, n. open sea, ocean. --syn. TAAW.

BAYENGBENG, adj. /-IMM-/ full and elongated: said especially of fruits.

BAYENGYENG, n. a bamboo container consisting of one or several internodes which is used generally for carrying water.

BAYO, v. /AG-/ to pound rice (PAGAY) in a mortar (ALSONG) with a pestle (AL-O). Inkam agbayo. We are going to pound rice. /AG-, MANG-:-EN/ to pound, especially rice in a mortar with a pestle. Maysa nga kaban nga pagay ti bay-oen mi. We will pound one sack of rice.

[1]BAYOG, adj. /NA-/ tall and slender, e.g. a bamboo.

[2]BAYOG, v. /MANGI-:I-/ to hoist, hang up on a pole. Ibayog mo dayta bandera. Hoist that flag.

BAYOG, n. a thornless climbing bamboo with thick walls. --syn. BIKAL.

BAYOKBOK, v. /AG-/ to bulge, swell sideways. Simpaem ta badom tapno saan nga agbayokbok. Fix your dress so that it won't bulge.

BAY-ON, n. a deep bag or sack generally made of strips of the leaves of the buri palm or of the pandanus.

BAYONETA [f. Sp.], n. bayonet.
v. /MANG-:-EN/ to stab, strike, injure or kill with a bayonet.

BAYOOT, adj. /NA-/ smelling like that of putrid urine, foul-smelling.

BAYYABAS [f. Sp.], n. guava.
v. /AG-/ to pick guavas. --var. BAYABAS.

BAYYEK, n. tadpole.

BEBEKKELAN, see under [1]BEKKEL.

BEDBED, n. band; string, rope, cord used for binding; bandage.

v. /MANG-:-AN/ to tie into a bundle; to bind; to tie a strong or bandage around. Bedbedam dagitoy kayo. Tie a string around these pieces of wood. /MANGI-:I-/ to tie or bind with, to use to bind. Barut ti imbedbed na kadagiti kayo. He used wire to bind the pieces of wood.

[1]BEDDENG, n. boundary, limit. --syn. INGGAAN.

[2]BEDDENG, v. /-UM-/ [= BUMDENG], to hesitate, be apprehensive. Saan ka nga bumdeng nga mangibaga kanyak iti kayatmo. Don't hesitate to tell me what you like.

BEDE, adj. stammerer, stutterer.

BEGBEG, v. /MANG-:-EN/ to reduce to small particles; to grind, mince. /MA-/ to be reduced to small particles; to be ground, minced.

BEGGANG, n. ember, live coal.
    v. /AG-/ to glow like ember or live coal.

BEGKET, v. /MANG-:-EN/ to cover, as the mouth of a jar or a head, by putting a piece of cloth, paper, leaf, etc. over and around it. Begketem dayta ngarab ti garapon ti lupot tapno saan nga agaw-aw ta naggian na. Cover the mouth of the jar with cloth so that its contents will not spill out. /MANGI-:I-/ to use to cover around (the mouth of a pot, a jar, etc.).

BEGNAT, v. /MA-/ to have a relapse (while recovering from an illness). Nabignat manen diay anak kon. My child had a relapse again.

BEKKAG, v. /AG-/ to burst open: said of cotton balls. No agbekkag dagidiay kapas mabalin ti agpurosen. When the cotton balls burst open we can then pick them.

[1]BEKKEL, v. /AG-/ to hang oneself; to commit suicide by hanging oneself. /-UM-, MANG-:-EN/ to strangle, strangulate.

BEBEKKELAN, n. the part of the windpipe situated in the throat.

[2]BEKKEL, n. kidney.

BEKLAT, n. boa, python.

BEL-A, v. /AG-/ to vomit. Sipsiputam no agbel-a ta
ubing. Watch if the child will vomit. /AG-, MANGI-:I-/
to vomit, throw out, spew. Nagbel-a ti dara diay lakay.
The old man vomitted blood. Adu ti inbel-a na. He
vomitted much. --syn. SARWA.

BELDAT, n. a large, edible, fresh water, lamellibranchiate
mollusk.

BELLAAK, n. uproar, tumult, turmoil, pandemonium.

PABLAAK, n. notice, announcement, proclamation.
v. /MANGI-:I-/ to announce, proclaim, give
notice of.

BELLAAY, n. flour, especially rice flour.

BELLAD, v. /-UM-/ [= BUMLAD] to swell due to being
soaked or boiled in water or any other liquid for
some time. /AG--AN/ to be oversated, to be heavy
due to overeating.

PABLAD [= PA- + BELLAD], v. /AG-/ to boil some
kernels of corn for PINABLAD preparation.
/MANGI-:I-/ to boil (kernels of corn) for
PINABLAD preparation. Mangipablad ka ti sanga
kap nga mais. Boil one cupful of corn kernels.

PINABLAD [= PA- + -IN- + BELLAD], n. a preparation
consisting of boiled kernels of corn which is
salted to taste and to which grated coconut is
mixed.

BELLENG, v. /AGI-, MANGI-:I-/ to throw away. Ibelleng
mo daydiay basura tayo. Throw our garbage away.
/MAI-/ to be spilled, thrown away, fall out.
Agin-inayad ka ta dinto maibelleng ta awit mo.
Move slowly so that what you are carrying will not
be spilled.

BENBEN, v. /MAKA-/ to be able to hold, last or do
its purpose. Saan nga makabenben dayta tali nga
pinanggalut mo. That string which you used in
tying cannot last. /MAKA-:MA--AN/ to be able to
cope with (one's task or duty). Saan ko nga

mabenbenan ti trabahok. I cannot cope with my work.

BENDISION [f. Sp.], n. benediction, absolution,
blessing.
v. /AG-/ to do the blessing, to give the
benediction. /MANG-:-AN/ to bless, to sprinkle holy
water at. Benindisionan nak daydiay nasingpet nga
padi. The kind priest blessed me.

BENDITA [f. Sp.], n. holy water.
adj. holy or blessed: said of St. Mary and other
women saints. --ant. BENDITO.

BENDITO [f. Sp.], n. holy or blessed: said of Jesus
and any of the saints. --ant. BENDITA.

BENNAL, n. sugarcane juice.

BENNAT, v. /MANG-:-EN/ to stretch, extend in length.
Bennatem daytoy goma. Stretch this rubber band.

BENNEG, n. section, division, department.

BENNEK, n. a small, edible, fresh water, lamellibranchiate
mollusk; it is much smaller than the BELDAT. --syn.
DUKIANG.

BENTE [béntɛ; f. Sp.], n. 1. twenty. 2. twenty centavos.

BENGBENG, adj. /NA-/ thick: said of boards, tissues,
books, etc. --ant. INGPIS.

BENGNGAT, n. accent, characteristic way of speaking or
pronouncing words. Iti bengngat ni Virginia, ammo
lattan ni Lakay Andres nga taga-Tarlac. From
Virginia's accent, old man Andre knew for sure that
she was from Tarlac.

BENGNGEG, adj. /NAG-/ hard of hearing, somewhat deaf.

BENGRAW, n. a large, greenish-looking fly. --see
NGILAW.

BERBER, v. /AG-/ to expose oneself to the wind, current,
etc. /MANGI-:I-/ to expose to the wind, current, etc.
/MAI-/ to be exposed to the wind, current, etc.

BERDE [bɛrdɛ; f. Sp.], adj. /NAG-/ green.

BERDIGONES [bɛrdigonɛs; f. Sp.], n. a lead pellet, especially that used in air guns or shotguns.

BESSAG, adj. /NA-/ pale, pallid, wan; lifeless.
    v. /-UM-/ [= BUMSAG], to turn pale, pallid, wan; to blench, flinch.

BESSANG, n. mountain pass.

BESTIDA [bɛstida; f. Sp.], n. women; dress.   --var. BESTIDO.

BESTIDO, var. of BESTIDA.

BETERANO [bɛtɛráno; f. Sp.], n. veteran.

BETTAK, v. /-UM-/ [= BUMTAK] 1. to crack. Bimtak diay baso idi natnag. The glass cracked when it fell. 2. to burst, explode. Bumtak ta lobom. Your balloon will burst. 3. to break out as war. Naiyanakak idi bimtak ti gubat. I was born when the war broke out. /MANG-:-EN/ or /MANGI-:I-/ 1. to cause to crack. 2. to cause to burst or explode. /MA-/ [= MABTAK] 1. to be caused to crack, to crack. 2. to be caused to burst or explode, to burst or explode. Nabtak diay lobo na. His balloon burst.

BETTED, var. of BETTEG.

BETTEG, n. cramp, a spasmodic painful involuntary contraction of a muscle.
    v. /AG-/ to have this.

BETTEK, n. 1. a strip of bamboo, vine or the like used for binding especially stalks of rice and leaves of the PAN-AW and LIDDA used for thatching. 2. a bundle of any of these.
    v. /MANG-:-EN/ to tie or bundle especially stalks of rice and leaves of the PAN-AW and LIDDA used for thatching.

BIAG, n. life. Narigat ti biag ditoy ili mi. Life is hard in our town.
    v. /AG-/ to live, remain alive, live on. Agbiag ngata daydiay immulak? Do you think what I planted

is going to live? /MANG-:-EN/ 1. to make live or
survive. Siak ti nangbiag kenka. I was the one who
made you live. 2. to revive. Biagen na daydiay apoy.
He will revive the fire. 3. to enliven; to give life,
action, or spirit to; to animate. Isu ti nangbiag
iti programa mi. He was the one who enlivened our
program.

BIAHE [biáhε; f. Sp.], n. trip, journey, voyage, travel.
    v. /AG-/ to travel, to make a trip or voyage. Kayat
ko ti agbiahe manen. I want to travel again.
/AGI-, MANGI-:I-/ 1. to transport to (another place)
in order to sell. Agibiaheak ti mais idiay Manila.
I will transport corn to Manila to sell. 2. to take
on a trip. Saan mo nga ibibiahe dayta anak mo ta
ubing pay la unay. Don't take your child on a trip
for he is still very young.

    BIAHERO n. one who is fond of traveling, one who
    travels a lot.

BIANG, n. concern, business, responsibility.
    v. /-UM-:-AN/ to concern oneself with, to interfere
with, meddle in. Saan mo nga biangan ti ania man nga
aramiden na. Don't concern yourself with anything
that he does.

BIBIG, n. lip, especially the underlip.

BIBINEG, v. /AG-/ to be numb, insensitive. Agbibineg
    dagitoy saksakak. My legs are numb. /MANG-:-EN/ to
    anaesthetize; to numb. Binibineg diay doktor daytoy
    imak. The doctor numbed my hand.
        adj. /NA-/ numb, insensitive. --syn. PIPIKEL.

BIBINGKA, n. 1. a kind of thick, flat and round cake
    made of glutinous rice (DIKET). --syn. BIKO. 2. a
    kind of flat and round cake made of non-glutinous
    rice and thinner and smaller than the BIKO.

BIBLIA [f. Sp.], n. Bible.

BIDA [f. Sp.], n. hero or heroine in a movie, the
    leading star in a movie. --ant. KONTRABIDA.

BIDANG, n. a broad band or sash worn by women around
    the body from the waist to the knee. /AG-/ to wear
    this. /MANG-:-AN/ to put this around (someone).

BIDDUT, n. mistake, error, sin. --syn. BASOL.
Liniklikan na ti biddut na idi napalabas nga bulan.
He avoided his mistakes last month.

BIDING, v. /MANG-:-EN/ to examine, scrutinize, inspect.
Bidingen yo nga nalaing dayta lupot tapno makita yo
amin nga rugit na. Inspect well that cloth so that
you can see all its dirt.

BIERNES [biérnɛs; f. Sp.], n. Friday.

BIERNES SANTO, Good Friday.

BIGAO, n. a large, circular or oval, shallow basket
made of strips of bamboo which are closely woven;
it is used principally as a winnowing basket.

BIGAT, n. morning, the period of the day between sunrise
and noon.

BIGATEN. It is already morning.

BIGAT KALMAN, yesterday morning.

BIGAT KASANGAALDAW, someday in the future.

BINIGAN-BIGAT, adv. every morning.

INTON(O) BIGAT, tomorrow.

INTON BIGAT TI AGSAPA or INTON AGSAPA NO BIGAT,
tomorrow morning.

INTON BIGAT TI MALEM or INTON MALEM NO BIGAT,
tomorrow afternoon.

KABIGATAN or KINABIGATAN, n. the next morning.

BIGBIG, v. /AG-/ to recognize or discriminate people.
Ammo na ti agbigbig dayta anak mon. Your child
already knows how to recognize people. /MANG-:-EN/
to recognize or acknowledge. Saan nak nga bigbigen
nga inam. Don't acknowledge me as your mother.
/MAKA-:MA-/ to be able to recognize, to discover.
Saan dak nga nabigbig. They were not able to recognize
me.

BIGLA, adj. sudden, abrupt.
v. /MANG-:-EN/ to surprise, startle by doing
something suddenly and unexpectedly. Saan mo nga
biglaen ta dinto ket agsakit. Don't startle him for
he might get sick.

BIIG, var. of BIN-IG.

BIIT, adj. /MA-/ to be brief or short in duration, to be away or stay for a short while. /NA-/ brief, short in duration (in the past). --ant. BAYAG.
n. the generic name for early rice. --ant. BAYAG.

(BI)BIIT, v. /MANG-:-EN/ to do briefly or within a short time. Binibiit na nga inibus diay dugo. He consumed within a short time the broth.

NABIIT, n. the recent past. ITAY NABIIT, a while ago, a few moments ago. Dimmaw-as ni Nora iti opisina itay nabiit. Nora passed by the office a few moments ago.

APAGBIIT, adv. for a short while, for a few moments.

BIKAL, n. 1. a climbing bamboo with thick walls. --syn. BAYOG. 2. a stake made of this.

BIKIAS, var. of BIKKIAS.

BIKKIAS, /AG-, -UM-/ to burst open. Irutem ti galut na dayta karton tapno saan nga bumikkias. Tighten the binding of that cardboard box so that it won't burst open.

BIKKOG, v. /MANG-:-EN/ to bend, curve. Bikkogem dayta landok. Bend that iron.
adj. /NAG-/ curved, crooked, bent. --syn. KILLO.

BIKO, n. native cake made of sticky rice, coconut milk and brown sugar cooked in a big, round and shallow pan. --syn. BIBINGKA 1.

BIKS [f. Eng.], n. Vicks ointment or any other similar ointment.

BIKTIMA [f. Sp.], n. victim.

BILADA, n. celebration, entertainment. Agsalaak to no bilada. I will dance during the celebration.

BILAG, n. a sunny place, a place hit directly by the rays of the sun. Saan ka nga aggian dita bilag. Don't stay in that sunny place.

v. /AG-/ to stay under the sun, to sunbathe.
Saan ka nga agbilag ta dinto agsakit ka. Don't stay
under the sun for you might get sick.
/AG-, MANGI-:I-/ to place under the sun, to dry
under the sun. Mapan na ibilag dagidiay nilabaan na.
She will go dry under the sun what she washed.

BILANG, n. number. Mano ti bilang da? What is their
number? or: How many are they?
v. /AG-/ to count, to recite the numbers in
succession. Diak pay ammo ti agbilang. I still don't
know how to count. /AG-, MANG-:-EN/ Bilangem ida.
Count them. /MANGI-:I-/ to consider, count as.
Ibilbilang ka nga gayyem ko. I consider you as my
friend.

BILEG, adj. /NA-/ strong, powerful, potent.

BILID, n. the peak of an angle, top of the end formed
by an angle.

BILIN, n. instruction, order, request. Ania ti bilin
mo? What are your instructions?
v. /MANG-:-EN/ to instruct, advise, counsel.
Bilinem bassit dayta anak mo, sa ka mapan. Counsel
your child a little and then go. /AGI-, MANGI-:I-/
to instruct or request to get, buy, do etc. Ania ti
imbilin mo kanyana? What did you request him to buy?

BILIS, n. a kind of sardine.

BILLIING, syn. of UWAO.

BILLIT, n. bird. --syn. TUMATAYAB.
BILLIT BALAY, house bird.

BILOG, n. a small boat made of the hollowed-out trunk
of a tree, or of boards put together; it has two
outriggers.

BIMDENG, pt. of BUMDENG.

BIMSAG, pt. of BUMSAG.

BIMTAK, pt. of BUMTAK.

BINAKLAG, v. /AG-/ to swell or become swollen due to bites or other injuries. Nagbinaklag dagitoy kinagat ti lamok. These ones bitten by mosquitoes became swollen.

BIN-I, n. seedling, seeds kept for the next planting season.

BIN-IG, adj. pure, nothing but. Bin-ig nga allid daytoy. This is pure beeswax.   --var. BIIG.

BINTING, n. twenty-five centavos, a quarter of a peso. Binting laeng ti kuartak. My money is only twenty-five centavos.   --see BENTE.

BINTOR, v. /AG-/ to roam around, wander about, rove. Isu ti nagbintor nga agsapul kenkuana. He was the one who wandered about looking for him.

BINUBUDAN, see under BUBUD.

BINUGBOG, n. leftovers kept to feed the pigs. Naimas nga binugbog ti ipakan na iti baboy na. He will feed his pig with tasty leftovers.

BINULLALO, see BULLALO.

BINGALO, n. the ARAMANG shrimp when large.

BINGAT, var. of BINGIT.

BINGAY, v. /MANG-:-EN/ to divide, share, split. Bingayem dayta inapoy. Divide that rice. /MANGI-:I-/ to give as one's share, to share with. Ibingay mo man la kanyak dayta bunga ti tarong yon? Will you please just give me that fruit of your eggplant as my share?   --syn. ATAY.   --var. BINGLAY.

BINGGAS, n. fiber of the body; grain of wood; white vein or streak of the betel nut.

BINGIT, v. /MANG-:-EN/ to stretch open especially with the hands.

BINGKOL, n. clod, a lump of earth which is hard and dry.

BINGLAY, var. of BINGAY.

BINGNGI, v. /AG-/ to open, break open. Umisem ka
inggana ti agbingngi ti bibig mo. Smile until your
lips break open.   /MANG-:-EN/ to open. Bingngiem
dagita bibig mo. Open your lips.

BINGRAW, var. of BENGRAW.

BIOGRAPIA [f. Sp.], n. biography.

BIOLIN [f. Sp.], n. violin.
    v. /AG-/ to play a violin.

BIOR, v. /MANG-:-EN/ 1. to control, cause to submit to
one's authority. Narigat nga mabior daytoy nga ubing.
It is hard to control this child. 2. to bend, e.g. a
wire, a piece of bamboo, wood, etc.

BIR [f. Eng.], n. beer.   --syn. SERBESA.

BIRABID, n. an edible, fresh water, gastropodous mollusk
with a round, thin shell. /MA-/ to feel dizzy and
feverish due to eating this. Saan mo nga kaaduen ti
mangan ti dayta ta dikanto mabirabid. Don't eat much
of that for you might feel dizzy and feverish
afterwards.

BIRAY, n. a small boat made of boards and with a flat
bottom which is used for long distances; it is much
larger than the BILOG and the BARANGAY.

BIRHINIA [f. Eng.], n. Virginia tobacco.

BIR-I, n. crack.
    v. /AG-/ to develop or have a crack. Nagbir-i
daydiay pinggan nga naytupak. The plate which was
dropped developed a crack.   --var. BIRRI.

BIRIA [f. Sp.], v. /MANG-:-AN/ to patch; to mend,
cover, or fill up a hole, crack or weak spot.
Biriaam dayta rata ti burnay. Patch that crack
of the jar.

BIRIT, n. a scar or scarlike indentation on the eyelid.

BIRKUG, adj. /NAG-/ derelict, negligent, being a
regular absentee. Maysa ka nga hues nga birkug. You
are one derelict judge.

BIRNGAS, n. nickname.
v. /MANG-:-EN/ 1. to call by one's nickname or
first name; hence, 2. to call or address impolitely.
Saan mo nga birbirngasen ni tatang ko. Don't call
my father by his nickname.

BIROK-, v. /AG-, -UM-, MANG-:-EN/ to look for, search.
Birokem daydiay lapis ko nga napukaw. Look for my
pencil which was lost. /MAKA-:MA--AN/ to be able to
find; to find by chance. Indiak nga mabirokan diay
lapis mo. I cannot find your pencil.

BIRRI, var. of BIR-I.

BIRTUD, [f. Sp.], adj. /NA-/ potent, effective: said
of medicine or poison.

BIRUT, n. a kind of small fresh water fish.

BISALEG, v. /AG-/ to have an acute pain: said of the
abdomen or stomach. Agbisaleg toy tian ko. My
stomach has an acute pain.

BISE [bíse; f. Sp.], n. vice-mayor or vice-president.

BISE-MAYOR, n. vice-mayor.

BISE-PRESIDENTE, n. vice-president.

BISIBIS, v. /MANGI-:-AN/ to sprinkle or spray with
water or any other liquid. Bisibisam dayta dalikan
tapno maepdep amin nga apoy na. Sprinkle the stove
with water so that the fire in it will be put out.
/MANGI-:I-/ to sprinkle or spray in or on. Daytoy
ti ibisbis mo idiay dalikan. Sprinkle this on the
stove.

BISIK, v. /MANGI-:I-/ to reveal. Isu ti nangibisik iti
gagara na. He was the one who revealed his mission.

BISIKLETA [bisikléta; f. Sp.], n. bicycle.
v. /AG-/ to use a bicycle, to ride on a bicycle.

BISIN, n. hunger.
v. /MA-/ to be hungry. Mabisinak. I am hungry.
/AG-/ to go hungry. Adu nga tao ti agbisin ita
umay nga bulan. Many people will go hungry this

coming month. /MANG-:-EN/ to cause or allow to go hungry, to starve. Saan mo nga bisbisinen dayta bagim. Don't allow yourself to go hungry. /MA--AN/ to suffer hunger, to go hungry. Nabisinanak ti kauuray kenka. I went hungry waiting for you.

BISIO [f. Sp.], n. vice. Nagadu la ket ti bisio mon. You have many vices indeed.
    adj. /NA-/ having many vices, idiosyncracies, or eccentricities. Nabisio la unay dayta lakay mo. Your husband is very eccentric.

BISIRO [f. Sp.?], n. young male of the horse, pony. --syn. BUMARO 2.

BISITA [f. Sp.], n. visitor, caller, guest. Agsubli tayo ta adda bisita da. Let's go back for they have a visitor.
    v. /-UM-, MANG-:-EN/ to visit, call on. Bisitaen nak met uray man no sagpaminsan laeng. Please visit me even if only once in a while.

BISKEG, adj. /NA-/ strong, powerful. Nabiskeg dagiti takiag na. His arms are strong. --syn. PIGSA.

BISKOTSO [f. Sp.], n. toasted bread.

BISLAK, n. a piece of split bamboo.

BISLIN, v. /-UM-/ to press or squeeze oneself in. Bumislin ka dita ta awan ti lugar mo ditoyen. Squeeze in there for you have no space here now. /MANGI-:I-/ to squeeze in. Isu ti nangibislin ti bagi na ditoy. It was he who squeezed himself in here.

BISNGAR, v. /AG-/ to turn up because of anger: said of the nose. Uray la nga nagbisngar ti agong na ti pungtot na. His nose turned up because of his anger.

BISNGAY, v. /MANG-:-EN/ to part especially the hair.

BISNGIT, v. /MANG-:-EN/ to part, push aside to make an opening. Bisngitem dayta sanga ta mula tapno makitam ida. Push aside that branch of that plant so that you can see them.

BISSAYOT, v. /AG-/ to hang downwards, droop. Sep-akem dayta sanga ti kayo tapno agbissayot ditoy daga. Break that branch of the tree so that it will hang downwards to the ground. /MANG-:-EN/ to keep aloft holding by the neck, hand or feet; to suspend in the air. Saan mo nga bissayoten dayta pusa. Don't suspend the cat in the air.

BISTI [f. Sp.], v. /AG-/ to dress oneself. Agbisti ka ta mapan tayon. Dress yourself for we are going. /AG-:PAG-/ to dress oneself with. Agbisti ka ti napintas. Dress yourself with something beautiful. Saan nga dayta ti pagbistim. Don't dress yourself with that. /MANG-:-AN/ to dress (someone). Bistiam dayta ubing ta adda papanan mi. Dress that child for we are going somewhere. /MANGI-:I-/ to dress with. Daytoy ti ibistim kanyana. Dress him with this. --syn. BADO.

BISTRAD, v. /MANG-:-EN/ 1. to spread out, as a piece of cloth. 2. to open, lay open, as a book, the eyes, etc.

BISUKOL, n. a kind of snail with smooth round shell.

BISUNG, n. kiss.
     v. /MANG-:-EN/ to kiss.   --syn. AGEK, ANGGO, UNGGO.

BITAMINA [f. Sp.], n. vitamin.

BITAY, v. /MANG-:-EN/ to hang by the neck until dead.

BITBIT, var. (dial.) of BITIBIT.

BITIBIT, v. /AG-, MANG-:-EN/ to carry or hold in the hand hanging or dangling. Binitibit na diay manok. He held the chicken in his hand dangling.

BITIK, v. /AG-/ to palpitate, throb: said of the heart or the chest. Agbitikbitik ti barukong na ti pannakakigtot na. His chest is palpitating due to his being surprised.

BITIN, v. /AG-/ to suspend oneself, to hang or remain suspended. Saan ka nga agbitin dita sanga ti kayo. Don't hang on the branch of that tree. /AGI-, MANGI-:I-/ to hang, suspend. Ibitin mo daytoy karne idiay adigi. Hang this meat on the post.

BITINBITIN, n. something hanging especially for a purpose.

BITLA, v. /AG-/ to discourse, deliver a speech or address. Isu ti nagbitla idi pabuya mi. He was the one who delivered an address during our show.

BITO, n. pit, hole. --syn. ABUT.

BITOR, v. /AGI-, MANGI-:I-/ to throw or toss to. Ibitor mo daytoy kuarta kanyada. Toss this money to them. --syn. BARANDIS.

BITTAYON, v. /AG-/ to hang or dangle downwards (out of an opening). Adda makitak nga agbittayon nga ima dita tawa. I can see a hand dangling out of that window. /MANG-:-EN/ or /MANGI-:I-/ to hang or dangle downwards (out of an opening). Saan mo nga bittayonen dayta ubing. Don't dangle that child (out of the window).

BITTAUG, n. 1. a tall tree which yields timber. 2. a fruit of this.

BITUKA, n. stomach.

BITWEN, n. star, planet.

BITWEN BAYBAY, starfish.

BLUMER [f. Eng.], n. bloomer.

BOA, n. 1. the betel-nut or areca-nut palm (Areca catechu. L.). 2. a fruit of this.

BOBONG, n. 1. the thatch that covers the ridge of a roof; hence, 2. the ridge of a roof.

BOBONGAN, n. the two beams at the ridge of the roof: the SALLABAWAN and the PAKABAYO.

BODEGA [bodéga; f. Sp.], n. warehouse, bodega.

BODI, v. /MAI-/ to be different, dissimilar. Maibodi ni Rosa kanyada. Rose is different from them.

BOGBOG, v. /MANG-:-EN/ 1. to cause to become pulpy, e.g. by cooking to excess or by beating; hence, 2. to maul, hit or beat repeatedly. /MA-/ 1. to be caused to become pulpy. 2. to be mauled, hit or beaten repeatedly.

[1]BOKA, v. /AG-/ to open (as a flower). Siguro agbuka dayta nalabaga nga sabong inton bigat. Maybe that red flower will open tomorrow.   --syn. UKRAD.

[2]BOKA, v. /MANG-:-EN/ to untie, unbind, unfasten, undo, loosen (a knot). Saan mo nga bokaen dayta galut ti aso. Don't untie the leash of the dog.   --syn. BUKRA, WARWAR. 2. to let loose or set free; to let go. Saan mo nga bokaen dayta aso nga naungit. Don't let loose that fierce dog.   --syn. LUBOS, [1]BUANG.

BOKAL [f. Sp.?], n. a provincial board member.

[1]BOKBOK, n. weevil or its larva; powder post beetle; woodworm.
    v. /-EN/ to be attacked by weevils: said of posts, boards, bamboos, etc.
    adj. /-IN-/ attacked by weevils, worm-eaten.

    BINOKBOK, n. a tooth with a cavity, a tooth with caries.   --syn. (dial.) BOKBOK.

[2]BOKBOK, n. a tooth with a cavity.   --syn. (dial.) of BINOKBOK n.

BOKRA, v. /MANG-:-EN/ to untie or undo (a knot); to unravel or untangle (a tangle). Bokraem man daytoy siglot ti talik? Will you please untie this knot in my rope?   --syn. BOKA.

BOLA [f. Sp.], n. 1. ball, any round object; sphere; globe. 2. any game using a ball.
    v. /AG-/ to play a game with a ball, especially baseball. Agbola tayo. Let's play a game with a ball.

    BOLABOLA, n. 1. a ball of sewing thread usually wound on a bobbin. 2. anything that is rounded, e.g. meatballs.

BOMBILIA [f. Sp.], n. light bulb.

BOOK, n. hair, mane.

BOONG, n. break, fracture, crack. Adda buong na dayta basom. Your glass has a crack.
v. /AG-, MANG-:-EN/ to break, fracture, crack. Saan mo nga boongen dayta baso. Don't break that glass. /MA-/ to be or get broken, fractured, cracked. Nadaras nga maboong dayta baso yo. Your glass gets broken easily.

BOONG TI ULO, source of problems, troubles or headache.

BOOS, n. a kind of large, red, stinging ant whose eggs are edible. --var. ABOOS.

BOOT, n. mold, mildew.
v. /-EN/ to be attacked by mold or mildew.

BORAR [f. Sp.], v. /AG-/ to erase something. /MANG-:-EN/ to erase, eradicate.

BOSES [bosɛs; f. Sp.], n. voice. --syn. TIMEK. Napintas ti boses mo. Your voice is beautiful.

BOTA, var. of BOTAS.

BOTANTE [f. Sp.], n. voter, elector. --syn. ELEKTOR.

BOTAS [f. Sp.], n. boot. /AG-/ to use or wear boots. --var. BOTA.

BOTE [bótɛ; f. Sp.], see BOTELYA.

BOTELYA [botélya; f. Sp.], n. bottle, any bottle container. --syn. BOTE.

BOTIKA [f. Sp.], n. drugstore.

BOTIKERO, n. druggist, pharmacist.

BOTO, var. of BOTOS.

BOTOS [f. Sp.], n. vote.
v. /-UM-/ to vote, to cast one's vote. Bomotosak inton bigat. I'll vote tomorrow. /UM-:-AN/ or /MANGI-:I-/ to vote for. Ibotos nak a. Vote for me, huh?

BRA [f. Eng.], n. bra, brassiere.

BRIAT, v. /MANG-:-EN/ to rip, tear or split open or apart. Isu ti nangbriat iti badok. He was the one who ripped my clothes. /MA-/ to be ripped, torn or split apart or open; to suffer a tear. Nabriat ti pantalon ko. The pants were ripped.

BRUHA [f. Sp.], n. an evil woman, a witch or sorceress.

BUABO, v. /AG-/ to gallop.

BUAL, v. /MA-/ to fall down. Nabual diay adigi. The post fell down. /MANG-:-EN/ or /MANGI-:I-/ to cause to fall down. Saan mo man nga bualen dayta mulak. Please don't cause my plant to fall down.

[1]BUANG, v. /MANG-:-AN/ 1. to open, remove the plug of. Buangan na dayta gripo. He will open that faucet. 2. to set loose. Buangan na diay kalding. He will set the goat loose. --syn. [2]BOKA.

[2]BUANG, v. /MANGI-:I-/ to let (newly hatched chicks) out of the nest. Ibuang mo dagita piek. You let the chicks out of the nest.

BUANGAY, v. /MANG-:-EN/ to do by oneself, be responsible for. Isu ti nangbuangay iti daytoy nga pabuya. He was responsible for this show.

BUAT, v. /MANG-:-AN/ to help (someone) lift a load on someone's head or shoulder. Buatan nak man. Will you please help me lift this load on my head? /MANGI-:I-/ to lift (a load) on the head or shoulder of. Narigat nga ibuat dayta karamba. It is hard to lift that jar on the head of someone.

BUAYA, n. crocodile, alligator.

BUBIDA, n. ceiling.

BUBO, n. a kind of large or small bow net made of bamboo which is used to catch fresh water shrimps or fish.

BUBO, v. /MANGI-:I-/ to expose to the wind. Saan mo nga ibubo dayta ubing. Don't expose that child to

the wind.   /MAI-/ to be exposed to the wind. Saan
ka nga agtugaw dita ta maibubo ka. Don't sit there
for you will be exposed to the wind.

BUBON, n. well, a hole sunk into the earth to reach a
supply of water.

BUBUD, n. yeast.

BINUBUDAN, n. cooked (non-glutinous) rice sprinkled
with yeast (BUBUD) and left in a cool place to
ferment for one or two days; fermented rice.

BUDO, n. hair on wormlike larvas or plants and fruits.
v. /AG-/ to itch, to become itchy.   /MAKA-/ to
cause to become itchy. Ania ti nakabudo kenka?
What caused you to become itchy?   /MA--AN/ to be
infected by itchiness. Nabudoan diay balasang idi
nagdigos idiay karayan. The young lady was infected
by itchiness when she bathed in the river.
adj. /MAKA-/ causing itchiness. Makabudo dayta.
That causes itchiness.   --syn. GATEL.

BUBUBUDO, n. a kind of large, soft, black or dark-brown,
hairy, stinging caterpillar.   --var. BUDUBUDOAN.

BUDUBUDOAN, var. of BUDUBUDO.

BUELTA [buélta; f. Sp.], v. /AG-/ to turn back, head
back, return. Agbuelta ka daras. Return at once.
/MANGI-:I-/ to turn (something) back; to take, drive
or cause to go back. Ibueltam dayta kotsem ditoy.
Drive your car back here.   --syn. SUBLI.

BUGAGAW, adj. gray; albino. Bugagaw ti mata na. His
eyes are gray.

BUGAS, n. 1. pith of plant stems. 2. core of fruits.
v. /AG-/ to develop (its) core: said of fruits.

BUGAW, v. /AG-, MANG-:-EN/ to drive or shoo away.

BUGAYONG, n. 1. a slender, leguminous vine with seeds
which are half black and half scarlet. 2. a seed of
this plant.

BUGBUGTONG, adj. only, sole, unique.

BUGGO, v. /AG-/ to wash one's hands or limbs.
/AG-, MANG-:-AN/ to wash (the hands or limbs of).
Buggoam dagita ima na. Wash his hands.

BUGGOONG, n. fish preserved in salt and slightly
fermented and used as sauce.

BUGI, n. the ovary or eggs of fishes, crabs, lobsters,
shrimps, etc.

BUGKAW, v. /-UM-, MANG-:-AN/ to shout, yell or bawl
at. Binugkawan na diay ubing nga natagari. He
bawled at the noisy child.

BUGNAW, var. of BAGNAW.

BUGNAY, n. a kind of tree which bears round, acidic,
edible fruits which turn red when ripe.

BUGSOT, /AG-/ to convulse, as when near death.
Agbugbugsotakon dinak pay nga arayaten. I am
already convulsing still you don't come to help
me. /MANG-:-AN/ to injure fatally.

BUGTAK, v. /MANG-:-EN/ 1. to scare away. Inka bugtaken
dagidiay babuy. Go scare away the pigs. --syn.
BUGAW. 2. to disturb. Saan nak man nga bugtaken ta
adu ti trabahok. Please don't disturb me for I have
much work to do.

BUGTONG, see BUGBUGTONG.

BUIS, n. tax paid to the government on incomes and
properties.
v. /AG-/ to pay taxes to the government.

BUISIT, adj. /NAG-/ unlucky, having bad luck (as in
gambling). Buisitak ita. I am unlucky today.
v. /MANG-:-EN/ 1. to cause (someone) to be unlucky
or have bad luck (as in gambling). 2. to irritate,
pester.

BUKAIT, v. /AG-, MANG-:-AN/ to open slightly by prying,
e.g. a package.

BUKAKAW, n. sorghum.

BUKAR, v. /AG-/ to burst open, break open. Saan pay
nga naloom dayta ta di pay nagbukar. That one is
not ripe yet for it has not yet burst open.

[1]BUKATOT, n. a kind of basket similar in shape to a
demijohn made of woven strips of bamboo and used
for holding fish by fishermen.   --syn. SUIKI.

[2]BUKATOT, adj. /NAG-/ avaricious, greedy, gluttonous.
--syn. RAWET.

BUKAYKAY, v. /MANG-:-AN/ to rip or cut open and spill
out the contents of. Binukaykayan na diay pungan.
He cut open the pillow and spilled out its contents.
/MA--AN/ to be ripped causing its contents to spill
out: said of pillows, sacks of rice, etc.
Nabukaykayan daydiay pungan na. His pillow was
ripped and its contents spilled out.

BUKAYO, n. a kind of sweet made of coconut meat and
sugar.

BUKBOK, v. /AGI-, MANGI-:I-/ to pour, spill. Ibukbok
mo kanyak dayta danom. Pour that water on me.
/MAI-/ to spill or flow out by accident. Naibukbok
diay danom nga pagdigos mo. The water for your bath
spilled out by accident.

[1]BUKEL, n. seed, kernel, grain.
    adj. /-AN/ having many seeds.

[2]BUKEL, v. /AG-/ to be formed, conceived; to take form.
Nagbukel daytoy nga panunot iti isip na. This thought
took form in his mind.   /MANG-:-EN/ to form, conceive
of, e.g. a thought, project, etc.
    adj. /NA-/ 1. round and solid (as an object). 2.
loud and clear (as voice). Nabukel ti panagbalikas
na iti nagan na. The way he uttered his name was
loud and clear.

BUKENG, adj. /NA-/ short and stocky; small-bodied.

BUKIBUK, v. /MANG-:-EN/ to turn over. Saan mo nga
bukibuken dagita nalabaan. Don't turn over the
washed clothes.

BUKINGKING, v. /MANG-:-EN/ to hit with the back of the
hand.

BUKIRAD, v. /AG-/ 1. to open wide, dilate (as the eyes do). Nagbukirad dagiti mata na. His eyes opened wide. 2. to break or burst (like a seed, kernel or grain). Nagbukirad diay mais. The corn kernel burst. /MANG-:-EN/ or /MANG-:I-/ to open wide, dilate. Bukiraden na dagiti mata na. He will dilate his eyes.

BUKITKIT, v. /MANG-:-EN/ to look for something through the contents of or inside (a box, a book, etc.) with the hand.

BUKKUAL, to dig or turn up. Bukkualem dayta daga ta ibunubon mo dagitoy bukel ti tarong. Turn up the soil and sow these eggplant seeds.

BUKLAN, = [1]BUKEL + -AN.

BUKLAW, adj. /NA-/; /-AN/ greedy, voracious.   --syn. BUKLIS, [2]BUKATOT, RAWET.

BUKLIS, adj. /NA-/ greedy, voracious.   --syn. BUKLAW, BUKATOT, RAWET.

BUKO, n. 1. knuckle. 2. node of plants or something similar to this. 3. bud.   --syn. BUSEL.

BUKOD, n. exclusive property.
    v. /AG-/ to be alone, stay alone, live alone. Agbukbukod ni Pedron. Peter is now living alone. /-UM-/ to live separately from. Bimmukod ni Pedro kadaydiay pamilya na. Pedro lived separately from his family. /MANG-:-AN/ to take or do by oneself excluding others; to monopolize. Binukudan na amin nga trabaho. He did all the work by himself excluding the others from it.

    KABUKBUKODAN, adj. exclusively owned. Adda met kabukbukodan nga balikas ti Iloko. The Ilokano has his own exclusive language.

BUKOL, n. hump, bump; a protuberance, a swelling.
    v. /MANG-:-AN/ to cause to have a bump; to strike or knock with force so as to produce a hump.

BUKOT, n. back (of a person, an animal, a book, etc.). --syn. LIKOD.

BUKRAD, var. of UKRAD.

[1]BUKSIL, n. the outer cover or integument of seeds.
v. /AG-, MANG-:-AN/ to remove this. Buksilam
daytoy bukel ko. Remove the integument of my seed.

[2]BUKSIL, v. /MANGI-:I-/ to explain, state succinctly,
e.g. one's desires.

BUKSIT, n. abdomen; belly, especially around the
umbilical region. --syn. TIAN.

BUKTO, n. a kind of small, whitish, fresh water fish.
--syn. BUNOG.

BULAN, n. 1. moon. 2. month.

BINULAN, adv. monthly, every month.

BINULAN-BULAN, adv. by the month.

BULAN-BULANEN, adj. lunatic, moonstruck.

MAKABULAN, adv. one month.

BULANOS, adj. /NA-/ voluntary, spontaneous. Maupayak
nga makaammo iti kaawan ti nabulanos nga tulong
dagiti dadduma nga ili. I am disappointed to know
about the lack of spontaneous help from the other
towns.

BULANG, v. /MAKI-/ to go to a cockfight, to engage in
cockfighting, to match one's gamecock with that of
another in a cockpit. Mapanak makibulang idiay ili
yo. I will go to a cockfight in your town.
/MANGI-:I-/ to match (a gamecock) in a cockfight.
--syn. TADI.

BULANGAN, n. cockpit, a place where cockfighting is
done. --syn. GALYERA.

BULBULLAGAW, n. a clown, jester, joker; a funny person.
v. /AG-/ to act like a clown.

BULDING, adj. one-eyed; blind in one eye. /MANG-:-AN/
to blind in one eye, to injure or destroy an eye of.

BULDOSER [f. Eng.], n. bulldozer.
v. /AG-, MANG-:-EN/ to use a bulldozer on; to
bulldoze. Binuldozer da diay balay ko. They bulldozed
my house.

BULI, n. lead.

BULIALA, n. a cock with yellowish plumage.

BULIBUL, n. remuneration in kind for work done, payment
in kind.
v. /MAKA-:MA-/ to receive (something other than
money) for work done, to earn (something other than
money). Adu ti nabulibul ko idi napalabas nga bulan.
I earned much (in kind) the past month.

BULIG, v. /AG-, MANG-:PAG--AN/ [with pl. actor] to
carry together. Agbulig kayo ti dayta nadagsen nga
kahon. Carry together that heavy box.

BULIG, n. one whole stem or cluster of banana fruits;
this consists of several rows or hands of bananas
each one called SAPAD.

BULILISING, n. a kind of green parrot.

BULILIT, adj. small, dwarfish, diminutive.

BULINTIK, n. a children's game played with marbles;
marbles.
v. /AG-/ [with pl. subject] to play marbles with
each other. /MAKI-:KA-/ to play marbles with.
--syn. (dial.) HOLEN.

BULLAGAW, see BULBULLAGAW.

BULLALAYAW, n. rainbow.

BULLALO, n. bobbin of thread.   --var. BINULLALO.
--syn. BOLABOLA.

BULLO, v. /MA-/ [= MABLO], to have a bone broken or
a joint dislocated; to have a sprain; hence, to be
crippled or disabled. /MANG-:-EN/ to break a bone
or dislocate a joint of; to sprain; hence, to
cripple or disable. Binullo na diay aso mi. He
crippled our dog.

MAMMULLO, n. a bone-setter, one who treats cases of
broken bones, dislocated joints or sprains.   --see
ILOT.

BULO, n. a slender, erect, thornless bamboo whose walls are thin.

BULOD, v. /-UM-:-EN/ to borrow. Bumulodak man ti asin yo. May I borrow some of your salt. --see PABULOD.

BULOG, n. male progenitor; uncastrated male carabao, pig, etc.

BULONG, n. leaf.

[1]BULOS, adj. loose, stray. --syn. WALANG.
    v. /MAKA-/ to break loose. Nakabulos diay aso da. Their dog broke loose. /MANG-:-AN/ or /AGI-, MANGI-:I-/ to set free, let loose. Saan da nga ibulbulos dayta nga aso. They don't let that dog loose.

[2]BULOS, v. /AG-/ to flow freely and profusely. Nagbulos di dara diay sugat na. The blood from his wound flowed freely and profusely. /MANGI-:I-/ to emit or flow from freely and profusely. Adu nga dara ti imbulos diay sugat na. Much blood flowed freely from his wound.

BULSA, n. pocket.
    v. /AGI-, MANGI-:I-/ to put or keep inside one's pocket. Ibulsam daytoy sabak. Put this banana of mine inside your pocket.

BULSEK, adj. totally blind; blind in both eyes.

BUMALASANG, n. 1. young woman below or at the age of puberty and usually though not necessarily unmarried; girl. --syn. BALASITANG; see BALASANG. 2. young female of the water buffalo or cow. --ant. BUMARO.

BUMARO, n. 1. young man below or at the age of puberty and usually though not necessarily unmarried; boy. --ant. BUMALASANG. --see BARO. 2. young male of the water buffalo or cow; pony.
    v. /AG-/ to be near or at the age of puberty: said of the male.

[1]BUMBA [f. Sp.], v. /AG-, MANG-:-EN/ to pump, especially a pump well (POSO). Binumba na daydiay poso. He pumped the pump well.

BUMBERO, n. fireman.

[2]BUMBA [f. Sp.], n. bomb.
    v. /AG-, MANG-:-EN/ to bomb, hit with bombs.
Bumbaen diay eroplano daytoy balay tayo. The
airplane will bomb our house.

BUMBERO, see under [1]BUMBA.

BUMBILIA, see BOMBILIA.

BUMDENG, = -UM- + BEDDENG.

BUMSAG, = -UM- + BESSAG.

BUMTAK, = -UM- + BETTAK.

BUNAG, v. /AG-, MANG-:-EN/ to transport, to carry from
    one place to another. Bunagen yo man dagitoy alikamen
    mi? Will you please transport our belongings?

BUNANNAG, v. /MANGI-:I-/ to proclaim, publish, extol.
    Ibunannag mo ti panangabak na. Proclaim his victory.

BUNAR, n. a red ant.

BUNENG [f. Sp.], n. bolo, a large, single-edged knife.

BUNIAG, see BUNYAG.

BUNOG, n. the BUKTO fish when at its largest size.

BUNONG, v. /AGI-, MANGI-:I-/ to apportion, distribute,
    allot. Ibunong mo dagitoy kadagiti ubbing. Distribute
    these to the children.

BUNOT, the outer husk of the coconut; coir.

BUNTIEK, n. the young of the fish called DALAG.

BUNTOG, adj. /NA-/ slow, sluggish.
    v. /-UM-/ to be like this.

[1]BUNTON, n. a small hill, hillock; a small hill built
    by termites.

[2]BUNTON, n. pile, heap, stack.
    v. /MANG-:-EN/ to lay or place in a pile, pile up,
    heap in abundance. /MA-/ to be placed in a pile; to

2
pile up. Nabunton ti trabahok. My work has piled
up.

BUNUBON, n. seedling, a plant grown from a seed for
transplanting.
v. /AG-/ to grow plants from seeds for transplanting;
to sow seeds for seedlings. Mabalin tayo ti
agbunubonen. We can sow seeds for seedlings now.

BUNYAG [f. Sp.], v. /AG-/ to baptize someone especially
in church. /MANG-:-AN/ to baptize. Daydiay lakay nga
padi ti mangbunyag ti anak ko. It is the old priest
who will baptize my child. /AGI-, MANGI-:I-/ to
give or bestow on as name or alias. Daytoy ti imbunyag
na kanyak. This is what he bestowed on me as an alias.

BUNGA, n. 1. fruit; result. 2. child - a term of
endearment used especially in literary works.
v. /AG-/ to bear fruits. Agbunga ti mangga min.
Our mango tree is now bearing fruits. /MANG-:-EN/
or /MANGI-:I-/ to bear, result to, lead to. Adu ti
bungaen dayta mangga yo. That mango tree of yours
will bear many fruits.

BUNGA TI MATA, n. sty.
v. /AG-/ to have or develop a sty. Agbunga ti mata
diay lalaki. The man's eye is developing a sty.

BUNGABONG, v. /MANGI-:I-/ to announce. Inbungabong na
ti gandat na nga agkandidato. He announced his
intention to run as a candidate.

BUNGAG, n. embryo of seed.

BUNGAW, adj. having one or both testicles swollen or
enlarged; having scrotal hernia.

BUNGDOL, adj. with tipless or blunt horn, as a cow or
water buffalo.

BUNGGOY, n. group, party, company, faction.
v. /MAKI-:PAKI--AN/, /-UM-:-AN/ to associate, join
with. Isuda ti nakibunggoyan na. Isuda ti binunggoyan
na. He joined with them. /-AG-/ [with pl. subject]
to join together. Nagbubunggoy da nga immay ditoy.
They joined together coming here.

BUNGKOL, n. a large piece of bone.

BUNGKONG, adj. /NA-/ bulky, large. Nabungkong dayta bungon mo. Your bundle is bulky.

BUNGLUG, adj. /NA-/ having the stench of rancid oil, lard, etc. --syn. BANGLIG.

BUNGON, n. 1. wrapper, covering. 2. package, bundle. v. /AG-, MANG-:-EN/ to wrap, bundle, package; to bundle up. Bungonem nga nalaing dayta anak mo ta lumamiis manen. Bundle up your child well for it is getting cold again.

BUNG-OR, v. /-UM-/ to become swollen and tender due to an injury or infection.

BUNGRO, n. jungle, wilderness.

BUNGSOT, adj. /NA-/ rotten, spoiled, decomposing, putrid, foul. --syn. LUNGSOT. v. /MANG-:-EN/ to cause to rot, become spoiled, putrid, foul. --var. BUNGTOT.

BUNGTOT, var. of BUNGSOT.

BUNGULAN, n. a kind of yellow, spotted, fragrant banana.

[1]BURAK, v. /-UM-, MANG-:-EN/ to break into bits, crush, shatter, crumble. Burakem daytoy yelo. Crush this ice. /MA-/ to be crushed, shattered, broken into pieces.

[2]BURAK, v. /AG-, MANG-:-EN/ to shake in order to collect the fish, shrimps, crabs, etc. caught in (the fagot). Binurak ko tay rama. I shook the fagots and collected the fish, shrimps, crabs, etc. caught in them. --syn. SANGAT.

BURANGEN, n. old male monkey.

BURANG-IT, v. /AG-/ to raise one's bottom or buttocks, to set oneself in a position with the bottom or buttocks up. Nagburang-it diay kabayo. The horse raised its bottom. /MANG-:-EN/ or /MANGI-:I-/ to set or place (someone or something) with the bottom

or buttocks up, to set or place upside down or
bottom up. Burang-item dayta burnay. Set that jar
upside down.   --syn. BALINSUEK.

BURARAWIT, n. a long slender branch; a pendulous top
of the bamboo.

BURAS, v. /AG-, MANG-:-EN/ to pick or gather (fruits),
especially when ripe or mature. Burasem dagiti
mangga tayon. Pick our mango fruits.

BURAY, v. /MANGI-:I-/ to give willingly. Iburay mo
ta kaasim kadakami. Give your pity to us willingly.

BURAYOK, n. an active spring, fountain.
v. /AG-/ to flow profusely, to gush out.
Nagburayok ti dara diay sugat na. The blood of his
wound gushed out.

BURBUR, n. down, soft fluffy hair, furry hair.
adj. /-AN/ having much of this.   --var. BARBURAN.

BURBURAN, n. 1. a kind of spaniel, poodle or
pekinese dog with long, thick wavy hair. 2. a
kind of shaggy blanket.

BURBURTIA, n. riddle.
v. /AG-/ to tell a riddle.   /MANG-:-AN/ to tell
a riddle to. Burburtiaan ka, Berto. I will tell you
a riddle, Bert.

BUREK, n. bubble, foam, froth, lather.
v. /AG-/ 1. to boil. Agburburek ti danomen. The
water is already boiling. 2. to foam, froth, lather,
bubble. Agburburek ti ngiwat na. His mouth is
foaming.

BURIAS, n. a young hog usually less than a year old,
shoat.   --var. BURYAS.

BURIDEK, n. the youngest child.   --syn. KIMMOT.

[1]BURIK, adj. dappled, motley, variegated in color.
n. a bird, a cock or rooster, with variegated
plumage.

[2]BURIK, v. /MANG-:-AN/ to engrave something on, to put an engraving on. Isu ti nangburik toy singsing ko. It was he who put an engraving on my ring. /MANGI-:I-/ to engrave. Iburik mo ti nagan ko ditoy singsing ko. Engrave my name on this ring of mine.

BURIS, n. loose bowel movement, watery excrement or feces.
v. /AG-/ to have loose bowel movement, to have diarrhea.

BURISANGSANG, n. brown sugar in loose form with big clods in it.

BURNAY, n. a kind of earthen jar.

BURO, n. fish, meat or fruit preserved in salt.
v. /AG-/ to make this. /MANG-:-EN/ to preserve in salt. --syn. ARTEM.

BURTIA, see BURBURTIA.

BURTONG, n. smallpox, chicken pox.
v. /AG-/ to have this.

BURYAS, var. of BURIAS.

BUS [f. Sp.], n. bus.
v. /AG-/ to go by bus, to take or ride on a bus. --syn. TRANSIT.

BUSA, n. cataract of the eye.

BUSAL, n. muzzle.
v. /MANG-:-AN/ to put a muzzle on.

BUSAT, n. 1. first sale of the day. 2. first sale of the day of a particular merchandise.

[1]BUSBUS, v. /MANG-:-EN/ to use up, consume completely. Isu ti nangbusbus iti amin nga kukua da. He was the one who used up all their properties.

[2]BUSBUS, v. /MANG-:-EN/ to loosen, slacken; to make loose or slack. Apay nga busbusem dayta galut ti kahon? Why are you making the binding of the box loose? /MA-/ to become loose or slack. Irutem

dayta galut ti kahon tapno saan nga mabusbus.
Tighten the band of the box so that it will not
become loose.

BUSEL, n. 1. flower bud of pistillate flowers. 2.
young coconut, melon, squash, etc.

BUSI, n. popped corn or rice.
    v. /-UM-/ to pop, as corn or rice. /AG-/ to pop
corn or rice.

BUSINA, n. horn, especially that of a car, truck or
carriage.
    v. /AG-/ to sound a horn.   /-UM-:-AN/ to sound a
horn at or for; to summon, drive away, or attract
the attention of by sounding a horn. Businaam dagita
nuang dita dalan. Sound your horn to drive away those
water buffaloes on the road.

BUSISERA [busiséra; f. Sp.?], adj. /NAG-/ fastidious.

BUSLON, adj. 1. wasteful, extravagant. 2. abundant,
teeming, abounding.
    v. /AG-, MANG-:-EN/ to waste; to use much more
than necessary.

BUSNAG, adj. /NA-/ light-colored, fair in complexion:
said of a person.

BUSOR, v. /-UM-, MANG-:-EN/ to oppose, contradict,
antagonize. Isu ti bimmusor kanyak. He was the one
who contradicted me. Saan mo nga busoren ti kayat
na. Don't oppose what he wants.

BUSSOG, v. /AG-/ to fill oneself with food, to satiate
oneself with food. Agbussog ka ta adayo ti papanan
tayo. Fill yourself with food for we are going far.
/MANG-:-EN/ to fill or satiate with food, to feed
until full. Saan mo nga busbussogen ta aso tapno
di nga maturog. Don't fill that dog with food so
that it will not go to sleep. /MA-/ [= MABSOG] to
be full. Nabsogakon. I am already full.

BUTAKA [f. Sp.], n. a lounging chair.

BUTBUT, n. hole, puncture.
    adj. having a hole or puncture.
    v. /MANG-:-AN/ to put a hole on; to puncture.

BUTEG, n. mucous nasal discharge; mucus.
v. /AG-/ to have nasal discharge.
adj. /MARA-/ like mucus: said especially of the
meat of young coconuts or betel nuts.

BUTENG, v. /AG-/ to be afraid, scared, alarmed. Saan
ka nga agbuteng. Don't be afraid. /MA-:KA-/ to be
afraid of, scared of, frightened by; to dread, fear.
Mabutengak kenka. I am afraid of you. Saan nak nga
kabuteng ta saanak nga mangan ti tao. Don't be
afraid of me for I don't eat people.

   BUTBUTENG, n. fear, alarm. Awan ti butbuteng na nga
   napan idiay sementerio. He went to the cementery
   without fear.
      v. /MANG-:-EN/ to frighten, scare, alarm. Saan
   nak nga butbutengen ta dinto atakien nak ti sakit
   ti puso. Don't scare me for I may have a heart
   attack.
      adj. /NAKA-/ frightening, scary, alarming;
   causing fear or fright.

BUTILAW, n. a protrusion of the uterus into the vagina.
v. /AG-/ to have this.

BUTINGGAN, n. wild tomato whose fruits are small,
round and smooth skinned.

BUTIT, see MARABUTIT.

BUTO, n. 1. penis. 2. style of the pistil. 3. tongue
of a bell.

BUTON [f. Sp.], n. something resembling a button;
button. Adda tinalmegan na nga buton. He pressed on
something like a button.

BUTONES [f. Sp.], n. button.
v. /AG-/ to button one's clothes. Agbutones ka pay
sa ka rumuar. Button your clothes before you come out.
/MANG-:-AN/ to put buttons on. Butonesan na daytoy
kamisadentrok. She will put buttons on my shirt.
/MANGI-:I-/ to button (a garment). Ibutones mo
dayta pantalon mo. Button your pants.

BUTONG, v. /MANG-:-EN/ to crowd around, press around.
Binutong da nga kasla ngilaw daydiay aglako ti ikan.
They crowded like flies around the one selling fish.

BUTOY, n. calf of the leg.

BUTTIAK, v. /MANG-:-AN/ to cut or slash open.   --var.
  BUTYAK.

BUTTIKI, n. cowry shell.   --syn. SIGAY.

BUTTIOG, adj. /NAG-/ pot-bellied, having a protuberant
  belly: said of adult persons especially the male.
  Buttiog ti tatang mo. Your father is pot-bellied.

BUTTOT, n. a person who is excused from doing manual
  work or house chores.   --syn. SENIORITO, SENIORITA.

BUTTUAN, n. corn, a local hardening and thickening of
  epidermis (as on'toe).
    v. /AG-/ to have this.

BUTWAN, var. of BUTTUAN.

BUTYAK, var. of BUTTIAK.

BUTYOG, var. of BUTTIOG.

BUYA, v. /AG-, MANG-:-EN/ to see, watch, look at,
  view. Agbuya tayo ti sine. Let's see a show.
    PABUYA, n. show; stage show.

BUYAT, v. /MANGI-:I-/ to pour out (water or any other
  liquid). Ditoy mo nga ibuyat dayta danum. Pour out
  that water here.   /MAI-/ to pour out accidentally.
  --syn. BUKBOK, SUYAT.

BUYBUY, n. fringe.
    adj. /-AN/ provided with this.

BUYOG, v. /MANG-:-EN/ to follow, comply with, fulfill,
  do accomplish. Laglagipem nga buyogen ti karim
  kadakami. Remember to fulfill your promise to us.

BUYOK, adj. /NA-/ fetid, having a bad smell; stinking.
  Nabuyok ta takkim. Your feces are fetid.
    v. /-UM-/ to be like this.

BUYON, v. /AG-/ to practice divination.

PABUYON, v. /MANGI-:I-/ to ask someone to find the location or situation (of a lost object or missing person or animal) by divination. --syn. PASILAW (under SILAW).

BUY-ONG, adj. /-AN/ big-bellied. --syn. BUTTIOG.

BUYOT, n. army, forces, troops; followers, adherents.

BUYUBOY, n. a kind of cup or dipper made of coconut shell.

BWAL, var. of BUAL.

BWAYA, var. of BUAYA.

[1]DA, pl. of [1]NI.

[2]DA, adv. a particle expressing affirmation. Da man dinak kikien. Please don't tickle me.

DAAN, adj. /NAG-/ old, ancient: said of inanimate objects.
    v. /-UM-/ to be like this. --syn. see BAAK, BAKET, LAKAY.

DAAN, v. /AG-, MANG-:-AN/ to wait for, watch for. Sino ti nangdaan kenka? Who waited for you?

  MADADAAN or SIDADAAN, adj. ready, prepared. Madadaan kami nga tumulong kenka. We are ready to help you.

DADAEL, v. /AG-, MANG-:-EN/ to destroy, ruin, damage, spoil. Saan mo nga dadaelen dayta relos ko. Don't destroy my watch. /MA-/ to be destroyed, ruined, damaged, spoiled. Nadadael daydiay relos ko. My watch was ruined.
    adj. destroyed, ruined, damaged, spoiled. Dadael daytoy relos kon. My watch is already ruined.

DADANES, v. /MANGI-:I-/ to insult, affront. Isu ti nangidadanes kadakami. He was the one who insulted us. /MAI-/ to be insulted, affronted. Narigat ti maidadanes. It is hard to be insulted.

DADANG, v. /AG-/ to go near a fire or any other source of heat. Saan ka nga agdadang ta dikanto nga agpanateng. Don't go near a fire for you might catch cold. /MANGI-:I-/ to heat, warm. Mangidadang ka ti danum nga pagdigus ko. Heat some water for my bath.

DADAPILAN, see under DAPIL.

DADAULO, pl. of DAULO.

DADDUMA, n. pl. others, some others, some. Napan ti dadduma kadagiti sangaili mi idiay kusina. Some of our guests went to the kitchen.

NO DADDUMA, sometimes, once in a while. No dadduma, agbasaak agingga ti agsapa. Sometimes, I read until morning.

DADI [f. Eng.], syn. of TATANG.

DADO, n. a die.

DAEG, adj. /NA-/ nice, graceful, elegant, majestic, grand, stately.

DAEG, v. /MANG-:-EN/ to surpass, excel, outdo. Sino ti nangdaeg kenka? Who outdid you? --syn. [1]ABAK.

DAEL, adv. inasmuch as, it is well that, it is fortunate that. Dael na pay ketdi ta nabaknang da. It is well that they are rich.

DAGA [f. Sp.], n. dagger. --syn. PUNYAL.

DAGA, n. 1. earth, soil, ground. Nagidda diay ubing idiay daga. The child lay on the ground. 2. land, especially agricultural land. Nalawa ti daga da. Their land is wide. 3. country. Ania nga daga ti naggapoam? What country did you come from?

DAGAANG, adj. /NA-/ sweltering hot, sultry: said of the weather. Nadagaang ita. It is sultry today.
    v. /-UM-/ to be sweltering hot, sultry: said of the weather. Dumagaang ti tiempo. The weather is becoming sultry. /AG-/ to feel sweltering hot, sultry: said of persons and animals. Agdagaang dayta balasang. That young woman feels sweltering hot.

DAGADAG, v. /MANGI-:I-/ to insist upon, press for or urge. Isu ti nangidagadag iti panagbangon ti eskuela ditoy barrio mi. He was the one who pressed for the construction of a schoolhouse in our barrio or village.

DAGAS, v. /-UM-/ to stop by, pass by, drop in for a while. Dumagas ka pay. Drop in for a while. /-UM-, MANG-:-EN/ to stop by for, to pick up, to stop by and fetch. Dagasen nak intono mapan ka. Stop by and fetch me when you go. /MANGI-:I-/ to stop by and deliver. Idagas mo daytoy idiay balay da intono mapan ka idiay plasa. Will you deliver this to their house when you go to the plaza.

DAGDAG, v. /AG-/ to hurry up someone, to impel or incite someone to act with greater speed. /MANG-:-EN/ to hurry up, to impel or incite to greater speed. Dagdagem ni Rosa nga aglaba. Incite Rose to greater speed in washing clothes.

DAGEL, v. /-UM-/ to grow worse, worsen. Dumagel ti sakit na. His sickness grew worse. /MANGI-:I-/ to make feel worse. Daytoy ti nangidagel kanyak. This made me feel worse.

DAGEM, v. /MANGI-:I-/ to take or do something intensely or seriously, to engage (oneself) on something intensely or seriously. Saan mo nga idagem ta bagim ti trabaho. Don't engage yourself in your work intensely.

DAGIDI, pl. of DAYDI.

DAGDAGIDI, pl. of DADDAYDI.

DAGIDIAY, 1. pl. of DAYDIAY. 2. var. of ADDAGIDIAY.

DAGDAGIDIAY, pl. of DADDADIAY.

DAGINSEN, v. /MANG-:-EN/ to press down, compress. Daginsenem dagita lupot tapno makaanay dayta kahon. Press down the clothes so that the box will be adequate to contain them. /MANGI-:I-/ to pack tightly or closely, to pile up neatly or tightly. Idaginsen mo dagita kayo ditoy. Pile up those pieces of wood neatly here.

DAGITA, 1. pl. of DAYTA. 2. var. of ADDAGITA.

   DAGDAGITA, pl. of DATDATA.

DAGITAY, pl. of DAYTAY.

   DAGDAGITAY, pl. of DATDATAY.

DAGITI, pl. of [1]TI.

DAGITOY, 1. pl. of DAYTOY. 2. var. of ADDAGITOY.

   DAGDAGITOY, pl. of DATDATOY.

DAGMEL, adj. /NA-/ stupid, dull, dense, obtuse.

DAGSEN, adj. /NA-/ 1. heavy, ponderous.   --syn. LAG-AN.
2. weighty, important, serious, deep, profound.
Nadagsen dayta imbagam. What you said is serious.
3. grievous, burdened. Nadagsen ti nakem ko nga
napan. My mind was burdened when I went. 4.
sluggish, slow or dull from loss of vitality.
Nadagsen ti riknak. I feel sluggish.

DAGULLIT, v. /MANG-:-EN/ to do often, to do repeatedly.
Saan mo nga dagulliten dayta nga aramid mo. Don't do
that act of yours repeatedly.
   adj. /(NA-)/ importunate, overly persistent in
request or demand.

DAGUM, n. needle.

   DAGUMDAGUM, n. sting of bees, wasps and other
   stinging insects.

DAGUP, n. sum, total. Mano ti dagup ti botos na? What
is the total of his votes?
   v. /MANG-:-EN/ to sum or add up, to total.
Dagupem amin nga utang ko kenka. Total all my debts
to you.   --cf. DARAGUP.

DAGUS, adv. immediately, at once, directly, straightaway,
forthwith.   --syn. DARAS.

DAGUS, v. /AG-/ to lodge, to stay or live in temporarily.
Agdagus ka idiay balay mi intono mapan ka idiay ili.
Lodge in our house when you go to town.

DAIB, v. /-UM-/ to dive. /MANG-:-EN/ to dive and
get, dive for. /MANGI-:I-/ to dive with in order
to put or give.

DAIG, v. /AG-/ to have tuberculosis, to be sick with
tuberculosis. Agdaig ti pusa no makasida iti siit
ti igat. A cat will have tuberculosis if it eats
the bones of an eel. --syn. SARUT, TISIS, TIBI.

DAING, n. dried fish, especially small ones. --syn.
see PINDANG.

DAIT, v. /AG-/ to sew garments. Ammo na ti agdait.
He knows how to sew garments. /-UM-, MANG-:-EN/
to sew (garments). Daytoy nga badok ti dinait na.
This is my dress which he sewed.

DAKEP, v. /MANG-:-EN/ [= DAKPEN] to catch, seize,
apprehend, capture. Apay nga dakpen da ka? Why will
they apprehend you?

DAKES, adj. /NAG-/ 1. bad, evil, wicked, sinful.
Dakes ka nga tao. You are a bad person. 2. defective,
faulty; unsound; damaged, spoiled. Dakes ti nagatang
ko nga kotse. The car that I bought is defective.

DAKIWAS, v. /AG-:-EN/ [with pl. goal] to go to one
after the other or to each one purposefully. Isuda
ti nagdakiwas kadagiti balbalay nga adda baboy na.
They were the ones who went to each one of the
houses which have pigs. Dinakiwas da amin nga
balbalay idiay ili. They went to each one of the
houses in town.

DAKKEL, adj. /NAG-/ 1. big, large (in size). --ant.
BASSIT. 2. great, grand.
   v. /-UM-/ 1. to become big, large. 2. to grow up.
Mangan ka ti adu tapno dardaras ka dumakkel. Eat
much so that you will grow up fast.
   n. [pl. DADAKKEL] parent, father, mother. --syn.
NAGANAK.

DAKLIS, n. a kind of seine used for fishing in the sea
near the shore.

DAKSANGASAT [cf. DAKES & GASAT], adj. unfortunate,
unlucky, ill-fated.

DAKULAP, n. palm (of hand).

DALAG, n. a kind of fresh water mudfish.   --syn. see
   LAMES.

DALAGA, see DUMALAGA.

DALAGAN, n. 1. the period after childbirth during which
   the mother is restricted from going out of her room.
   2. also, the inclined bed in which the mother stays
   most of the time during this period.
   v. /AG-/ to spend this period, to be in this
   period.

DALAGUDUG, n. a kind of tree whose branches are used
   for fencing and whose flowers are sometimes eaten.
   --syn. KAWKAWATI, (dial.) PASAKUATIT.

DALAN, n. road, way, passage, track, path.   --syn.
   KALSADA, DANA.

DALAN, v. /MANGI-:I-/ to advise, counsel. Isu ti
   nangidalan kanyak. It was he who advised me.   --syn.
   BAGBAGA.

DALANDAN, n. orange.   --syn. DALANGHITA, KAHEL,
   KAMUYAW.

DALANGHITA, n. orange.   --syn. DALANDAN.

DALAPUS, v. /-UM-, MANG-:-EN/ to collide with, bump.
   Saan nak man nga dalapusen. Don't collide with me
   please.   /MAKA-/ to collide with a spirit or ghost,
   to become sick because of colliding with a spirit
   or ghost.

DALAYAP, n. 1. a kind of citrus tree (Citrus lima.
   Lunan.). 2. a fruit of this.

DALAYDAY, v. /MANGI-:I-/ to hang in a careless or
   disorderly manner on a clothesline, a fence, etc.
   /MAI-/ to be hung in a careless or disorderly manner.
   --syn. see SALAPAY.

DALAYUDOY, v. /AG-/ to be spongy, pulpy: said of meat,
   fish, fruits, etc. Agdalayudoy diay ikan nga
   nagatang ko. The meat that I bought was spongy.

DALDAL, v. /MANGI-:I-/ to soil, sully, besmirch
especially by dragging on a dirty surface. Saan
mo nga idaldal dayta lupot. Don't soil that piece
of cloth.

DALEB, v. /MANGI-:I-/ to cause to fall forward on
one's face. Isu ti nangidaleb kanyak. It was he who
caused me to fall forward on my face. /MAI-/ to
fall forward on one's face. Aluadam ta dikanto
maidaleb. Be careful so that you won't fall forward
on your face.

DALEM, n. liver.

DALEPDEP, v. /MANG-:-EN/ to press the flat side or
handle of a big knife (BUNENG) on a person with
flu who is lying down in order to prevent his
sickness from becoming worse.

DALIASAT, v. /AG-/ to go across, go through. Annadam
ti agdaliasat dita kalsada ta adu ti aglabas nga
lugan. Be careful in going across the street for
there are many vehicles passing through. /AG-:-EN/
to cross, traverse. Agdaliasat kami ti taaw no
mapan kami diay lugar da. We cross an ocean when we
go to their place. --syn. LASAT, BALLASIW, BALIW.

DALIKAN, n. stove; fireplace; hearth.

DALIKEPKEP, v. /AG-/ to cross the arms on the breast.
/MANG-:-AN/ to hold with the arms around against the
breast, to hug like a bear. Saan mo nga dalikepkepan
dayta ubing. Don't hold the child with your arms
around against your breast.

DALIMANEK, adj. /NA-/ orderly, well-arranged, neat.
Nadalimanek ti ayan ti panganan da. The place where
they eat is orderly.
    v. /AG-, AGI-/ to put things in order, to arrange
things neatly. Ammo na ti agdalimanek. He knows how
to put things in order.

DALIMUGTONG, v. /MANG-:-EN/ to pile up, stack.
Dalimugtongem dagita kayo ditoy. Pile up those pieces
of wood here.

DALINGDING, n. drapes, curtain.
    v. /MANG-:-EN/ to drape, provide with a curtain.

DALIPATU, n. a flake of fire, especially one floating
in the air; a flying ember.

DALIT, v. /MANGI-:I-/ to crush, press, squeeze (on
something). Idalit mo daytoy suman dita bulong.
Press this rice cake on that leaf.

DALLOT, n. a kind of native song or chant.
v. /AG-/ to sing or chant this.

DALLUYON, n. a wave breaking into foam; a breaker.

DALUBDUB, v. /MANGI-:I-/ to prick, to pierce slightly
with a sharp point. Idalubdub mo daytoy dagum dita.
Prick the needle there. /MA--AN/ to be pricked, to
be pierced slightly with a sharp point. Nadalubduban
daytoy sakak ti siit. My foot was pricked by a thorn.
n. the result of this action, a prick. Adda
dalubdub daytoy sakak. My foot has a prick.

DALUNGDONG, n. head covering, e.g. a bandana.
v. /AG-/ to cover the head with this. /MANG-:-AN/
to cover someone's head with this.

DALUPINGPING, v. /MANG-:-EN/ to gather up, draw
together a section of one's skirt. Dalupingpingem
dayta pandiling mo. Gather up a section of your
skirt. /MANGI-:I-/ to gather up or draw together
a section of one's skirt and tuck this in the
waist. Idalupingping mo dayta pandiling mo. Gather
up a section of your skirt and tuck this in your
waist.

DALUPISAK, v. /AG-/ to sit on one's hunches on the
floor. --var. LUPISAK.

DALUS, adj. /NA-/ clean. Nadalus ka nga babai. You
are a clean woman.
v. /-UM-/ to become clean. /AG-, MANG-:-AN/ to
clean. Dalusam ta kuartom. Clean your room.

DALUSON, v. /AG-/ [with pl. subject] to congregate,
assemble, come together. Saan kayo nga agdadaluson
dita. Don't congregate there. /MANGI-:I-/ [with
pl. goal] to gather, bring or put together. Sino
ti nangidaluson iti luplupot ditoy? Who gathered
the clothes here?

DALUTAYTAY, v. /AG-/ 1. to be weak, feeble, exhausted; hence, 2. to swoon or collapse due to weakness or exhaustion.

DAMA, n. draughts, checkers.
v. /AG-/ [with pl. subject] to play draughts or checkers. Agdama ta. Let's play checkers.
/MAKI-:KA-/ to play draughts or checkers with. Makidamaak kanyana. I'll play checkers with him.

DAMA, adj. /MA-/ actually going on or happening, in progress, going on just now or at the present time or moment. Madama ti kasar da. Their wedding is in progress.
adv. /AG-/ at the present time, presently, right now, at this very moment, currently. Agdama nga maturog diay lakay. The old man is at the present time sleeping. /MA- + R1/ in a little while, by and by, soon. Innawak dagita inton madamdama. I will wash those in a little while.

DAMAG, n. news, information; rumor, hearsay; gossip.
v. /-UM-/ to ask for news, information, rumor, or gossip. Dumamag ka man kanyana. Will you ask for some news from him? /-UM-:-EN/ to ask for or solicit (news, information, etc.), inquire about. Damagem no kaano ti panagsubli na. Inquire when he is coming back.

AGDINDINAMAG, adj. renowned, famous, popular; notorious; well-known. Isu ti agdindinamag nga bandido. He is the notorious bandit.

DAMAHUANA [f. Sp.], demijohn.

DAMDAM, v. /MANGI-:I-/ to bake, roast or cook in hot ashes. Idamdam mo dagita kamotit. Roast those sweet potatoes in hot ashes.

DAMDAMO, see under DAMO.

DAM-EG, adj. /NA-/ damp, moist.

[1]DAMGIS, v. /-UM-/ to make a brief stop; to stop by or go inside someone's house or place for a moment. Dumamgis ka pay. Stop by for a moment.

[2]DAMGIS, v. /MAKA-:MA--AN/ to brush against slightly, to scratch. Nadamgisan diay pingping na ti bala. His cheek was scratched by a bullet.

DAMILI, n. earthenware.
v. /AG-/ to make this. /MANG-:-EN/ to make as earthenware.

AGDAMDAMILI, n. potter.

DAMIT, v. /MANG-:-EN/ to receive or collect the benefits or rewards of, to profit from, to reap or enjoy the benefits of. Ania ti damiten iti dayta nga ar-aramidem? What benefits will you receive from what you are doing? Isu ti nangdamit iti nagbannogan ni tatang na. He was the one who reaped the benefits of what his father labored for.

DAMKA, adj. /NA-/ malicious, wicked, vicious.

DAMO, n. the first time; the beginning with reference to time. Damo ni Rita ti sumbrek iti eskuela..It was the first time for Rita to go to school.

ITI DAMO NA, at first, in the beginning.

DAMDAMO, var. of DAMO.

AGDADAMO, n. beginner, tyro, novice.

DAMORTIS, n. a leguminous tree with spiny branches and turgid pods with seeds surrounded by an edible, whitish, pulpy arillus. --syn. KAMANTIRIS.

DAMSAK, adj. /NA-/ 1. spendthrift, wasteful. 2. dissolute, dissipated.

DANA, n. footpath, trail; track. --syn. DALAN, DASDAS.

DANAG, v. /AG-, MA--AN/ to worry, be worried, anxious, troubled, uneasy. Saan ka nga madanagan ta umay ti ambulansian. Don't be worried for the ambulance is coming. --syn. DANAG.

DANDANI, adj. near, almost here. Dandani ti piesta min. Our festival is almost here.
adv. almost, nearly. Dandani natay diay anak na. His child almost died. --syn. NAGISTAYAN. --var. NGANNGANI.

DANES, see DADANES.

DANI, see DANDANI.

DANIW, n. poem, verse, rhyme.
   v. /AG-/ to sing, especially ditties. Nalaing nga
agdaniw diay baro. The young man is good in singing.
--syn. KANSION, KANTA.

DANON, v. /-UM-/ to come inside or enter a building,
   especially a house. Dumanon ka. Come inside.
   /-UM-:-EN/ often /MAKA-:MA-/ 1. to reach, arrive at,
   come to, go as far as. Ti la Manilan ti diko pay
   nadanon. Manila is the only place that I have not
   reached so far. 2. to see or find in a place upon
   arriving there. Nadanon nak idiay balay da meyor.
   He found me in the house of the mayor (upon his
   arrival there). /-UM-:-EN/ to ask for the hand of
   a girl in marriage for someone, to propose marriage
   to a girl for someone. Mapan da danonen ni Maria.
   They will go ask for the hand of Mary in marriage
   (for someone). /AGI-, MANGI-:I-/ 1. to take to,
   cause to reach. Idanon mo man daytoy librok idiay
   balay mi. Will you please take my book to our house.
   2. to report to someone, cause to reach someone.
   Saan mo nga idanon kanyana dayta nga damag. Don't
   report that news to him.

DANUG, v. /AG-, MANG-:-EN/ to hit with the fist.   --syn.
   DISNUG.

DANUM, n. water.
   v. /MANG-:-AN/ to add water to. Danumam dayta
lutlutoem. Add water to what you are cooking.

   DINANUMAN, n. a dish consisting of roasted fish
      boiled in water and seasoned with sour fruits
      or vegetables.

   PADANUM, n. irrigation.   --syn. PALAYAS.
      v. /AG-, MANG-:-AN/ to irrigate.

   TARINDANUM, n. itchiness between the toes or fingers
      caused by prolonged soaking in water.
      v. /AG-/ to have this, be affected with this.

DANGADANG, n. battle, fight, combat. Iti dayta a nadara
   nga dangadang, nauloyan ni Heneral Evangelista. In
   that bloody battle, General Evangelista was killed.

v. /MAKI-:KA-/ to fight, battle, combat with, to
contend or compete with. Apay nga makidangadang ka
kanyak? Why do you fight with me? /AG-/ [with pl.
subject] to fight each other, to contend or compete
with each other. Agdangadang dagiti dua nga nalaing
nga kumanta. The two who are good in singing will
compete with each other.

DANGAN, n. the distance from the tip of the thumb to
the tip of the middle finger. Igupungan nak ti dua
nga dangan dita talim. Cut for me two tip-of-thumb-
to-tip-of-middle-finger measures of your rope.
v. /MANG-:-EN/ to measure using this.

DANGAW, n. a kind of stinkbug.
v. /-EN/ to be attacked by or infested with this.
Dinangaw daydiay tabungaw da. Their white squash
plant was attacked by stinkbugs.

DANGER, v. /MANG-:-AN/ [= DANGRAN] to hurt, injure,
bruise. /MA--AN/ [= MADANGRAN] to be hurt, injured,
bruised. Adu ti nadangran nga Kristiano. Many
Christians were hurt. --syn. DUNOR, DUNGIR.

DANGGAY, v. /AG-/ [with pl. subject] to sing together
harmoniously. Nagdanggay da nga nagkanta. They sang
together harmoniously. /-UM-, MANG-:-AN/ to
accompany, especially with a musical instrument.
Danggayan na dagiti kanta na iti gitara. He
accompanies his songs with a guitar.

DANGKOK, adj. /NA-/ bad, evil, vile, wicked, depraved.

DANGRAN, = DANGER + -AN.

DANGRO, adj. /NA-/ having the stench of spoiled meat
or fish. --syn. LAES.

DAO, n. a kind of tree which gives valuable timber.

DAPADAP, v. /MANG-:-EN/ to feel or explore by touching
with the hand. Dapadapem dayta datar. Feel that
floor with your hand.

DAPAG, v. /MANGI-:I-/ to place, put or set down
squarely, firmly or solidly.

DAPAK; DAPAKDAPAK, v. /AG-/ to make a flapping or trotting sound especially when walking. Sino ti agdapakdapak dita? Who is making a trotting sound there?

DAPAN, n. sole of foot.

PADAPAN, n. 1. runner of a sledge. 2. presser foot of a sewing machine.

DAPANDAPAN, n. a kind of cake shaped like a sole.

DAPAT, n. 1. plain, level land. 2. a kind of native woven blanket.

DAP-AW, v. /-UM-/ to step in for a moment, to pay a short visit. Immay kay la dimmap-aw. You just step in for a moment. /-UM-:-AN/ to step on for a moment. Dinap-awan ti ngilaw daytoy. This was stepped on for a moment by flies. /MA--AN/ to be stepped on by flies. Kitaem ta madap-awan. Watch it for it may be stepped on by flies.

DAPIG, v. /AG-, MANG-:-EN/ to hit with the flat side of a large knife (BUNENG).

DAPIL, v. /AG-/ to press out the juice of the sugarcane using a machine with rollers called DADAPILAN. /AG-, MANG-:-EN/ to press out the juice of (the sugarcane) in the DADAPILAN. Dinapil na dagiti unas ko. He pressed out the juice of my sugarcane in the DADAPILAN.

DADAPILAN, n. sugar mill; a machine with rollers used to press out the juice of the sugar cane; it is operated by a water buffalo attached to the end of the beam (TANGBAW) walking in a circle.

DAPIL, adj. half-rounded, semicircular, flattish: said especially of the head. --syn. DIPPIG.

DAPILAG, n. a kind of shallow basket, more or less resembling a big winnow.

DAPILUS, v. /MANG-:-EN/ to demolish, cause to collapse. Dinapilus na diay lamisaan. He caused the table to collapse. /MA-/ to collapse, especially due to weakness. Nadapilusak. I collapsed.

DAPLA, v. /AG-/ to lie prone especially with the arms
  spread. Sino dayta nagdapla dita? Who is that lying
  prone there? /MAI-/ to fall prone. Nakitak nga
  naidapla idiay datar. I saw him fall prone on the
  floor.

DAPO, n. ashes, adj. /-EN/ ash-colored, ashen; gray.

DAPOGAN, n. the part of a stove or fireplace before
  the hearthstones where the ashes are collected.

DAPPOOR, v. /AG-/ to stamp on the ground.

DARA, n. blood.
    v. /AG-/ to bleed. Nagdara diay sugat na. His
  wound bled. /MANGI-:I-/ to bleed. Adu ti indara
  diay sugat na. His wound bled much.
    adj. /NA-/ bloody.

  PADARA, v. /AG-/ to have a hemorrhage.

DARADDAN, v. /MANG-:-EN/ to do one after the other,
  to do successively.

DARAGUP, v. /AG-/ [with pl. subject] to join together,
  unite; to pile up, accumulate. Agdaragup ti sakit na.
  His ailments are accumulating. Nagdaragup da nga
  nakimisa. They joined together in going to mass.
  --cf. DAGUP.

DARAMUDUM, v. /MAI-/ to trip, stumble.

DARAN, v. /MAI-/ to increase, become greater in
  intensity, to worsen. Naidaran ti sakit na. His
  sickness worsened.

DARANUDOR, v. /AG-/ to make a roaring or rumbling
  sound. Nagdaranudor daydiay trak. The truck made
  a roaring sound.

DARANGIDANGAN, adj. ripening, almost ripe, nearly
  ripe: said of fruits. Darangidangan dayta papayan.
  That papaya is almost ripe.

DARANGIDONG, n. the middle part of the nose from the
  bridge to the tip.

DARAS, n. times, instances. Mamin-ano nga daras nga
  nagsubli. How many times did he come back?

[1]DARAS, adj. /NA-/ 1. easy, not difficult; fast.
Nadaras nga basaen dayta librom. It is easy to read
your book. 2. often, frequently. Nadaras nga mangan
ditoy diay baro. The young man eats here often.
v. /-UM-/ to become often or frequent.

DARDARAS, v. /AG-:-EN/ to hurry, hasten; to do in a
hurry. Nagdardaras nga nagdigos diay balasang.
The young woman took a bath hurriedly. Dinardaras
na ti nagdigos. She took a bath in a hurry.

[2]DARAS, adv. quickly, rapidly, swiftly, fast; immediately,
promptly. Naturog daras diay ubing. The child slept
immediately.

DARASUDOS, adj. /NAG-/ over hasty, rash.
v. /AG-/ to do hastily, hurriedly, rashly; to
rush. Saan ka nga agdarasudos nga mapan dita kalsada.
Don't rush going to the street.

DARAT, n. sand, silt.

DARAUDO, v. /AG-/ to suffer a morbidly copious discharge
of the menses, especially after having lifted a heavy
object or after being injured. Agdaraudo ni Rosa. Rose
is having a heavy discharge of the menses.

DAR-AW, v. /-UM-:-AN/ to look at or watch from an
elevated position, to look down at. Dar-awam
dagidiay agsalsala. Look down toward the persons
dancing.

DAR-AY, v. /MANG-:-AN/ to help, assist. Immay na
dinar-ayan ni Rosa. He came to help Rose. --syn.
TULONG.

DARDARAS, see under DARAS.

DAREKDEK, n. a long and slender stake, especially one
used to support a fence.

DAREPDEP, n. dream, aspiration, ambition; imagination,
vision. --TAGTAGAINEP.

DARIKMAT; APAGDARIKMAT, adv. in a little while, a
moment. Rimmuar diay balasang iti apagdarikmat.
The young woman came out a moment. --syn. APAGBIIT.

DARINGONGO, v. /AG-/ to bleed in the nose, to have a
nosebleed.

DARIPESPES, v. /MANG-:-EN/ to wet thoroughly, soak.
Dinaripespes na diay lupot ti napudot nga danum.
He wet the cloth thoroughly with hot water. /MA-/
to be thoroughly wet, to be drenched or soaking wet.
Nadaripespes ni Jose ti ling-et. Jose is drenched
with perspiration.

DARISAY, v. /NA-/ of good quality, pure, clear: said
of the climate, air, etc.

DARISAYEN, n. a cock with black and white plumage.

DARISDIS, adj. /NA-/ sloping, slanting, inclining.
PADARISDIS, v. /MANGI-:I-/ to put in a horizontal
position.

DARISON, v. /AG-/ to push oneself in, to squeeze in.
Saan kay nga agdadarison dita. Don't squeeze in
there. /MANGI-:I-/ to push, cram or squeeze in.
Isu ti nangidarison kadagiti lupot ditoy. He was
the one who pushed in the clothes here.

DARIWIS, adj. diagonal, slanting, oblique (in shape).

DARONDON, adj. producing a second crop: said of
fruit bearing trees.

DAROY, adj. /NA-/ thin, watery, weak: said of gruel,
chocolate, soup, and the like.

DARUM, v. /AGI-, MANGI-:I-/ to accuse of or charge
with an offense or any transgression; to sue in
court. Uray no idarum nak indiak nga bayadan diay
utang ko. Even if you sue me I will not pay my
debts.

DARUMISA, adj. /NA-/ clumsy and dirty or slovenly:
as, to spill food, drink, water, when washing the
dishes. Nagdarumisa ka ket nga aginnawen. You are
very clumsy and dirty in washing in the dishes.

DARUNDUN, v. /AG-/ to push someone standing in a crowd
or in line. Saan ka nga agdarundun. Don't push

someone in a crowd. /-UM-, MANG-:-EN/ to push
(someone standing in a crowd or in line). Sino
ti nangdarundun kenka? Who pushed you?

DARUP, v. /-UM-/ to come or approach impetuously
or precipitately. Saan kayo nga dumarup. Don't
approach precipitately. /-UM-:-EN/ to go to or
approach impetuously or precipitately. Saan yo
nga darupen dagita sangaili. Don't approach the
guests impetuously.

DARUSDUS, n. a trowel.

DAS, v. /-UM-/ to be enough, sufficient, adequate.
Adda met la ngata umdas nga kired ti pakinakem
na ket maitured nak nga palubosan? Do you think
his will power is strong enough that he can bear
to let me go?

DASAR, v. /MANG-:-AN/ to set (the table) for eating.
Dasaram ta lamisaan ta mangan tayon. Set the table
and let's eat. /MANGI-:I-/ to set out or prepare
for use. Indasar na dagiti pinggan. He set out
the plates. --syn. PUNI.

DASAY, v. /MAI-/ to be weakened, overpowered or
prostrated (by a sickness, drunkenness, etc.);
to be caused to stay in bed or lie down. Naidasay
ti sakit. He was caused to stay in bed by sickness.

DASDAS, n. footpath, trail. --syn. DANA, DESDES.

DASI, v. /MAI-/ to slip and fall on the back, to
fall supine. Annadam ta dikanto maidasi dita.
Be careful lest you might slip and fall on your
back. --syn. DATA.

DASIG, n. row, file, line.
     v. /MANG-:-EN/ or /MANGI-:I-/ to separate into
groups, classify and separate accordingly.

DATA, v. /AG-/ to lie on one's back, lie supine.
/MANGI-:I-/ to cause (someone) to lie on his back.
--var. PADATA.

DATAG, v. /MANGI-:I-/ to submit, offer, deliver, give.
Indatag na ti papeles na kadagiti agtuturay. He

submitted his papers to the government officials.
--syn. TED.

DATAO, pron. 1. one: an indefinite pronoun. 2. I: an
indirect pronoun for the first person singular.
Masapul nga aginana bassit datao. It is necessary
that I rest for a while.

DATAR, v. /MANGI-:I-/ to display, exhibit, expose,
show, present to view. Idatar mo dagita tagilakom
ditoy. Display your merchandise here.

DATAR, n. floor.

DATDATLAG, n. mystery, miracle, wonder, phenomenon.
--syn. MISTERIO.
   adj. /MAKA-/ mysterious, fantastic, miraculous,
phenomenal, wondrous.

DATENG, v. /-UM-/ [= DUMTENG] to arrive, come. --syn.
SANGPET.

DATLAG, see DATDATLAG.

DATO, n. a Moslem ruler.

DATON, v. /MANGI-:I-/ to give, present, offer as a
sacrifice or token of something. --syn. DIAYA.

DATOY, var. of DAYTOY.

DAULO, n. [pl. DADAULO], head, leader.
   v. /MANGI-:I-/ to lead, direct, guide, be in the
vanguard of. Isu ti nangidaulo ti gimong mi. It was
he who led our group.

DAWA, n. an ear of grain, especially of rice; spike.
   v. /AG-/ to develop spikes: said especially of
rice.

DAWADAW, v. /AG-/ to jut, project, protrude, stick
out; to exceed in length or height. Adda agdawadaw
nga kayo idiay tuktok ti balay da. There is a piece
of wood jutting from the top of their house.
/MANGI-:I-/ to project; to cause to stick out, jut,
protrude; to cause to be longer (as the wick of a
lamp). Idawadaw mo dayta kayo. Cause that piece of
wood to stick out.

DAW-AS, v. /-UM-/ to make a detour to (a place), to
make a brief stop in (a place), to go to (a place)
for a moment. /MANG-:-EN/ to make a detour to or
a brief stop in (a place) in order to get (something
or someone), to go to (a place) for a moment in
order to get (something or someone). Mapan ko
daw-asen diay ragadi mi idiay balay da. I am going
to go get our saw at their house. /MANGI-:I-/ to
make a detour to a brief stop at (a place) in order
to give or deliver (something or someone), to go to
(a place) for a moment in order to deliver or give
(something or someone). Idaw-as mo man diay ragadi
mi idiay balay da. Will you please make a detour
to their house and deliver our saw.   --see DAGAS.

DAWAT, v. /-UM-/ to ask for, beg, request. Kayat na ti
dumawat ti bawang. He wants to ask for garlic.

DAWEL, adj. /NA-/ 1. cruel, merciless, savage, inhuman.
Nadawel dayta anak mo. Your child is cruel. 2.
harmful, noxious, injurious. 2. inclement, stormy,
rough, unfavorable. Nadawel ti tiempo ita. The
weather today is unfavorable.

DAWENG; DAWENGDAWENG, v. /AG-/ to swim, to have a
hazy, reeling, or whirling appearance. Agdawengdaweng
ti makitak. The ones that I see are swimming.

[1]DAWI, v. /-UM-/ to bite a baited hook: said in fishing.
Nabayagak ditoyen ngem awan pay ti dimmawi. I have
been here for a long time but not one has taken a
bite at my bait.

[2]DAWI, adj. /NA-/ usual, common, customary, ordinary,
normal. Daytoy ti nadawi nga aramiden na. This is
what he usually does.

DAWIS, adj. /NA-/ pointed.

DAYA, n. east; eastern region.

[1]DAYA, n. feast, festival, banquet.
     v. /AG-/ to have this.

[2]DAYA; SIDADAYA, adj. exposed, laid bare, presented to
view.

DAYAG, adj. /NA-/ grave, grand, stately, majestic.

DAYAMUDOM, v. /AG-, -UM-/ to mumble, mutter. /-AN/
to growl at. Saan nak man nga dayamudoman. Don't
growl at me.

DAYANG; DAYANGDAYANG, adj. without walls, exposed.
v. /AG-/ to be without walls, exposed.

DAYAS, v. /MANG-:-AN/ to wash, bathe, cleanse. Dinayasan
na diay sugat na. He washed his wound. /MANGI-:I-/ to
use to wash, bathe or cleanse; to wash, bathe or
cleanse with. Danum nga napudot ti idayas mo ti dayta
sugat na. Wash his wound with hot water.

DAYAW, n. honor, reputation.
v. /-UM-, MANG-:-EN/ to honor, respect; to show
respect or reverence for; to esteem, revere; to
praise, exalt.
adj. /NA-/ 1. respectful, polite, courteous. 2.
great, grand, eminent, illustrious.

MADAYDAYAW, adj. honorable, reputable, famous.

PAMMADAYAW, n. acknowledgments.

DAYDAY, v. /MANGI-:I-/ to spread. Idayday mo dagita
lupot tapno agmaga da. Spread the clothes so that
they will get dry.

DAYDI [pl. DAGIDI], dem. 1. that, that one: no longer
extant, remote in time. --var. DEYDI, DEDI, ADI, DI.

DADDAYDI, that only, nothing but that: no longer
extant, remote in time. --var. DEDDEYDI.

DAYDIAY [pl. DAGIDIAY], dem. 1. that, that one: far
from both speaker and hearer. 2. of that, of that
one: far from both speaker and hearer. --var.
DEYDIAY, DEDIAY, ADIAY, DIAY.

DADDADIAY, that only, nothing but that: far from
both speaker and hearer. --var. DEDDEDIAY,
DEDEDIAY, DEDDEYDIAY.

DAYENGDENG, v. /AG-:-AN/ to complain about, scold,
rebuke, reprimand. Saan nak nga dagengdengan.
Don't scold me.

DAYO, v. /-UM-/ to go to (another place).

DAYO, v. /AG- + R2/ to compete with each other, to rival each other. Agdidinnayo dagiti tallo nga ili. The three towns are competing with one another. /-UM-/ to compete, enter into or be in rivalry, to enter or participate in a contest, athletic meet, etc. Napan kami dimmayo ti kanta idiay ili da. We went to participate in a singing contest in their town. /MANG-:-EN/ to compete or vie with (in a contest, athletic meet, etc.)

DAYTA [pl. DAGITA], dem. 1. that, that one: near the hearer. 2. of that, of that one: near the hearer. --var. DEYTA, DETA, ATA, TA.

DATDATA, that only, nothing but that: near the hearer. --var. DETDETA.

DAYTAY [pl. DAGITAY], dem. 1. that, that one: extant but not seen. 2. of that, of that one: extant but not seen. --var. DEYTAY, DETAY, DATAY, ATAY, TAY.

DATDATAY, that only, nothing but that: extant but not seen. --var. DETDETAY, DEDETAY.

DAYTOY [pl. DAGITOY], dem. 1. this, this one: near the speaker. 2. of this, of this one: near the speaker. --var. DEYTOY, DETOY, DATOY, ATOY, TOY.

DATDATOY, this only, nothing but this. --var. DETDETOY.

DAYYENG, v. /AG-/ to sing a song by humming and mumbling the lyrics. /MANG-:-EN/ to sing by humming and mumbling the lyrics.

DE [dɛ; f. Sp.], an adjectivizing affix meaning: equipped with, provided with, wearing, using, etc. De-armas ken de-uniporme dagiti tattao. The people were equipped with arms and were wearing uniforms.

DEBATE [dɛbáte; f. Sp.], n. debate, argument. v. /AG-/ [with pl. subject] to debate or argue with each other. /MAKI-:KA-/ to debate or argue with.

DEBORSIO [diborsio; f. Sp.], n. divorce.

DEBOSION [dibosion; f. Sp.], n. devotion, dedication,
loyalty.

DEBOSIONADO [dibosionado; f. Sp.], adj. pious, devout,
religious.

DEDDEDIAY, var. of DADDADIAY.

DEDDEYDI, var. of DADDAYDI.

DEDDEYDIAY, var. of DADDADIAY.

DEDEDIAY, var. of DADDADIAY.

DEDETAY, var. of DATDATAY.

DEDI, var. of DEYDI.

DEDIAY, var. of DEYDIAY.

DEGDEG, v. /-UM-/ to increase in degree or intensity;
to worsen. Dimmegdeg ti sakit na. His sickness
worsened. /MANG-:-EN/ to cause to increase in
degree or intensity; to make worse. Saan mo nga
degdegen toy nasakit ko. Don't make my sickness
worse.

DEGGES, v. /-UM-/ to gush out, flow copiously.

DEKDEK, v. /MANG-:-EN/ to pound. Dinekdek na diay
bagas. He pounded the rice.

DEKKET, adj. /NA-/ 1. sticky, gluey. 2. close, intimate.
--syn. NAASIDEG.
    v. /-UM-/ to stick, adhere. /MANGI-:I-/ to stick,
paste, glue (something).

DEL-AG, v. /AG-/ to shout, yell, shriek. Saan ka nga
agdel-ag ta dinto ket makariing diay ubing. Don't
shout lest the child wake up. /-AN/ to shout or
yell at. Dinel-agan nak ni Rosa. Rose shouted at me.

DELATA [dɛláta; f. Sp.], n. canned food. --see LATA.

DELIKADO [dɛlikádo; f. Sp.], adj. 1. delicate, frail,
weak. Delikado la unay dayta anak mo. Your child is
very frail. 2. serious, grave. Delikado ti sakit na.

His sickness is serious.   /NA-/ 1. delicate, having
or showing a sensitive distaste for anything
offensive or improper. Nagdelikado dayta nga
balasang. That woman is very delicate. 2. dangerous,
perilous, uncertain. Delikado ti magna iti rabii.
It is dangerous to travel at night.

DEMDEM, v. /MANG-:-EN/ to repress. Nabayag nga
demdemdemen na ti pungtot na. He has been repressing
his anger for a long time now.

DEMOKRASIA [dɛmokrasia; f. Sp.], n. democracy.

DEMONYO [dɛmonio; f. Sp.], n. demon, devil.   --syn.
DIABLO.

DEMONYO KA! You devil!

DEMONSTRASION [dɛmonstrasion; f. Sp.], n. demonstration.

DENDEN, v. /-UM-/ to move by sliding, as when one is
sitting on a bench; to go or come nearer a certain
point. Dumenden ka man bassit ta makatugawak met.
Will you please move a little bit so that I can
sit down also.   /MANGI-:I-/ to move (someone or
something) by sliding toward a certain point.

DENNET, v. /MANGI-:I-/ to put in contact with, to
cause to come in contact with. Saan mo nga idennet
dayta badom dita kape. Don't cause your dress to
come in contact with the coffee.   /MAI-/ to come
in contact with. Aluadam no maidennet ta imam dita
agburburek nga danum. Be careful lest your hand
come in contact with the boiling water.

DENGDENG, v. /AG-/ to cook a vegetable dish.
/MANG-:-EN/ to cook (vegetables) into a vegetable
dish.   --syn. ABRAW.

DINENGDENG, n. a vegetable dish.   --syn. INABRAW.

DENGNGEG, v. /-UM-:-EN/ [= DUMNGEG : DENGGEN] 1. to
listen to, pay attention to; hence, 2. to heed,
obey. Denggen yo ti ibagbaga da. Listen to what
they are saying.   /MAKA-:MA-/ [= MAKANGEG :
MANGNGEG] to be able to hear. Indiak nga mangngeg
ti boses mo. I cannot hear your voice.

DENGNGEP, v. /MANG-:-EN/ to apply ointment, poultice and the like (to an injury).

DEPARTAMENTO [dɛpartamɛnto; f. Sp.], n. department.
DEPARTAMENTO EHEKUTIBO, executive department.

DEPDEP, syn. of IDDEP.

DEPPA, n. span or distance measured by both arms extended sideways.
    v. /AG-/ to extend both arms sideways.
/MANG-:-EN/ to measure by the two arms extended sideways.

DEPPAAG, v. /-UM-, MA-/ [= DUMPAAG] to collapse, topple. Tallo nga balay ti dimpaag kalpasan ti uram. Three houses collapsed after the fire.
/MANG-:-EN/ to cause to collapse or topple. Saan nga deppaagen ti angin dayta abulog yo ta nalagda. The wind won't cause your fence to collapse for it is strong.

DEPPAAR, n. side (of an object or place).

DEPPEL, v. /AG-/ to imprint or put one's thumbprint. Agdeppel ka ditoy. Imprint your thumbprint here.
/MANG-:-AN/ to imprint one's thumbprint on.
Deppelam daytoy. Imprint your thumbprint here.
--syn. TIMBRE.   /MANGI-:I-/ to press on, apply pressure on.

DEPPES, v. /AG-/ to bend downward.   /MANG-:-EN/ to cause to bend backward; to push down or close to the surface. Deppesem dagita ruot. Push down those weeds.

DERDER, v. /MANG-:-EN/ to cause to become pulpy by beating, cooking, etc.   /MA-/ to become pulpy due to beating, overcooking, etc.

DERRAAS, n. precipice, cliff.

DESDES, n. footpath, trail.   --syn. DANA, DASDAS.
    v. /MA--AN/ to be streaked with, have trails of.
Nadesdesanak ti ling-et. I am streaked with sweat.

DESISION [dɛsision; f. Sp.], n. decision.

DETA, var. of DEYTA.

DETAY, var. of DEYTAY.

DETDETA, var. of DATDATA.

DETDETAY, var. of DATDATAY.

DETDETOY, var. of DATDATOY.

DETI, var. of DEYTI.

DETOY, var. of DEYTOY.

DEYDI, var. of DAYDI.

DEYDIAY, var. of DAYDIAY.

DEYTA, var. of DAYTA.

DEYTAY, var. of DAYTAY.

DEYTI, var. of DAYTI.

DEYTOY, var. of DAYTOY.

[1]DI, adv. no, not: var. of SAAN. --see MADI, INDIAK.

[2]DI, adv. a particle expressing indifference, defiance or encouragement. Di makitaray ka no isu ti kayat mo. Then elope (with someone) if that is what you want to do.

[3]DI, var. of DAYDI.

[4]DI, var. of IDI.

DIABLES, n. form of DIABLO used in cursing. Naggaset ket ti diables nga Paulon. That devil Paul is indeed very lucky.

DIABLO [f. Sp.], n. devil, demon. --syn. DEMONYO.

DIAKET [diákɛt; f. Eng.], n. jacket.
    v. /AG-/ to use or wear this.

DIANITOR [f. Eng.], n. janitor. --var. DYANITOR.

DIARYO [f. Sp.], n. newspaper.
v. /MAI-/ appear or be published in a newspaper.

DIASKE, n. a curse word synonymous with DIABLES; devil. Kasla napukaw nga asok ti diaske. The devil disappeared like smoke.

DIAY, var. of DAYDIAY or IDIAY.

DIAYA, n. gift, offering.
v. /MANGI-:I-/ to offer, give or present as an act of worship or devotion. Indiaya na amin nga kukua na nga pangtulong kadakuada. He offered all his properties in order to help them. --syn. DATON.

DIDAL, n. thimble.
v. /AG-/ to use or wear this. /MANG-:-AN/ to provide with this.

DIDIAY, var. of IDIAY.

DIDIGRA, n. disaster, calamity, catastrophe.
v. /MA-/ to be frightened, scared, startled. Nadidigra kami itay napalabas nga gerra. We were scared during the past war.

DIDING, n. wall.
v. /AG-/ to put up a wall. /MANG-:-AN/ to provide with a wall, put a wall to. Didingan mi daytoy balay mi inton bigat. We will put a wall to our house tomorrow.

DIDIOSEN, pl. of DIOSEN.

DIENWAIN [dienwa?in, dienwain; f. Eng.], adj. genuine, not imitation.

DIES [diεs; f. Sp.], num. ten; 10. ALAS DIES, ten o'clock. --syn. PULLO, SANGAPULO.

DIGO, n. 1. broth; the liquid of a dish. 2. coconut water.
PADIGO, v. /MANG-:-AN/ [= MAMADIGO, MANGPADIGO] to share one's food (with another). Isu ti namadigo

kadakami. It was he who shared us some of his food. /MANGI-:I-/ to share (a portion of one's food) (with another). Adu ti impadigo na kanyak. He shared with me much of his food.

DIGOS, v. /AG-/ to take a bath, to bathe oneself. Mapan da agdigos idiay karayan. They are going to take a bath in the river. /MANG-:-EN/ to give (a person or animal) a bath, to bathe (a person or animal). Mapan da digosen diay nuang da idiay waig. They are going to bathe their water buffalo in the brook.

DIGRA, see DIDIGRA.

DIKEN, n. pad: a circlet of cloth placed on top of the head on which a load is set; this protects the crown of the head from injury and at the same time stabilizes the load.

DIKEN-DIKEN, n. milliped.

DIKET, n. 1. sticky or glutinous rice. 2. sticky variety of corn. 3. sticky variety of cassava.

DIKIDIK, v. /MANG-:-EN/ to grind into powder form. Dikidiken na dayta nakirog nga bagas. He will grind that toasted rice into powder.

DIKKI, n. soft deposit on the surface of the teeth, as when one does not brush his teeth.

DIKORASION [f. Sp.], n. decoration, ornament. v. /MANG-:-AN/ to decorate, adorn. /MANGI-:I-/ to decorate or adorn with, to use as decoration. /MA--AN/ to be decorated with. --syn. ARKOS.

DILA, n. tongue; anything resembling a tongue.

DILAMUT, v. /MANG-:-AN/ often /MAKA-:MA--AN/ to (be able to) gather with difficulty from a scant supply; to scrape; to benefit or be given a share of something that is scant or meager. Awan ti nadilamutan mi ti daydiay inted na nga kuarta. We were not given a share of the money that he gave.

DILANA [f. Sp.], adj. woolen.

[1]DILAP, n. flood, inundation.
   v. /AG-/ to flood, inundate; to have a flood.
   --syn. LAYOS.

[2]DILAP, v. /AG-/ to stick out one's tongue at someone.
   /MANG-:-AN/ to stick out one's tongue at (someone).
   Isu ti dinilapan na. It was he at whom he stuck out
   his tongue.   --var. (dial.) DILAT.

DILAT, var. (dial.) of [2]DILAP.

DILDIL, v. /MANG-:-AN/ to lick. Saan mo nga dildilan
   dayta pinggan. Don't lick that plate.   --syn.
   DILPAT.

DILI, adj. /NA-/ stony. Ammo na ti nadili nga paset
   ti dalan. He knows the stony stretch of the road.

[1]DILIG, v. /MANGI-:I-/ to compare (to someone or
   something).

[2]DILIG, syn. (dial.) of SIBUG.

DILLAW, v. /MANG-:-EN/ to notice, observe, see,
   perceive; hence, 2. to call attention to, remark
   or comment on; to criticize, complain about. Saan
   mo nga dildillawen ti pannangan na. Don't notice
   or make any comment on his manner of eating.
   /MAKA-:MA-/ [= MAKADLAW : MADLAW] to notice or
   observe by chance; to perceive. Nadlaw ko nga
   adda kayat na nga ibaga diay baro. I noticed by
   chance that the young man wants to say something.

   PADLAW [= PA- + DILLAW], v. /MANGI-:I-/ to cause
      someone to notice or perceive; to show, reveal,
      display.

DILPAT, v. /AG-/ to lick someone. /-UM-:-AN/ to lick
   (someone or something).   --syn. DILDIL.

DIMTENG, pt. of DUMTENG.

DINENGDENG, see under DENGDENG.

DINNA, n. side (of).   --syn. ABAY, SIBAY, SIKIG.
   v. /-UM-:-AN/ to put or place oneself at the side
   of, to go and stay at the side of. Saan mo nga
   dinnaan dayta balasang ko. Don't go and stay at the
   side of my daughter.

DINGPIL, v. /MANG-:-EN/ to press, squeeze. Dingpilen yo dagita pias tapno maikkat ti tubbog na. Squeeze those sour fruits so as to remove their juice.

DINGO; PADINGO, v. /MANG-:-EN/ to take care of, to feed. Isu ti nangpadingo kadaydiay baboy. It was he who fed the pig.

DINGOEN, n. animals, especially hogs, raised for meat.

DIOS [f. Sp.], n. deity; god.

DIOS TI AGNGINA. Thank you.

DIOSA [f. Sp.], n. goddess.

DIOSEN]pl. DIDIOSEN], n. a minor deity; idol.

DIPAS; APAGDIPAS, adv. in a short time. Apagdipas nga naibus ti saba. The bananas were consumed in a short time. --syn. APAGKANITO.

DIPPIG, adj. /NAG-/ flat, compressed. --syn. DAPIL. n. a kind of banana which is flat in shape. It is usually boiled or fried before it is eaten.

DIPPIT, v. /-UM-:-AN/ to press near, crowd in. Saan ka nga dumippit kadagita agtartarabaho. Don't press near those who are working. /AG- + R2/ to be pressed together. Uray la nga agdidipiit ti tao ti kaadu ti nagbuya. The people were pressed together due to the great number of those who went to see the show. /MANG-:-EN/ to press, crush. Saan mo nga dippiten dayta badok. Don't crush my dress.

DIPUTADO [f. Sp.], n. representative, delegate. --syn. REPRESENTANTE.

DIRAM-US, v. /AG-/ to wash one's face. Apagriing mo agdiram-us ka. As soon as you wake up wash your face. /MANG-:-AN/ to wash the face (of someone). Diram-usam dayta kabsat mo intono makariing. Wash the face of your brother (or sister) when he (or she) wakes up.

DIREKSION [direksión; f. Sp.], n. direction.

DIREKTOR [direktór; f. Sp.], n. director.

DIREKTOR [dirɛktór; f. Sp.], n. director.

DIREKTORIO [dirɛktório; f. Sp.], n. directory.

DIR-I, v. /AG-/ to shout, shriek. Nagdir-i da nga namimpinsan. They shouted all at once.

DIRO, n. honey.

DISGRASIA [f. Sp.], n. accident, misfortune, evil.
v. /MANG-:-EN/ 1. to inflict injury on, to cause to have an accident or misfortune. 2. to assault or molest sexually. /MA-/ 1. to meet a misfortune or accident, to be injured. 2. to be assaulted or molested sexually.

DISIEMBRE [disiémbrɛ; f. Sp.], n. December.

DISIPLINA [f. Sp.], n. discipline.
DISIPLINADO, adj. disciplined.

DISIPULO [f. Sp.], n. disciple, follower.

DISKURSO [f. Sp.], n. discourse, speech, oration.
v. /AG-/ to make a speech or oration.

DISMAYA, v. /MANG-:-EN/ to upset, perturb, discompose, distress. /MA-/ to be upset, perturbed, discomposed, distressed.

DISNOG, v. /MANG-:-EN/ to hit with the fists; to punch.

DISSAAG, v. /-UM-/ to get down or off, alight, descend, dismount. /MANGI-:I-/ to take, put or place down from a higher place.

DISSAAR, v. /MANGI-:I-/ to put or place on the floor. Idissaar mo dayta ubing. Place that child on the floor.

DISSO, n. spot, site, region, place, location. Immuna nga impabuya da dagiti napintas nga disso ditoy Pilipinas. They first showed the beautiful spots in the Philippines.
v. /AG-/ to alight, to set (on a place), to land. Nagdisso diay billit ditoy abagak. The bird alighted on my shoulder. /MANGI-:I-/ to set down on, put or

place down on or in. Idissom ta kargam ditoy.
Put down your load here. /MANG-:-AN/ to set, put
or place down the load of. Idissoan nak man. Please
put down my load.

DISSOOR, v. /AG-/ to fall suddenly and heavily.
/MANGI-:I-/ to cause to fall suddenly and heavily,
to put down suddenly and heavily. Isu ti nangidissoor
ti dakkel nga kahon. It was he who put down the big
box suddenly and heavily.

DISTRITO [f. Sp.], n. district.

DISTURBO [f. Sp.], n. disturbance, nuisance, trouble.
v. /MANG-:-EN/ to disturb, bother, trouble. Saan
nak man nga disturboen ta adu ti trabahok. Please
don't disturb me for I have much work to do.

DITA, var. (dial.) of GITA.

DITA, adv. there: near the hearer. --var. IDTA.

DITOY, adv. here: hear the speaker. --var. IDTOY.

DIWIG, adj. 1. wry, twisted, contorted: said of the
mouth of a person, a jar, a basket, etc. 2. crooked,
not straight: said of the way an object is cut.
3. having a wry mouth: said of a person.

DLAW, see under DILLAW.

DODOL, n. a kind of pudding made of rice, either
ground or pounded into powder, GETTA and sugar.

DODOOMEN, see under DOOM.

DOKTOR [f. Sp.], n. doctor; physician. --syn. MANGNGAGAS.

DOKTRINA [f. Sp.], n. doctrine.

DOKUMENTO [dukuménto; f. Sp.], n. document.

DOMINGGO [f. Sp.], n. 1. Sunday. 2. week. --syn. LAWAS,
SEMANA.

DINOMINGGO, every week, weekly, by the week.

KADA DOMINGGO, every week, weekly.

DOMINGGO RAMOS, Palm Sunday.

DON [f. Sp.], n. 1. Sir; Mr.: a title of respect, used with the first name. 2. a distinguished man. --see SENYOR.

DONYA [f. Sp.], n. 1. Madam; Mrs.: a title of respect, used with the first name. 2. a distinguished woman. 3. rat, mouse. --see SENYORA.

DOOL, v. /MANG-:-AN/ to feed, especially by putting the food to the mouth.

DOOM, v. /AG-/ to eat or chew immature rice or uncooked rice after removing the husk. /MANG-:-EN/ to eat or chew: said of immature rice or uncooked rice after removing the husk.

DODOOMEN, adj. rice near maturity whose grain is already fully formed.

DOOY, adj. /NA-/ wanting attention, care or show of affection: usually said of children. Nakadodooy ka nga anak. You are a child who wants so much attention.

DOS [f. Sp.], num. two; 2. ALAS DOS, two o'clock. --syn. DUA.

DOSE [dose; f. Sp.], num. twelve; 12. ALAS DOSE, twelve o'clock. --syn. SANGAPULO KET DUA.

DRAM [f. Eng.], n. drum: a barrellike metal container for oil, etc.

DRAMA [f. Sp.], n. drama.

DUA, num. two; 2. --syn. DOS.

DUADUA, n. doubt, hesitation, indecision.
v. /AG-/ to be doubtful, hesitant, undecided.

DUAG, n. porch, balcony. --syn. BALKON.

DUAYA, n. lullaby. --syn. LALLAY.
v. /AG-/ to sing a lullaby. --var. DUAYYA.

DUAYYA, var. of DUAYA.

DUBLI [f. Sp.], adj. double.
v. /MANG-:-EN/ to repeat, to do, say, etc. again.
--syn. DUPAG.

DUDA, n. suspicion, doubt. --syn. ATAP, DUADUA,
SUSPITSA.
v. /AG-/ to have doubts, be doubtful, suspicious.

DUDUN, n. locust.

DUDUOGAN, adj. very old, decrepit.

DUGDUG, v. /MA-/ to decay, decompose, rot, dissolve,
melt.

DUGGONG, n. dried mucus.

DUGMAM, v. /MAI-/ to fall forward or prone. /MANGI-:I-/
to cause to fall forward or prone.

DUGMON, n. nest of a wild boar or a hog.
v. /AG-/ to wallow, to roll oneself about in an
indolent or ungainly manner. /MANG-:-EN/ to collect
or gather for making a DUGMON.

DUGUDUG, n. northeast wind.

DUGUL, n. a hump, protuberance, swelling; a node.
DUGULDUGUL, adj. full of humps or nodes.

DUGYOT, adj. /NAG-/ filthy, dirty, untidy. --syn.
BABOY 2.

DUKANG, adj. /NA-/ bulky, piled in a big heap.

DUKINAR, v. /MANG-:-EN/ or /MANG-:I-/ to strew around,
scatter. Apay nga dukinaren yo dagita lupot? Why are
you strewing around the clothes?

DUKIT, v. /MANGI-:I-/ to reopen a subject, to mention
again; to recall, to remind someone of. Saan mo nga
idukit dayta ta nalipatakon. Don't mention that
again for I have already forgotten it.

DUKLUS, v. /-UM-:-EN/ to attack, assault. Isu ti
dimmuklus kanyak. It was he who attacked me.

DUKO, v. /-UM-/ to recur: said of an ailment, hunger, etc. Madanaganak no dumuko ti sakit ko. I am worried lest my sickness recurs.

DUKOL, v. /-UM-/ to produce a hump disclosing its presence; to protrude, jut out. Ania dayta dumukol dita ikamen? What is that producing a hump on the mat?

DUKOT, v. /MA--AN/ to be worried, distressed, uneasy, perturbed, anxious, impatient. --syn. DANAG.

DUKYANG, n. a kind of small clam found in brooks and rivers.

DULANG, n. a low table.

DULDOG, adj. /NA-/ 1. dirty, filthy. --syn DUNGRIT. 2. dumb.

DULIAN; DULDULIANAN, n. difference, distinguishing trait. Awan duldulianan na. He has not a distinguishing trait.

DULIDUL, v. /MANGI-:I-/ to urge, press, insist, or force on (someone). Saan mo nga idulidul kanyak dayta saan ko nga kayat. Don't force on me that which I don't like.

DULIN, v. /AG-/ to hide, stay away from view. Agdulin ka ta biroken ka. You hide and I will look for you. /MANGI-:I-/ to hide or keep away from view (someone or something). --syn. LIMMENG. /AGI-:I-/ to put away, put aside (plates or bedding). Nagidulin kami kadagiti nagturogan mi. We put away our bedding.

DULING, adj. slightly cross-eyed. --syn. GILAB; see also PANGKIS.

DULLOOG, syn. (dial.) of GURROOD.

DUL-OK, v. /AG-/ to retch.

DULON, n. 1. limit, boundary. 2. landmark, monument.

DULPET, adj. /NA-/ dirty, filthy. --syn. RUGIT, DUNGRIT, DUGYOT.

DUMA, v. /AG-/ to differ, be different, dissimilar, unlike. Agduma ti pintas da. They differ in beauty.

DUMADUMA, adj. /NA-/ [with pl. subject] different, various, diverse. Nadumaduma nga nateng ti immula da. They planted different vegetables.

DUMDUMA or DADUMA, v. /MAI-/ to be regarded differently, to be distinguishable, to stand out. Naidumduma ti pintas na. Her beauty stood out.

DUMALAGA, n. pullet, young hen.

DUMTENG, = -UM- + DATENG.

DUMUDUM, v. /MAI-/ to fall prone.   --syn. DUGMAM.

DUMUG, v. /AG-/ to bend or incline the head, to bow; to look down. Nagdumug idi nakita nak. He looked down when he saw me.   /MANGI-:I-/ to bend or incline down, to cause to bend or incline down.

DUNOR, v. /MANG-:-EN/ to hurt, injure, bruise.   /MA-/ to be hurt, injured, bruised.   --syn. DANGER, DUNGIR.

DUNG-AW, v. /AG-/ to wail, lament, mourn aloud which may include singing a dirge.   /-AN/ to lament for (someone or something).

DUNGDUNG, n. a very large pot used for cooking rice, meat, vegetables, etc.

DUNGER, v. /AG-/ to shake the head forward and backward rapidly, to nod rapidly and continuously.   /MAI-/ to have the head drop forward involuntarily due to drowsiness, etc.   --syn. TANG-ED.
adj. /AG- + R2/ drowsy, sleepy.   --syn. DUNGSA.

DUNGET, v. /MANGI-:I-/ to cut near or close to the trunk, origin or beginning. Isu ti nangidunget ti sanga ti kayo. It was he who cut close the branches of the tree.

DUNGGIAL, v. /MANG-:-AN/ to hurt, injure.   /MA--AN/ to get hurt or injured.

DUNGIR, v. /MANG-:-AN/ to hurt, injure, bruise. /MA--AN/ to get hurt, injured or bruised. Saan ka nga

agtartaray ta dikanto madungiran. Don't run for you
might get hurt. --syn. DANGER, DUNOR.

DUNGNGO, n. beloved, dear one.
   adj. /NA-/ loving, devoted, affectionate.
   v. /MANG-:-EN/ to love deeply, dote on. Dungdungngoen
kanto unay unay. I shall love you very, very deeply.

DUNGPAR, v. /MANG-:-EN/ to bump, collide with. --syn.
DUNGSO, BANGDOL.

DUNGRIT, adj. /NA-/ filthy, dirty, untidy, especially
   on the face. --syn. DULPET, DUGYOT, DUNGRIT.

DUNGSA, v. /AG-/ to become drowsy or sleepy.
   adj. /AG- + R2/ drowsy, sleepy. /MAKA- + R1/
becoming drowsy, sleepy. --syn. DUNGER.

DUNGSO, v. /MANG-:-EN/ to crash (oneself or itself)
   into, to ram (oneself or itself) against, to cause
   (oneself) to collide with. Apay nga dinungso nak?
   Why did you collide with me? /MAI-/ to crash into,
   ram against, collide with. Naidungso diay lugan da
   ti poste. Their vehicle crashed into a post. --syn.
DUNGPAR.

DUNGSOL, n. blacksmith's hammer.
   v. /MANG-:-EN/ to hit with this. /MANGI-:I-/ to
   use as this (on someone or something), to hit
   (someone or something) with this.

DUOG, see DUDUOGAN.

DUPAG, v. /MANG-:-EN/ to repeat, do again, say again.
   Dupagem man tay imbagam kanyak? Will you please
   repeat what you said to me. --syn. DUBLI.

DUPAK, adj. flat, flattened. --syn. DIPPIG, DAPIL.

DUPIR, v. /MANG-:-EN/ to push, shove, move. Saan nak
   nga dupiren. Don't push me. /MANGI-:I-/ to push,
   shove or move to (a place). Idupir mo dayta bangko
   dita diding. Push that bench to that wall. --syn.
DURON.

DUPRAK, v. /MANG-:-EN/ to demolish, raze. Dupraken
   danto daytoy balay mi. They will raze our house.
   --syn. REBBA.

DUPUDUP, v. /AG- + R2/ to be, go or come together.
Nagdudupudup da nga immay gimmatang ti lupot. They
came together to buy clothes.

DUR-AS, adj. /NA-/ progressive, advanced, modern.

DUREK, n. pus in the ear.
   v. /AG-/ to have this: said of the ear.

DURI, n. spinal column, vertebral column, spine,
backbone.

DURIRI, adj. having protruding buttocks.
   v. /AG-/ to protrude the buttocks. /MANGI-:I-/ to
protrude the buttocks (of someone).

DURON, v. /AGI-, MANGI-:I-/ to push, shove. Saan nak
man nga iduron. Please don't push me. --syn. DUPIR.

DURSOK, adj. /NA-/ impulsive, fiery, ardent, fervent.

DURUDOR, n. spit (made of bamboo or iron).
   v. /MANG-:-EN/ 1. to put on a spit. 2. to poke
with a spit.

DUSA, n. punishment, chastisement, penalty.
   v. /MANG-:-EN/ to punish, chastise, discipline.

DUSAG, v. /MANG-:-EN/ to elbow, hit with the elbow.
Saan nak nga dusagen. Don't hit me with your elbow.

[1]DUTDUT, n. 1. feather. 2. body hair.
   adj. /-AN/ full of this.
   v. /MANG-:-AN/ to remove the feather of, to dress
(a chicken, etc.).

[2]DUTDUT, v. /MANG-:-EN/ to extract, draw out, pick off.

DUTOK, v. /MANG-:-AN/ to designate, appoint, assign.
Ni Pedro ti dinutokan mi nga presidente. We
appointed Peter president. /MA--AN/ to be appointed,
designated, assigned (as president, etc.). Isu ti
nadutokan nga presidente. He was appointed president.

DUYAW, adj. yellow, gold-colored; yellowish, golden.

DUYDUY, v. /MANG-:-EN/ to mash.

   DINUYDUY, n. a kind of sweet made of boiled ripe
   squash mixed with coconut meat and either sugar
   or salt.

DUYOG, n. 1. half of coconut shell used as dish. 2.
dish.

DUYOK, v. /-UM-/ to produce or cause a sharp or
stabbing pain. Dumuyok manen ti sakit na daytoy
tian ko. My stomach ailment is producing again a
sharp pain. /MANG-:-EN/ to stab or pierce.
Dinuyok na daydiay baboy ti natirad nga imuko.
He stabbed the pig with a sharp knife.

DUYOS, n. /PAG--AN/ that to which one's feelings,
sympathy, etc. flows. Isu ti pagduyosan ti riknak.
It is he to whom my feelings flow.

DYADS [f. Eng.], (rare) syn. of HUES.

DYANITOR, var. of DIANITOR.

DYIP [f. Eng.], n. jeep.

DYINWAIN, var. of DIENWAIN.

EBBAL, n. beriberi.
   v. /-UM-/ [= UMBAL] to swell, to become tumescent
or swollen due to beriberi or any internal injury.
Imbal ti rupa na. His face became swollen.

EBIDENSIA [εbidénsia; f. Sp.], n. evidence, proof,
sign.

EBKAS, v. /MANGI-:I-/ to say, pronounce, utter, express,
state. Isu ti mangiyebkas ti panggep na. It was he
who stated his aim. --syn. BAGA, KUNA.

EDAD [εdad; f. Sp.], n. age. --syn. TAWEN.
   v. /AG-/ to be as old as, to have as age. Agedad
ti lima nga tawen diay anak na. His child is five
years old. --var. IDAD.

EDITOR [εditor; f. Sp.], n. editor.

EHE [éhε; f. Sp.], n. axle of a cart with springs.

EHEKUTIBO [εhεkutibo; f. Sp.], n. executive.
DEPARTAMENTO EHEKUTIBO, executive department.

EKONOMIA [εkonomia; f. Sp.], n. economy.

EKSAMEN [εksamεn; f. Sp.], n. examination, test.
   v. /AG-/ to take a test or examination.
/MANG-:-EN/ to test or examine, to give a test or
examination to; to investigate, cross-examine.
Apay nga ek-eksamenen nak? Why are you cross-
examining me?

EKSPERTO [εkspεrto; f. Sp.], adj. skilled, expert,
proficient. Eksperto nga agluto diay baket ko.
My wife is expert in cooking.

EKTARIA [εktaria; f. Sp.], n. hectare.

ELEKSION [εlεksión; f. Sp.], n. election.
   v. /AG-/ to hold an election.
ELEKTOR [εlεktor; f. Sp.], n. elector, voter.   --syn.
BOTANTE.

ELEKTRISIAN [εlεktrisian; f. Eng.], n. electrician.
--syn. ELEKTRISISTA.

ELEKTRISIDAD [εlεktrisidád; f. Sp.], n. electricity.

ELEKTRISISTA [εlεktrisista; f. Sp.], n. electrician.
--syn. ELEKTRISIAN.

EL-EL, n. 1. any temporary mark, impression or line
produced on the skin by a string, rope or any other
object pressed on it. 2. groove at the base of the
glans penis.
   v. /MANG-:-AN/ to etch or engrave something on.
/MA--AN/ to have something etched or engraved on.

ELEMENTARIA [εlεmεntaria; f. Sp.], n. elementary
school.

ELLAY, v. /-UM-/ [= UMLAY] 1. to droop, to hang or
incline downward. 2. to droop, to become depressed
or weakened.

ELLEK, v. /-UM-/ [=UMLEK] to become mute or speechless
due to anger, happiness or sorrow; to laugh or weep
intensely producing only a slight sound.

EMBARGO [εmbargo; f. Sp.], v. /MANG-:-EN/ to seize,
commandeer.

EMMA, adj. /NA-/ kind, gentle, meek, mild, amiable,
affable.

EMMAK, v. /AG-/ to bleat, moo or low. Apay nga agemmak
diay baka? Why is the cow mooing?

EMPLEADO [εmplεado; f. Sp.], n. employee.

EMPLEO [εmplεo; f. Sp.], n. employment.

EMPLEO [εmplεo; f. Sp.], n. employment.
    v. /MANGI-:I-/ to employ, secure a job for. Awan
ti mayat nga mangiyempleo kenka no kasta ka nga
sadut. Nobody will want to employ you if you are
as lazy as that.

[1]-EN [pt. -IN-, prp. R1 + -EN, ptp. R1 + -IN-], a
passive verbalizing affix which generally places
the goal of the verb in focus or subject position.
It has various special meanings such as the
following. 1. to make or fashion into, transform
into, or equate with the thing referred to by the
(nominal) stem. Badoen da diay lupot nga inted mo.
They will make into a dress the cloth that you gave.
2. to use the thing referred to by the (nominal)
stem as tool or implement to do something. Imaen
tayo ti mangan. Let's use our hands to eat. 3. to
affect with the disease or ailment named by the
(nominal) stem. Burtongen ta ubing. That child has
chicken pox. 4. to be attacked, injured or eaten
by the animal, insect, pest, etc. named by the
(nominal)·stem. Kutonen dayta no dimo nga ingato.
That will be attacked by ants if you don't put it
up. 5. to consider as having the quality or
attribute indicated by the (adjectival) stem.
Pintasen da daytoy. They consider this beautiful.
6. to cause the number indicated by the (numeral)
stem to be reached. Sangapuloen da ti ited da kenka.
They will make ten what they are going to give you.

[2]-EN, adv. now, already; as of now; as of this or that moment. --var. -N (after a vowel), -ON (after pronoun -AK).

ENBELOP [ɛnbelop; f. Eng.], n. envelope. --syn. SOBRE.

ENERO [ɛnɛro; f. Sp.], n. January.

ENTABLADO [ɛntablado; f. Sp.], n. a raised platform, dais; stage.

EP-EP, v. /MANG-:-EN/ to mitigate, repress, check. Daytoy ti agas nga nag-ep-ep ti sakit ti ngipen ko. This is the medicine that repressed my toothache. /MA-/ to be repressed, checked, mitigated. Agasam dayta sugat mo tapno maep-ep ti sakit na. Apply medicine on your wound so that its pain will be repressed.

EPPES, adj. 1. without any content or substance: said especially of rice grains and the like. 2. empty, such as words.
    v. /-UM-/ [= UMPES] to subside, flatten: said of swellings.

ERBULARIO [ɛrbulario; f. Sp.], n. herb doctor, quack doctor.

ERGO [ɛrgo; f. Sp.], v. /AG-/ [with pl. subject] to argue, to dispute with each other, to debate. Apay nga agergo kayo? Why are you arguing? /MANG-:-EN/ to argue, dispute or debate with (someone). Apay nga ergoen nak? Why do you argue with me? --syn. DEBATE.

EROPLANO [ɛropláno; f. Sp.], n. airplane.
    v. /AG-/ to go by airplane.

ERRES, v. /-UM-/ [= UMRES] to shrink. Umres to dayta kayo inton magango. That wood will shrink when it is dry. --syn. ES-ES.

ERTENG, var. of IRTENG.

ES-ES, v. /AG-/ to shrink, contract. --syn. ERRES. /MANG-:-EN/ to put closer together, as pieces of boards after shrinking.

ESKANDALO [εskandálo; f. Sp.], n. scandal, trouble,
disturbance, uproar.
v. /AG-/ to create a scandal, trouble, disturbance
or uproar. Intayo man ketdi iyawid amangan no
ageskandalo manen sadiay. We'd better take him home
lest he creates trouble there again.

ESKOBA [εskóba; f. Sp.], n. brush for cleaning clothes,
shoes, etc.
v. /MANG-:-EN/ to brush.

ESKOLAR [εskolar; f. Eng.], n. scholar.

ESKRIBIENTE [εskribiénte; f. Sp.], n. clerk, scribe.

ESKUELA [εskuéla; f. Sp.], 1. school, schoolhouse.
--var. ESKUELAAN. 2. school child, pupil, student.
--syn. ESTUDIANTE.
v. /AG-/ to attend school.

ESKUELAAN [εskuεlaan; f. Sp.], var. of ESKUELA n. 1.

ESPESIAL [εspεsiál; f. Sp.], adj. special.

ESPESIALISTA [εspεsialista; f. Sp.], n. a specialist,
especially in medicine.

ESPIA [εspia], var. of ISPIA.

ESSEM, n. desire, wish.
adj. /NA-/ desirous; greedy, covetous, avaricious.
v. /MANG-:-AN/ [= ESMAN] to desire, long for; to
covet. Saan mo nga esman ti agkandidato. Don't
desire to become a candidate.

ESTADIUM [εstádium; f. Eng.], n. stadium.

ESTADO [εstádo; f. Sp.], n. state.

ESTADOS UNIDOS [f. Sp.], n. the United States of
America.

ESTANTE [εstante; f. Sp.], n. a showcase; a cabinet
to display and protect wares in a store.

ESTASION [εstasión; f. Sp.], n. station.

ESTATUA [εstátua; f. Sp.], n. statue.

ESTETSAID [εstetsaid; f. Eng.], adj. coming from or made in the United States of America.

ESTILO [εstílo; f. Sp.], n. style.
    adj. /NA-/ stylish, tasteful, elegant, refined.

ESTUDIANTE [εstudiantε; f. Sp.], n. student, pupil.
    --syn. ESKUELA n. 2.

ESTUDIO [εstudio; f. Eng.], n. studio.

ET-ET, adj. /NA-/ tight.
    v. /MANG-:-AN/ to tighten, to cause to become tight, to make tight. Saan mo nga et-etan ti galut dayta kahon. Don't make the binding of that box tight.

EUROPA [yorópa; f. Sp.], n. Europe.

FIESTA [fiεsta; f. Sp.], n. feast, festival. --var. PIESTA.

FILIPINA [f. Sp.], n. a female Filipino. --var. PILIPINA.

FILIPINAS [f. Sp.], n. the Philippines. --var. PILIPINAS.

FILIPINO [f. Sp.], n. a male Filipino. --var. PILIPINO.

GAAS, var. of GAS.

GABAY, v. /MA-/ to be late or tardy. Idardaras mo ti agrubbuat tapno ditay magabay. Get dressed in a hurry so that we won't be late.

GABBO, v. /AG-/ [with pl. subject] to wrestle, grapple.
    /MANG-:-EN/ to grapple and throw down (someone).

GABSOON, v. /MANG-:-EN/ or /MANGI-:I-/ to heap, pile up. Saan mo nga gabsoonen ti basura dita. Don't pile up the rubbish there.

GABUR, v. /MANG-:-AN/ to fill up, cover, dump something
on or into. Saan mo nga gaburan dayta kinalik nga
abut. Don't fill up that hole which I dug.

GABUT, v. /MANG-:-EN/ to pull up, uproot.   --syn. PAG-UT.

GABYON, n. hoe.
   v. /MANG-:-EN/ to dig or hit with a hoe.

GADDIL, n. scabies, itch, sarna; mange.
   v. /AG-, -EN/ to be affected with this.

GADGAD, v. /MANGI-:I-/ to whet, to cause to become
smooth, e.g. tools.   --syn. ASA.

GAED, v. /MANG-:-AN/ or /MANGI-:I-/ to do eagerly,
seriously, diligently. Igaed mo ti agadal. Study
diligently.

GAGA, adj. /NAG-/ coquettish, flirtatious.

GAGA, v. /MANGI-:I-/ to esteem, value, care for.
Igagam dayta karadkad mo. Value your prayer.

GAGA, v. /MANGI-:I-/ to protect from, lead away from.
Isu ti nangigaga kanyak ti disgrasia. It was he who
led me away from danger.

GAGANGAY, adj. usual, ordinary, normal. Dagiti nailanad
nga sarsarita ditoy nga libro, dagitay gagangay nga
aramiden dagiti ubbing iti inaldaw. The stories
written in this book are the usual things that
children do every day.

GAGAR, v. /AG-, MANG-:-EN/ to wish or desire strongly,
to crave. Aggagarak nga makakita kenkuana. I wish so
much to see her.

GAGARA, v. /MANG-:-EN/ to overuse, to use roughly.
/MA-/ to be overused, to be used roughly.

GAGARA, n. aim, purpose, mission.
   v. /MANG-:-EN/ or /MANGI-:I-/ to do on purpose, to
do intentionally or knowingly. Inggagara na nga sinaktan
diay ubing. He hurt the child on purpose.

GAGEM, n. intention, motive, object, aim, purpose.
--syn. GAGARA.

GAGET, adj. /NA-/ industrious, hard-working, assiduous,
diligent.

GAKAT, n. plan, proposal.
v. /MANG-:-EN/ or /MANGI-:I-/ to plan or propose to
do or carry out. Saan mo unay nga kaaduen ti igakat
mo nga trabaho. Don't plan on doing too much work.

GAKGAK, v. /AG-/ to croak: said of frogs; to produce a
similar sound.

GALASUGAS, adj. /NAG-/ obstinate, stubborn.

GALBA [f. Sp.], n. galvanized iron sheet used for
roofing. Nagatep ti galba ti balay mi. Our house is
roofed with galvanized iron sheets. --syn. YERO, SIM.

GALYERA [galyɛra; f. Sp.], n. cockpit, the place where
cockfighting is held. --syn. BULANGAN, SABUNGAN.

GALGALING, var. of GALING-GALING.

GALING-GALING, n. amulet, charm, talisman.

GALIP, v. /MANG-:-EN/ to slice, cut into slices.

GALIS, adj. /NA-/ slippery.
v. /MAI-/ to slip, to slide down.

GALUT, n. anything used for tying or binding. --SINGDAN.
v. /MANGI-:I-/ to tie, bind.

GALYETAS [f. Sp.], n. a kind of flat round bread.

GAMAT, n. 1. tendril. 2. arm of cuttlefish, octopus, etc.

GAMAY, v. /MANG-:-EN/ to knead, e.g. flour.

GAMED, v. /-UM-:-AN/ to desire, wish, want.

GAMENG, n. treasure, precious objects.

GAMER, v. /MANGI-:I-/ to mix, blend, mingle; to get
mixed up with. Saan mo nga igamer ta bagim ti kinadakes.
Don't get yourself mixed up with evil.

GAMGAM, v. /MANG-:-EN/ to desire, covet, e.g. a
position, an office, etc.

GAMIT, var. (dial.) of ARAMAT, USAR.

GAMMAL, v. /MANG-:-AN/ to grasp, to take hold of
firmly with the hand. Darasem nga gammalan dayta
tukak. Hurry up and grasp that frog. --var. (dial.)
GAMMAT.

GAMMAT, var. (dial.) of GAMMAL.

GAMPANG, var. of AMPANG.
MARAGAMPANG, adj. frivolous, silly.

GAMOLO, v. /MANG-:-EN/ to turn over, to turn to the
other side. Saan mo nga gamoloen dayta ikan. Don't
turn over that fish.

GAMOLO, v. /AG-:-EN/ to manage, take charge of, be
responsible for. Isu ti naggamolo ti sagana mi ti
piesta. It was he who took charge of our preparation
for the festival.

GAMUD, v. /-UM-, MANG-:-EN/ to bewitch: to influence
or affect especially injuriously by witchcraft. Saan
mo nga gamuden ni nanang ko. Don't bewitch my mother.
/MA-/ to be bewitched.

MANGGAGAMUD, n. a person who practices or is familiar
with witchcraft.

GAM-UD, v. /MANG-:-EN/ to obtain, get. Narigat nga
gam-uden ti dawdawatek kenkuana. It is hard to
obtain what I am asking from him.

GAM-UD, v. /-UM-:-AN/ often /MAKA-:MA--AN/ 1. to catch
up with, to arrive early for. Diak nga nagam-udan ti
rugi ·ti pabuya. I did not arrive early for the
beginning of the show. 2. to reach, go as far as.
Isu ti nakagam-ud ti ungto ti dalan. It was he who
reached the end of the road.

GAMUT, n. poison.
v. /MANG-:-EN/ to poison. /MA-/ to be poisoned.
adj. /MAKA-/ poisonous.

GANA, var. of GANANSI or GANAS.

GANAB   n. gain, benefit, profit.
   v. /-UM-:-EN/ to gain, to receive as benefit.

GANADOR, n. 1. a gamecock which has won at least
   twice. 2. an established winner.

GANAGAN, n. fertilizer. Agusar kami ti ganagan. We
   use fertilizers.

GANAKGAK, v. /AG-/ to produce a loud, deep and
   reverberating sound like that of bells.

GANANSIA, n. gain, profit.
   v. /AG-:-EN/ to gain, earn as profit.   --syn.
   GANAB.

GANAS, n. appetite, desire, urge to do something.
   Awan ti ganas ko nga mangan. I have no appetite
   to eat.
      adj. /NA-/ pleasing, satisfying, exciting.
   Naganas ti mangan iti panganan nga nadalimanek.
   It is pleasing to eat in an eating place that is
   clean and neat.
      v. /AG-:-EN/ to enjoy, relish; to find pleasure
   or satisfaction in doing. Nagganganas da nga
   nangan. They enjoyed eating.

GANAT, v. /AG-, -UM-/ to be in a hurry, to hasten.
   Gimmanat da nga nagawid. They hastened to go home.

GAN-AY, v. /MANG-:-EN/ or /MANGI-:I-/ to fix fibers
   ready for weaving.

GANAYGAY, n. spirit, vigor, enthusiasm. Awan ti
   ganaygay na nga nagsao. He talked without enthusiasm.
      v. /AG-, -UM-/ to be lively, full of life, full of
   spirit, full of enthusiasm.   /MANG-:-EN/ to animate,
   to cause to be lively, full of life, etc.

GANDAT, n. intention, project, plan. Napaay dayta nga
   gandat na. That plan of his was rebuffed.
      v. /MANG-:-EN/ to plan, design.

GANETGET, adj. /NA-/ careful, diligent, earnest,
   assiduous.   --syn. GAGET.

GANNA, n. defect, flaw, blemish.

GANNAET, n. alien, foreigner, stranger.

GANSA, n. gong.

GANSILIO [f. Sp.], n. crotchet, a hooked instrument used in crocheting.
   v. /AG-/ to crochet.   /MANG-:-EN/ to make by crocheting, to crochet.

GANSO, n. goose, gander.

GANSA, var. (dial.) of GANSO.

GANTING, v. /MANG-:-EN/ to weigh.
   GAGANTINGAN, n. any weighing machine.

GAGANTINGAN, see under GANTING.

GALAS, var. (dial.) of ¹ALAS.

GANUS, adj. /NA-/ 1. immature, unripe, green: said of fruits. 2. young, immature: said of persons.

GANOT, v. /MANG-:-EN/ to pull off forcibly. Ganotem amin nga kumalkalatkat dita alad. Pull off forcibly all those climbing on the fence.

GANGAT, v. /AG-, MANG-:-AN/ to light, set fire to, kindle. Saan na kayat nga gangtan diay silaw. He does not want to light the lamp.   /MANGI-:I-/ to light or kindle (a lamp, candle, etc.) with another light.

GANGO, v. /MA-/ to become dry: said of leaves.   --cf. MAGA.

GAO, v. /AG-/ to draw out food, especially rice, from the pot or pan in order to serve. Aggao kayon ta mangan tayon. Draw out the food so that we can eat. /MANG-:-EN/ to draw out (food) from the pot or pan in order to serve. Saan mo pay nga gaoen dayta ta saan pay nga naluto. Don't draw that out yet from the pot for it is not yet cooked.

GAPAGAP, v. /MANG-:-EN/ to cut into thin slices with a knife moving it as though using a saw. Gapagaem dayta nambaan. Cut that banana trunk into thin slices.

GAPAS, v. /AG-/ to harvest rice by cutting the upper part of the stalks where the grains are attached with a sickle. /MANG-:-EN/ 1. to cut the top part of (rice or any other plant) with a sickle. 2. to cut or attack with a sickle.

GAPO, n. cause, motive, reason, origin.
    v. /AG-/ to come from. Naggapoak idiay simbaan. I came from the church. /MANG-/ to begin, set about, start; to be about to. Manggapoak nga maturogen. I am about to go to sleep. /MANGI-:I-/ to do something for the sake of (someone). /MAI-/ to be done because of, for the sake of, on account of.

    GAPO TA, conj. because, since, inasmuch as, for, as.

    NAGGAPPOAM? Where have you been? or: Where did you come from? - a usual greeting equivalent to: How are you?

GARADGAD, n. a light scratch. --GARUMYAD.
    v. /MAKA-:MA--AN/ to be scratched lightly.

GARADUGUD, v. /AG-/ to produce a gurgling or rumbling sound. Aggaradugud ti tian ko. My stomach is producing a rumbling sound.

GARAIGI, v. /AG-/ 1. to neigh, whinny. 2. to laugh like a horse.
    n. a neigh, a whinny.

GARAKGAK, v. /AG-/ to laugh loudly.
    n. this kind of laugh.

GARAMI, n. rice stalk, straw.

GARAMPANG, syn. of AMPANG.

GARAMPINGAT, syn. of AMPANG.

GARAMUGAM, adj. /NAG-/ always moving about and touching things. --syn. GARAWIGAW.

GARANTIA [f. Sp.], n. guarantee.
   v. /MANG-:-AN/ to guarantee.
   GARANTISADO, adj. guaranteed.

GARANGOGONG, v. /AG-/ to slide down into a pit, hole,
   etc. /MANGI-:I-/ to slide (something) down into a
   pit, hole, etc. Igarangogong mo dayta basura dita
   abut. You slide down the garbage into the hole.

GARAPON, n. a glass jar where bread, sugar, etc. are
   stored.

GARAW, v. /AG-/ to move, stir. Matnag ka no aggaraw ka.
   You will fall if you move. /-UM-, MANG-:-EN/ 1. to
   move, to change the place or position of. 2. to touch,
   molest. Patayen ka no garawem diay balasang ko. I will
   kill you if you molest my daughter.
      adj. /NA-/ 1. always moving or stirring. 2. always
   touching someone.

GARAWIGAW, adj. /NA-/ syn. of GARAMUGAM.

GARES, adj. /NA-/ soft, watery and friable: said
   especially of squashes, which are considered not very
   tasty to eat. --ant. KINTAL.

GARET, see GARGARET.

GARISON [f. Eng.], n. garrison.

GARGARET, n. pl. furniture, jewels; tools, implements,
   utensils; household belongings.

GARGARI, v. /-UM-, MANG-:-EN/ to incite, provoke, goad,
   stir up. Saan mo nga gargarien dayta pusa. Don't
   incite that cat.

GARI, see GARGARI.

GARIT, adj. striped, streaked.

GARRETA, n. a small store.

GARUGAD, n. file (a tool).
   v. /AG-/ to use a file; to rub, smooth or cut away
   something with a file. /MANG-:-EN/ to rub, smooth
   or cut away with a file; to file.

GARUT, v. /-UM-/ to break loose by breaking or untying
its leash or pulling out the tether: said of animals,
chickens, etc. on a leash. /MAKA-/ to succeed in
breaking loose by breaking or untying its leash.
Igalut mo nga nasayaat dayta manok tapno saan nga
makagarut. Tie that chicken well so that it won't
succeed in breaking loose. /MANG-:-EN/ to snap or
break suddenly a string, thread, etc.).

GAS, n. kerosene.   --var. GAAS.

GASAGAS, v. /MANG-:-EN/ to sift. Ginasagas na diay
bellaay. He sifted the flour.

GASANG, adj. /NA-/ hot: producing a burning sensation
in the mouth, throat, etc.; pungent; piquant; biting.

GASAT, n. luck, fortune; destiny, fate; chance.
adj. /NA-/ lucky, fortunate.

NAIGASATAN or NAPAGASATAN, adj. blessed with good
luck or fortune.

GASANG-GASAT, v. /MAKI-/ to take chances, take the
risk, go on an adventure. Mapanak makigasang-gasat
diay Manila. I will go take my chances in Manila.

GASGAS, v. /MANG-:-EN/ to wear off by rubbing; to
scrape. /MA-/ to be worn off by rubbing or friction.

GASOLINA [f. Sp.], n. gasoline.

GASTO [f. Sp.], v. /-UM-:-EN/ to spend. Mano ti gastoen
yo nga mapan idiay Manila? How much will you spend to
go to Manila?   --cf. GASTOS.

GASTOS [f. Sp.], n. expense, cost, expenditure. Ti
gastoen nga agpaaramid iti kasilyas maksay iti
gastos nga pagpaagas. What will be spent in having
a toilet made is less than the medical expenses.
--cf. GASTO.

GASUT, num. hundreds, times one hundred. SANGAGASUT,
one hundred; DUA GASUT, two hundred; TALLO GASUT,
three hundred.

GATAD, n. price, value.   --syn. PRESIO, BALOR, PATEG.
v. /MANG-:-AN/ to set a price or value on, to

appraise. /MA--AN/ to be priced or valued, to be
appraised. --syn. PABALOR.

GATANG, v. /-UM-, MANG-:-EN/ to buy, purchase.
n. purchase; anything obtained by buying. Adda pay
baul nga gatang pay laeng da lolo ken lola. There is
also a chest which was bought by grandfather and
grandmother.

GATAS, n. milk.
v. /AG-, MANG-:-AN/ 1. to milk. Kugtaran na ka
dayta nuang no padasem nga gatasan. That water
buffalo will kick you if you try to milk her. 2. to
put or add milk to.

MARAGATAS, adj. resembling milk.

GATEL, adj. /NA-/ 1. itchy. 2. lustful, hot.
v. /AG-/ 1. to be itchy. 2. to be hot.

GATUD, v. /AG-, MANG-:-EN/ to cull, pick, pluck, gather
with fingers. Mabalin nga gatuden dagidiay tabakon.
The tobacco plants can be culled now.

GATUT, adj. /NA-/ rash, precipitate, overhasty,
impatient; impulsive.

GAUD, n. oar, paddle.

GAWANG, v. /MANG-:-AN/ to put a hole or holes on, to
perforate. /MA--AN/ to be perforated.

GAWANGGAWANG, adj. full of holes.

GAWAT, n. any period during which food is scarce; a
period of drought.

GAW-AT, v. /-UM-, MANG-:-EN/ to reach for; to thrust
out or extend the hand to get (something).

GAWAWA, v. /-UM-:-EN/ to ask for, request (something)
earnestly or urgently. Isu ti gumawgawawa ti tulong.
It is he who is asking for help urgently.

GAWAY, v. /MAKA-/ to be able to manage; to be able to
conduct or direct affairs, carry on business; to
contrive to get along, succeed in handling matters.
Dika makagaway nga meymeysa. You cannot manage alone.

GAWED, var. of GAWWED.

GAWGAW, v. /AG-, MANG-:-AN/ to rinse in water.   --syn. BEGNAW, BELNAS.

GAWGAW, n. starch, especially corn starch, used primarily for starching clothes.

GAWID, v. /MANGI-:I-/ to restrain, hold back. No diko la nga inggawid, pinatay na ka kuma. If only I did not restrain him he would have killed you.

GAW-IS, v. /MANG-:-EN/ to reach for and cut or hit with a glancing blow.

GAWWED, n. betel leaf.   --var. GAWED.

GAY-AB, v. /MANG-:-EN/ to tear, rip by pulling violently. Ginay-ab na diay bado na. He ripped his clothes.

GAYABANG, v. /MA-/ to be torn into shreds, to be shredded.

GAYAD, adj. /NA-/ sufficiently long: said of garments, eaves, etc.

GAYADAN, n. hem. Impunas na ti gayadan ti bado na iti mata na. She wiped her eyes with the hem of her dress.

GAYAGAY, v. /AG-, MANG-:-EN/ or /MANGI-:I-/ to initiate, begin; to urge. Ingayagay na ti pannakabangon ti escuela. He initiated the construction of a schoolhouse.

GAYAM, adv. a particle expressing mild surprise or wonder about something unexpected or not previously known. Isu gayam ti gobernador tayo. I did not know he is our governor.

GAYAMAN, n. centipede.

GAYANG, n. spear, lance, arrow.   --syn. PIKA.

GAY-AT, v. /MANG-:-EN/ to reach for to grasp, to thrust out or extend the hand to grasp (something). Idi gay-aten na ti imak, nagtarayak a dagus. When he

reached for my hand to grasp it, I ran away at once.
--syn. GAW-AT.

GAY-AT, v. /MANG-:-EN/ or /MANGI-:I-/ to try to do,
start to do. Igay-at ko kuma ti agawiden ngem adu
pay la ti tao. I started to go home but there were
still many people.

GAYYEM, n. [pl. GAGAYYEM] friend.
    v. /MAKI-/ to befriend, to be a friend of (someone).
Kayat ko ti makigayyem kenka. I want to be your
friend.

    AGGAYYEM, n. [pl. AGGAGAYYEM] mutual friends.
    Aggayyem kami laeng. We are only mutual friends.

GEBGEB, v. /MAKA-:MA--AN/ to be able to do or manage.
Diak nga magebgeban amin nga trabahok. I cannot do
all my work. --syn. see GAWAY.

GEDGED, v. /MANG-:-EN/ to cut with a knife but with
motions as though using a saw. Gedgedem ta tengnged
ti manok. Cut the neck of that chicken.

GEKGEK, v. /-UM-/ to go deep inside (a forest, a cave,
etc.). Saan kay nga gumekgek ta dikay to mapukaw.
Don't go deep inside lest you get lost.

GELGEL, v. /MANG-:-EN/ or /MANGI-:I-/ to rub with the
hands, as when handwashing clothes.

GEMGEM, n. fist.
    v. /MANG-:-AN/ to hold, grasp, grip, clasp, clutch.
Isu ti nanggemgem toy imak. It was he who grasped my
hand. --syn. IGGEM.

GEPPAS, v. /MANG-:-EN/ to cut with rough sweeping
strokes, to slash. Geppasem amin nga ruot dita.
Slash all the grasses there.

GERGER, n. line, groove. --var. GETGET.

GERILYA [gɛrília; f. Eng.], n. guerilla.

GERRA [gɛrra; f. Sp.], n. war. --syn. GUBAT.
    v. /AG-/ to have a war.

GERRET, n. slice.
v. /MANG-:-EN/ to slice; to cut into slices.

GESSAT, v. /MANG-:-EN/ to cause (a strong, etc.) to
snap or break suddenly; to cut. Gessatem dayta sagut
nga agbitbitin dita. Cut that fiber that is hanging
there. /MA-/ to snap or break suddenly. Nagsat ti
tali nga pinaggalut ko. The string which I used to
tie something snapped.

MAGSAT TI ANGES or MAGSAT TI BIAG, to die, expire.

GETGET, var. of GERGER.

GETTA, n. coconut milk obtained by pressing the grated
coconut meat.

GINETTAAN, n. a native cake usually eaten for
mid-afternoon snacks. It is made of sliced GABI,
bananas, sweet potatoes with coconut milk (GETTA)
and sugar. This preparation is boiled until the
coconut milk thickens on top.

GETTEB, v. /MANG-:-EN/ to snap, break or cut (a string,
thread, etc.). Saan mo nga getteben ta lubid ti ullaw
ko. Don't cut the string of my kite.

GETTENG, n. scissors, shears. --syn. KARTIB.
v. /MANG-:-EN/ to cut with scissors.

GIAN, v. /AG-/ to stay, reside, live, dwell. Aggian ka
dita. You stay there. --cf. AYAN.

GIBAK, n. potsherd. --see RIBAK.

GIBUS, n. end, conclusion, termination, ending.

GIDDAN, v. /AG-/ [with pl. subject] to do something at
the same time. Aggiddan kayo nga mangan. You eat
at the same time. /-UM-:-AN/ to do something at the
same time with (someone). /MANGI-:I-/ to do
(something) simultaneously with something.

GIDDIAT, n. difference.
v. /AG-/ [with pl. subject] to be different, unlike,
distinct, unequal. --var. GIDIAT.

GIDDATO, v. /MANGI-:I-/ to do instantly or immediately.
Igiddato na ti agawid. He will go home instantly.

GIDGID, v. /AG-/ to rub one's body against (something
or someone). /MANGI-:I-/ to rub (one's body)
against (something or someone). Inggidgid diay
baboy ti bagi na diay abulog. The pig rubbed its
body against the house fence. --var. GIDIGID.

GIDIAT, var. of GIDDIAT.

GIDIGID, var. of GIDGID.

GIEM, adv. a particle expressing cautious confidence
or uncertainty. Matay giem dayta immulam. It seems
that what you planted will die.

GILAB, adj. having an eye defect in which the lower
eyelid is pulled down.

GIL-AYAB, v. /-UM-/ to burst into flame, to blaze.
Gimmil-ayab diay apoy itay naanginan. The fire
burst into flame when the wind blew into it.

GILING, v. /AG-, MANG-:-EN/ to grind.
GILINGAN, n. grinder, mill.

GIMONG, n. community, society, group, crowd; any
gathering of people.

GINA, v. /MANGI-:I-/ to mind, bother about, pay
attention to, attend to, take care of. Saan na
nga ingginggina ti nasakit na isu nga kimmaro.
He did not attend to his sickness, that's why
it became worse.

GIN-AWA, n. relief, comfort, ease.
adj. /NA-/ comfortable, full of ease, pleasant.
v. /-UM-/ 1. to become comfortable or pleasant.
Sapay kuma ta gumin-awa met ti biag tayo. I hope
our life will become comfortable. 2. to improve
or feel better: said of a sick person.

GINGINED, n. earthquake.
v. /AG-/ to have an earthquake.

GIRAY, v. /MA-/ to be tilted, slanted, inclined.

GIRGIR, v. /MANGI-:I-/ to be careful about, to take care of. No dimo nga igirgir ta nasakit mo, kumaronto. If you don't take care of your sickness it will get worse.

GIRIT, n. a hide-and-seek game.   --syn. SITSITBONG, KIRIKIT.
   v. /AG-/ [with pl. subject], to play this game.

GISGIS, v. /MANG-:-EN/ to tear up. Saan mo nga gisgisen dayta peryodiko. Don't tear up that newspaper.   --syn. PIGIS.

GISIGIS, n. toothbrush.   --syn. SIPILYO.
   v. /AG-/ to brush one's teeth.   /MANG-:-EN/ to brush, especially the teeth.

GISLA, n. a piece of split bamboo.   --syn. BISLAK.
   v. /MANG-:-EN/ to split into small pieces. Gislaem dayta kawayan. Split that bamboo.

GISTAY, short for NAGISTAYAN.

GITA, n. 1. venom of snakes.   --var. (dial.) DITA. 2. poison in general.

GITA, adj. /NA-/ oily to the taste, e.g. nuts.

GITARA [f. Sp.], n. guitar.

GIWANG, v. /MANG-:-AN/ to make an opening or hole through; to make a breach in.   --syn. ABUT.

GLAB [f. Eng.], n. a fighting glove.

GLORIA [f. Sp.], n. 1. heaven.   --syn. LANGIT. 2. a girl's name.

GOBERNADOR [gobεrnador; f. Sp.], n. governor.

GOBIERNO [gobiεrno; f. Sp.], n. government.

GRADO [f. Sp.], n. 1. grade in school; a class organized for the work of a particular year of a school course. 2. a mark indicating a degree of accomplishment in school. 3. a position in a scale of ranks or qualities
   v. /MANG-:-EN/ to grade, sort, arrange in a scale or ranks of qualities.

GRASA [f. Sp.], n. grease.

GRASIA [f. Sp.], n. grace.

GRIEGO [griégo; f. Sp.], n. Greek

GRIPO [f. Sp.], n. faucet, tap.

GRUPO [f. Sp.], n. group.

GUAPO [f. Sp.], adj. /NAG-/ handsome, good-looking.
   --syn. NAPINTAS.

GUARDIA [f. Sp.], n. guard, watch.   --syn. BANTAY.
   v. /AG-/ to stand guard.   /MANG-:-AN/ to guard,
   watch.

GUBAL, v. /AG-/ [with pl. subject] to wrestle, grapple.
   /MANG-:-EN/ to wrestle, grapple.   /MAKI-:KA-/ to
   wrestle with, grapple with.   --syn. GABBO.

[1]GUBANG, adj. /-IMM-/ burnt, charred.

[2]GUBANG, adj. /NA-/ coarse, unpolished: said of the
   texture of cloth, skin, etc.

GUBAT, n. war, fight, battle.   --syn. GERRA.
   v. /AG-/ to have a war, fight, battle.

GUBBUAY, v. /AG-/ to originate, rise, issue, spring
   from. Aggabbuay ti danum dita ringgat. Water will
   issue from that crack.

GUBSANG, adj. /NA-/ 1. coarse, rough (to the touch).
   2. coarse, ill-mannered: said of a person's action
   or manner.

GUDAS, v. /MANG-:-EN/ to put an end to, get rid of,
   eradicate, stop. Ginudas na ti nasayaat nga
   panaggagayyem da. He put to an end their
   beautiful friendship.

GUDDUA, v. /AG-/ [with dual subject] to share, to
   divide between themselves. Agguddua kayo ti maysa
   nga mansanas. Divide between yourselves one apple.
   /MANG-:-EN/ to divide into two.

KAGUDDUA, n. one-half.

GUDDUAGUDDUA, v. /MANG-:-EN/ to divide into several parts or shares. Ginudduaguddua da dagiti dagdaga da. They divided into their lands into several parts.

GUDGUD, n. herpes; an itchy skin disease; mange. v. /AG-/ to be affected with this.

GUGOT, n. gum: the tissue that surrounds the necks of teeth and covers the alveolar parts of the jaw.

GUKAYAB, n. cave; grotto.   --syn. RUKIB.

GULAMAN, n. AGAR-AGAR.   --var. GURAMAN.

GULGOL, n. a kind of tree whose macerated bark is used to make hair shampoo. v. /AG-/ to wash the hair with this shampoo; to shampoo the hair.   /MANG-:-AN/ to wash with shampoo, to shampoo (the hair).

GULIB, adj. /NA-/ traitorous, treacherous, disloyal, unfaithful.

GULLUONG, v. /-UM-/ [= GUMLUONG] to resound, reverberate. Gumluong ti timek na nga nagdiskurso. His voice resounded when he delivered a speech.

GULO, n. disorder, uprising, revolt, rebellion. adj. /NA-/ disorderly, confused and noisy. v. /AG-/ to create disorder, confusion and noise. /MANG-:-EN/ to put into disorder. Saan mo nga guloen daytoy grupo mi. Don't put our group into disorder.

GUMA [f. Sp.], n. 1. rubber. 2. rubber tire.

GUMAMELA, n. hibiscus.   --syn. KAYANGA.

GUMES, v. /MANGI-:I-/ to wash (clothes, etc.) by squeezing in water.

GUMINTANG, v. /AG-/ to move the arms and hands in different directions as in native dances. /MANGI-:I-/ to move (the arms and hands) as in native dances.

GUMLUONG, = -UM- + GULLUONG.

GUNAM; GUNAMGUNAM, v. /MANGI-:I-/ to express, make
known, show. Inggunamgunam na ti ipapan mi. He made
known our departure.

GUNAY, v. /AG-/ to move, stir. Saan ka nga aggungunay.
Don't move. /MANG-:-EN/ to move, stir (someone or
something). Saan nak nga gunayen. Don't move me.
--syn. GARAW.

GUNDAWAY, n. 1. privilege, prerogative, distinction.
2. superiority. 3. chance, occasion.
v. /MA--AN/ to be given the privilege or
distinction (to do something).

GUNNOT, n. fiber.
adj. /NA-/ or /-AN/ fibrous, full of fibers.
v. /MANG-:-EN/ to pull by combing through with
the fingers.

GUN-OD, v. /MANG-:-EN/ to obtain, get acquire; to
earn, win. Masapul nga gun-odem ti kangatoan nga
grado. It is necessary that you obtain the highest
grade.

GUNGGON, v. /MANG-:-EN/ to shake, to cause to quake,
to rock. Saan mo nga gunggonen toy balay mi ta
dinto marba. Don't rock our house lest it collapse.

GUNGGUNA, n. reward, pay; prize.
v. /MANG-:-AN/ to reward, recompense, pay.
Gunggunaan na kanto ti Dios no naasi ka ti padam
nga tao. God will reward you if you are merciful
to your fellow men. --var. GONGGONA.

GUNGGONG, adj. /NAG-/ stupid, ignorant, silly.

GUNGLO, n. association. --syn. ASOSASION.

[1]GUPED, v. /MANG-:-EN/ [= GUPDEN] to cut breadthwise
(any elongated object), to cut shorter. Gupden na
dayta kawayan. He will cut that bamboo shorter.

[2]GUPED, n. obstruction. --syn. LAPPED.
v. /MAKA-/ to obstruct, hinder; stop. Dayta ti
nakaguped ti panagasawa da. That obstructed their
getting married.

GUPUGOP, v. /MANG-:-EN/ to saw, cut with a saw. --syn. RAGADI.

GUPUNG, v. /MANG-:-EN/ to cut off with a knife, a saw, etc. --syn. [1]GUPED.

GURA, n. anger, irritation; hate, dislike.
   v. /-UM-/ to become angry. /-UM-:-EN/ to be angered, annoyed or irritated by (something said or done), to hate or dislike (something said or done). /MA-:KA-/ to be angered, annoyed or irritated by (someone or something), to hate or dislike (someone or something).

GURAMAN, var. of GULAMAN.

GURGUR, v. /MANG-:-AN/ to refine; to reduce to a pure state; to free from impurities: said of metals. Ginurguran na daydiay balitok. He refined the gold.

GURGURMUT, n. roots of the BALLAIBA which are eaten.

GURIGOR, n. fever.
   v. /AG-/ to have a fever especially due to an infection.

GURMUT, see GURGURMUT.

GURONG, n. the lower part of the leg between the knee and the ankle.

GURRUOD, n. thunder.
   v. /AG-/ to thunder, to produce a thunder.

GUSAB, adj. with cut lips, having the lips cut.
   v. /MANG-:-AN/ to cut the lips (of someone), to cause the lips (of someone) to be cut. /MA--AN/ to have one's lips cut through an accident.

GUSING, adj. 1. harelipped. 2. chipped or notched at the rim: said of pots, plates, etc.

GUSO; GUSOGUSO, adj. /NA-/ disorderly, disarrayed, dishevelled, tousled.
   v. /MANG-:-EN/ to cause to become disorderly, disarrayed, dishevelled, tousled.

GUSUD, v. /MANG-:-EN/ to spear, to hit with a spear or
a similar instrument. /MANGI-:I-/ to use to spear
with, to spear into.

GUSUGUS, v. /MANG-:-AN/ to rub. Gusugusan na dayta
tabla ti nabasa nga lupot. He will rub that board
with a wet piece of cloth. /MANGI-:I-/ to rub on
(something). Igusugus na dayta nabasa nga lupot dita
tabla. He will rub that wet piece of cloth on that
board.

GUTAB, v. /MANG-:-AN/ 1. to chip the rim of the mouth
or edge of (a plate, a bowl, a coconut shell, etc.).
Sino ti nanggutab ditoy ungot? Who chipped this
coconut shell? 2. to cut (hair) unevenly. /MA--AN/
to be chipped along the rim or edge.
adj. not smoothly cut, especially hair.

GUTAD, v. /-UM-, MANG-:-EN/ to pull with a quick sharp
motion, to pull with a flick or a jerk.

GUTOK; GUTOKGUTOK, v. /AG-/ to throb, palpitate,
pulsate.

GUTTA, v. /MANG-:-EN/ to pull hard especially with a
jerk, to tug.

GUTUGUT, v. /MANG-:-EN/ to importune, incite, provoke,
spur.

GUYAB, v. /AG-/ to thrust or stick out the tongue at,
to make faces at which includes sticking the tongue
out. Ni Rosa ti nangguyab kanyak. It was Rose who
made faces at me.

GUYUD, v. /-UM-, MANG-:-EN/ to pull, tug, drag.

GUYUGUY, v. /MANG-:-EN/ to invite, attract, entice,
allure. Guyuguyen nak nga mangan dayta naimas nga
sida. That delicious sidedish entices me to eat.
adj. /MAKA-/ inviting, attractive, enticing,
alluring.

HAAN, var. of SAAN.

HAISKUL [f. Eng.], n. high school.

HAMON [f. Sp.], n. ham.

HANMAN, var. of SANMAN.

HAPON [f. Sp.], n. 1. Japan. 2. Japanese.
  HAPONESA [haponɛsa; f. Sp.], n. a female Japanese.

HARDIN [f. Sp.], n. garden.

HENERAL [hɛnɛral; f. Sp.], n. general.

HEPE [hɛpɛ; f. Sp.], n. chief, chief of police.
  --syn. TSIP.

HERPIN [hɛrpin; f. Eng.], n. hairpin. --syn. ARIPIT.

HIGANTE [higantɛ; f. Sp.], n. a giant.

HIMNO [f. Sp.], n. hymn, anthem.
  HIMNO FILIPINO, Philippine (National) Anthem.

HOLEN [holɛn; f. Eng.], n. 1. a marble, a little ball
  made of a hard substance (usually glass) used in
  various games. 2. a children's game played with
  marbles. --syn. BULINTIK.
    v. /AG-/ [with pl. subject] to play marbles.
  /MAKI-:KA-/ to play marbles with. --syn. BULINTIK.
  /MANGI-:I-/ in a game of marbles, to roll or toss
  a marble into a hole.

HUDIO [f. Sp.], n. a Jew.

HUEBES [huɛbɛs; f. Sp.], n. Thursday.

HUES [huɛs; f. Sp.], n. judge. --syn. UKOM.

HUISIO [f. Sp.], n. arraignment.

HUK [f. Tag.], n. an outlawed organization operating
  principally in Central Luzon.

HULYO [f. Sp.], n. July.

HUNTA [f. Sp.], n. board.

HUNYO [f. Sp.], n. June.

HURADO [f. Sp.], n. 1. jury. 2. board of judges.

HURNO [f. Sp.], n. any of several kinds of containers in which cake is baked.

HUSGADO [f. Sp.], n. court of justice.

HUSTISIA [f. Sp.], n. justice.

HUSTO, var. of KUSTO.

I [a prolonged shrill sound], interj. an exclamation expressing surprise and wonder.

[1]I- [pt. IN-, prp. I- + R1, ptp. IN- + R1], a passive verbalizing affix that generally places in focus or subject position the goal of the action expressed by the verb, or that with which the action is done or which effect the performance of the action. --var. [1]IY- [1]Y- (before a vowel). --see -EN.

[2]I- [pt. IN-, prp. I- + R1, ptp. IN- + R1], a passive verbalizing affix which places the cause or agent of the action expressed by the verb in focus or subject position. Daytoy ti ipatay mo. This is what you will die of. --var. [1]IY-, [1]Y-.

[3]I- (+ R2), a nominalizing affix which combines with certain verb stems to form verbal nouns with the meaning: process or manner of the action expressed by the verb stem. --var. [2]IY- (+ R2), [2]Y- (+ R2) (before a vowel).

I--AN [pt. IN--AN, prp. I- + R1 + -AN, ptp. IN- + R1 + -AN], a passive verbalizing affix which places in focus or subject position the beneficiary of the action expressed by the verb. Idawatan nak ti asin. You ask for some salt for me.

IBAR, v. /AG-/ to incline, bend, sway.

IBAR-IBAR, v. /AG-/ to totter, stagger, sway, wobble as in walking. Agibar-ibar diay nabartek. The drunk person is tottering.

IBBAT, v. /-UM-/ to stop holding onto something with the hand or hands. /MANGI-:I-/ to release one's hold of, to let go, fall, drop, etc. by releasing one's hold of.

IBBUNG, adj. spoiled: said of eggs.
v. /AG-/ to become spoiled as an egg or as like an egg. Nagibbung amin nga itlog ti manok da. All the eggs of their hen became spoiled.

IBIT, v. /AG-/ to cry, weep, whimper.   --syn. SANGIT.

IBLENG, v. /AG-/ to have diarrhea, to have loose bowel movement.   --syn. see TAKKI, BURIS.

IBO, n. awn, especially that of rice.

IBTUR, v. /MANG-:-EN, -AN/ to tolerate, endure, bear, suffer, withstand. Ibturem ti sakit na. Bear its pain.

IBUS, v. /MANG-:-EN/ to consume completely, to dispose of completely, to finish; to eat all. Inibus na diay sida. He ate all the sidedish. /MA-/ to be completely consumed or disposed of; to be completely eaten. Naibus ti sida. The sidedish was completely consumed.

IDA, pron. they, them (in passive sentences): the enclitic nominative of ISUDA.   --see DA.

IDAD, var. of EDAD.

IDDA, v. /AG-/ to lie down, recline. /MANG-:-EN/ to cause to lie down, be prostrate; to lay down in horizontal position, to lay prostrate.

KAIDDA, n. that with whom one sleeps, that sleeping by the side of oneself.
v. /MAKI-:KA-/ to sleep with, to sleep by the side of /AG-/ [with pl. subject] to sleep side by side, to sleep together.

IDDAL, var. of IKDAL.

IDDEP, v. /AG-, MANG-:-EN/ to put off, extinguish (light). Sino ti nangiddep ti silaw ko? Who put off my light? /MA-/ to be put off, extinguished.
--var. DEDDEP.

IDEA [idɛa; f. Sp.], n. idea.

[1]IDI, v. /MANGI-:I-/ to give up, leave off; to stop from doing. Inidian na ti panaginum. He stopped drinking (alcoholic beverages).

[2]IDI, adv. in the distant or remote past, formerly, then. Pulis idi daydi tatang ko. My father then was a policeman.

[3]IDI, prep. last, the past (night, morning, etc.): forms prepositional phrases expressing past time.

IDI KALMAN, yesterday.

IDI UN-UNANA, in the beginning.

[4]IDI, conj. when (in the remote past). Matmaturogak idi immay kayo. I was sleeping when you came.

[5]IDI, form of DAYDI postposed to a noun expressing emphasis.

[1]IDIAY, dem. there, yonder. --var. DIAY, DIDIAY.

[2]IDIAY, prep. to, in, at, from, toward, away from. --var. DIAY.

[3]IDIAY, form of DAYDIAY postposed to a noun expressing emphasis.

IDINTO TA, whereas (past). --see ITA TA.

IDNA, v. /MAKA-/ to be quiet, calm, still, tranquil. Diak nga makaidna ti danag ko. I cannot keep calm on account of my worry.

IDOLO [f. Sp.], n. idol, hero.

IDOS, v. /MANG-:-EN/ to spoon; to take up with or as with a spoon. Idosem dayta sida. Take some of the sidedish with a spoon.

SANGKAIDOS, n. one spoonful.

IDTA, var. of DITA.

IDTOY, var. of DITOY.

IGAD, n. coconut grater.
   v. /AG-/ to grate coconut meat. /AG-, MANG-:-EN/ to grate (coconut meat or something else).

IGAM, n. weapon, arms. --syn. ARMAS.

IGAT, n. eel.

IGGAM, var. of IGGEM before [1]-AN.

IGGAN, var. of IGGEM before [1]-AN.

IGGEM, v. /-UM-/ to hold on. /MANG-:-AN/ [IGGAMAN, IGGANAN] to hold, grasp or clutch (someone or something). Iniggaman na ti imak. He held my hand.

IGGES, n. worm.

[1]IGID, n. edge, brink, side.
   v. /-UM-/ to go to the edge, brink or side (of).

[2]IGID, v. /-UM-/ to defecate. --syn. TAKKI.

IGLESIA FILIPINA INDEPENDIENTE, the Philippine Independent Church, also known as the Aglipayan Church. --see AGLIPAY.

IGLESIA NI KRISTO (CHURCH OF CHRIST), 1. a church founded in the Philippines. 2. (often shortened to IGLESIA) a member of this church.

IGOROT, n. a general name for the natives of the Mountain Province.

IGPIL, v. /AG-, MANG-:-AN/ to carry under the armpit.

IGUP, v. /-UM-:-EN/ to sip, suck; to draw liquid into the mouth by sucking and/or by letting the liquid flow into it. Umigup ka ti digo. Sip some broth.

IHONG, n. son: familiar term.

IIL, v. /AG-, -UM-/ to whimper or whine importunately or annoyingly. Apay nga umaniil ka? Why are you whining?

IIT, n. midrib of coconut or buri leaf.

IKA-, a verbalizing affix occurring with adjective
roots which expresses the meaning: in the manner
or with the characteristic indicated by the root.

IKAB, v. /AG-/ to eat something surreptitiously or
secretly. /MANG-:-EN/ to eat surreptitiously or
secretly. Inikab na amin nga sida nga indulin ko.
He ate surreptitiously all the sidedish which I hid.

IKAMEN, n. mat made of the leaves of the buri palm or
any similar material.

IKAN, n. fish, usually salt water fish. --see LAMES.

IKDAL, n. fishbone, or something similar to it, caught
in the alimentary canal in the region of the throat.
v. /MA--AN/ to have a fishbone or something similar
caught in the alimentary canal in the region of the
throat.

IKET, n. any net used for catching fish, shrimps, etc.

IKING, n. edge of a board, book, etc.

IKIT, n. aunt. --syn. TIA.

IKK-, v. /-An/ to be given, granted, bestowed, conferred
(something). --var. of ITDAN (?). Ikkan nak man ti
kanek. Please give me something to eat.

IKKAN, see IKK-.

[1]IKKAT, v. /MANG-:-EN/ to remove, take away. Ikkaten na
diay ridaw ti balay da. He will remove the door of
their house. /MA-/ to be removed, taken away.

[2]IKKAT, v. /AG-/ to resign from (a position, a job, etc.).
Nagikkat nga maestra ni Maria. Mary resigned as
teacher. /MA-/ to be removed from (a position. a job,
etc.). Maikkat nga maestra ni Maria. Mary was removed
as teacher.

IKKIS, v. /AG-/ to shriek, scream. --syn. see RIAW.

IKUB, n. inside, within. Adda da iti ikub ti estudio.
They are inside the studio.

IKUT, v. /AG-, MANG-:-AN/ to hold or keep in one's possession; to have, possess. Dakes nga ikutan ti saan mo nga kukua. It is bad to hold in one's possession what one does not own.

ILAD, v. /AG-/ 1. to lie and rub the body on the floor lazily. Nagil-ilad la ti inaramid na. All he did was to lie and rub his body on the floor lazily. 2. to lie prostrate due to pain, exhaustion, etc. Uray la nga nagilad diay aso idi bauten na. The dog lay prostrate when he beat it.   /MANGI-:I-/ to lie and rub the body on the floor lazily with, to be wearing (it) when lying and rubbing the body on the floor lazily. Saan mo nga iyilad dayta baro nga badom. Don't lie and rub your body lazily on the floor with your new clothes.

ILALA, v. /AG-, MANG-:-EN/ to value, treasure; to cherish, esteem; to take care of dearly; to hold and keep with affection; to appreciate. Ilalaem ti inted ko kenka. You treasure what I gave you.

ILALA PAY, interj. alas!, what a pity!, it's a pity! --var. KAILALA PAY.

ILANG-ILANG, n. 1. a tree that bears fragrant flowers. 2. a flower of this tree.

ILEM, adj. /NA-/ jealous; suspicious.
    v. /AG-/ to be jealous, suspicious.   --syn. IMON.

ILET, adj. /NA-/ tight, narrow.   --syn. KITING.   --ant. LAWA.
    v. /-UM-/ to become like this.

ILI, n. 1. town. 2. country.
    v. /-UM-/ to go to town.   --var. PAILI.

    KAILIAN, n. 1. coming from the same town, townmate. 2. coming from the same country.

    PAGILIAN, n. 1. town, township. 2. country.

    UMILI, n. pl. the inhabitants of a town or country; townspeople.

    INILIN-ILI, n. every town, each town.

ILIW, v. /MA-/ to be homesick (for someone or something), to be nostalgic, to be lonesome for.

ILO, v. /AG-/ to wipe the anus after defecating. /MANG-:-AN/ to wipe the anus (of someone) after defecating.

ILOKANO, n. 1. one of the Philippine languages spoken principally in Northern Luzon. 2. a speaker, especially a native speaker, of this language.   --var. ILOKO, ILUKANO, ILUKO.

ILOKO, var. of ILOKANO.

ILOT, v. /AG-, MANG-:-EN/ 1. to rub, massage.   --syn. MASAHE. 2. to set (broken bones) by massaging. 3. to deliver a baby by massaging and pushing.

MANGNGILOT, n. 1. one who sets broken bones or treats muscle sprains by massaging.   --syn. MAMMULLO. 2. a woman who delivers babies by massaging and pushing; a midwife.   --syn. MAMMALTOT.

ILUKANO, var. of ILOKANO.

ILUKO, var. of ILOKANO.

IM-, var. of IN- occurring before P or B.

-IM-, var. of -IMM- before a consonant.

[1]IMA, n. 1. arm. 2. hand. 3. something like or corresponding to an arm.

[2]IMA, see IM-IMA.

IMAS, adj. /NA-/ delicious, tasty, savory, appetizing. v. /-UM-/ to become like this.   /MANG-:-EN/ to enjoy, relish. Imasen ti aggian idiay bakir. He enjoys staying in the forest.

IMATANG, n. attention, mind, sight. Dina isina ti imatang na ken ni Maria. He won't remove his sight from Mary. v. /MANG-:-AN/ to pay attention to, watch, see, witness, observe. Imatangam diay agsarsarita. Pay attention to the one speaking.

IMATON, v. /MANG-:-AN/ to watch, see; to attend, e.g. a show.

IMBAG, adj. /NA-/ good: 1. kind. 2. skillful, competent, efficient. 3. pleasing, gratifying, enjoyable. 4. well, no longer sick. 5. proper, becoming, right. --syn. SAYAAT.
  v. /-UM-/ to become any of these.

IMBAL, pt. of UMBAL.

IMBES [imbɛs; f. Sp.], prep. instead of.

IMBESTIGA [imbɛstiga; f. Sp.], v. /AG-, MANG-:-EN/ to investigate, look into.
  IMBESTIGASION, n. investigation.

IMBITAR [f. Sp.], v. to invite. --syn. ANGAY. --var. IMBITA.

IMBITASION [f. Sp.], n. invitation. --cf. IMBITAR.

IMENG, adj. /NA-/ safe, secure.

IM-IMA, v. /MANG-:-EN/ to thwart, frustrate, bring to naught, cause to fail. /MA-/ to be thwarted, frustrated, brought to naught, caused to fail.

IMING, n. 1. beard. 2. moustache. 3. whiskers. --syn. BARBAS.

IMIS, adj. /NA-/ affected, prudish, fastidious, squeamish, finicky.

IMLAY, pt. of UMLAY.

IMLEK, pt. of UMLEK.

-IMM-, pt. of -UM-. --var. -IM- (before a consonant).

-IMM--AN, an adjectival affix meaning: to be truly in the state or condition described by the stem. Limmalakian ka ket natakrot ka. You are truly a man and yet you are cowardly.

IMNA, adj. /NA-/ elegant, handsome, comely, graceful.

IMNAS, n. muse. --syn. SANIATA.

IMNO, pt. of UMNO.

IMOKO, n. a small knife.

IMON, adj. /NA-/ jealous, envious.
   v. /AG-/ to be jealous, envious.

IMPEKSION [impɛksion; f. Eng.], n. infection.

IMPES, pt. of UMPES.

IMPIERNO [impiɛrno; f. Sp.], n. hell, purgatory.

IMPIS, var. of INGPIS.

IMPLUENSIA [impluɛnsia; f. Sp.], n. influence.

IMPORMASION [f. Sp.], n. information.

IMPUSUAN [cf. PUSO], adj. /AN-/ hearty, cordial;
   sincere, whole-hearted. Inted na kanyana ti
   naimpusuan nga tulong na. He gave him his whole-
   hearted support.

IMRES, pt. of UMRES.

IMUT, adj. /NA-/ selfish, stingy, miserly. --syn
   KIRMUT.

[1]IN-, v. to go, proceed.   --var. INN- (before pronoun
   -AK).   --syn. PAPAN.

[2]IN-, pt. of [1,2]I-.

[1]-IN-, pt. of -EN.

[2]-IN-, a nominalizing affix identical to the pt. form
   of -EN; the meaning is: one that has undergone the
   action or process expressed by the verb stem.

[3]-IN-, an adverbial affix meaning: every, each. Tinawen
   nga aganak diay baket na. Every year his wife gives
   birth to a child.

[4]-IN-(+ R1), an adjective affix meaning: to tend to be
   what the stem describes. Linoloko dayta nga aramid.
   That action tends to be foolish.

[5]-IN-(+ Rt), an adverbial affix meaning: every, each
   (day, week, year, etc.) without fail; an emphatic
   form of -IN-.

⁶-IN- + R1, ptp. of -EN.

¹ÍNA, interj. an exclamation expressing mild displeasure or impatience; usually preceded by AY. Ay ina, nagbuntog kan! Oh my, you are so slow!

²ÍNA, n. a girl, one's young daughter: used affectionately.

³ÍNA, n. a title of respect for an older woman.

INÁ, n. mother. --syn. INANG, NANANG.
AGINA, [pl. AGIINA], n. pl. a mother and one of her children. AGIINA, pl. of AGINA: a mother and two or more of her children.
INA TI BUNYAG, godmother.

INAKA; NAKAIN-INAKA, adj. pitiful, deplorable.

INAKBAY, v. /AG-/ to diffuse, spread, e.g. odors, smoke, etc. Aginakbay ti angot ti sida ditoy. The smell of the sidedish is spreading here.

INALADAN [= ALAD + -IN- + -AN], n. fenced portion of a yard or lot.

-IN--AN, pt. of ¹-AN.

INANA, v. /AD-/ to rest, to cease from action or motion. Aginana tayo pay ta nabannogakon. Let's rest for I am already tired.

INANAK, see under ANAK.

INANAMA, n. hope, confidence, trust.
v. /MANG-:-EN/ to hope, trust, rely on, have confidence in. --syn. NAMNAMA.

INANG, syn. of INA: usually used as a term of address.

INAPOY [= -IN- + APOY], n. cooked, boiled or steamed rice. --var. INNAPOY.

INASAR [cf. ASAR], n. roast pig. --syn. LITSON n.

INASITGAN, = ASIDEG + -IN--AN.

INAT, v. /AG-/ to stretch oneself. --see UNNAT.

INAUDI [cf. UDI], n. 1. a younger brother or sister.
2. youngest child.   --syn. KMAUDIANAN, BURIDEK,
KIMMOT.

INAUNA [cf. UNA], n. 1. elder brother or sister. 2.
eldest child; first-born child.

INAW, v. /AG-, MANG-/ to be at the early period of
conception characterized by vomiting and/or
capricious desire to eat certain foods; to conceive,
become pregnant.

INAWGURASION [f. Sp.], inauguration.

INAYAD, adj. /NA-/ slow and gentle; careful, deliberate.
IN-INAYAD, v. /AG-/ to move or do something slowly,
gently and carefully.   /AG-:-EN/ to do slowly,
gently and carefully. In-inayaden yo nga bagkaten
dayta maletak ta adda mabuong. Carry my suitcase
slowly, gently and carefully for there is
something breakable inside it.

INDAKLAN [cf. DAKKEL], adj. /NA-/ great, eminent,
illustrious.

INDAYON, n. cradle, hammock.
v. /AG-/ 1. to use a swing or cradle for
recreation. 2. to swing, sway.   /MANG-:-EN/ to put
in a cradle or hammock, to rock in a cradle or
hammock.

INDENG, v. /MANG-:-AN/ to listen to, heed; to hearken.
Indengam ti saok. Listen to my words.   --syn.
DENGNGEG.

INDEPENDIENTE [indεpεndiεntε; f. Sp.], adj. independent.

INDIAK, I don't want to, I refuse (to do it).   --var.
MANDIAK.   --see MADI.

INDUSTRIA [f. Sp.], n. industry.

INHENIERIA [inhεniεria; f. Sp.], n. engineering.

INHENIERO [inhεniεro; f. Sp.], n. engineer.

INIIN, v. /AG-/ to shake or be unstable due to the
uneven distribution of its weight or contents: said
of containers. Pekpekem dayta kahon tapno saan nga
aginiin. Compress the contents of that box so that
it won't shake.

IN-INUT, see under INUT.

INIRUBAN, see under IRUB.

INIT, n. the sun.
   adj. /NA-/ sunny.
   v. /AG-/ to shine, to have the sun shining. Aginit
ngata inton bigat? Do you think the sun will shine
tomorrow? /MA--AN/ to be exposed to the sun, to be
hit or burned by the sun. Intayo idiay sirok ti kayo
tapno saan tayo nga mainitan. Let's go under the tree
so that we will not be hit by the sun.

INKIWAR [cf. KIWAR], n. a kind of rice pudding.

INN-, var. of IN- before pronoun -AK.

INNADAW [= cf. ^{2}ADAW], n. a children's game played with
the fingers.

INNAPOY, var. of INAPOY.

INNAW, v. /AG-/ to wash plates, bowls, and other things
used in eating a meal. /AG-:-AN/ to wash (things
used in eating a meal).

INNEM, num. six; 6. --var. -NEM. --syn. SEIS.

-INN-, a verbal affix indicating reciprocity in the
performance of the action expressed by the (verbal)
stem.
   -INN- + -AN, 1. with a verbal stem, a var. of -INN-.
   2. with an adjectival stem, it indicates competition
   or rivalry in showing the quality or attribute
   expressed by the stem.

INNO, var. (dial.) of ANIA.

INNUDO, var. of INUDO.

INNUROG [cf. TUROG], v. /AG-/ to spin smoothly: said
of tops and similar objects.

INSARABASAB, n. broiled meat or fish.

INSEKTO [insɛkto; f. Sp.], n. insect.

INSIGIDA [f. Sp.], adv. at once, immediately, right
away. --syn. DARAS.

INSIK, n. 1. the Chinese language. 2. a Chinese person. 3. figuratively: a cunning person especially in business, a cheater especially in business.

INSTRUMENTO [instrumɛnto; f. Sp.], n. instrument.

INTAR, v. /AG- + R2/ to fall in line, stand in a line or row. /MAKI-/ to fall in line with others, stand in a line with others. /MANG-:-EN/ to place in a line or row, to file. Intaren na dagidiay pinggan ditoy. He will place the plates in a row here. /MA-/ to be standing in a line, to be placed in a row. Adu ti naintar nga lugan iti arubayan ti balay. There are many cars placed in a row within the premises of the house.

INTEK, v. /AG-/ to stay, remain. Saan ka nga agintek idiay papanam. Don't stay where you are going.

[1]INTERES [intɛrɛs; f. Sp.], n. interest: readiness to be concerned with or moved by an object or class of object. Awan ti interes ko dita ar-aramidem. I have no interest in what you are doing.

[2]INTERES [intɛrɛs; f. Sp.], n. a charge for borrowed money.

INTERESADO [intɛrɛsado; f. Sp.], adj. interested.

INTERMEDIA [intɛrmɛdia; f. Sp.], n. the intermediate stage in the elementary school; the fifth and sixth grades and also seventh grade (if any) in the elementary school. --var. INTERMEDIET.

INTERMEDIET [intɛrmɛdiɛt; f. Eng.], var. of INTERMEDIA.

INTO; INTONO, prep. at (some future time), in (the future). --var. INTON, TONO.

INTO KET NO, lest.

INTO NGARUD NO, if.

INTONO KUAN, then, subsequently.

INTON, var. of [1,2]INTONO.

[1]INTONO, conj. when (in the future). Intono umayak ditoy, adda ka ngata? When I come here do you think you will be here? --var. INTON, TONO.

[2]INTONO, conj. lest. Saan ka nga natagari intono agunget. Don't be noisy lest he gets angry.   --var. INTON.

INTONANO, INTON-ANO, inter. when?, at what time? (in the future).   --syn. KAANO.

INTRIMITIDA [f. Sp.?], adj. /NAG-/ inquisitive, observant, curious.

INTUOD, v. /AG-, MANG-:-EN/ to ask, inquire about. --syn. SALUDSUD. Intuodem no ania ti kayat na. Ask what he wants.

INUDO, v. /AG-/ to warm oneself in front of a fire or any other hot object.   --var. INNUDO.

INUM, v. /-UM-:-EN/ to drink.   /AG-/ to drink alcoholic beverages.   --syn. BARTEK.
INUMEN, n. something to drink; drink. Adda inumen yo? Do you have something to drink?

INUT, adj. thrifty, economical, not wasteful.
IN-INUT, v. /AG-/ to be like this.   /MANG-:-EN/ 1. to do little by little, every now and then, a little at a time. 2. to use or consume economically, a little at a time, little by little. In-inuten yo dayta sida ta awanen. Eat that sidedish economically for there is no more.

INYOG, var. of NIOG.

ING-, var. of IN- occurring before K or G.

INGAR, v. /-UM-/ to growl.   /-AN/ to be growled at.

INGAS, n. /KA-/ one similar or resembling (another one) in physical features. Kaingas na diay tatang na. He resembles his father in physical features.
v. /AG-/ [with pl. subject] to be similar, to resemble each other in physical features.

INGAT, n. toothpick; wedge; splinter.
v. /AG-/ to pick the teeth.   /AG-:-AN/ to insert something in (an opening).

INGEL, adj. /MA-/ brave, courageous, valiant, daring, bold, heroic. /NA-/ strong: said of liquors, tobacco, etc.   --syn. SANGER.

INGEP, v. /MANG-:-EN/ [= INGPEN] to imagine, dream
about. Letson ti ing-ingpek. What I am imagining is
roast pig.

INGET, adj. /NA-/ strict, severe, firm.

[1]INGGA, n. end, conclusion, ending.

INGGAAN, n. boundary, limit.

[2]INGGA, adv. until, till, up to (a place, time).   --var.
INGGANA, AGINGGA, AGINGGANA.

INGGA TI, until, till the time that, up to the time
that.   --var. INGGANA TI, AGINGGA TI, AGINGGANA TI,
INGGAT, INGGANAT, AGINGGAT, AGINGGANAT.

INGGANAT, var. of INGGA TI.

INGGAT, var. of INGGA TI.

INGGANA, var. of INGGA.

INGGET, adv. very: the absolute superlative. Ingget
pintas diay balasang. The young lady is very very
beautiful.

INGGLATERA [ingglatera; f. Sp.], n. England.

INGPIS, adj. /NA-/ thin.   --var. IMPIS.   --ant. PUSKOL.

INGUNGOT, v. /MANG-:-EN/ to love dearly, to be very
fond of. Ing-ingungotek ni nanang ko. I love my
mother dearly.

KAINGUNGOT, n. loved one, beloved, sweetheart.
    v. /AG-/ [with pl. subject] to be sweethearts.

IPA-, = 1. I- + PA- (causative): the goal of the
noncausative verb is placed in focus or subject
position. 2. I- + PA (to go): the goal of the verb
(PA) is placed in focus or subject position. 3.
I- + PA- (to use or put as): the goal of the verb is
placed in focus or subject position.

IPAG, n. sister-in-law.   --ant. BAYAW.

IPAKIN, = I- + PAKIN-.

IPASTREK, = I- + PASTREK.

IPDOOK, v. /MAKA-:MA--AN/ to choke.   /MA--AN/ to be choked.

IPES, n. cockroach.

IPIL, n. a leguminous tree which yields valuable timber.

IPIT, n. 1. pincers: a grasping claw, as of a crab or lobster; chela. 2. var. of SIPIT.
    v. /MANG-:-EN/ to pinch: to squeeze between two surfaces, two edges, etc.   /MA-/ to be pinched.

IPON, n. shrimp.   --syn. KURUS.

IPUS, n. tail.
    adj. /-AN/ having a large tail.
    v. /MANG-:-EN/ to tail, follow behind.   /MANG-:-AN/ to put a tail on or to.

IRAY, v. /AG-/ to incline, lean, slant. Nagiray diay balay da kalpasan ti bagyo. Their house inclined after the typhoon.   /MANGI-:I-/ to cause to incline, lean, slant. Iyiray mo dayta taleb. You cause that wall to incline.

IRI, v. /AG-/ to produce a long shrill cry.

IRIG, v. /AG-/ to incline, bend down on one side. /MANGI-:I-/ to cause to incline, bend down on one side.

IRIGASION [f. Sp.], n. irrigation.   --syn. PADANUM, PALAYAS.

IRIID, v. /AG-:-EN/ to crush, grind. Nagiridiid ti balatong. He crushed some mongo beans.

IRIK, n. unhusked rice.
    v. /AG-/ separate rice grains from the harvested stalks especially with the feet.   /AG-:-EN/ to separate the grains of (harvested rice), to thresh rice grains.
    IRIK-IRIK, v. /MANG-:-EN/ to step on or trample someone moving the feet as when separating rice grains from the stalks.

IRIS, n. greenish feces of infants.

IRO, n. soot.

IRTENG, adj. /NA-/ tightly drawn, taut, not loose, stretched tightly.
v. /MANG-:-EN/ to stretch tightly, draw tightly.

IRUB, v. /AG-/ to roast young or immature rice grains which are pounded afterwards in order to flatten the grains and separate the husks. /MANG-:-EN/ to roast (rice grains, etc.).

INIRUBAN, n. the rice resulting from such action.

IRUT, adj. /NA-/ tight.
v. /-UM-/ to become like this. /MANG-:-EN/ to tighten, make tight. Irutem dayta tali ti sapatos mo. Tighten the tie of your shoes.

ISAR, v. /AG-/ to ravel, fray. Saan nga nagisar ti badok. My clothes did not fray.

ISBO, n. urine.
v. /-UM-/ to urinate, wet. /-UM-:-AN/ to urinate or wet on (someone or something). Inisboan diay asom ta mulak. Your dog wetted on my plant.

ISEK, v. /-UM-/ [= UMSEK] to fit, to be correctly adjusted to or shaped for. Saan nga umsek dayta sapatos mo kanyak. Your shoes won't fit me. /MANGI-:-/ to make fit in or on, to put on (shoes). Iyesek mo dayta sapatos mo. Put on your shoes.

ISEM, n. smile.
adj. /NA-/ always smiling, full of smiles; cheerful. Naisem ni Berto uray kasano ti bannog na. Bert is always smiling no matter how tired he is.
v. /-UM-/ to smile. /-UM-:-AN/ [= ISMAN] to smile to (someone).

ISIIS, v. /MANG-:-EN/ to sift (flour). Inisiis na diay bellaay. He sifted the flour.

ISIP, n. mind, thought, intellect.
adj. /NA-/ intelligent, bright, keen.
v. /AG-:-EN/ to think of, consider, ponder, reflect upon (what to do). --syn. PANUNOT.

IS-ISO, see ISO.

ISLAID [f. Eng.?], n. trombone. --var. TRUMBON.

ISO; IS-ISO, v. /AG-/ to rub the dirt off one's body, to scrub oneself. /MANG-:-AN/ to rub the dirt off (someone's) body, to scrub.

[1]ISPAL, v. /MAKA-:MA--AN/ to obstruct the throat of, to choke. /MA--AN/ to have the throat obstructed by food, to be choked by food.

[2]ISPAL, v. /MANG-:-EN/ to protect, defend, guard against. Ispalen na kami ti nakaro nga sakit. Protect us from serious sicknesses. /MA-/ to be protected, defended.

ISPELING [ispɛling; f. Eng.], n. spelling.
    v. /AG-:-EN/ to spell.

ISPIA [ispia; f. Sp.], n. spy.

ISTAM [f. Eng.], n. stamp. --syn. SELYO.

ISTAY, var. of NAGISTAYAN.

ISTRIKTO [f. Eng.?], adj. /NA-/ strict, severe.

ISTORYA [f. Sp.], n. story, narrative.
    v. /AG-/ to tell a story. /MANGI-:I-/ or
    /MANG-:-EN/ to tell, relate, narrate.

[1]ISU, pron. he, she; him, her: the person previously mentioned. ISU is the full nominative case form, ISU or zero (nothing) the enclitic nominative, KUKUANA the full possessive, NA the enclitic possessive and the agent, and KANYANA or KENKUANA the oblique.
--var. ISUNA.

    IS-ISU, he or she only, he or she alone.

[2]ISU, pron. it, that. No isu ti kayat ti dios, awan ti maaramid tayo. If it is the will of God, we can't do anything.

[3]ISU, v. /-UM-/ to be enough or sufficient, to fit.

    APAGISU, adj. just right, just enough.

    ISUN or ISUNAN, that's enough now, all right.

[4]ISU, adv. an emphatic particle; it is followed by NGA before a clause. Isu dayta ti paggapoan ti kirokiro

ita. It is that from which problems come. Isu nga
addaak ditoy ta kayat ka nga makita. That I am here
is because I want to see you. --var. ISUNA.

ISUDA, pron. they; them: the persons previously
mentioned. ISUDA is the full nominative case form,
DA or IDA the enclitic nominative, KUKUADA the full
possessive, DA the enclitic possessive and the agent,
and KANYADA or KENKUADA the oblique.

IS-ISUDA, they only, they alone.

[1]ISUNA, var. of [1]ISU.

[2]ISUNA, see KAKAISUNA.

IT [í:t], interj. a sound that someone makes to tell
someone else that he is hiding and that the other
should look for him. If the person hiding comes out
suddenly and wishes to startle the other, he cries
BA [ba:].

[1]ITA, var. of [1,2]ITATTA.

[2]ITA, form of DAYTA postposed to a noun expressing
emphasis. Ta ubing ita ti naariwawa. That child there
is the one who is noisy.

ITA TA, var. of ITATTA TA.

[1]ITATTA, adv. now, at the present time, at this moment.
--var. ITA.

[2]ITATTA, prep. this (morning, night, etc.): forms
prepositional phrases expressing present time. --var.
ITA.

ITATTA TA, whereas (present). --var. ITA TA. --see
IDINTO TA.

[1]ITATTAY, adv. in the immediate past, in the near past,
a moment ago. Adda itattay diay anak mo ditoy. Your
child was here a moment ago. --var. ITAY.

[2]ITATTAY, prep. last, the immediate or near past (morning,
night, etc.): forms prepositional phrases expressing
immediate or near past time. --var. ITAY.

[3]ITATTAY, conj. when (in the immediate or near past).
--var. ITAY.

[1]ITAY, var. of [1,2,3]ITATTAY.

[2]ITAY, form of DAYTAY postposed to a noun expressing emphasis.

ITDEN, = ITED + -EN: often replaced by ITED.

ITED, v. /MANG-:-EN/ [= MANGTED : ITED, ITDEN] to give, grant (something) to; to confer, bestow (something) on. Saan na kayat ti mangted ti kuarta idiay baket na. He does not want to give money to his wife. --see IKK-.

[1]ITI, cm. indefinite goal marker. --var. TI.

[2]ITI, prep. as for, concerning (a person, place or thing). Iti lalaki, napigpigsa ngem ti babai. As for a man, he is stronger than a woman.

[3]ITI, conj. because of, on account of, due to, in. Iti rurod na, kayat na nga tiritiren ti tengnged ko. In his irritation, he wanted to twist my neck. --var. TI. --syn. GAPO TI.

ITIK, n. duck with speckled plumage.

IT-IT, v. /AG-/ to produce a thin high-pitched sound like the cry of snakes, rats, etc.

ITLOG, n. egg.
v. /AG-/ to lay an egg. /MANGI-:I-/ to lay (an egg or eggs).

ITNEG, n. a name applied to the natives of the province of Abra.

ITOY, form of DAYTOY postposed to a noun expressing emphasis.

ITSURA [f. Sp.], n. form, figure, appearance, feature, mien.

ITTA, n. in milled rice, unhusked grains mixed with the husked ones.
v. /AG-/ in milled rice, to remove remaining unhusked grains from the husked ones. /MANG-:-AN/ to remove unhusked grains from (milled rice).

ITTIP, n. crust of rice found at the bottom of the pot; it is usually harder and slightly burned.

ITUM, v. /MANG-:-EN/ to close (mouth, etc.). Itumem ta
ngiwat mo. Close your mouth.

IWA, n. slice of something.
  v. /MANG-:-EN/ to slice, cut open.

SANGKAIWA, n. one slice.

[1]IY-, var. of [1,2]I- occurring before a vowel. --see Y-.

[2]IY- (+ R2), var. of [3]I- (+ R2) before a vowel. --see
Y- + R2.

IYAAY [I- + R2 + AY], nominalized form of AY: the
coming or arrival (of). --var. YAAY.

IYOT, v. /-UM-:-EN/ to copulate with, to engage in
sexual intercourse with. /AG-/ [with pl. subject] to
copulate or engage in sexual intercourse with each
other. --var. YOT, IYYOT.

IYYOT, var. of IYOT.

-K, var. of KO after a vowel.

-K, var. of -AK after the possessive pron. NA (by him
or her) or DA (by them).

KA, pron. you (sg.): the enclitic nominative of SIKA.

KA-, a ligature prefixed to mensural nouns preceded by
a numeral.

KA-, a prefix that combines with (1) the full
nominative pronouns with DA- to form the corresponding
oblique pronouns, (2) the indefinite pronoun DATAO
to form its oblique, and (3) the plural article and
demonstrative pronouns to form their oblique. --see
KANYA-, KEN-, KENUA-.

KA-, a prefix which occurs with adjective roots forming
verb stems which in turn take the verbalizing affix
-EN to form verbs meaning (1) to make like what the
adjective root describes when the subject is a noun
phrase, and (2) to do in the manner described by the
adjective root when the subject is a verb phrase.

KA- + R1-, nom. af. the doing of the action expressed
by the verb continuously. Nabisinanak ti kauuray
kenka. I went hungry waiting for you.

KA- [pt. KINA-, prp. KA- + R1, ptp. KINA- + R1], a
verbalizing affix which places the reciprocal actor
or accessory of the action expressed by the verb in
focus or subject position.

KA-, a nominalizing affix occurring with adjective
roots which expresses the degree or extent of the
quality or trait indicated by the root.

KA-, a nominalizing affix which occurs with verb stems
and nouns. With verb stems, it expresses the
performance of the action expressed by the verb stem
together with someone or close to someone; with
nouns, it expresses the sharing of the object
referred to be the noun with someone, or being or
living in the place referred to by the noun with
someone.

KA- +R1, a prefix occurring with verb stems which
indicates recent completion of the action expressed
by the verb stem. --var. KAI- R1.

KAALDAWAN [cf. ALDAW], n. the very day (od). Ita ti
kaaldawan ti piesta mi. Today is the very day of our
fiesta.

KAAMAAN, see under AMA.

KAAN, v. /AG-/ to eat, feed on (something). /MANG-:-EN/
[= MANGKAAN or MANGAN : KANEN] to eat. --see PANGAN.

KA--AN, a verbalizing affix occurring with numeral roots
which expresses the meaning: to increase or bring to
the number indicated by the numeral stem.

KA--AN, a nominalizing affix occurring with temporal
nouns which expresses the meaning: at the actual
time of the period or event indicated by the noun
stem.

KA--AN, the superlative affix of adjectives: most.
--var. KA- + R1 + -AN.

KA--AN, the superlative adjectival affix. --var.
KA--AN + R1.

KA--AN, a nominalizing affix occurring with nouns which indicates the place where the objects referred to by its noun stem are numerous or plentiful.

KA- + R2 + -AN, var. of KA--AN.

KA--AN + R1, var. of the superlative adjective affix KA--AN.

KAANAKAN [cf. ANAK], n. nephew, niece.

KAANATUP, KAANATUPAN, see under ANATUP.

KAANNAWIDAN, n. something done habitually, customarily or regularly. Saan ko nga kaannawidan ti magna ditoy nga dalan. It is not my custom to walk on this road.

KAANO, interr. when?, at what time? --see INTONANO.

KAARUBA, var. of KARRUBA.

KAASI, KAKAASI, see under ASI.

KAASMANG, see under ASMANG.

KAAYAN-AYAT [AYAN + AYAT], n. sweetheart, betrothed. --syn. KOBIO, NOBIA.

KABABALIN [cf. BALIN], n. habit, custom (of).

KABABAGAS [cf. BAGAS], n. the essence, pitch, meaning (of).

KABADDUNGAL, v. /AG-/ [with pl. subject] to belong to the same age group, to be contemporaries.

KABAELAN, see under BAELAN.

KABAG, n. gas pain.
    v. /-AN/ to be afflicted with this.

KABAGIAN, see under BAGI.

KABAGIS [rt. BAGIS?], n. brother, sister; sibling. --syn. KABSAT.
    KABAGIS ITI BUNYAG, child of one's godparents.

KABALYO [f. Sp.], n. horse. --var. (rare) KABAYO.

KABAN, n. a dry measure approximately 75 liters.

KABARBARO, see under BARO.

KABARET [kabarɛt; f. Eng.], n. cabaret.
    v. /AG-, MAKI-/ to go to a cabaret.

KABASI, n. a kind of large marine fish whose meat is
    esteemed.

KABATITI, n. a scandent, cucurbitaceous, herbaceous
    vine with large leaves, yellow flowers and oblong
    cylindric, green, ribbed or smooth, edible fruits.

KABAW, adj. /NAG-/ 1. feebleminded, senile. 2. absent-
    minded, often forgetful.
    v. /AG-/ 1. to be feebleminded, senile. 2. to be
    absent-minded, often forgetful.

KABAW, adj. /NA-/ mild, as tobacco; weak, as wine.
    v. /-UM-/ to become this.

KABAYO, var. (rare) of KABALYO.
    PAKABAYO, v. /MANGI-:I-/ to put astride (something).
    /MAI-/ to be put astride (something).

KABBALAY [rt. BALAY], n. 1. housemate, one who lives in
    the same house. 2. concubine, mistress.   --syn.
    BABAI 2., KERIDA.
    v. /MANG-:-EN/, /MAKI-:KA-/ 1. to live in the same
    house with. 2. to be one's concubine or mistress:
    said of women.

KABBI, n. mumps.
    v. /AG-/ to be afflicted with this.

KABBIBAW, adj. wry, twisted, contorted: said especially
    of the mouth of a person, a pot, etc.   --syn. DIWIG.
    v. /-UM-/ to become like this.

KABBOT, v. /AG-/ to bubble like boiling sugar, honey,
    etc. No agkabbot dayta tagapulot, adawemon. When that
    sugar bubbles, take it out of the fire.

KABESA [kabésa; f. Sp.], v. /MANGI-:I-/ to memorize,
    commit to memory, learn by heart.

KABESERA [kabɛsɛra; f. Sp.], n. 1. capital. 2. head of
    the dining table.
    v. /AG-/ to sit at the head of the dining table.

KABIBI, n. a kind of very large, brown, lamellibranchiate mollusk.

[1]KABIL, v. /MANGI-:I-/ to put, place, lay, set in or on something.

[2]KABIL, v. /AG-/ to punish or maltreat someone. /MANG-:-EN/ to punish, hit, strike. Kabilen ka no di nak nga patien. I will punish you if you won't believe me. /MAKI-:KA-/ to fight with someone. /AG-/ [with pl. subject] to fight with one another.

KABIT, v. /MANGI-:I-/ to fasten on a wall, post, etc. /MAI-/ to be caught by a hook or as by a hook.

KABITI, v. /MANG-:-EN/ to cement, concrete.

KABKAB, n. body dirt, skin dirt.

NAKAKABKABKAB, adj. full of dirt on the body or skin.

KABKABANGA, n. skull.

KABLAAW, v. /AG-, -UM-:-AN/ to greet, salute, congratulate, felicitate, compliment. Adu ti immay kimmablaaw kenkuana. There were many who came to greet him.

KABO [f. Sp.], n. corporal.

KABSAT [pl. KAKABSAT], n. a brother or sister, a sib, sibling. --syn. KABAGIS.

AGKABSAT [pl. AGKAKABASAT], n. to be brothers or sisters or brothers and sisters.

KABSAT TI AMA, a half brother or sister with the same father.

KABSAT TI INA, a half brother or sister with the same mother.

KABUKAB, v. /AG-/ to grit, gnash, grind the teeth. Apay nga agkabkabukab ka? Why are you gnashing your teeth? /MANG-:-EN/ to grind with the teeth. Ania ti kabkabukabem? What are you grinding with your teeth?

KABUL; KABULKABUL, v. /AG-/ to masticate or chew food slowly and with difficulty, as a toothless person. Agkabulkabul ni lelang na. His grandmother is chewing her food slowly and with difficulty. /AG-, MANG-:-EN/

to masticate or chew (food) without using the teeth,
to masticate or chew (food) as a toothless person
does.

KABUS, n. the period when the moon is full. Kabus ita.
This is the period when the moon is full.
v. /AG-/ to become full: said of the moon.

KABUSOR [rt. BUSOR], n. enemy.

KAD, var. of KADI.

KADA [f. Sp.], prep. each, every; as in KADA MALEM,
every afternoon.

KADA, pl. of KEN NI, the oblique or locative form of
DA.

KADAGIDI, pl. of ITI DAYDI; the oblique or locative
form of DAGIDI: in, at, to, of those (which are now
extinct).

KADAGIDIAY, pl. of ITI DAYDIAY; the oblique or locative
form of DAGIDIAY: in, at, to, of those (far from both
speaker and hearer).

KADAGITA, pl. of ITI DAYTA; the oblique or locative
form of DAGITA: in, at, to, of those (near hearer).

KADAGITAY, pl. of ITI DAYTAY; the oblique or locative
form of DAGITAY: in, at, to, of those (not in sight).

KADAGITI, pl. of ITI; the oblique or locative form of
DAGITI: in, at, to, of those.

KADAGITOY, pl. of ITI DAYTOY; the oblique or locative
form of DAGITOY: in, at, to, of these (near the
speaker).

KADAKAM, var. of KADAKAMI.

KADAKAMI, var. of KANYAMI.   --var. KADAKAM.

KADAKAY, var. of KADAKAYO.

KADAKAYO, var. of KANYAYO.   --var. KADAKAY.

KADAKLAN [cf. DAKKEL], n. the principal part of the
house, the house proper. Naglampaso tay ubing iti

kadaklan. The child scrubbed or polished the principal part of the house.

KADANG-KADANG, n. stilts. --syn. see TEKKEN.
v. /AG-/ to walk on stilts.

KADAPA; KADKADAPA, v. /AG-, -UM-/ to move forward heavily, to drag oneself forward. Kumadkadapa ti rigat na. He moves forward heavily because of his difficulties.

KADAS, v. /MANG-:-AN/ to sweep away the dirt of or on. Isu ti nangkadas diay datar. It was he who swept away the dirt on the floor.

KADATA, var. of KANYATA.

KADATAO, the oblique of the pronoun DATAO.

KADATAY, var. of KADATAYO.

KADATAYO, var. of KANYATAYO. --var. KADATAY.

[1]KADAWYAN, adj. regular, normal, ordinary.

[2]KADAWYAN, n. custom, habit, practice, usage.

[3]KADAWYAN, n. menses, the menstruous flow.
v. /AG-/ to menstruate.

KADI, adv. 1. a word that makes a sentence interrogative. 2. a word entreating someone to act: with imperative sentences. Alaem kadi diay sarming ko. Will you please get my glasses. --var. KAD.

KADKAD, v. /MANG-:-AN/ to remove or rake off the ashes (of the stove). Kadkadam nga umuna dayta dalikan. Remove first the ashes of the stove. /MANGI-:I-/ to remove or rake off. Ikadkad mo dagita dapo. Rake off those ashes.

KADKADUA [cf. KADUA], n. afterbirth, placenta.

KADTA, short for UMALIS KA DITA, go away from there.

KADUA [cf. DUA], companion, mate, one of a pair.
v. /-UM-/ to go with, pair with, join the company of. /MANG-:-EN/ to accompany. Sino to kaduaem nga mapan idiay pasala? Whom will you accompany to the dance?

KAEM, v. /MANG-:-Eɴ/ to put together; to close, shut.
Isu ti nangkaem diay bibig na. It was he who put his
lips together. /AG-/ [with pl. subject] to come
together, unite, join. Nagkaem dagidiay bibig na.
His lips came together.

KA--EN, see under KA-.

KAFE [kafɛ; f. Sp.], var. of KAPE.

KAGAT, v. /AG-/ to bite someone. Agkkagat dayta asom.
Your dog bites people. /-UM-, AG-:-EN/ to bite, to
cut or wound with the teeth.

KAGAW, n. germ; itch mite.

KAGAY, n. cape, cloak, mantle, wrap.
   v. /AG-/ to wrap round oneself, to cover oneself
with this. /MANGI-:I-/ to wrap (this) round
(someone), to use (this) to cover or wrap (someone).

KAGKAG, v. /MANGI-:I-/ to shake or beat vigorously as
to remove dirt or something else. Ikagkag mo dayta
labba. Shake that basket.

KAGLIS, v. /MAI-/ to slide, slip. /-UM-/ to deflect,
deviate, swerve. --syn. GALIS.

KAGUD, v. /MANGI-:I-/ to finish (one's work, doing
something) on time. Ikagud mo bassit daytoy badok
nga para inton bigat. Please finish my dress which
is for tomorrow.

KAGUMAAN, v. /MANGI-:I-/ to make an effort, try,
endeavor (to do something). Ikagumaan na ti umay
diay pabuya. He will make an effort to go to the
show.

KAHA [f. Sp.], n. case, box, pack (or cigarettes).
--see KAHITA.

KAHITA [f. Sp.], n. diminutive of KAHA: a small case
or box.

KAHON [f. Sp.], a box much bigger than a KAHA. --syn.
KARTON.

KAI- + R1, var. of KA- + R1.

KAI--AN, a nominalizing affix occurring with verb roots
which expresses the destination, termination or
direction of the action expressed by the stem.

KAIBATUGAN, see under BATUG.

KAILALA, var. of ILALA.

KAILIAN, see under ILI.

KAIMITO, n. 1. a star-apple tree. 2. a fruit of this.

KAIN, n. skirt.   --syn. PANDILING.

KAINGUNGOT, see under INGUNGOT.

KAKA, n. 1. an elder brother or sister. 2. also, anyone
older than oneself or as old as one's elder brother
or sister.

AGKAKA, n. a brother and a sister, two brothers, or
two sisters one of whom is older.

KÁKAB, n. a cage for chickens.

KAKABSAT, pl. of KABSAT.

[1]KAKAISUNA, adj. one and only, sole, unique.

[2]KAKAISUNA, conj. since, inasmuch as, now that.

KAKAK, v. /AG-/ to cluck, to make a slow and prolonged
sound as when looking for a nest or just roaming
around: said of a hen.   --var. KAKKAK.

KAKAW [f. Sp.], n. cacao.

KAKKAK, var. of KAKAK.

[1]KAKOK, n. a kind of cuckoo.

[2]KAKOK, v. /-UM-:-EN/ to knock or strike sharply
(something). Saan mo nga kakoken ti ulo ni Pedro.
Don't knock on the head of Peter. /MANG-:-EN/ to
knock or strike sharply (a part of someone or
something). Saan mo nga kakokan ni Pedro. Don't
knock Peter (on his head).

KALA, see KALKALA.

KALABUS [f. Sp.], n. jail, prison.   --syn. PRISO,
  KARSEL, PAGBALUDAN.
    v. /MANGI-:I-/ to imprison.   --syn. PRISO, BALUD.

KALADKAD, v. /AG-, -UM-/ to climb using hands and feet,
  to climb awkwardly, to clamber.   /MANG-:-EN/ to
  climb on or over (something) using hands and feet.
  --syn. KALAY-AT.

KALAKAL, v. /MANG-:-EN/ to transplant, especially a
  young plant. Isu ti nangkalakal kadagidiay tarong.
  It was he who transplanted those eggplants.

KALALAINGAN [cf. LAING], adj. just the right amount,
  time, length, etc.: usually with the possessive
  pronoun NA after it.

KALAMANSI, n. 1. a citrus tree. 2. also, the fruit of
  this.   --see DALAYAP.

KALAMAY, n. a kind of thick sweet made of rice flour,
  sugar, and water.

KALAM-IT, v. /MAKAI-:MAI-/ to implicate or involve
  (someone), as in a case, plot, etc.   /MAI-/ to be
  implicated or involved (in a case, plot, etc.).
  Narigat ti maikalam-it kadagita nga banag. It is
  difficult to get involved in those things.

KALANTAY, n. bridge, especially a temporary one.
  --syn. RANGTAY.
    v. /AG-/ to walk as on a bridge.   /MANG-:-EN/ to
  walk on (something) as a bridge.

KALANGAKANG, adj. overripe and almost dry: said of the
  fruit of the tamarind tree.
    v. /-UM-/ to become like this.   /AG-/ to be this.

KALANGKANG, v. /MANG-:-EN/ to form into a ring, to
  wind, to turn completely or repeatedly about an
  object, e.g. coil, twine. Kalangkangem dayta sagut.
  Wind that fiber.

KALANGIKING, v. /AG-/ to jingle like coins or metal.

KALANGOKONG, v. /AG-/ to produce a deep rattling sound,
  as a coconut shell inside an earthen jar.

KALANGTAY, var. of KALANTAY.

KALAP, v. /AG-/ to catch fish.   /MANG-:-EN/ to catch (fish).

KALAPATI, n. dove, pigeon.

KALAPAW, n. shed, hut, hovel; a temporary shelter.

KALASAG, n. shield.

KALASKAS, v. /MANG-:-EN/ to gather up (things that are disarranged or scattered about). Kalaskasem amin nga lupot dita. Gather up all the clothes there.

KALASUGAN, n. rain pipe, rain gutter.

KALATKAT, v. /-UM-/ to climb as vines and other plants.

KALAW, n. a kind of hornbill.

KALAWASAN, v. /AG-/ [with pl. subject] to have more than enough room. Agkalkalawasan kami idiay balay da. We have more than enough room in their house.

KALAWIKIW, v. /AG-, -UM-/ to wag: said especially of the tail of a dog.

KALAWKAW, v. /MANG-:-EN/ to stir (liquid) especially with the hand.

KALAY-AT, v. /AG-, -UM-/ to climb awkwardly and with difficulty.   /MANG-:-EN/ to climb (something) awkwardly and with difficulty.   --syn. KALADKAD.

[1]KALBIT, v. /AG-/ to nudge someone with the tip of a finger, usually the index finger.   /MANG-:-EN/ to nudge (someone) with the tip of a finger, usually the index finger.

[2]KALBIT, v. /MANG-:-EN/ to pull the trigger of: said of guns.

KALBO, adj. bald, having the hair of the head completely shaved off.
     v. /MANG-:-EN/ to shave completely the hair of the head.

KALDERO [kaldɛro; f. Sp.], n. kettle, cauldron.

KALDING, n. goat.

KALENKEN, v. /MANG-:-EN/ to draw aside, as a curtain or
like a curtain. Kalenkenen na dayta kurtina. He will
draw aside that curtain. /MA-/ to be drawn aside,
as a curtain or like a curtain.

KALESA [kalɛsa; f. Sp.], n. a kind of two-wheeled
calash opening at the back; a kind of horse-drawn
two-wheeled carriage with one row of seats; it is
smaller, lighter, and lower than the KAROMATA.

KALGAW, n. dry season, drought.

[1]KALI, v. /AG-, MANG-:-EN/ 1. to dig, to make by digging.
Agkali ka ti abut. Dig a hole. 2. to get by digging,
to dig out. Agkali ka ti mani. Dig out some peanuts. 3.
to put in the ground or as if in the ground by digging
a hole. Ikalim daytoy bukel. Put this seed in the
ground.

[2]KALI, n. a pond or lagoon. especially a man-made one.

[3]KALI, n. a kind of hawk.

KALIBRE [kalibrɛ; f. Sp.], n. caliber.

KALIDAD [f. Sp.], n. quality.

KALIKAGUM, v. /AG-:-AN/ to wish, desire (to do something
or something to happen). Kalikaguman na ti makisao
kenka. He desires to speak to you.

KALINDARIO [f. Sp.], n. calendar.

KALINTEGAN [cf. LINTEG], n. legal right.

KALINTUDO [cf. TUDO], v. /AG-/ to walk in the rain
without an umbrella or any covering.

KALIPIKASION [f. Sp.], n. qualification.

KALIPKIP, v. /AG-, -UM-/ to climb up, ascend especially
a mountain. Narigat ti agkalipkip dita bambantay. It
is difficult to climb up those mountains. /MANG-:-EN/
to climb, ascend (a mountain or as if a mountain).
Narigat nga kalipkipen dayta nga bantay. It is
difficult to climb that mountain.

KALAG, v. /MANGI-:I-/ to bump against the ground or as
if against the ground in order to remove dirt: said
especially of boxes and other containers.

KALKAL, v. /AG-/ to be in heat, to be sexually excited. Agkalkal daydiay aso. The dog is sexually excited.

KALKALA, adj. 1. happening a long time ago: said of an act or event. Kalkala pay ti isasangpet ko. I arrived a long time ago. 2. being present or being in a place a long time ago: said of a person or thing. Kalkala ka pay ditoy? Were you here a long time ago?

KALKALPAS, = KA- + R1 + -AN + LEPPAS.

KALLAMO, n. preserved fish or BUGGOONG which has not been in a jar long enough and has not fermented sufficiently.

KALLATIK, v. /AG-/ to rebound, to spring back after hitting something. Nagkallatik daydiay kuarta nga imbato na. The coin which he threw rebounded.

KALLATOK, v. /AG-/ to drop or fall on: said of a thrown or projected object. Nagkallatok ti dakkel nga bato idiay toktok ti balay da. A big stone fell on top of their house.

KALLAUTANG, v. /AG-/ 1. to float in a random way, to drift. 2. to travel about in a random way, to wander about, drift.

KALLAUTIT, n. 1. a kind of tree. 2. also, the fruit of this.

KALLAWIT, n. hook.
    v. /MANG-:-EN/ to catch with a hook.

KALLAYSA, v. /MANGI-:I-/ to marry, wed (someone). Ingkallaysa na ti Rosa. He married Rose. /AG-/ [with pl. subject] to get married. Nagkallasya da itay napan nga bulan. They got married the past month. --syn. KASAR. /-UM-/ to be in harmony or agreement with, to be one with: said of one's mind, feelings, desires. Kimmallaysa ti nakem na kenkuana. His mind is in agreement with hers.

KALLID, n. dimple. --var. KALLIT.

KALLIT, var. of KALLID.

KALLUGONG, n. hat. --syn. BALANGGOT, SOMBRERO.

KALLONG, v. /AG-/ to eat food surreptitiously especially between meals. /MANG-:-EN/ to eat (food) surreptitiously especially between meals.

KALMA [f. Sp.], adj. /NA-/ calm, tranquil, serene, peaceful, quiet. --syn. KAPIA.

KALMAN, n. The day before today, yesterday.

IDI KALMAN, yesterday.

BIGAT KALMAN, yesterday morning.

KALNAAWAN, see under LINNAAW.

KALOG, v. /MANG-:-EN/ to shake. Saan mo nga kalogen dayta basket nga napno ti itlog. Don't shake that basket that is full of eggs.

KALOGKALOG, /AG-/ to wobble, waggle. Agkalogkalog dayta tugaw. That chair wobbles.

KALPASAN [cf. LEPPAS], n. the period after the conclusion, end or termination of.

KALPASANNA, adv. afterwards.

KALSADA [f. Sp.], n. street, road. --syn. DALAN. --var. KARSADA.

KALSON [f. Sp.], n. trousers or drawers provided with buttons and coming to the ankle. --see KALSONSILIO.

KALSONSILIO [f. Sp.], n. drawers, knee breeches. --var. KARSONSILIO. --see KALSON.

KALTAANG, n. middle (of night), midnight.

KALTI, v. /AG-/ to cook sliced sweet potatoes, unripe papayas, unripe bananas, etc. in boiling sugar. /AG-, MANG-:-EN/ to slice and cook in boiling sugar.

KINALTI, n. sliced sweet potatoes, unripe papayas, unripe bananas, etc. cooked in boiling sugar.

KALUB, n. cover, lid.
v. /MANG-:-AN/ to cover, especially an opening or hole. /MANGI-:I-/ to use to cover (something) with, to put or place on (something) as cover or screen.

KALUB TI MATA, eyelid.

KANIKA-, a numeral prefix used to form ordinal numbers.
--syn. MAIKA-.

KALUBBABA, var. of KALUMBABA.

KALUKBABA, v. /AG-/ to lean out of the window or as out
of the window with almost half of the body outside.

KALULOT, n. ferrule.

KALUMBABA, v. /AG-/ to rest the chin on one or both
hands.

KALUNAY, n. a spiny herb (Amaranthus spinosus) with
long petioled leaves.

KALUNKON, v. /AG-/ to clear the dining table after a
meal. /MANG-:-EN/ to gather or stack up and put
away (object, especially dishes) after using. --var.
KALUNKON.

KALONG; KALONG-KALONG, adj. loose-fitting, as shoes.

KALUNGKON, var. of KALUNKON.

KALUPAPIS, v. /AGI-:I-/ to do in a roundabout or
circuitous way, to do indirectly, to make (one's
speech) circuitous. Ikalkalupapis na ti sarita na.
He is making his speech circuitous.

KALUPI, n. a kind of basket with a flat rectangular
bottom used primarily for storing rice.

KALUPKUP, v. /MANG-:-AN/ to cover or overlay (with
something), to encrust. Kalupkupan na daytoy sagaysay
ko ti balitok. He will encrust my comb with gold.
/MANGI-:I-/ to use to encrust (something) with, to
encrust on (something). Balitok ti inkalupkup na ti
daytoy sagaysay ko. He encrusted my comb with gold.
/MA--AN/ to be encrusted (with something).

KALUYA, v. /MANGI-:I-/ to prohibit, hinder, obstruct
(someone from doing something).

KAM, var. of KAMI.

KAMA [f. Sp.], n. cot, bed.

KAMAKAM, v./AG-/ to catch up with someone, as in a race. /AG- + R2/ to come or occur in rapid succession. Agkakamakam ti nangngeg ko nga putok. The shots that I heard occurred in rapid succession. /MANG-:-EN/ to catch up with (someone or an event). Kamakamen tayo ida idiay airport. We will catch up with them at the airport.

KAMALI, n. mistake, error.   --syn. BIDDUT.
  v. /AG-/ to commit an error, to be mistaken.

KAMALIG, n. granary, warehouse.   --syn. AGAMANG.

KAMAN, n. family, a household. Naimbag nga pagtuladan ti kaman da. Their family is a good model or example.

KAMANAW, n. patches of discolored skin, much paler than the rest of the skin, caused usually by tinea.

KAMANTIGI, n. a common ornamental plant, Impatiens.

KAMANTIRIS, syn. of DAMORTIS.

KAMANG, var. of AMANG.

KAMARIN, n. barn, granary.   --syn. KAMALIG, SARUSAR.

KAMAT, v. /AG-, -UM-/ to run after, pursue or chase someone or something.   /-UM-, MANG-:-EN/ to run after, chase, pursue.

KAMATA [cf. MATA], n. an infection of the eye characterized by redness of the eyeball and an abundant discharge of gum; ophthalmia.

KAMATIS, n. tomato.
  v. /AG-/ to become swollen big and soft like a tomato: said of the penis of a person who has been circumcized a few days ago.

KAMAUDI [cf. UDI], n. hindleg.   --ant. KAMAUNA.   --var. KAMMAUDI.

KAMAUDIANAN [cf. UDI], n. the end, conclusion, termination (of).

KAMAUNA [cf. UNA], n. foreleg.   --ant. KAMAUDI.   --var. KAMMAUNA.

KAMAY, n. a young head louse.

KAMBAL, adj. 1. twin. 2. having two of something, as an egg with two yolks.

KAMEN, short of IKAMEN.

KÁMENG, n. genitals.

KAMENG, n. member, delegate or representative of an organization, association, union, etc. --syn. MIEMBRO.

KAMERA [kamɛra; f. Eng.], n. camera. --syn. KODAK.

KAMET, v. /AG- + R2/ [with pl. subject] to stick to each other in a disorderly manner. Nagkakamet dagiti sagut. The threads stuck to each other.

KAMI, pron. we, us (excl.): the enclitic nominative of DAKAMI. --var. KAM.

KAMIRING, n. a kind of shrub with large leaves crowded at the apices of the branches; it causes some persons to develop rashes upon contact with it.
v. /MA--AN/ to develop rashes due to contact with this shrub.

KAMISA [f. Sp.], n. an outer garment worn by women to cover the upper part of the body, a kind of blouse worn especially by elder women.

KAMISADENTRO [kamisadɛntro; f. Sp.], n. a dress shirt.

KAMISATSINO [f. Sp.], n. a kind of undershirt similar to a T-shirt except that it has buttons below the front part of the neck and the sleeves are tight-fitting.

KAMISETA [kamisɛta; f. Sp.], n. a sleeveless undershirt.

KAMISOLA [f. Sp.], n. an undergarment worn by women to cover the upper part of the body of adult women and the whole body of little girls.

KAMISON [f. Sp.], n. a long undergarment worn by women; slip, chemise.

KAMIT, v. /AG-:-EN/ to profit or gain something from. Awan ti kamiten ti tao nga agtatakaw. A person who is a thief will not gain anything.

KAMKAM, v. /AG-, MANG-:-EN/ to acquire or seize unjustly or illegally.

KAMKAMPILAN, n. 1. a tree bearing big pods. 2. a fruit of this.

KAMLOS, v. /AG-/ to slip, slide out of place. Agkamlos daydiay preno ti dyip. The brakes of the jeep are slipping.

KAMMADANG, n. wooden shoe.   --syn. SUEKOS, BAKYA.

KAMMAUDI, var. of KAMAUDI.

KAMMAUNA, var. of KAMAUNA.

KAMMEL, v. /AG-/ to catch fish with the hands. /MANG-:-EN/ often /MAKA-:MA-/ to catch or be able to catch with the hands in the water as a fish or as one like a fish.

KAMMET, v. /AG-/ to use the hands as in eating. Adkammet tayo nga mangan. Let's use our hands in eating. /MANG-:-EN/ to grasp or seize (something) with the hand.

KAMMO, short for INDIAK AMMO, I don't know.

KAMMUOL, n. welt.

KAMOTI, var. of KAMOTIT.

KAMOTIT, n. sweet potato (Ipomea batatas).   --var. KAMOTI.

KAMPANA [f. Sp.], n. bell, especially a big one. --syn. BATINGTING.   --see also KAMPANILYA.

KAMPANILYA [f. Sp.], n. a small bell.   --see KAMPANA.

KAMPANYA [f. Sp.], n. campaign. v. /AG-/ to campaign.

KAMPAY, short form of KANO PAY, also as they say.

KAMPEON; KAMPION [f. Sp.], n. champion. --var. SAMPION, TSAMPION.

KAMPILAN, n. sword, saber, cutlass, machete.

[1]KAMPIT, v. /-UM-/ to meddle, interfere. Saan ka nga kumampit ta riri da. Don't meddle in their quarrel. /MANGI-:I-/ to get (oneself or someone) entangled.

[2]KAMPIT, n. kitchen knife.

KAMPO [f. Sp.], n. camp.

KAMPUSANTO [f. Sp.], n. cemetery.

KAMURAS, n. measles.
    v. /AG-/ to have the measles.

KAMURO, n. pimple.
    v. /AG-/ to develop pimples.

KAMUTING-KAHOY [f. Tag.], n. cassava.

KAMUYAW, n. a kind of wild orange.

KAN, var. of KANO.

KANA, adj. /NA-/ sharp, piercing, intense (as pain).

KANABTUOG, n. a kind of noise or sound like that produced when running and stamping on the floor, when falling down heavily especially from a high place, etc.
    v. /AG-/ to make noise like this. Saan kay nga agkanabtuog dita batug ti matmaturog. Don't make noise above that sleeping person. /M-/ [= MANABTUOG] to fall down with a thud especially when falling from a high place. Nanabtuog diay ubing ditoy. The child fell down here with a thud.

KANADA, v. /MAI-/ to be appropriate, fit, proper. Saan nga maikanada dayta inaramid mo. What you did is not appropriate.

KANAL [f. Eng.], n. canal.
    v. /AG-/ to make a canal. /MANG-:-AN/ to make a canal in (a place).

KANALBUONG, n. a succession of explosions.
    v. /AG-/ to produce this.

KANALPAAK, v. /AG-/ to produce a succession of slapping or clapping sounds, to clap repeatedly.

KANALPIIT [cf. LIPPIIT], v. /AG-/ to produce a succession of snapping sounds.

KANALPUOT, v. /AG-/ to bluster, to blow stormily: said of wind.

KANALTAAK [cf. LITTAAK], v. /AG-/ to produce a succession of popping sounds as a small stone falling on a roof made of galvanized iron sheets.

KANALTIIK [cf. LITTIIK], v. /AG-/ to produce a succession of snipping or snapping sounds.

KANALTUOG, v. /AG-/ to produce a succession of exploding or thumping sounds. --cf. LANITOG.

KANALTUOK, v. /AG-/ to produce a succession of hollow metallic sounds, as a stone rolling on a roof made of galvanized iron sheets.

KANATAD, adj. /NA-/ orderly, accurate, correct.

KANAWA, v. /MANGI-:I-/ to defend, protect, guard. Ikanawa na kami ti peggad. Protect us from danger. /MAI-/ to be protected. Apay nga saan mo nga kayat ti maikanawa? Why don't you want to be protected?

KANAWAN, n. the right side.
    adj. 1. of, relating to, or being the stronger hand in most persons. 2. located nearer to the right hand than to the left. --var. KANNAWAN. --ant. KANIGID.

KANAYON, adv. always; often, frequently. Kanayon nga makitak ni Rosa idiay simbaan. I always see Rose in church. --syn. PATINAYON.
    v. /MANG-:-EN/ or /MANGI-:I-/ to do always or often. Kanayonen na ti agbuya ti sine. He goes to a movie always.

KANDADO [f. Sp.], n. lock.
    v. /AGI-, MANGI-:I-/ to lock.

KANDILA [f. Sp.], n. candle.

KANDIDATO [f. Sp.], n. candidate.
   v. /-UM-/ to be a candidate (for a position).

KANDIDATURA [f. Sp.], n. candidacy

KANEN [cf. KAAN], n. food.
   KANKANEN, n. cake, sweet.

KANEN, = KAAN + -EN.

KANIBUSANAN, n. end of life, or of the world.

KANIGID, n. the left side.
   adj. 1. of, relating to, or being the weaker hand
in most persons. 2. located nearer to the left than
to the right. --var. KANNIGID. --ant. KANAWAN.

KANITO, n. moment, instant.
   APAGKANITO, in a short time, in a moment. Sumangpet
   to ni nanang mo iti apagkanito. Your mother will
   arrive in a short time. --syn. APAGDIPAS.

KANIWAS, v. /MAI-/ to be against, in opposition, or
   contrary to, to be adverse to. Saan ka nga agaramid
   ti maikaniwas ti linteg. Don't do anything that is
   contrary to law.

KANKANEN, see under KANEN.

KANNAWAN, var. of KANAWAN.

KANNAWAY, n. a kind of heron, egret.

KANNIGID, var. of KANIGID.

[1]KANO, adv. the quotative adverb: it is said, they say.

[2]KANO, var. of AMERIKANO, usually with a pejorative
   meaning.

[3]KANO, v. /MANGI-:I-/ to mind, pay attention to, treat
   with respect, heed. Saan na nga inkankano diay
   nasakit na. He did not mind his sickness. --syn.
   KASO.

[4]KANO; KINNANO, v. /AG- + R2/ [with pl. subject] in
   certain games, to throw flattened metals, stones,
   coins, etc. to determine the order in which the
   players are to play. --syn. MANO.

KANTA [f. Sp.], n. song.
     v. /AG-, -UM-/ to sing a song.   /AG-, -UM-:-EN/ to
sing or chant.   --syn. KANSION.

KANTINA [f. Sp.], n. a general store which is usually
     small.

KANUNONG, v. /-UM-, MANG-:-AN/ to accede to, yield to,
     acquiesce to. Dimo nga kanunongan amin nga kayat na.
     Don't acquiesce to all his wishes.

KANYA-, a prefix that combines with the enclitic
     possessive pronouns to form the corresponding oblique
     pronouns.   --see KEN-, KENKUA-, KA-.

KANYADA, pron. to, toward, from, with, etc. them: the
     oblique of ISUDA.   --var. KENKUADA.

KANYAK, pron. to, toward, from, with, etc. me: the
     oblique of SIAK.

KANYAM, var. of KENKA.

KANYAMI, pron. to, toward, from, with, etc. us (excl.):
     the oblique of DAKAMI.   --var. KADAKAMI.

KANYANA, pron. to, toward, from, with, etc. him or her:
     the oblique of ISU.   --var. KENKUANA.

KANYATA, pron. to, toward, from with, etc. the two of
     us: the oblique of DATA.   --var. KADATA.

KANYATAY, var. of KANYATAYO.

KANYATAYO, pron. to, toward, from, with, etc. us
     (incl.): the oblique of DATAYO.   --var. KANYATAY,
     KADATAYO.

KANYAYO, pron. to, toward, from, with, etc. you (pl.):
     the oblique of DAKAYO.   --var. KADAKAYO.

KANYON [f. Sp.], n. cannon.
     v. /AG-, -UM-:-EN/ to hit with a cannon.

KANGKONG, n. water spinach.   --syn. BALANGEG.

KANGRUNAAN [cf. NANGRUNA], adj. most important, primary,
     principal. Ti kano agrikultura ti kangrunaan nga
     pagsapulan dagiti umili. They say that agriculture

is the most important means of livelihood of the townspeople.

KAP [f. Eng.], n. cup. --syn. TASA.

KAPANAGAN, n. plain. Ibulos na ti kalding na idiay kapanagan. He will let his goat loose in the plain.

KAPARANGET, n. neighbor; someone or something situated near another.
  v. /AG- + R2/ [with pl. subject] to be situated near or adjacent to each other. Agkakaparanget dagiti il-ili mi. Our towns are adjacent to each other.

KAPAS, n. 1. the cotton plant (Gossypium paniculatum). 2. cotton boll.

KAPASANGLAY, n. the silk-cotton or kapok tree (Ceiba pentandra).

KAPATADAN, n. one with the same age as the subject.

KAPATAS, n. overseer, supervisor, superintendent.

KAPE [kapɛ; f. Sp.], n. coffee. --var. KAFE, KAPI.
  v. /AG-/ to drink coffee.

KAPER, n. 1. smegma; the sebaceous substance which collects between the glans penis and the foreskin. 2. a curse word.

KAPET, v. /-UM-/ [= KUMPET] 1. to hold on or cling to something. 2. to fit well, as a dress. /-UM-:-EN/ [= KUMPET : KAPTEN] 1. to hold on, cling to. 2. to transfer to (someone), as a disease or sickness, to infect: said of a disease or sickness. Saan nga nalaka nga kapten ti sakit ti agsida ti natnateng. One who eats vegetables will not easily be infected by a disease.

KAPI, var. of KAPE.

KAPIA, adj. /NA-/ calm, quiet, peaceful. --syn. KALMA.

KAPIDUA [cf. DUA], n. second cousin.

KAPILITAN, see under PILIT.

KAPINANO, KAPIN-ANO, inter. what is your relation to

(someone)? how are you related to (someone)?

KAPITAN [f. Sp.], n. captain.

KAPITLO [cf. TALLO], n. third cousin.

KAPITOLIO [f. Sp.], n. capitol.

KAPKAP, v. /AG-/ to grope or feel something or someone with the hand. /MANG-:-EN/ to grope or feel for (something) with the hand. /MANG-:-AN/ to frisk.

KAPOTE [kapotε; f. Sp.], n. raincoat.

KAPPI, n. a kind of small edible fresh-water crab.

KAPPON, v. /-UM-:-AN/ to join with (a party, an association, etc.). Kimmappon da ti sabali nga partido. They joined another party. /MANGI-:I-/ to put together with, to add to. Inkappon ko ti kuartak ti kapital da. I put my money together with their capital.

KAPSUT, adj. /NA-/ weak, feeble, frail.
    v. /-UM-/ to become this. /AG-/ to tend to be like this. /AG- + R2/ to feel weak, exhausted. --syn. KAPUY.

KAPUTOTAN, see under PUTOT.

KAPUY, adj. /NA-/ 1. weak, feeble. 2. slow, not fast or clever.
    v. /-UM-/ to become adj. 1 or 2. /AG-/ to tend to be like adj. 1 or 2. /AG- + R2/ to feel weak or exhausted. --syn. KAPSUT.

KAPUYO, n. blister.
    v. /AG-/ to develop a blister, to become blistered.

KARA-, a prefix occurring with verb roots which expresses the constant, frequent or habitual repetition of the action indicated by the stem.

KARABA, v. /-UM-:-EN/ to beg for, ask for (help, a job, etc.). Adu ti kumaraba ti tulong na. There are many who ask for his help.

KARAB-AS, v. /AG-/ to put the hands or forelegs heavily on someone or something. Adayoam dayta aso

ta agkarab-as. Go away from that dog for he will put
his forelegs on you. /-UM-:-EN/ to put the hands or
forelegs on (someone or something).

KARABASA [f. Sp.], n. 1. the squash plant (Cucurbita
pepo.). 2. the fruit of this.

KARABUKOB, n. throat, esophagus, gullet.
     v. /-EN/ to have or develop a sore throat. Saan ka
nga agiri ta dikanto karabukoben. Don't cry loud lest
you develop a sore throat.

KARADAKAD, n. the sound produced when walking on gravel
with wooden shoes on, the sound of a cart running on
gravel.
     v. /-UM-/ to produce this sound.

KARADAP, v. /-UM-/ to creep, crawl. /MANG-:-EN/ to
reach (a person, thing, or place) by creeping or
crawling, to crawl or creep to (a person, thing, or
place).

KARADKAD, adj. /NA-/ healthy, robust, active, lively.
     v. /-UM-/ to become alive, lively. Kimmaradkad ni
Rosa idi nangngeg na ti timek ko. Rose became lively
when she heard my voice. /-AN/ to do something in a
lively manner.

KARADUKUD, n. a rumbling sound.

KARAI-, a prefix occurring with verb roots which
indicates repetition of the action expressed by the
verb root.

KARAKARAN, n. crop, craw of a bird.

KARAKATAK, n. snare drum.

KARAMBA, n. a large jar with a wide mouth used especially
for fetching and storing water.

PAGKARAMBAAN, n. 1. a stand or support for this jar.
2. the place where this jar is located.

KARAMUKOM, adj. being in the state before ripening,
not mature, not yet ripening: said of a guava.

KARAMUT, v. /AG-/ to scratch someone. /MANG-:-AN/ to
scratch. /MANGI-:I-/ to scratch with on (someone or
something), to use to scratch (someone or something).

KARANTIWAY, adj. having long thin legs, shanks, stalk, etc.

KARARAG, n. prayer, supplication, plea, petition.
v. /AG-/ to pray. /-UM-:-AN/ to pray to, entreat, implore, beseech. Kumararag tayo ken ni apo Dios. Let's pray to God. /MANGI-:-/ to pray for (something to happen). Ikararag tayo nga agtudo inton bigat. Let's pray for it to rain tomorrow.

KARARIT, n. pulley, a wheel.

KARARWA, n. soul, spirit, ghost.
v. /MANG-/ to serenade a house on the eve of All Souls' Day or shortly before usually for money or food.

KARAS, v. /AG-/ to catch fish by bailing or scooping water from the place where the fish are. /MANG-:-EN/ to bail or scoop (as water or like water). /MANG-:-AN/ to bail or scoop the water content of.

KARASAEN, n. a kind of poisonous snake.

KARASAKAS, v. /AG-/ to rustle like leaves, grass, or pieces of paper.

KARASIKIS, v. /AG-/ to make a thin, crispy sound.

KARASOKOS, v. /AG-/ to slide down a slope. Saan kay nga agkarasokos dita. Don't slide down there.

KARATAKAT, v. /AG-/ to produce a clinking sound, as coins in a wooden box, a cart running over gravel.

KARATIKIT, v. /AG-, -UM-/ to give out a tinkling sound, as coins when jingled.

KARATOKOT, v. /AG-/ to produce a cracking sound, to shake, tremble: said of the knees. Agkaratokot dagitoy tumeng kon. My knees are already shaking.

KARAWA, v. /AG-/ to feel or touch some part of someone with the hand. /-UM-, MANG-:-EN/ to feel or touch with the hand.

KARAYAM, v. /AG-/ to creep, crawl.

KARAYAN, n. river.

KARAYKAY, n. 1. the foot of a bird or fowl. 2. rake.
v. /AG-/ to scratch as a chicken does. /MANG-:-EN/
to scratch (something) as a chicken does.

KARAYO, v. /-UM-/ to strongly and eagerly want to be
with someone or go to someone. Kumarayo dayta anak
mo kanyak. Your child wants eagerly and strongly to
come to me.

KARBENGAN, see under REBBENG.

KAREMKEM, v. /AG-, MANG-:-EN/ to crush or grind with
the teeth.

[1]KARERA, n. course, profession, degree.
v. /-UM-/ to pursue a course, profession or degree.

[2]KARERA [karɛra; f. Sp.], v. (dial.) /MAKI-:KA-/ to run
a race with, to race with. /AG-/ [with pl. subject]
to run a race against each other. --syn. LUMBA.

KARETELA [karɛtɛla; f. Sp.], n. syn. of KAROMATA.

KARETKET, v. /AG-/ to wrinkle, to pucker. Agkaretket
diay muging na. His forehead wrinkles. /MANG-:-EN/
to cause to wrinkle or pucker, to wrinkle, pucker.
Apay nga karetketem ta muging mo? Why do you cause
your forehead to wrinkle?

KARETON [karɛton; f. Sp.], n. a kind of cart pulled by
a carabao or cow. --var. KARITON, KARISON.

KARGA [f. Sp.], n. var. of KARGADA.
v. /AG-, MANG-:-EN/ to carry. --syn. BAKLAY.

KARGADA [f. Sp.], n. load, cargo. Imbati na dagiti
kargada na. He left his cargo. --see KARGAMENTO.

KARGAMENTO [f. Sp.], n. cargo, luggage. --see KARGADA.

KARGO [f. Sp.], charge, obligation, responsibility.

KARI, n. promise.
v. /MANGI-:I-/ to promise (something, or to do
something). Inkari na ti makimisa inton dominggo.
He promised to attend mass on Sunday. /MAI-/ to be
destined, worthy, fitting for (a position, role,
etc.).

KARIBUSO, v. to hustle and bustle, to move briskly. Kumaribuso dagiti tao idiay bodaan. The people in the ball are hustling and bustling.

KARIG [cf. ARIG], adv. like, similar to. Karig la bituen nga rumimatrimat diay bado na. Her dress is like a star that is twinkling. --syn. KAS.

KARIMBUAYA, n. a cactus-like plant (Euphorbia trigona).

KAR-IN, v. /MANGI-:I-/ to turn over the food content of with a spatula or ladle, to turn over (food in a pot, pan, etc.) with a spatula or ladle. Ikar-in mo diay banga. Turn over the food in the pot with a ladle.

KARINYO [f. Sp.], adj. /NA-/ fond of caressing or teasing the opposite sex. --syn. KARINYOSO.

KARINYOSO [f. Sp.], adj. habitually fond of caressing or teasing the opposite sex.

KARISON, var. of KARETON.

KARIT, adj. /NA-/ impudent, defiant, bold, brash, daring.
v. /-UM-, MANG-:-EN/ to dare, defy, challenge, provoke, incite. Saan mo nga kariten dayta aso ta kumagat. Don't incite that dog for it will bite.

KARITON, var. of KARETON.

KARKAR, v. /-UM-:-AN/ to erode. /MA--AN/ to be eroded. Nakarkaran dayta pagayan ti danum. Water eroded that rice field.

KARMAY, n. 1. a kind of tree. 2. the fruit of this tree.

KARNABAL [f. Sp.], n. carnival.

KARNE [karnε; f. Sp.], n. meat.
  KARNE TI BABOY, pork.
  KARNE TI BAKA, beef.

KARNERO [karnεro; f. Sp.], n. sheep.

[1]KARO, adj. /NA-/ excessive, too much, too severe. Saan
nak nga nakastrek ti eskuela gapo ti nakaro nga
uyek. I was not able to go to school because of
excessive coughing.
   v. /-UM-/ to worsen. Kumaro ti sakit na. His
sickness is worsening.

[2]KARO, v. /MANGI-:I-/ to atone for, expiate, make
satisfaction for. Ikarom to met la ta basol mo. You
will also atone for your sin.

KAROMATA [f. Sp.], n. a kind of horse-drawn two-wheeled
carriage with two or three rows of seats. --syn.
KARETELA.

KARRO [f. Sp.], n. 1. a four-wheeled vehicle without
body used for floats. 2. a funeral carriage. 3. a
car. --syn. KOTSE.

KARRUBA, n. neighbor, a person or thing located near
another. --var. KAARUBA.

KARSADA, var. of KALSADA.

KARSEL [karsεl; f. Sp.], n. prison, jail.
   v. /MANGI-:I-/ to imprison. --syn. KALABUS,
PRESO.

KARSO, see PAKARSO.

KARSONSILIO, var. of KALSONSILIO.

KARTERO [kartεro; f. Sp.], n. mailman, mail carrier.

KARTIB, n. scissors, shears. --syn. GETTENG.
   v. /MANG-:-EN/ to cut with a pair of scissors or
shears.

KARTILYA [f. Sp.], n. a syllabary. Nagbasa da iti
kartilya. They read a syllabary.

KARTING, adj. /NA-/ brisk, alert, active, lively, fast.

KARUKAY, v. /AG-/ to scratch as a chicken does. Dagidiay
manok ti nagkarukay ditoy. The chickens were the ones
that scratched here. /MANG-:-EN/ Dagidiay manok ti
nangkarukay kadagidiay mula. The chickens were the
ones that scratched the plants. --syn. KARAYKAY.

[1]KARUS, n. a scraper.
    v. /AG-, MANG-:-EN/ to scrape.

[2]KARUS, n. strickle.
    v. /MANG-:-EN/ to level with a strickle, to gather
or form with a strickle.

[3]KARUS, v. /MANG-:-EN/ to scrape in order to get part
of.   --syn. KARUSAKIS.

KARUSAKIS, v. /MANG-:-EN/ to get some of by scraping,
    to scrape some of. Karusakisem dayta tagapulot.
    Scrape some of that hard sugar.   --syn. KARUS.

KARUSKUS, v. /AG-/ to slide down a tree, a rope, a
    slope, etc. Saan kay nga agkaruskus dita. Don't
    slide down there.

KARUT-OM, v. /AG-:-EN/ to crunch or grind with the
    teeth: said of uncooked rice. Isu ti nagkarut-om ti
    bagas. It was he who crunched rice.

KARUY, v. to take out (something soft) with or as with
    a scoop, to scoop. Karuyem daytoy niog nga naganus.
    Take out with a scoop this soft coconut meat.

KAS, adv. like, similar to: usually followed by LA.
    Kas ka la ubing. You are like a child.   --syn. KARIG.

KASABA; KASKASABA, v. /MANG-/ [= MANGASKASABA] to
    preach to, deliver a sermon to. Napan nangaskasaba
    kadagiti tattao idiay baryo. He went and preached to
    the people in the barrio.   /MANGI-:I-/ to indoctrinate,
    proselytize. Isu ti nangikaskasaba kadagiti tattao
    idiay baryo. It was he who proselytized the people
    in the barrio.

KASADAR, n. a contemporary.
    v. /AG-/ [with pl. subject] to be of the same age,
coetaneous, contemporary.

KASAG, n. a kind of dome-shaped trap for fish set down
    on the bottom of rivers, brooks, lakes, etc.
    v. /AG-/ to catch fish with this.   /MANG-:-EN/
often   /MAKA-:MA-/ to catch or be able to catch fish
with this. Adu ti nakasag na. He was able to catch
many fish with the KASAG.

KASAKBAYAN [cf. SAKBAY], n. the period before an event.
--syn. KASANGOANAN.

KASAMAK, n. a farm tenant, sharecropper.

KASANO, inter. how?, in what manner?
  URAY KASANO, KASANO MAN, howsoever.

KAS-ANG, adj. /NA-/ painful, hurting. Nakas-ang ta
  imbagam. What you said is painful.

KASANGAALDAW [cf. ALDAW], n. the day before.

KASANGOANAN [cf. SANGO], n. the period before an event.
--syn. KASAKBAYAN.

KASAPULAN [cf. SAPUL], n. something needed, something
  requisite, desirable, or useful; need. Dioty ti
  pakaipangagan dagiti asug ken kasapulan dagiti
  taga-away. This is where the complaints and needs of
  the farm people can be heard.

KASAR [f. Sp.], n. wedding
     v. /MAKI-:KA-/ to marry, wed. /AG-/ [with pl.
  subject] to get married. /MANGI-:I-/ to marry, wed.
  --syn. KALLAYSA.

KASASAAD [cf. SAAD], n. position, social standing,
  situation.

[1]KASDI, dem. like that one in the remote past.
     v. /MANGI-:I-/ to do or make like that one in the
  remote past.

[2]KASDI, see KASKASDI.

KASDIAY, dem. like that one yonder.
     v. /MANGI-:I-/ to do or make like that one yonder.
  NO KASDIAY, in that case, thus.

KASILYAS [f. Sp.], n. outhouse, privy, toilet.

KASINSIN [pl. KAKASINSIN], n. first cousin, cousin-
  german.

KASIR, v. /-UM-:-EN/ to provoke, incense, irritate.
  Saan mo nga kasiren dayta adim. Don't irritate your
  younger brother (or sister).

KASKARON [f. Sp.], n. a kind of sweet made of rice flour boiled in sugar.

KASKAS, v. /MANG-:-EN/ to gather in one place. Kaskasem amin nga agkaiwara nga basura. Gather in one place all the rubbish that is strewn around.

KASKASABA, see KASABA.

KASKASDI, adv. nevertheless, just the same.

KASO [f. Sp.], n. 1. case (in court). Adda kasok idiay ili mi. I have a case in our town. 2. value, importance. Awan ti kaso na dayta. That is of no importance.
     v. /MANGI-:I-/ to mind, pay attention to. Saan mo nga ikaskaso ni baket ko ta nagapa kami. Don't mind my wife for we quarreled.

KASSIET, var. of KISSIT.

KASTA, dem. like that one near the hearer.
     v. /MANGI-:I-/ to do or make like that one near the speaker.

     NO KASTA, in that case, thus.

     KASTA UNAY, very much, excessively so. Kasta unay ti kaadu ti tao idiay. The people there were excessively numerous.

KASTAY, dem. like that one not now visible.
     v. /MANGI-:I-/ to do or make like that one not now visible.

KASTILA [f. Sp.], n. 1. Spaniard. 2. the Spanish language.
     v. /AG-/ to speak the Spanish language. /MANG-:-EN/ 1. to speak to (someone) in Spanish. 2. to render in the Spanish language.

KASTOY, dem. like this one near the speaker.
     v. /MANGI-:I-/ to do or make like this one near the speaker.

KASUGPON, n. a helper in farming.

KASUNO, n. substitute, successor. --syn. KASUKAT.

KASUORAN, n. the part of the roof which is over the hearth.

KATAKAT, v. /MA--AN/ to diminish, lessen, to become fewer. Saan nga makatakatan ti tao nga aggatang ti bagas. The people who are buying rice are not getting any fewer.

KATAM, n. carpenter's plane.
  v. /MANG-:-EN/ to shave with a plane.

NAGKATAMAN, n. shavings.

KATANG; KATANG-KATANG, v. /AG-/ to float in a random manner, to drift. Agkatang-katang ti taaw diay biray nga nagluganan da. The boat on which they were riding drifted in the ocean.

KATATAO [cf. TAO], n. one's nature or trait as a human being.

KATAWA, v. /AG-/ to laugh. Saan ka nga agkatkatawa. Don't laugh. /:-AN/ to laugh at (someone or something). Saan nak nga katkatawaan. Don't laugh at me.
  adj. /NAKA-R3-/ funny, ludicrous, laughable. Nakakatkatawa ka. You are funny. --syn. GARAKGAK.

KATAWTAW-AN [cf. TAO], n. a supernatural being.

KATAY, n. saliva, spittle.
  v. /AG-/ to have saliva flowing out of the mouth. /-AN/ to drop saliva on.

KATIGID, var. of KANIGID.
  adj. left-handed. --var. KATTIGID.

KATIKAT, v. /MANG-:-EN/ to wind, coil. Katikatem dayta barot. Wind that wire.

KATIL, v. /MANG-:-EN/ to fight with, quarrel with: especially said of children. Saan mo nga katilen ta adim. Don't fight with your younger brother (or sister). /AG-(-INN-) + R2/ [with pl. subject] to fight with one another. Saan kayo nga agkikinnatil. Don't fight with one another.

KATING, v. /AG-/ to have leprosy, to be leprous. Saan ka nga umasideg kanyana ta agkatil. Don't go near him for he has leprosy. --syn. KUTEL.

KATOLIKO [f. Sp.], adj. Catholic, being a member of the Roman Catholic Church. --syn. ROMANO.

KATRE [katrɛ; f. Sp.], n. a kind of bed.

KATTIGID, var. of KATIGID.

KATUDAY, n. a leguminous tree (Sesbania grandiflora) with large white or white and violet flowers and long linear edible pods.

KATUGANGAN [pl. KAKATUGANGAN], n. father-in-law, mother-in-law, the father or mother of one's spouse.

KATULAGAN [cf. TULAG], n. agreement, contract. --syn. KONTRATO, KONTRATA.

KAUT, v. /AG-, -UM-, MANG-:-EN/ to draw out from a hole, pocket, jar. etc.

KAWA, v. /MAI-/ 1. to feel strange or lost (being in a place or with someone). 2. to do (an unexpected or sinful act) inadvertently or accidentally, to happen (to do something). Naikawa ka man nga immay ditoy? Did you happen to come here?

KAWAL, v. /MANG-:-EN/ to touch or feel with the fingers, to finger. Saan mo nga kawalen ta sida. Don't finger the sidedish.

KAWAR, n. chain.
    v. /MANG-:-AN/ to put a chain on, to chain.

KAWAS, adj. /NA-/ tall. --syn. TAYAG, NGATO.

KAWAYAN, n. bamboo. --see SIITAN, BAYUG, KILING.

KAWES, n. clothing, garment, apparel, clothes, dress. --syn. BADO.

KAWIKAW, v. /MANG-:-EN/ to twist into a coil, to coil.

KAWIL, v. /MANG-:-EN/ to hold fast with a leg or both legs. /AG-(-INN-)/ to hold each other fast with the legs.

KAWILI, v. /MA-/ to be possible to reach and return to the original point of departure on the same day. Saan nga makawili ta adayo. It is not possible to reach it and return from it (to this place) on the same day.

KAWING, adj. crooked, bent, curved. --syn. KILLO.
   v. /AG-/ to bend, curve.

KAWIT, n. hook.
   v. /MANG-:-EN/ to seize with a hook, to hook.

KAWITAN, n. cock, rooster.

KAWIWIT, v. /-UM-:-AN/ to hold onto by putting the arms
   and legs around. Kumawiwit ka dita poon ti kayo. Hold
   onto that trunk of the tree by putting your arms and
   legs around it.

KAWKAW, v. /MANG-:-EN/ to touch or stir with the
   fingers or hand. /MANG-:I-/ to dip (especially one's
   fingers or hands) into a liquid (especially water).

KAWKAWATI, n. syn. of DALAGUDOG.

KAWWET, n. the spur of a cock.

KAY, var. of KAYO.

KAYAB, v. /-UM-/ to flap the wings rapidly, to flutter.
   Abbungam dayta alat tapno saan nga kumayab dagita
   manok. Cover that basket so that the chickens will
   not flutter.
   KAYABKAYAB, v. /AG/ to float in the air, to be
      wafted. Adu ti agkayabkayab nga dutdot ditoy.
      There are many feathers floating in the air here.

KAYABKAB, v. /AG-/ to flap the wings, to flutter:
   said of a hen.

KAYAKAY, adj. /NA-/ remote. Nangngeg ti kanalbuong
   uray kadagiti nakayakay nga ili. The explosions were
   heard even in the remote towns.

KAYAM, v. /MANG-:-AN/ to influence or affect especially
   injuriously by witchcraft, to bewitch. /MA--AN/ to
   be influenced or affected especially injuriously by
   witchcraft, to be bewitched. Nakayaman diay balasang.
   The young woman was bewitched.

KAYAMKAM, v. /-UM-/ to spread, as fire, water, ink,
   diseases, etc. Sibugam dayta apoy ta di kumayamkam.
   Splash water on that fire so that it won't spread.
   /MANG-:-EN/ to spread over, engulf. Kinayamkam ti
   apoy amin nga bulbulong. The fire spread over all
   the leaves and burned them.

KAYANG, v. /AG-/ to straddle, to part the legs wide.

KAYANGA, n. a large showy-flowered Asiatic hibiscus (Hibiscus rosa-sinensis), China rose. --syn. GUMAMELA.

KAYAS, v. /AG-, MANG-:-AN/ to whittle.

KAYASKAS, v. /MANG-:-EN/ to gather, put together (objects that are scattered). Kayaskasem aming nga narugit nga pinggan. Gather all the dirty plates.

KAYAT, n. desire, wish; something desired, longed for or wanted. Kayat ko ti mangan. I want to eat.
    v. /M-/ [= MAYAT] to be willing; to consent or allow oneself (to do something). Mayat nga agkumpisar diay baro. The young man is willing to go on confession. --ant. MADI. --see AYAT.

KAYKAYAT, n. someone or something desired more.

KAYAW, v. /MANG-:-AN/ to captivate, fascinate, charm. Isu ti nangkayaw ti riknak. It was she who captivated my feelings.
    adj. /MAKA-/ captivating, fascinating, charming. Makakayaw ti panagkanta na. Her singing is captivating.

KAYAW-AT, v. /-UM-/ to move the hand or arm to and fro especially in order to call someone's attention. Kumaykayaw-at idi nakita mi. He was moving his hand to and fro when we saw him. /MANGI-:I-/ to move (the hand or arm) to and fro. Inkayaw-at na ti ima na tapno makita da. He moved his hand to and fro so that they could see him.

KAYETKET, v. /AG-, -UM-/ to shrink or contract due to exposure to or contact with heat or water. Nagkayetket diay singsing na idi napuoran. His ring contracted when it was burned. Kimmayetket ti bado na idi nabasa. Her dress shrank when it got wet.

KAYKAY, n. broom
    v. /AG-:-AN/ to sweep (in a place). --syn. SAGAD.

[1]KAYO, n. 1. tree, a big plant. 2. wood, timber, log.

[2]KAYO, pron. you (pl.): the enclitic nominative of DAKAYO. --var. KAY.

[3]KAYO, n. a roll of cloth woven in the native loom.

KAY-O, v. /MANGI-:I-/ to remove, throw away. Ikay-om dayta danum dita bakka. Throw away the water in that big basin.

KAYONG, n. brother-in-law, the husband of one's sister or cousin. --syn. BAYAW.

KAYSA; KAYKAYSA [cf. MAYSA], v. /AG-/ 1. to become one, unite, coalesce. 2. to agree.

KAYUMANGGI, adj. brown, tan, swarthy.

KAYUMKOM, v. /MANG-:-EN/ to gather.

KAYUSKUS, v. /MANG-:-EN/ to sweep together, gather. Kayuskusem amin nga nagkayasan. Gather all the whittlings.

KAYYANAK [cf. ANAK], adj. newly born.

KEBBA; KEGGAKEBBA, v. /AG-/ to heave, to rise or swell and fall rapidly and strongly: said of the chest. Agkebbakebba ti barukong ko ti kigtot ko. My chest is heaving due to my having been startled.

KEBBES, v. /MANG-:-EN/ to measure by grasping with hand, to grasp a handful of. Mangkebbes ka ti balangeg nga itedmo kanyana. Grasp a handful of water spinach.

KEBBET, v. /-UM-/ [= KUMBET] to shrink, contract, wrinkle.

KEDDEL, v. /AG-/ to pinch or squeeze someone between the nails painfully. /MANG-:-EN/ to pinch or squeeze (someone or something) between the nails.

KEDDENG, n. wish, desire, decision, resolution. --syn. KAYAT.
    v. /MANGI-:I-/ to determine, decide, settle, resolve. Isu ti mangikeddeng no mano ti pagbayad mo. It is he who will determine how much you should pay.

KEDKED, v. /AG-/ to refuse or resist (to do something). Saan ka nga agkedked nga umawat ti daytoy kuarta. Don't refuse to receive this money. /AG-:-AN/ to refuse or resist to give (something). Kinedkedan na ti rasyon mi. He refused to give our ration.

KEGGANG, n. scab, a crust of hardened blood and serum over a wound.
v. /AG-/ to form this: said of a wound. /-AN/ to remove this over a wound.

KEKEK, v. /-UM-/ to cluck.

KELLAAT, adj. sudden, instant, fast. Kellaat ti panagadu ti tao iti ili mi. The increase of people in our town was sudden.
v. /MANG-:-EN/ to surprise, to come upon (someone) suddenly, unexpectedly, or abruptly. Saan mo nga kellaaten ni nanang mo no aglutluto. Don't surprise your mother when she is cooking. /MA-/ [= MAKELLAAT or MAKLAAT] to be surprised due to the suddenness or unexpectedness. Nakellaat kami ti isasangpet mo. The unexpectedness of your arrival surprised us.

KELLAD, v. /AG-, MANG-:-AN/ to scrape with the teeth. Narigat ti agkellad ti bunga ti marunggay ngem naimas. It is difficult to scrape with the teeth the fruit of the MARUNGGAY, but it is delicious.

[1]KELLEB, see PAKLEB.

[2]KELLEB, n. the cover of an earthen jar, pot, or pan.
v. /MANG-:-AN/ to cover (a jar, pot, or pan).
--syn. KALUB.

KELLENG; KINELLENG, n. rice field. Isu ti agtaltalon iti kinelleng mi. It is he who farms our rice field.
--syn. TALON.

KELNAT, v. /AG-, MANG-:-EN/ to parboil (a vegetable).

KELTAY, v. /MANG-:-EN/ to frustrate, destroy, ruin, dash. Saan mo nga keltayen ti ganas ko nga mangan. Don't ruin my appetite to eat.

KEMKEM, v. /MANG-:-EN/ to chew, masticate. Kemkemem nga nalaing ta kanem. Chew well what you eat. --syn. NGALNGAL.

KEMMA, v. /MANG-:-EN/ to examine or treat (a sore eye). Isu ti nangkemma ti mata ni Ana. It was he who examined the sore eye of Ann.

KEMMAKEM, v. /AG-/ to open and close the hand. Ammo na ti agkemmakem ta anak mon. Your child already knows how to open and close his hands.

KEMMEG, v. /MANG-:-EN/ to catch, seize, capture.

¹KEN, prep. to, in, at, toward, from (before a proper name).

²KEN, conj. 1. and. Sika ken siak ti mabati ditoy. You and I will be left here (before a proper name). 2. including, together with. Dakami ken ni Maria ti mapan. Mary and I will go.

KEN-, a prefix that combines with the second person singular enclitic nominative pronoun (KA) to form the corresponding full oblique pronouns. --see KANYA-, KENKUA-, KA-.

KENDI [kɛndi; f. Eng], n. candy.

KENKA, pron. to, toward, from, with, etc. you (sg.): the oblique of SIKA. --var. KANYAM.

KENKUA-, a prefix that combines with the third person pronouns to form the corresponding oblique pronouns. --see KANYA-, KEN-, KA-.

KENKUADA, var. of KANYADA.

KENKUANA, var. of KANYANA.

KEPKEP, v. /AG-/ to fold the arms over the chest. /MANG-:-AN/ to hold close to the chest with the arms around, to embrace, hug.

KEPPES, v. /-UM-/ [= KUMPES] to shrink, cower (especially from fear). Kumkumpes kami ti buteng mi. We were cowering due to our fear.

KEPPET, v. /AG-/ to close, shut. Nagkeppet ti mata na. His eyes closed.

KERKER, n. bundle, bunch.

KERRAAD, v. /-UM-/ [= KUMRAAD] to creak. Nangngeg ko nga kimraad idiay ruangan. I heard it creak in the gate. --syn. RANITRIT.

KERRAANG, v. /-UM-/ [= KUMRAANG] to become completely dry. Ibilag mo dagita kayo inggana ti kumraang da. Expose those pieces of wood in the sun until they are completely dry.

KERRAAY, v. /MA--AN/ [= MAKRAAYAN] to be depleted, ravaged. Nakraayan ti bunga daydiay mangga mi. Our mango tree was depleted of its fruits.

KERRAS, v. /MANG-:-AN/ to level with a strickle. Kerrasam dayta salop no agsuksukat ka ti bagas. Level the SALOP with a strickle when you measure rice.

KERRET, n. anus. --var. KIRRET.

KERSANG, adj. /NA-/ rough, coarse to the touch.

KESSEN, v. /-AG-, -UM-/ [= KUMSEN] to shrink, contract; to become warped. Kimsen daytoy badok. My dress shrank.

KESSET, v. /MANG-:-EN/ to burn, scorch, char through overcooking. /MA-/ [= MAKSET] to be burned, scorched, or charred due to overcooking.

INPAKSET, n. burned or scorched rice or meat.

[1]KET, conj. and. --syn. KEN.

[2]KET, adv. of emphasis.

[3]KET, lig. standing between the subject and the predicate.

KETDI, adv. implying opposition, contrariness, or an alternative to what is expected or planned or happening. Inta ketdi ida biroken. Let's go look for them instead.

KETTA, v. /MANG-:-EN/ to disunite, separate, take apart, disassemble. /MA-/ [= MAKTA] to be disassembled, taken apart. Nakta diay kuentas na. Her necklace was disassembled.

KETTANG, v. /MA-/ [= MAKTANG] to tire being in the same position for some time.

KETTAT, v. /-UM-/ [= KUMTAT] to shrink or recoil from due to fear. Saan nga kumtat diay balasang nga agiggem ti paltog. The young woman does not shrink from holding a gun.

KETTEL, v. /MANG-:-EN/ to nip by squeezing between the
  nails or fingers.

KETTER, v. /-UM-/ [= KUMTER] to shrivel, wrinkle,
  shrink due to being soaked in water or to the
  coldness.

KIAD, adj. having the abdomen protruding.

KIAK, n. the cry of a chicken when caught or injured.
  v. /AG-/ to make this sound.

KIAW, adj. yellow.
  n. a kind of oriole with yellow and black plumage.

KIBAAN, n. leprechaun-like supernatural being, an elf.

KIBBO, v. /AG-, -UM-/ to bend. /MANG-:-EN/ to cause
  to bend, to bend. Kibboem man daytoy barut. Will you
  please bend this wire.
  adj. bent, curved, twisted.

KIBIN, v. /MANG-:-EN/ to guide by holding the hand.
  /AG- + R2/ [with pl. subject] to hold hands.

KIBIT; KIBITKIBIT, v. /AG-/ to draw near, approach
  (death). Agkibitkibit ken patay. He is approaching
  death.

KIBKIB, v. /AG-/ to nibble. /MANG-:-EN/ to eat in
  small bits, to nibble. Ania ti kibkibkibem dita?
  What are you nibbling there? /MANG-:-AN/ to nibble
  a part of. Kinibkiban ni Pedro daytoy. Peter nibbled
  a part of this.

KIBONG; KIBONGKOBONG, n. the superior part of the
  buttocks where they inflect toward the back.

KIBOR, v. /MANG-:-EN/ to stir, agitate, upset, confuse.

KIDAG, v. /-UM-, MANG-:-EN/ to hit with the elbow or
  knee.

KIDAY, n. eyebrow.

KIDDAW, n. petition, plea, request.
  v. /AG-, MANG-:-EN/ to beg, request, plead,
  petition, solicit. Kayat ko nga kiddawen ti yaay mo

inton piesta mi. I would like to request your coming
during our fiesta.

KIDDAY, v. /AG-/ to wink at someone. /MANG-:-AN/ to
wink at.

KIDDIAS, v. /-UM-/ [= KUMDIAS] to turn aside, deflect,
deviate from (as a bullet). Kimdias ti bala idiay
balay da. The bullet turned aside from their house.

KIDDIS, n. a pinch: used with a numeral.
    v. /MANG-:-EN/ to pinch off, to remove by pinching.
Kiddisem dayta ukis ti manok. Pinch off that skin of
the chicken. /MANG-:-AN/ to pinch off a part of, to
remove a part of by pinching. Saan mo nga kiddisan
daytoy bagik. Don't pinch off a part of my share.
--see KEDDEL.

KIDEM, v. /AG-/ to close the eyes. /MANGI-:I-/ to
close (the eyes or something like the eyes).

KIGAW, n. 1. fawn. 2. a person who tries to avoid
people.

KIGTOT, v. /AG-, MANG-:-EN/ to surprise, startle.
/MA-/ to be startled, surprised.

KIKI, v. /AG-, MANG-:-EN/ to tickle, titillate.

KIKIT, n. 1. the little finger, auricular finger. 2.
the little toe.

    KIKIT TI IMA, the little finger.

    KIKIT TI SAKA, the little toe.

KILABBAN, n. cold cooked rice usually what is left
after a meal.
    v. /AG-/ to eat usually between meals with cold
rice. /MANG-:-EN/ to eat usually between meals
(cold rice with something).

KILANG, v. /MANGI-:I-/ to toll the bells for (someone
who is dead). /MAI-/ to announce the death of by
tolling the bells. Naikilang ni Pedro itay malem.
The death of Peter was announced by tolling the
bells this afternoon.

KILAP, adj. /NA-/ shiny, brilliant, glittering,

sparkling.
   v. /-UM-/ to shine, gleam, glitter, sparkle.

[1]KILAT, adj. having one or both lower eyelids stretched
   or pulled downwards.

[2]KILAT, interj. an exclamation used in sneering.

KILAW, v. /AG-, MANG-:-EN/ to eat (meat or fish) raw
   or uncooked or half cooked.

KILAWEN, n. a kind of meat dish.

KILGA, v. /MANG-:-EN/ to confuse, disturb. Saan mo nga
   kilgaen dagita manok. Don't disturb those chickens.

KILIKIL, v. /-UM-/ to contort the body, to writhe.
   Kumilikil ni Rosa ti sakit ti tian na. Rose is
   writhing because of her stomach ache.

KILIKILI, n. armpit, axilla.
   v. /AG-/ to tickle or titillate someone. /MANG-:-EN/
   to tickle, titillate.

KILILING, n. 1. a small bell. --syn. KAMPANILYA. 2.
   the ringing of a small bell. Addaak pay laeng iti
   balay idi mangngeg ko ti kililing. I was still in
   the house when I heard the ringing of a small bell.
   v. /AG-/ to ring: said of a small bell. /MANG-:-EN/
   to ring (a small bell). Sino ti nangkiling diay
   kampanilya? Who rang the small bell? --var. KILING,
   KULILING.

[1]KILING, var. of KILILING.

[2]KILING, n. an erect, slender, and spineless bamboo
   (Bambusa vulgaris).

KILLO, v. /MANG-:-EN/ to bend, curve, twist, cause to
   become crooked. /MA-/ to become crooked, bent,
   curved, twisted.
   adj. crooked, bent, curved, twisted.

KILNET, adj. /NA-/ thick and sticky, gluey.

KILO [f. Sp.], v. /AG-, MANG-:-EN/ to weigh in a
   weighing machine.

PAGKILOAN, n. a weighing machine.

KILOMETRO [kilomɛtro; f. Sp.], n. kilometer.

KIMAT, n. lightning.
v. /AG-/ to strike: said of lightning. /-EN/ often /MA-/ to be struck or injured by lightning. Nakimat diay nuang na. His water buffalo was struck by lightning.

KIMAW, v. /AG-/ to bob or jump to the surface of the water and back: said of a fish.

KIMDIAS, pt. of KUMDIAS.

KIMIKA [f. Sp.], n. chemistry.

KIMKIM, adj. /NA-/ frugal, thrifty.

KIMMOL, n. coccyx.

[1]KIMMOT, n. the youngest child. --syn. BURIDEK.

[2]KIMMOT, n. anus.

KIMMOKIMMOT, v. /AG-/ to dilate and contract alternately like the anus of a chicken.

[1]KINA-, pt. of KA-.

[2]KINA-, a nominalizing affix used with nouns and adjective roots to form abstract quality nouns.

KINABITI, see KABITI.

KINELLENG, see KELLENG.

KINNI, v. /AG-/ to wiggle the hips, as in dancing or walking.

KINNIT, v. /AG-, MANG-:-EN/ to pull with the teeth. Saan ka nga agkinnit ti karne. Don't pull meat with your teeth.

KINOD, v. /AG-/ to move the pelvic region forward and backward as in sexual intercourse. /-UM-:-AN/ to do this toward the direction of (someone or something). --var. KIN-OD.

KINTAL, adj. /NA-/ sticky and firm: said of the meat of a squash. --ant. GARES.

KINTAYEG, adj. /NA-/ jerky, full of jogs.
v. /AG-/ to shake, tremble, quiver, shiver.
Agkintayeg ti laslasag ko no kumitaak ti baba. My
muscles quiver when I look down.

KINGKI, n. lamp. --syn. SILAW, LAMPARA.

KINGKING, v. /AG-/ to hop.
n. a children's game played mostly by hopping,
hopscotch. --syn. PIKO.
v. /AG-/ [with pl. subject] to play this game.

KIPET, adj. /NA-/ tight, narrow. --syn. KITING.

KIPUT, adj. /NA-/ tight, tight-fitting, as a dress.

KÍRANG, adj. /NA-/ scarce, scanty.

KIRAOD, n. 1. a cuplike instrument used to scoop rice,
water, etc. from a container. 2. a unit of dry
measure chiefly for rice, a cupful. --var. KIRAOS.

KIRAOS, var. (dial.) of KIRAOD.

KIRAS, v. /AG-/ to walk by dragging the feet or causing
them to scrape the ground or floor. /MANGI-:I-/ to
scrape against the ground or floor when walking.
Saan mo nga ikiras dayta sinelas mo. Don't scrape
your slippers against the floor while walking.

KIRAT, v. /MANG-:-EN/ to kill or knock down all at
one stroke. /MA-/ [with pl. subject] to be killed
or knocked down at one stroke.

KIRAY, n. twinkle, twinkling. Kayat mo nga makita iti
kiray dagiti bituen? Do you want to see the twinkling
of the stars?
v. /AG-/ to twinkle, wave, blink, glint. Adda
nakitak nga nagkiray dita. I saw something glint
there.

KIRAYKIRAY, v. /AG-/ to flicker, to blink repeatedly.
Apay nga agkiraykiray dayta silaw? Why is that
lamp flickering?

KIRED, n. strength, vigor, endurance.
adj. /NA-/ strong, vigorous, robust, durable.

KIREM, v. /AG-/ to wink or blink one's eyes.   /MANG-:-EN/
or /MANGI-:I-/ to wink, blink (one's eyes).

KIRIKET, var. (dial.) of GIRIT.

KIR-IN, v. /AG-/ to move slightly. Awan pay ti nagkir-in
kadagidiay agbuybuya. No one of those watching made
a slight stir.

[1]KIRKIR, v. /MANG-:-AN/ to scrub. Kirkiran dayta datar.
Scrub that floor!

[2]KIRKIR, n. carpenter's file.   --syn. GARUGAD.
v. /MANG-:-AN/ to file.

KIRMET, adj. /NA-/ stingy, selfish, miserly.   --syn.
IMOT.

KIRO, adj. /NA-/ disorderly, confused, entangled.
v. /MANG-:-EN/ to cause to become disorderly,
confused, or entangled.

KIROKIRO, n.pl. problems, disorders, disturbances.

KIROG, v. /AG-, MANG-:-EN/ to roast or toast in a pan.

KIR-OS, v. /AG-/ to pound rice the third and usually
the last time.   /MANG-:-EN/ to pound (incompletely
pounded rice) for the third and usually last time.

KIRRET, var. of KERRET.

KIRRIIT, v. /-UM-/ to dry up under the sun. Akasem to
dagita longboy inton kumriit da. Take those blackberries
in from the sun for they might dry up.   /MANG-:-EN/
to dry up (e.g. a fruit) under the sun. Kirriitem
dagita longboy. Dry up those blackberries under the
sun.

KIRUS, n. 1. a strickle. 2. a scraper especially of
coconut meat or coconut shell.
v. /MANG-:-EN/ to scrape off.   /MANG-:-AN/ to
level with or as if with a strickle.

KISAME [kisamɛ; f. Sp.], n. ceiling.   --syn. BUBIDA.

KISANG, adj. /NA-/ insufficient, inadequate, deficient.

KISAP, v. /MANG-:-EN/ or /MANGI-:I-/ to consume,

shear, or get rid of completely. Inkisap na amin nga
bunga ti mangga. He consumed all the mango fruits.
/MAI-/ to be completely consumed, shorn, or destroyed.

KISKIS, v. /AG-/ to shave one's beard with a razor or
shaver. /MANG-:-EN/ to cut off (hair, especially
the beard) at the surface of the skin. Kiskisem ti
barbas na. Shave his beard. /MANG-:-AN/ to cut the
beard of (a person). Kiskisan nak ni Pedro. Peter
will shave my beard.

KISSAY, v. /AG-/ to reduce what one has. /MANG-:-AN/
to take from, reduce, decrease. Kinissayan na ti
kuartak. He took some from my money. /MANG-:-EN/
to take away from in order to lessen. Mano ti
kinissay na idiay kuartam? How much did he take
from your money? --syn. KURANG.

KISSIAL, v. /-UM-/ [= KUMSIAL] to harden. Kunsial diay
inapoy. The cooked rice hardened.

KISSIIM, v. /MANG-:-AN/ to whisper something to, to
tell something to secretly. Kinssiiman nak ni Huana.
Joan whispered something to me. /MANGI-:I-/ to
whisper to (someone), to tell to (someone) secretly.
Isu ti nangikissiim ken ni Rosa nga agawid tayon. It
was he who whispered to Rose that we are going home.

KISSIT, var. of KASSIT.

KISSIW, n. epilepsy.
    v. /AG-/ 1. to be afflicted with this sickness.
    2. to have a fit, to convulse.

[1]KITA, n. kind, sort. Umay agalako ti adu nga kita nga
agas. He will come to sell many kinds of medicine.

[2]KITA, v. /-UM-:-EN/ 1. to look at, watch, observe.
Kitaen nak. Look at me. 2. to examine. Kitaem man
bassit daytoy rilok. Will you please examine my
watch a while. 3. to look for, search. Inka man
kitaen ni tatang ko idiay galyera. Will you please
look for my father in the cockpit. /MAKA-:MA-/ to
see. Nakakitaak ti al-alya idi rabii. I saw a ghost
last night.

[3]KITA, v. /-UM-:-EN/ to earn as wages. Mano ti kinitam
ita? How much in wages did you earn today?

n. earning, wages, salary. Dakkel ti kitak ita. I
have earned a lot today.

KITAKIT, v. /AG-/ to excuse oneself from an obligation,
to avoid an obligation or responsibility. Saan ka nga
agkitakit. Don't avoid your responsibilities.

KITANG, n. a long fishing line to which many hooks are
attached, a boulter, trawl.

[1]KITEB, n. a bedbug.

[2]KITEB, v. /AG-/ to palpitate, throb. Agkitebkiteb
daytoy sugat ko. My wound is throbbing continuously.

KITIK, v. /AG-/ to tick (as a clock or like a clock).
Agkitikkitik diay relo na. His clock ticks
continuously.

KITIKIT, n. groove.

KITING, adj. /NA-/ 1. tight and short (as a garment).
Nakiting ta badom. Your dress is short and tight.
2. narrow, not spacious. --syn. KIPET.

KITKIT, v. /MANG-:-EN/ to gnaw, nibble. Sino ti
nangkitkit ti daytoy mais? Who nibbled this corn?

KITTAB, v. /MANG-:-EN/ to take a bite on, to bite.
Saan mo nga kittaben ta pinggan mo. Don't bite your
plate. /-UM-:-AN/ to bite something off. Saan mo
nga kittaban ta mansanas ko. Don't bite some off my
apple.
n. a bite.

KITTIB, v. /MANG-:-EN/ to bite off little by little,
to nibble. Kinittib na diay tagapulot. He nibbled
the hard sugar.

KIUTEKS [kiutɛks; f. Eng.], n. nail polish.

KIWAR, v. /MANG-:-EN/ to stir in order to mix, to turn
over.

KIWER, adj. curved or coiled at the top end, as the
tail of some dogs.

KIWING, adj. /NAG-/ crooked, bent, curved. --syn. KILLO.

KIWKIW, v. /MANG-:-AN/ to incite, stir up. Saan mo nga
kiwkiwan dayta aso ta dinto kumagat. Don't incite
that dog lest it bites.

KLABODEKOMER [klabodɛkomɛr; f. Sp.], n. clove.

KLARINETE [klarinɛtɛ; f. Sp.], n. clarinet.

KLASE [klasɛ; f. Sp.], n. 1. class, kind, sort. --syn.
KITA. 2. class, a group of students taught together.

KLIMA [f. Sp.], n. climate.

KLINIKA [f. Sp.], n. clinic.

¹KO, pron. by me, I (as actor): the agent of SIAK.
--var. -K (after a vowel).

²KO, pron. my: the enclitic possessive of SIAK. --var.
-K (after a vowel).

KOBER [kobɛr; f. Eng.], n. cover (of a book, notebook,
etc.).
    v. /AG-, MANG-:-AN/ to cover (a book, notebook, etc.).
Koberam ta librom. Cover your book. /MANGI-:I-/ to
use to cover (a book, notebook, etc.) with. Daytoy
ti ikober mo dita librom. Use this to cover your
book with. --syn. KALUB.

KOBOY [f. Eng.], n. cowboy.

KODAK [f. Eng.], n. camera. --syn. KAMERA.
    v. /AG-, MANG-:-EN/ to photograph, to take a
picture of. Kodaken nak man. Will you please take a
picture of me.

KOKOMBAN [f. Eng.], n. bond paper.

KOLADA [f. Sp.], v. /AGI-, MANGI-:I-/ to bleach (as
clothes or like clothes). Ikoladam dagita lupot
tapno pumudaw da. Bleach those clothes so that they
will get whiter. --var. KULA.

KOLEHIALA [kolɛhiala; f. Sp.], n. a coed, a female
college student.

KOLEHIO [kolɛhio; f. Sp.], n. college.

KOLERA [kolɛra; f. Sp.], n. cholera.
  v. /MA-/ to be afflicted with this, to have this.

KOLORETE [kolorɛtɛ; f. Sp.], n. rouge.

KOMADRE [komadrɛ; f. Sp.], n. 1. the godmother of one's
  child. Komadrek ni Marya. Mary is the godmother of
  my child. 2. a title of address or reference for the
  godmother of one's child (sometimes followed by the
  first name or nickname of the godmother). Sumrek ka,
  Komadre Marya. Come inside, KOMADRE Mary. --var.
  KOMARE. --ant. KOMPADRE.

KOMANDER [komandɛr; f. Eng.], n. commander.

KOMARE [komarɛ], var. of KOMADRE.

KOMBENSION [kombɛnsion; f. Sp.], n. convention.
  v. /AG-/ to have or hold a convention.

KOMBENTO [kombɛnto; f. Sp.], n. convent, cloister.

KOMENTARIO [komɛntario; f. Sp.], n. commentary.

KOMERSIANTE [komɛrsiantɛ; f. Sp.], n. merchant.

KOMERSIO [komɛrsio; f. Sp.], n. commerce, business.

KOMIKS [f. Eng.], n. comics, funnies.

KOMISIONADA [f. Sp.], n. commission.

KOMPADRE [kompadrɛ; f. Sp.], n. 1. the godfather of
  one's child. Kompadrek diay presidente. The president
  is the godfather of my child. 2. a title of address
  or reference for the godfather of one's child
  (sometimes followed by the first name or nickname
  of the godfather). Dumagas ka pay, Kompadre Huan.
  Come in for awhile, KOMPADRE John. --var. KOMPARE.
  --ant. KOMADRE.

KOMPARE, var. of KOMPADRE.

KOMPERENSIA [kompɛrɛnsia; f. Sp.], n. conference.
  v. /MAKI-:KA-/ to confer with. /AG-/ [with pl.
  subject] to confer with each other.

KOMPLETO [komplɛto; f. Sp.], adj. complete, whole.

KOMPLIKASION [f. Sp.], n. complication.

KOMPRADOR [f. Sp.], n. a trader, buyer and seller, merchant. --syn. KOMERSIANTE.

KOMUNISMO [f. Sp.], n. 1. communism. 2. a communist.

KONDISION [f. Sp.], n. condition.

KONEHO [konɛho; f. Sp.], n. rabbit.

KONGRESO [koŋgréso; f. Sp.], n. congress.

KONKRETO [koŋkrɛto; f. Sp.], n. concrete. --syn. SEMENTO.

KONSEHAL [konsɛhal; f. Sp.], n. councilor.

KONSEHALA [konsɛhala; f. Sp.], n. a female councilor.

KONSEHO [konsɛho; f. Sp.], n. council.

KONSIDERAR [konsidɛrar; f. Sp.], v. /MANG-:-EN/ to consider.

KONSIDERASION [konsidɛrasion; f. Sp.], n. consideration.

KONSIENSIA [konsiɛnsia; f. Sp.], n. conscience.

KONSTABULARIA; KONSTABULARIO [f. Sp.], n. constabulary. --var. KOSTABULARIO.

KONTRA [f. Sp.], n. contrary (to), something against.

KONTRABANDO [f. Sp.], n. contraband.

KONTRABIDA [f. Sp.], n. a villain, especially in a film. --ant. BIDA.

KONTRATA; KONTRATO [f. Sp.], n. contract.

KONGKONG, v. /MANG-:-AN/ to provide with a canal or groove, to make a canal or groove at. Kongkongam ditoy tapno adda pagayusan ti danum. Make a canal here so that water can flow through it.

KOPA [f. Sp.], n. cup, goblet. --syn. TASA.

KOPIA [f. Sp.], n. copy.
   v. /AG-/ to copy someone's answer to a question in
an examination. /MANG-:-EN/ to copy, imitate.

KOPITA [f. Sp.], n. a small cup or goblet.

KORBATA [f. Sp.], n. cravat, tie.
   v. /AG-/ to wear a cravat or tie.

KORDERO [kordεro; f. Sp.], n. lamb.

KOREA [korεa; f. Sp.], n. belt, a continuous band of
   tough material for transmitting motion and power or
   conveying materials, a belt chain.

KOREO [korεo; f. Sp.], n. mail.

KORNETEN [kornεtεn; f. Sp.], n. trumpet, bugle.

KORONEL [koronεl; f. Sp.], n. colonel.

KORTAPLUMA [f. Sp.], n. pocketknife, penknife.

KORTAR [f. Sp.], v. /MANG-:-AN/ to cut the hair of, to
   give (someone) a haircut. Sino ti nangkortar kenka?
   Who cut your hair? --syn. PUKIS.

KORTE [kortε; f. Sp.], n. court.

   KORTE SUPREMA [kortε suprεma; f. Sp.], the Supreme
   Court.

KOSMOS [f. Eng.], n. 1. the cosmos plant. 2. the flower
   of a cosmos.

KOSTABULARIO, var. of KONSTABULARIO.

KOSTUMBRE [kostumbrε; f. Sp.], n. custom, habit.

KOTA [f. Sp.], n. fort, rampart, fortress.

KOTSE [ḳotsε; f. Sp.], n. car, automobile. --syn.
   OTO, ᶟKARRO.

KRAYOLA [f. Eng.], n. crayon.

KRIMINAL [f. Eng.], n. criminal.

KRISTIANO [f. Sp.], n. Christian.

KRISTO [f. Sp.], n. Christ.

HESUKRISTO [hɛsukristo; f. Sp.], n. Jesus Christ.

KROS [f. Eng.], n. that which is marked with a cross to indicate that it is wrong or that it is stricken out.
v. /MANG-:-EN/ to cancel or strike out by marking a cross on or drawing a line through, to cross. Saan mo nga krosen ta nagan ko dita listaan. Don't cross my name from the list.

KROSING [f. Eng.], n. crossing, especially road crossing.

[1]KRUDO [f. Sp.], n. brown sugar.

[2]KRUDO [f. Sp.], n. crude oil.

KRUS [f. Sp.], n. cross.   --var. KURUS.

KUA, n. var. of KUKUA.
pron. substitute for noun, verb root, or adjective root. Ni kua ti mapan. So-and-so will go. Ania ti kukuaen na? What is he doing? Adda daydiay nakua nga ubing. The such-and-such child is here.

KUKUA, n. property, possession.

KUADA, var. of KUKUADA.

KUADRA [f. Sp.], n. stable.

KUADRO [f. Sp.], n. picture frame.

KUAK, var. of KUKUAK.

KUAM, var. of KUKUAM.

KUAMI, var. of KUKUAMI.

KUANA, var. of KUKUANA.

KUARESMA [kuarɛsma; f. Sp.], n. 1. Lent. 2. the dry season.   --syn. GAWAT.

KUARTA [f. Sp.], n. money.   --syn. PIRAK.
v. /-EN/ to substitute or pay in money for. Kuartaem laengen daydiay binulod kanyak nga bagas.

You may pay in money for the rice that you borrowed from me.

KUARTEL [kuartɛl; f. Sp.], n. quarters, especially army quarters.

KUARTO [f. Sp.], n. room especially bedroom.   --syn. SILED.

KUAT, see PAMKUATAN.

KUATA, var. of KUKUATA.

KUATAYO, var. of KUKUATAYO.

KUATRO [f. Sp.], num. four; 4. ALAS KUATRO, 4 o'clock. --syn. UPPAT.

KUAYO, var. of KUKUAYO.

KUBBO, adj. humpbacked, hunchbacked, stooping. v. /AG-, MA-/ to become like this.

KUBBUAR, v. /AG-/ to spurt upwards, shoot upwards, spout upwards, jet upwards. Umadayo ka tapno dika mabasa no agkubbuar ta danum. Stay far away so that you won't get wet when the water shoots upwards. /MANG-:-EN/ to agitate or stir vigorously (as water or like water). Sino ti nangkubbuar toy danum? Who agitated this water vigorously?   --syn. KIBOR.

[1]KUBKUB, v. /-UM-:-EN/ to surround, lay siege on.

[2]KUBKUB, v. /AG-/ to dig a hole by scratching with the toes. Nagkobkob diay aso da. Their dog dug a hole by scratching with its toes.

KUBO, n. hut, a small house.

KUBÓNG; KUBONGKUBONG, n. a bed curtain, a mosquito net.

KUBRA [f. Sp.], v. /AG-/ to collect payment of debt, rent, bet, etc. /MANG-:-EN/ 1. to collect payment from (someone). Inka kubraen ni Pedro. Go collect payment from Peter. 2. to collect (payment from someone). Pisos ti kubraem ken ni Pedro. Collect one peso from Peter.

KUBRADOR, n. bill collector.

KUBUKUB, v. /AG-/ to curl up, cuddle. Apay nga
   agkubkubukub ka dita? Why are you cuddling there?

KUDAG, adj. /NA-/ slow, dull: said of the sale of
   merchandise. --ant. BILI.

KUDDAY; KUDDAKUDDAY, v. /MANG-/ [= MANGUDDAKUDDAY] to
   totter, stagger, sway. Manguddakudday nga nagna. He
   swayed as he walked.

KUDDOT, v. /AG-, MANG-:-EN/ to pinch. Kinuddot nak diay
   maestra tayo. Our teacher pinched me.

KUDIDIT, adj. /NA-/ stunted, dwarfed.

KUDIL, n. skin (of a person or an animal). --see LALAT.

KUDING, v. /-UM-:-EN/ to tinker with. Ania ti
   kudkudingem dita? What are you tinkering with there?

KUDIS, v. /MANG-:-AN/ to remove part of skin or peelings
   usually by pinching. /MA--AN/ to have part of skin
   or peelings removed usually by pinching.

KUDIT, v. /AG-/ to do, work, be active. Saan nga
   masapul nga agkudit ka dita. It is not necessary
   that you work there. /-UM-:-EN/ to do, work on.
   Adu ti kinudit na isu nga nabannog. He did many
   things, so he is tired.

KUDKUD, v. /AG-/ to scratch or rub a part of one's
   body. /MANG-:-EN/ to scratch or rub. Kudkudem man
   ti likod ko. Will you please rub my back.

KUDREP, adj. /NA-/ dim, not bright (as a lamp).
   Nakudrep ta silaw mo. Your light is dim. --ant.
   LAWAG, SILLAG.

KUDUG, v. /MANGI-:I-/ to ingratiate (one's self).

KUEBA [kuɛba; f. Sp.], n. cave. --syn. RUKIB.

KUELYO [kuɛlyo; f. Sp.], n. collar.

KUENTA [kuɛnta; f. Sp.], n. 1. account, bill. 2. value,
   importance, import. Awan ti kuenta na dayta. That is
   of no importance.
      v. /AG-/ to compute, count. /MANG-:-EN/ to count,
   compute, calculate. Kuentaem man no mano ti utang mi
   kenka. Will you please compute how much we owe you.

KUENTAS [kuɛntas; f. Sp.], n. necklace.
v. /AG-/ to wear a necklace. /MANG-:-AN/ to put
a necklace around the neck of. /MANGI-:I-/ to put
around one's neck as or as like a necklace.

KUERDAS [kuɛrdas; f. Sp.], n. 1. a string or cord of
a musical instrument as a guitar. 2. The coil of a
timepiece.
v. /AG-, MANG-:-AN/ to wind (a timepiece).

KUETES [kuɛtɛs; f. Sp.], n. a small rocket made to
burst in the air in order to produce noise or a
brilliant lighting effect.

KUGIT, v. /-UM-, MANG-:-EN/ to circumcise.
adj. circumcised. --ant. SUPOT.

KUGTAR, v. /-UM-:-AN/ to kick. /MANGI-:I-/ to kick
(something) toward (someone or something).

KUKOD, n. shank, shin of an animal.

KUKOT, v. /AG-/ to curl up, huddle up; to bend the
arms and legs close to the body. /MANGI-:I-/ to
bend, fold: said of the arms and legs.

KUKU, n. 1. a finger nail. 2. a claw. 3. a hoof.

KUKUA, see under KUA.

KUKUADA, pron. theirs; their property; their own: the
full possessive of ISUDA. --var. KUADA.

KUKUAK, pron. mine, my property, my own: the full
possessive of SIAK. --var. KUAK.

KUKUAM, pron. yours (sg.), your property, your own:
the full possessive of SIKA. --var. KUAM.

KUKUAMI, pron. ours (excl.), our (excl.) property, our
(excl.) own: the full possessive of DAKAMI. --var.
KUAMI.

KUKUANA, pron. his, hers; his or her property; his or
her own: the full possessive of ISU. --var. KUANA.

KUKUATA, pron. ours, yours (sg.) and mine, your (sg.)
and my property, your (sg.) and my own: the full

possessive of DATA. --var. KUATA.

KUKUATAYO, pron. ours (incl.), our (incl.) property, our (incl.) own: the full possessive of DATAYO. --var. KUATAYO.

KUKUAYO, pron. yours (pl.), your (pl.) property, your (pl.) own: the full possessive of DAKAYO. --var. KUAYO.

KUKUMER, v. /AG-/ to walk unsteadily, weakly. Apay nga agkukumer diay manok? Why is the chicken walking unsteadily?

KULA, var. (dial.) of KOLADA.

KULAGTIT, v. /AG-/ to lift or raise one's feet abruptly as when startled, to gambol.

KULAIDAG, v. /AG-/ to lie and stretch oneself on the floor or ground. --syn. ILAD.

KULALANTI, n. firefly. --syn. KULINTABA.

KULAM, v. /MANG-:-EN/ to harm (someone) through witchcraft.
MANGKUKULAM, n. one who practices black magic.

KULAMBO, n. mosquito net. --syn. MUSKITERO.
v. /AG-/ to use a mosquito net. /MANG-:-AN/ to put a mosquito net over (someone).

KULANIT, n. membrane.

KULATLAT, v. /MANG-:-AN/ to peel off a portion of the skin, to flay. /MA--AN/ to be flayed, skinned.

KULAY-ONG, n. the depression in the flank of a quadruped, e.g. a water buffalo.

KULBET, adj. /NA-/ tough, resilient, leathery. Nakulbet daytoy karne nga nilutom. This meat that you cooked is tough.

KULBO, v. /MANGI-:I-/ to put (someone) in a bad predicament, to endanger (someone). Isu ti nangikulbo kanyak. It was he who put me in a bad predicament.

KULDING, v. /-UM-, MANG-:-EN/ to touch lightly with the tip of a finger.

KULIBANGBANG, n. butterfly.

KULILING, var. (dial.) of KILILING.

KULIMBITIN, v. /AG-/ to dangle. /MANG-:-EN/ or /MANGI-:I-/ to cause to dangle.

KULINTABA, n. firefly, glowworm.

KULINTIPAY, n. a piece of translucent shell used as window glass.

KULIPAG, adj. /NA-/ dehydrated, dried up.

KULIPAGPAG, v. /AG-/ to flutter as a chicken when killed.

KULKUL, v. /MANG-:-EN/ to entangle or mess up. Kinulkul na diay sagut ko. He entangled my thread. /MA--AN/ to be confused, to become tangled. Makulkulan toy panunot ko. My mind is confused.

KULKULANIOG, n. cartilege.

KULLAAP, v. /MA--AN/ to be made or become dim, unclear, hazy. Nakullaapan ti isip na. His mind became hazy.

KULLAAW, n. a kind of owl.

KULLALONG, v. /MANG-:-EN/ to lift up by holding both hands and feet.

KULLAPIT, adj. thin, without meat or substance: said of the pod of the KAMATIRIS when young or undeveloped.

KULLAYAW, v. /AG-/ to inhale air through the mouth and check it, as when frightened; to be checked, to stop: said of the breath. Nagkullayaw ti anges ko. My breath stopped.

KULLAYOT, adj. /-IMM-/ slim, slender: said of the body.

KULLUONG, n. 1. a large hollowed-out log in which rice
is pounded to separate the grains from the stalks.
2. a wooden trough used to hold fodder for pigs.

KULMEG, v. /AG-/ to stoop, crouch, bend down the body
usually behind something to avoid being seen.

KUL-OB, v. /AG-/ to lie down face forward with the arms
crossed under the head. Agkul-ob ka tapno saan na ka
nga makita. Lie down with your face forward and
your arms crossed under your head so that he cannot
see you.

KULOR [f. Sp.], n. color, hue.
   v. /MANG-:-AN/ to color.

KULOS, n. brook, creek.   --see WAIG.

[1]KULOT, adj. curly, wavy. Kulot ti book na. His hair is
curly.
   v. /MANG-:-EN/ to curl, to cause to become curly
or wavy. Saan mo nga kuloten toy book ko. Don't curl
my hair.

[2]KULOT, n. a Negrito or one like a Negrito.

KULPI, v. /MANG-:-EN/ to fold (a dress, a piece of
paper, etc.). Saan mo pay nga kulpien ta badok.
Don't fold my dress yet.

KULTURA [f. Sp.], n. culture.

KULUG, v. /MANG-:-EN/ to shake. Kinulug na diay lata.
He shook the can.

KULUKUL, n. gimlet, auger.
   v. /MANG-:-EN/ to bore a hole through with or as
if with an auger.

KULUNG, v. /MANG-:-EN/ or /MANGI-:I-/ to confine, put
in a cage, imprison.
   KULUNGAN, n. a cage for birds or animals.

KUMA, adv. expresses wish, intention, or hope.

KUMAW, n. a kidnapper especially of small children.

KUMDIAS, = -UM- + KIDDIAS.

KUMINTANG, v. /AG-/ to swing the arms and hands rhythmically as is done in some dances.   --see GUMINTANG.

KUMIT, v. /MANGI-:I-/ to entrust, give for safekeeping. Inkumit kanyak ni Pedro daytoy tulbek ti balay da. Peter entrusted me with this key to their house.

KUMPAY, n. a sickle with toothed blade.

KUMPIANG, n. a cymbal.
   v. /MANG-:-EN/ to strike with or as if with a cymbal.

KUMON, n. toilet, privy, outhouse.   --syn. KASILYAS.

KUMUSTA, interr. a word used in greeting someone: how. Kumusta ka? How are you? Kumusta ni baket mo? How is your wife?
   v. /MANG-:-EN/ to greet, hail. Sino daydiay nangkumusta kenka? Who was that who greeted you?

KUMUT, v. /AG-/ to wrap oneself with or as if with a blanket. /MANGI-:I-/ to use (a blanket) to wrap oneself with. Apay nga ikumut mo dayta ules? Why do you wrap yourself with that blanket?

KUNA, v. /AG-:-EN/ [= KUNAEN or KUNA] to say, state. --syn. BAGA.

KUNAIL, v. /MAKA-/ to be able to move slowly: usually used negatively. Saan nga makakunail ni Pedro ti bannog na. Peter can hardly move even slowly because of his weariness.

KUNDIDIT, n. cicada.   --syn. ANDIDIT.

KUNDUYOT, n. a children's hand game.

KUNEM, adj. /NA-/ overcast, cloudy.   --syn. KUYEMYEM.

KUNENG, adj. /NA-/ dull, thickheaded, dense, stupid.

KUNIKON, v. /MANG-:-EN/ to roll (a piece of string, thread, etc.) into a ball, to wind.

KUNING, var. of KUTING.

KUNOL; KUNOLKUNOL, v. /AG-/ to squirm, wriggle. Apay
nga kumunolkunol kay la dita? Why are you squirming
there?

KUNUKON, v. /MANG-:-AN/ to fill up (with something).
Kunukonan na ti bato daydiay sirok ti balay da. He
will fill up the space under their house with stones.
/MANGI-:I-/ to use to fill up (a place), to fill up
(a place) with. Apay nga inkunukon mo dagitoy bato
ditoy sirok ti balay mi? Why did you fill up the
space under our house with these stones?

KUNUT, v. /MANG-:-EN/ to suck, chew. Saan mo nga
kunuten ta tangan mo. Don't suck your thumb.

KUPAG, n. grated coconut meat from which the milk has
been pressed.

KUPIN, v. /AG-, MANG-:-EN/ to fold, usually in order
to store away.   --syn. KULPI.

KUPIT, v. /-UM-:-EN/ to filch (money).

KUPKOP, v. /MANG-:-AN/ to enclose with the arms or
wings.

KUPLAT, v. /MA--AN/ to have part of skin or surface of
peeled off, to have an abrasion.

KUPPIT, v. /MANG-:-EN/ to dent, misshape. Kinuppit na
diay balde. He dented the big can. /MA-/ to be
dented, misshapen. Nakuppit diay balde idi imbarsak
na. The big can was dented when he dropped it
heavily.

KURA [f. Sp.], n. curate, priest, friar.

KURAD, n. a skin disease, eczema, ringworm.
   v. /AG-/ to be infected with this skin disease.

KURANG, n. what is missing or lacking, shortage.
   v. /AG-/ to be short of, to be wanting, to be in
need of. Agkurang ti dua daytoy. This is short of
two. /-UM-, MANG-:-AN/ to reduce, lessen, decrease,
take from. Kurangan na ti tallo dayta bagim. He will
reduce by three your share. /MANG-:-EN/ to take
away from in order to reduce or lessen. Mano ti
kurangem ditoy bagik? How many will you take away

from my share?   --syn. KISSAY.   --ant. NAYON.
   adj. being short of, lacking, deficient, inadequate.

KURANG; KURKURANG, n. mental deficiency, stupidity.

KURAPAY, adj. /NA-/ poor, indigent, needy, impoverished.
   --syn. POBRE, MARIGRIGAT.   --ant. BAKNANG.

KURARAP, adj. having a defective eyesight, shortsighted,
   myopic.

KURARAPNIT, n. bat, a nocturnal placental mammal with
   forelimbs modified to form wings.   --var. KURARATNIT.

KURARATNIT, var. of KURARAPNIT.

KURARET, v. /AG-/ to become shrunk or wrinkled due to
   coldness. Agkuraret dagitoy laslasag ko. My muscles
   are shrunk.

KURAY, v. /AG-/ to scratch as a hen.   /MANG-:-AN/ to
   scratch something toward (someone).

KURDON, n. cord, string; shoestring.   --syn. ASINTOS.
   v. /MANG-:-AN/ to provide with a cord, string, or
   shoestring.

KURET; KUKURET, v. /AG-/ to be huddled up and shivering
   especially when drenched or sick: said of a chicken.

KURIAT, n. cricket.

KURIB, v. /MANG-:-AN/ to gnaw a hole in. Kinuriban ti
   marabutit diay sako. A mouse gnawed a hole in the
   sack.   /MA--AN/ to have a hole gnawed in it.

KURIBETBET, n. a kind of shrub (Tabernaemontana
   pandacaqui) with shining leaves, white flowers and
   red or yellowish-red follicles.

KURIBOT, n. a kind of large basket about a yard high.

KURIDEMDEM, adj. /NA-/ weak and flickering: said of a
   light.
   v. /AG- + R1/ to become weak and flickering. Apay
   nga agkurkuridemdem diay silaw? Why has the light
   become weak and flickering?

KURIKUR, n. a toothpick or one like it used to remove adhering matter from the ear hole.
v. /AG-/ to remove adhering matter from one's ear holes. /MANG-:-AN/ to clean or remove adhering matter from (a narrow hole, especially an ear hole). Kurikuran na ta lapayag mo. He will clean your ear holes.

KURIMATMAT, n. eyelash.

KURIPASPAS, v. /AG-/ to writhe violently due to extreme pain or injury. Nagkuripaspas diay manok nga binatom. The chicken that you hit with a stone writhed violently.

KUR-IT, v. /MANG-:-AN/ to scratch or mark with a sharp point.

KURITA, n. a kind of squid.

KURKUR, v. /AG-/ to call and feed a chicken. /AG-:-AN/ to call and feed (a chicken or like a chicken).

KURKURATTOT, adj. spinning jerkily as or like a spinning top.

KURKURUS, see under KURUS.

KURNO, v. /AG-/ to genuflect.

KURSING, n. dead epidermis that is peeling off.

KURSONG, v. /MANGI-:I-/ to push or thrust inside a container. Ikorsong mo daytoy dita bay-on mo. Push this inside your bag.

KURTINA [f. Sp.], n. curtain, screen.

KURUNIKON, v. /AG-/ to curl up, cuddle.

KURUROT, v. /AG-/ to cover the head with something as a piece of cloth. /MANGI-:I-/ to use to cover the head with. Saan mo nga ikururot day tualya. Don't cover your head with that towel.

[1]KURUS, n. shrimp. --syn. IPON.

[2]KURUS, n. var. of KRUS.
v. /AG-/ to make the sign of the cross, to cross

oneself.

KURKURUS, n. Ash Wednesday.

KUSAPO, adj. /NA-/ dull, not shiny.
v. /-UM-, AG-/ to become dull, not shiny. Apay nga kimmusapo dayta datar? Why did that floor become dull?

KUSAY, v. /AG-/ to kick forwards. /MANG-:-AN/ to kick. Saan mo nga kusayan ta pusa. Don't kick that cat. /MANGI-:I-/ to kick off or away (something). Saan mo nga ikusay ta sapatos mo. Don't kick away your shoe.

KUSBO, v. /MA-/ 1. to collapse, as a building. 2. to be bent double, as a person. Saan mo nga danugen ta bukot ko ta diak to makosbo. Don't hit my back with your fist lest I be bent double.

KUSEL, adj. /NA-/ half-cooked: said of rice and rice cakes.

KUSEP, adj. /NA-/ not burning well: said of firewood that is difficult to kindle and produces a lot of smoke due especially to its not being dry.

KUSIKUS, v. /MANG-:-EN/ to make into a funnel. Isu ti nangkusikus diay bulong. It was he who made the leaf into a funnel.

KUSILAP, v. /-UM-:-AN/ to glare at, leer at. Apay nga kusilapan nak? Why do you glare at me?

KUSIM, adj. /NA-/ finicky, fastidious, not having a good appetite in eating.

KUSINA [f. Sp.], n. kitchen.

KUSINERA [kusinɛra; f. Sp.], n. a female cook. --see KUSINERO.

KUSINERO [kusinɛro; f. Sp.], n. a cook especially a male one. --syn. PARALUTO.

KUSIPET, adj. having one or both eyes smaller than the normal ones, almond-eyed.

KUSIT, adj. /(NA-)/ deceitful, being a cheater especially in a game of chance.

v. /AG-/ to cheat especially in a game of chance.
/MANG-:-EN/ to cheat (someone) especially in a game
of chance. Nangabakak kuma no di nak nga kinusit. I
would have won if you did not cheat me.

[1]KUSKUS, v. /MANG-:-EN/ to scrape, rasp, scrub.

[2]KUSKUS, v. /MANG-:-AN/ to remove the hair from the
head or body completely.

KUSNAW, adj. /NA-/ not clearly visible, hazy.

KUSO; KUSOKUSO, v. /MANG-:-EN/ to dishevel, disarray,
crumple.
adj. /NA-/ dishevelled, disarrayed, crumpled.

KUSPAG, adj. /NA-/ arrogant, haughty, insolent.

KUSPIL, v. /MANGI-:I-/ to prevent (someone) from
advancing or progressing. /MAI-/ to be prevented
from advancing or progressing.

KUSPILO, v. /MA-/ to twist one's ankle while walking.
/MANG-:-EN/ to bend, twist.

KUSTO, adj. 1. right, correct. Kusto ti imbagam.
What you said is right. 2. enough, sufficient.
Kusto daytan. That's enough.
v. /-UM-/ to be enough or sufficient. Kumusto met
la ngata ti niluto tayo? Do you think what we cooked
will be enough?

KUTA, interj. a sound that one makes to call dogs.

KUTAK, n. the sharp broken noise or cry characteristic
of a hen especially after laying.
v. /AG-/ to make this noise or cry, to cackle.
Apay nga agkutkutak dayta manok? Why is that hen
cackling?

KUTEL; AGKUKUTEL, n. leper.

KUTENGTENG, v. /AG-/ to pluck the strings of a guitar.
/MANG-:-EN/ to pluck, as the strings of a guitar.

KUTI, v. /AG-/ to move, stir. Saan ka nga agkuti ta
matmaturogakon. Don't move for I am already sleeping.
/MANG-:-EN/ to move, change the position of.

adj. /NA-/ always moving or shifting. Nakuti ka nga mangan. You are always moving while eating.

KUTIBENG, n. any stringed instrument, a guitar.

KUTIKUT, v. /MANG-:-EN/ to wind. Sino ti nangkutikut di daydiay barot? Who wound the wire?   --syn. KUNIKON.

KUTING, n. kitten.   --var. KUNING.

KUTKOT, n. a grooving plane.
    v. /MANG-:-EN/ to cut a groove or rabbet in.

KUTSON [f. Sp.], n. cushion.

KUTUKUT, n. a kind of punch used for widening or enlarging holes.

KUT-IM, v. /AG-/ to remove the shell of rice or nuts with the teeth.

KUTING, v. /MANG-:-EN/ to handle, to repair, adjust, or experiment with. Saan mo nga kutingen dayta? Don't tinker with that.

KUTIT, n. the end of a row, a file, etc., the end part of a cart, the back of a water buffalo, etc.
    adj. last in a row, a line, etc.

KUTKUT, v. /AG-/ to dig a hole by scratching. /AG-:-EN/ 1. to dig by scratching. 2. to erode, wash away: said of a current of water.

KUTSARA [f. Sp.], n. spoon.
    v. /AG-/ to use a spoon especially in eating.
    /MANG-:-EN/ 1. to take with a spoon. 2. to hit with a spoon.

KUTSARITA [f. Sp.], n. teaspoon.

KUTSILIO [f. Sp.], n. table knife.

KUTSERO [kutsɛro; f. Sp.], n. the driver of a horse-drawn carriage.

KUTO, n. louse.
    v. /MANG-:-AN/ to pick lice from the head of.

KUTOG; KUTOGKUTOG, v. /AG-/ to shake, quake, vibrate
violently. Agkutogkutog ti batukong ko ta nakigtotak.
My chest is quaking for I was startled.

KUTON, n. ant, pismire.
v. /-EN/ to be attacked or eaten by ants.

KUTOR, v. /MA--AN/ to shiver due to being wet.
Nakutoran diay manok. The chicken is shivering and
wet.

KUTTONG, adj. /NA-/ thin, lean, slender. Nakuttong
dayta anak mo. Your child is thin.
v. /-UM-/ to become like this.

KUTUKOT, v. /-UM-/ to be piercing, as pain. Kumutukot
ti sakit na daytoy ngipen ko. The pain of my
tooth(ache) is piercing. /MANG-:-AN/ to pierce,
bore, make a hole in, on, or through.

KUYAKUY, v. /AG-/ to move the legs to and fro while
suspended in mid air. /MANGI-:I-/ to move (the legs)
to and fro while suspended in mid air.

KUYAS, adj. /NA-/ sharp-faced, thin-faced: said of a
person.

KUY-AT, v. /MANGI-:I-/ to raise, lift up, as one's
foot. Ikuy-at mo ta sakam. Lift up your foot.

KUYEGYEG, adj. /NA-/ jerky, joggy.

KUYEM, adj. /NA-/ overcast, cloudy. --var. KUYEMYEM.

KUYEMYEM, var. of KUYEM.

KUYEP, adj. having eyes that are almost shut and
always blinking.

KUYKUY, v. /MANG-:-EN/ to gather, push together with
the fingers. Kuykuyem ta inapoy dita pinggan mo.
Push together the rice in your plate.

KUYOG, v. /MANG-:-EN/ to accompany, go with, escort.
Kuyugen nak man nga mapan idiay Manila. Will you
accompany me in going to Manila. /-UM-:-AN/ to go
with. Kumuyog ka la idiay soldado. Just go with the
soldier. /AG-/ [with pl. subject] to go together,

be together in doing something. Agkuyog ta nga
agbuya ti sine. Let's go together to see a movie.

KUYYAKUY, var. of KUYAKUY.

LA, var. of LAENG.

LAAD, adj. /NA-/ ugly, unsightly, disgusting.   --syn.
ALAS.   --ant. PINTAS.

LAAW, v. /AG-/ to shout, vociferate. Apay nga naglaaw
ka? Why did you shout? /MANGI-:I-/ to say or tell
by shouting, to shout, vociferate (something). Saan
mo nga ilaaw ti nagan ko. Don't shout my name.

LABAG, n. a bundle of thread or fiber, a strand.
Iyalaan nak ti maysa nga labag nga panait. Get me a
strand of sewing thread.

LINABAG, n. thread-like or fine strand.

LABAGA, adj. /NA-/ red in color. Nalabaga ti matam.
Your eyes are red.
v. /-UM-/ to become this.   --var. LABBAGA.

LABAK, v. /MANG-:-EN/ to abuse, treat roughly; to
maltreat. Saan mo nga labaken ta ubing. Don't
maltreat that child.

LABAN, v. /-UM-/ to fight or compete with someone.
Apay nga lumaban ka? Why do you fight? /-UM-, MANG-:-AN/
to fight or compete with. Labanan na ka ni Pedro.
Peter will fight with you. /AG-/ [with pl. subject]
to fight or compete with one another.

LABANAG, v. /AG-/ to start ripening. Aglabanag
dagidiay manggan. The mangoes are starting to ripen.

LABANG, adj. spotted, dappled, speckled, mottled.

LABAS, v. /-UM-/ 1. to pass, go by, move by or past;
to pass by or through. Saan kay nga lumabas ditoy
inaladan mi. Don't pass through our yard. 2. to pass,
slip by, elapse. Nakalabas manen ti maysa nga aldaw.
One day again has passed. /MANGI-:I-/ to cause (a
parade, procession, etc.) to pass by or through.
Ilabas mo diay parada ditoy balay mi. Have the parade

pass by our house.

IDI NAPALABAS NGA (ALDAW, BULAN, TAWEN), during the
past (day, month, year).

LABASIT, adj. /NA-/ red, reddish.   --var. LABBASIT.
--syn. LABAGA.

LABATIBA, n. enema.
v. /AG-/ to have an enema, to give oneself an
enema. /MANG-:-EN/ to give (someone) an enema.
Bumulod ka ti labatiba ta labatibaek toy anak ko.
Borrow an enema for I shall give my child an enema.

[1]LABAY, n. skein, hank of cotton yarn.

[2]LABAY, n. cooked rice with broth mixed in it.
v. /AG-/ to mix broth in one's cooked rice.
/MANGI-:I-/ to mix (broth) in (cooked rice).
/MANG-:-AN/ to mix (broth) in (cooked rice). Labayam
ta inapoy mo ti digo ti sinigang. Mix the broth of
SINIGANG in your rice.

LAB-AY, adj. /NA-/ 1. flat, not tasty. Nalab-ay ti
linutom. What you cooked tastes flat. 2. bland,
mild, dull, not exciting. Nalabay daydi napalabas nga
eleksion. The past election was not exciting.

LABBA, n. a large deep closely-woven basket.

LABBAGA, var. of LABAGA.

LABBASIT, var. of LABASIT.

LABBEG, v. /AG-/ to agitate the water to make any fish
in it dizzy. Saan kay nga aglabbeg dita. Don't
agitate the water there. /MANG-:-EN/ to agitate
(the water).

LABBET, v. /AG- +R2/ [with pl. subject] to gather in
crowds, to flock together.

LABEG, v. /MANG-:-EN/ often /MAKA-:MA-/ to muddle,
confuse, bewilder (the mind). Ania ti nakalabeg ti
panunot mo? What confused your mind? /MA--AN/ to be
muddled, confused, bewildered. Nalabegan ti panunot
na. His mind was muddled.

[1]LABES, adj. /NA-/ excessive, overmuch. Nalabes ti
    kinasadut mo. Your laziness is excessive.

[2]LABES, n. any place past or beyond something. Adda diay
    labes ti rangtay ti balay mi. Our house is in a place
    past the bridge.
        v. /-UM-/ to go past or beyond. Limmabes diay lugan
    mi diay papanan mi. Our vehicle went past the place
    where we were going.   /MANGI-:I-/ to cause to go
    beyond or past.

LABI, see MALABI.

[1]LABID, adj. /NA-/ always tattling, prating, chattering;
    being an idle talker. Nalabid daytoy nga ubing.
    This child is a tattler.

[2]LABID, n. a species of tall and slender palm tree.
    --syn. ANAAW.

LABINTADOR [f. Sp.], n. firecracker.

LABIT, adj. /NA-/ probable (followed by NGA): said of
    an event or action. Nalabit nga simmangpeten. It is
    probable that he has arrived.

LABLAB, v. /AG-, MANG-:-EN/ to lick. Saan mo nga
    lablaban ta kutsaram. Don't lick your spoon.

LABNAW, adj. /NA-/ thin: said of liquids. Nalabnaw
    dayta inaramid mo nga tsokolate. The chocolate that
    you made is thin.

LABO, v. /MANG-:-EN/ to annoint or rub with (oil,
    lard, medicine, etc.). Laboem dayta barukong mo ti
    biks. Rub your chest with Vicks.
        adj. /NA-/ covered thickly with oil or grease.
    Nalabo dayta buok mo. Your hair is covered thickly
    with oil.

LABÓN, v. /AG-/ to be in abundance, to abound.
    Aglablabon ti sida diay bodaan. There is an
    abundance of food at the wedding.
        adj. /NA-/ abundant, plentiful. Nalabon ti bunga
    ti mangga. The fruits of the mango tree are
    plentiful.

LABONG; LABONGLABONG, v. /AG-/ to be ill-fitting,

loose. Aglabonglabong toy sapatos ko. My shoes are loose.

LAB-ONG, var. of PALAB-ONG v. 1.

LABORATORIO [f. Sp.], n. laboratory.

LABSING, v. /-UM-/ to deviate, slide out of place. Saan kayo nga lumabsing ti dayta dalan. Don't deviate from that road. /MANG-:-EN/ to go against, hence to disobey. Saan yo nga labsingen ti kayat dagita nagannak kenka. Don't go against the wishes of your parents.

LABUDOY, adj. /NA-/ soft, not firm or stiff. Nalabudoy daytoy badok. My dress is soft.

LABUS, v. /AG-/ 1. to remove one's garments, hence to strip oneself naked; to be naked. 2. to remove one's lower garments, hence to be naked from the waist down; to be half-naked. /MANG-:-AN/ 1. to remove (someone's) garments, hence to make (someone) nude or naked. 2. to remove the lower garments (of someone), hence to make (someone) naked from the waist down.

    LABUS or SILALABUS, adj. 1. nude, naked. 2. without the lower garments, naked from the waist down, half-naked.

LABUTAB, n. foam, bubble.
    v. /AG-/ to bubble, foam. Kiwarem ta danum inggana ti aglabutab. Stir the water until it bubbles.

LADAM, v. /MANG-:-AN/ to scorch, singe, burn. /MA--AN/ to be scorched, singed, burned. Naladaman diay badok ti plantsa. My dress was scorched by the iron.

LADAW, adj. /NA-, MA-/ late, tardy, delayed. Kanayon nga naladaw ni Rosa. Rose is always late.

LADAWAN, n. picture, photograph, image, likeness. Ladawan ni nanang ko dayta. That is a picture of my mother.
    v. /MANGI-:I-/ to picture, illustrate, describe, depict, imagine. Narigat nga iladawan ti pintas ti balay da. It is difficult to depict the beauty of their house.

LADDIT, v. /MANG-:-EN/ 1. to crush, crumble, grind.
Ladditen yo dayta bawang. Crush the garlic. 2. to gin
(cotton).

LADEK, n. scum of coconut, the solid particles formed
with the oil after boiling coconut milk.

LADINGIT, adj. /NA-/ sad, grievous, mournful, gloomy,
dreary. Naladingit ti pangsisina da. Their parting
was sad.
    v. /AG-/ to be sad, mournful. Saan ka nga agladingit
ta agsubliak met laeng. Don't be sad for I am coming
back. /MANG-:-EN/ to be sad or mournful about, to
grieve for, mourn for; to be sorry for. Ladingetek
ti napasamak kenka. I am sorry for what happened to
you.

LADLAD, v. /MANG-:-AN/ to scrape the skin; hence to
skin, flay. /MA--AN/ to be skinned, flayed.

LADUT; LALADUT, v. /AG-/ to feel dull, sluggish,
spiritless, heavy. Aglaladutak. I feel sluggish.

LAENG, adv. only, merely, solely. Dua laeng ti immay.
Only two came.

MET LAENG, anyway, nevertheless, however.

LAES, adj. /NA-/ beginning to putrefy, putrid; hence,
spoiled: said usually of fish. Nalaes daytoy ikan
nga ginatang mo. This fish that you bought is spoiled.

LAGA, v. /AG-, MANG-:-EN/ to weave: said of baskets.
Naglaga kami ti adu nga labba. We wove plenty of
baskets.
    n. a (woven) basket.
    v. /MANGI-:I-/ to put inside a (woven) basket.
Inlagana dagiti bangbanga. He put the pots inside a
(woven) basket.

LAG-AN, adj. /NA-/ 1. light, not heavy. Nalag-an daytoy
maletak. My suitcase is light. 2. nimble. Nalag-an
nga aggungunay ni Rosa. Rose moves around nimbly.

LAGANGAN, n. a circlet made of cloth, bamboo strips,
dried banana leaves, etc. on which big pots or jars
are placed. --syn. SAGAPA.

¹LAGAW, adj. /NA-/ impatient, in a hurry; restless.
Natalna da nga mangan. Awan nalagaw. They eat
peacefully. Nobody is in a hurry (to eat).
v. /AG-/ to be impatient, in a hurry, or restless.

²LAGAW, v. /AG-, MA--AN/ to be stunned, stupefied,
dumbfounded, confused. Apay nga malagawan ka? Why
are you confused?

LAGDA, adj. /NA-/ strong, durable. Nalagda daytoy datar
mi. Our floor is strong. --ant. RUKOP.

LAGDAW, n. a small shrimp. --syn. KURUS.

LAGID, v. /MANGI-:I-/ 1. to rub against (something);
hence, 2. to sharpen (a knife) by rubbing against a
whetting stone. Ilagid mo daytoy buneng tapno tumadem.
You rub this big knife against a whetting stone so
that it will become sharp.

LAGIP, v. /MANG-:-EN/ often /MAKA-:MA-/ to remember,
recall, be reminded of. Lagipem amin nga bilin ko
kenka. Remember all the things I ordered you to do.
PAKALAGLAGIPAN, n. remembrance, reminder, souvenir.

LAGISI, v. /MAI-/ to slip, slide down; slip off.
Nailagisi diay ubing. The child slipped.

LAGLAG, adj. /(NA-)/ idiotic, imbecile, dumb, moronic.
Nalaglag ka la unay. You are very dumb.

LAG-OY, v. /AG-/ to walk or move in a swaying manner.
Saan ka nga aglag-oy. Don't sway while walking.
/MANGI-:I-/ to sway in one's arms. Saan mo nga
ilag-oy dayta ubing. Don't sway that child in your
arms.

LAGTO, v. /AG-, -UM-/ to jump, leap, spring. Aglagto
ka. or Lumagto ka. Jump. /MANG-:-EN/ to jump, leap
over or across; to jump for, to get by jumping.
Lagtoen na dayta mangga nga agbitbitin. He jumped
in order to get that hanging mango. /MANGI-:I-/
to jump with.

LAGUD; LAGUDLAGUD, v. /AG-/ to caper, gambol, frisk,
frolic. Aglalagudlagud ti madumaduma nga tattao
idiay tiendaan. Various sorts of people are
frolicking in the market.

LAGUERTA [laguɛrta; f. Sp.], n. garden.

LAILO, adj. /NA-/ affectionate, caressive.
    v. /AG-, MANG-:-EN/ to express one's affection to, to caress, fondle. /MAKI-:KA-/ to exchange affection with.

LAING, adj. /NA-/ 1. able, competent, capable, skillful. 2. good, desirable.

LAIS, v. /MANG-:-EN/ to despise, degrade, depreciate, belittle. Saan mo nga laisen dagita napanglaw. Don't despise the poor.

LAKA, adj. /NA-/ 1. easy, not difficult. 2. cheap, low-priced.
    v. /-UM-/ 1. to become easy. 2. to become cheap.

[1]LAK-AM, v. /AG-:-EN/ to gain, reap, obtain. Awan ti lak-amen. He who steals will gain nothing.

[2]LAK-AM, v. /MANGI-:I-/ to include in the reckoning or preparation. Ilak-am tayo ida iti pammigat. Let's include them for breakfast.

LAKASA [f. Sp.], n. chest, trunk usually made of wood. --syn. BAUL.

LAKATAN, n. a variety of thick-skinned yellow banana.

LAKAY, adj. /NAG-/ old: said of male (animate) things, especially persons and animals.
    n. 1. an old man. 2. husband. Isu dayta ti lakay. That one is my husband.
    v. /-UM-/ to become old: said of male (animate) things, especially persons and animals. --ant. BAKET.

    PANGLAKAYEN, n. an elder, an old headman.

LAKIEN [cf. LALAKI], adj. tomboyish, masculine, mannish: said of a woman.

LAKO, v. /AG-, MANGI-:I-/ to sell. Kayat na nga ilako ti balay na kenka. He wants to sell his house to you.

LAKSA [rare], num. ten thousand, times ten thousand.

    SANGALAKSA, ten thousand.

    DUA NGA LAKSA, twenty thousand.

LAKSID, n. any place beyond or outside another place.
   v. /MANG-:-EN/ 1. to eliminate, remove, get rid of,
   to stop considering as such. Laksiden na nga anak ni
   Pedro. He stopped considering Peter as his child.
   2. to stop doing, to cease from. Laksidem nga
   pampanunuten diay pimmanaw nga gayyem mon. Stop
   thinking of your friend who left. /MANGI-:I-/ to set
   aside, separate. Ilaksid mo dayta nareppet nga kayo.
   Set aside those pieces of wood that are bundled.

   MALAKSID, prep. except. Nagdigos da amin malaksid ni
   Maria. They all took a bath except Mary.

LAKTAW, v. /MANG-:-EN/ to jump, leap over, step over.
   --syn. LAGTO. /MANG-:-AN/ to skip, omit.

LAKUB, v. /MANG-:-EN/ to encircle, surround. Saan yo
   nga lakuben dayta mula. Don't surround that plant.
   /MA-/ to be encircled, surrounded. Nalakub kami ti
   soldado. We were surrounded by soldiers.

LALAKI, n. a male, a man.

LALAT, n. 1. skin, hide. 2. leather. --syn. KUDIL.
   v. /MANG-:-EN/ to make into or use as leather.
   /MANG-:-AN/ to remove the skin of, to skin.

LÁLAW, v. /MANG-:-EN/ to cause to become soft through
   handling, as a fruit. Sino ti nanglalaw daytoy
   papaya? Who caused this papaya to become soft?
   /MA-/ to become soft through handling or falling on
   the ground.

LALI, v. /MANG-:-EN/ to squeeze with the hands through
   the fingers. Lalien na daydiay almidor. He will
   squeeze the clothes starch with his hands.

LALLAY, n. lullaby. --syn. DUAYA.
   v. /AG-/ to sing a lullaby.

LALO, adj. /NA-/ serious, grave: said of an illness or
   sickness. Nalalo si sakit. His sickness is serious.
   v. /-UM-/ to become serious, grave: said of an
   illness or sickness.

   AGLALO, adv. especially.

   --see PALALO.

LAMANO, [f. Sp.], n. handshake.
v. /MAKI-:KA-/ to shake hands with. /AG-/ [with pl. subject] to shake hands.

LAMAW, v. /MANG-:-EN/ to scald. /MA-/ to be scalded. Nalamaw ti saka na. His foot was scalded.

LAMBI; LAMBILAMBI, n. wattle, dewlap.

LAMBONG, v. /MANGI-:I-/ to boil in plain water: said especially of vegetables.

LAM-EK, adj. /NA-/ cold (in temperature). Nalam-ek itay bigat. It was cold this morning.
v. /MA-, -EN/ to feel cold. Lam-ekenak. I feel cold. --syn. LAMMIN.

LAMES, n. fish. --syn. IKAN.

LAMIGONG, v. /AG-/ to be afflicted with a chronic disease.

LAMIIS, adj. /NA-/ cool, cold: said of the weather or objects.
v. /-UM-/ to become cool, cold.

LAMISAAN [f. Sp.], n. table.

LAMISITA [f. Sp.], n. small table.

LAMLAM, v. /MAKA-:MA--AN/ to gain, obtain, benefit. Awan ti nalamlaman mi diay inabak na ti sugal. We did not benefit anything from what he won in gambling.
PALAMLAM, v. /MANG-:-AN/ to give a bit of (something). Saan na kami nga pulos pinalamlaman ti mangga da. He did not give us even a bit of the fruits of their mango tree.

LAMMIN, v. /AG-/ to feel cold, chilly.
adj. /MA-/ feeling cold, chilly. --syn. LAM-EK.

LAMO; LAMOLAMO, adj. naked, nude. --syn. LABUS.
v. /AG-/ to become naked, nude.

LAMOK, n. mosquito.
v. /-EN/ to be bitten or attacked by mosquitoes.

LAMPARA, n. lamp.   --syn. SILAW.

LAMPAY, adj. /(NA-)/ weak, easily falls or stumbles.

LAMPIN, n. diaper.
   v. /MANG-:-AN/ to put a diaper around.

LAMPONG, adj. /NAG-/ having long, bushy, disorderly
   hair.

LAMUT, n. food.
   v. /MANG-:-EN/ to eat in a coarse manner: a
   derogatory term.   --syn. KAAN.

LAMUYOT, adj. /NA-/ soft and smooth.
   v. /-UM-/ to become this.

LANA, n. coconut oil.
   v. /MANG-:-AN/ 1. to put oil in, to oil. 2. to
   flatter, coax.

   LALANAAN, n. oil gland, especially of fowls.

LANAD, v. /MANGI-:I-/ to write, inscribe. Ilanad mo
   dita papel ti kayat mo nga ibaga. Write on that
   paper what you want to say.   /MAI-/ to be written,
   inscribed.

LANANG, v. /MANG-:-EN/ to solder. Lanangem man daytoy
   nakta nga singsing ko. Will you please solder my
   ring which cracked.

LANAT, v. /MANGI-:I-/ to expose to a fire or scorch
   to make soft and pliable: said of leaves especially
   banana leaves.

LANAY, adj. /NA-/ mild, gentle, charming (as eyes).
   Nalanay dagita matam. Your eyes are charming.

LANDAG, n. a wood block on which clothes are beaten
   when washing them.

   PAGLANDAGAN, n. anything on which something is
   placed to be cut, chopped, etc.

LANDOK, n. iron.

LANIT, adj. /NA-/ oily, greasy.

LANITOG, v. /-UM-/ [LUMANITOG] to produce an exploding
sound.   --see KANALTUOG.

LANLAN, v. /-UM-/ to worsen, become aggravated.
Limmanlan ti sakit ni Ana. Ann's sickness worsened.

LANSA, n. nail.
   v. /MANGI-:I-/ to nail.
LANSALANSA, n. ankle.

LANSAD, n. 1. base of a mountain, etc. 2. level of a
well.
   v. /AG-, -UM-/ to descend in, come down to or upon.
Rabiin idi limmansad kami idiay ili. It was already
night when we descended in town.

LANSANGAN, n. street, thoroughfare.   --syn. KALSADA.

LANSITA [f. Sp.], n. pocket knife.

LANTAG, adj. /(NA-)/ level, flat, even, plane.

LANTIP, v. /MANGI-:I-/ to fit (a member of a pair or
set) with (the other). /AG-/ to fit, get into its
place. Saan nga aglantip daydiay rikep ti bintana.
The window cover won't fit.

LANUT, n. vine.

LANGA, n. personal appearance, looks.
   adj. /NA-/ good-looking, handsome.

LANG-AB, v. /-UM-/ to inhale or breathe air.
/-UM-:-EN/ to inhale, breathe. Napresko ti angin nga
lang-aben mi ditoy. The air that we breathe here is
fresh.

LANGAN, n. an act of skipping or not doing something
at the usual time.
   v. /AG-, -UM-/ to skip, miss, or fail to do
(something) at the usual time, to skip or be absent
in (a place) at the usual time. Limmangan ni Pedro
idiay eskuela. Peter skipped school.

LANGAY; LANG-AY, v. /AG-/ to run at full speed in a
carefree manner; to gallop, romp.

LANGDET, n. chopping board or block.

v. /MANGI-:I-/ to cut, chop, slice, pound, etc. on a chopping board. /PAG--AN/ to throw the blame on, to accuse.

LANGEB, v. /MANG-/ to be cloudy, overcast. Nanglangeb itay malem. It was cloudy the past afternoon.

LANGEN; LANGEN-LANGEN, v. /MAKI-/ to deal, associate or socialize with (others); to get along with (others). Dika makilangen-langen kadakuada. Don't deal with them. /AG-/ [with pl. subject] to deal, associate or socialize with each other; to get along together.

LANG-ES, adj. /NA-/ smelling like fish, slimy. --syn. LANGSI.

LANGGONG, adj. foolish, stupid, idiotic, imbecile.

LANGGUSTI [f. Sp.], n. a sack usually made of maguey fiber and usually used as a container for rice. --var. LANGGUTSI.

LANGGUTSI, var. of LANGGUSTI.

LANGIT, n. sky, heaven, paradise.

LANGKA, n. 1. jack tree. 2. its fruit. --var. NANGKA.

[1]LANGLANG, n. an uninhabited, unfrequented, and remote place.

[2]LANGLANG, n. the space between the front of the hearth and the fire.

[3]LANGLANG, v. /MAKI-:KA-/ to eat with, sit at the dining table with. Isuda ti kinalanglang ko nga nangan. There were the ones with whom I ate. /AG- + R2/ to eat together, to sit together at the dining table to eat. Naglalanglang kami idiay balay ti meyor. We ate together at the house of the mayor.

LANGOY, v. /AG-/ to swim. Indiak ammo ti aglangoy. I don't know how to swim. /-UM-, MANG-:-EN/ 1. to swim across, to cross by swimming; to swim. Kayat na nga langoyen dayta nalawa nga karayan. He wants to swim that wide river. 2. to swim for, to get by swimming. Langoyem man diay sapatos ko nga impalapal na idiay karayan. Will you please swim for my shoe which he threw into the river.

LANGSI, adj. /NA-/ smelling like fish, slimy.   --syn.
  LANG-ES.

LANGSOT, adj. /NA-/ boastful, bragging.   --syn. TANGSIT.

LANGTO, adj. /NA-/ fresh, green: said of plants.

LAON, v. /AG-:-EN/ to hold, contain.   --syn. LAS-UD.

LAPA, v. /MAI-/ to be deprived of the chance to do,
  experience, see, taste, etc. something. Nailapa da
  ti naimas nga sida. They were deprived of the chance
  of eating a delicious dish.

LAPÁG, v. /MANGI-:I-/ to set out, spread out.

LÁPAT, adj. /NA-/ 1. thin, fine (as thread). 2. subtle,
  tactful. Makisao ka ti nalapat kadakuada. Talk to
  them in a tactful manner.

LAPAYAG, n. ear, something resembling an ear.

LAPDUG, v. /MAKA-:MA--AN/ to cause to peel or the skin
  to come off by scorching or burning. /MA--AN/ to
  peel or be skinned due to scorching or burning.
  Nalapdugan daytoy natuno nga takkiag ko. My burned
  arm was skinned.

LAPGIS, v. /MANG-:-EN/ to tear off, remove by force.
  Lapgisen na dayta kudil ti letson. He will tear off
  the skin of the roast pig. /MA-/ to be torn off.
  Nalapgis diay kudil na. His skin was torn off.

LAPIGOS, n. /MANG-:-EN/ to pinch or tweak the ear.

LAPIOT, see LAPPIOT.

LAPIS [f. Sp.], n. pencil.

LAP-IT, n. the top part of a branch of a tree which is
  very flexible.
    adj. /NA-/ flexible, easily bent and broken.   --syn.
  LAPPIOT.

LAPLAP, v. /MANG-:-EN/ to cut into a thin slice across
  the surface, as the skin of roast pig. /MA-/ to be
  sliced across the surface.

LAPOG, n. a piece of land used for planting tobacco, corn, cotton, or vegetables.
   v. /MANG-:-EN/ to till or cultivate for planting.

LAPPED, n. obstacle, obstruction, hindrance.
   v. /MANG-:-AN/ to block, obstruct, hinder. Dika lappedan ti kayat na nga aramiden. Don't obstruct what he wants to do. /MANGI-:I-/ to use to obstruct, block, hinder, to put (in a place) as an obstruction or obstacle. Ilapped mo daytoy labba dita ruangan. Put this big basket at the gate as an obstruction.

LAPPIOT, adj. /NA-/ flexible, easily bent.
   v. /AG-/ to bend. Dika tugawan dayta sanga ti kayo ta aglappiot. Don't sit on that branch of the tree for it will bend.

LAPSAK, adj. /NA-/ robust, lusty, vigorous: said especially of plants. --var. LAPSAT.

LAPSAT, var. of LAPSAK.

LAPSI, v. /MANG-:-EN/ to tear off with the hands. Lapsiem dayta naipigket nga papel dita diding. Tear off that paper sticking on the wall. /MA-/ to be torn off.

LAPSUT, v. /AG-/ to attempt to go free or slip off when tied or when being held. /MAKA-/ to go free, slip off. /MANG-:-EN/ to slip off, draw, pull out. Lapsuten na diay baina ti buneng na. He will draw the sheath of his big knife. /MA-/ to be drawn, to slip off. --syn. UKSOT.

LARGABISTA [f. Sp.], n. binoculars.

LASAG, n. flesh, meat (not bone), muscle.

LASAK, n. a cock with black and white plumage and white legs.

LASANG, v. /MANG-:-EN/ to break apart, tear apart, destroy. /MA-/ to be broken apart, torn apart, destroyed.

LASAT, v. /AG-, -UM-/ to go across, pass through, cross (a place). /-UM-, MANG-:-EN/ to cross, go from one side to the other of, go across. /MAKA-:MA-/

to live through or survive an illness. /MANGI-:I-/ to take across, take from one side to the other of.

LASAW, adj. /NA-/ thin, watery (as chocolate). --syn. LABNAW.

LASBANG, adj. /NA-/ luxuriant, exuberant, fresh, lush, rank. --syn. LAPSAK.

LASI, n. dandruff.

[1]LASIN, v. /-UM-, MAKI-/ to separate from (one's group, company, family, etc.). /MANGI-:I-/ to separate, set apart, segregate.

[2]LASIN, v. /MAKA-:MA-/ or /MAKAI-:MAI-/ to recognize, perceive, discern. Mailasin na ka diay tatang na. His father will recognize you.

LASO [f. Sp.], n. ribbon. --syn. RIBON.

LASONA, n. small onion, scallion.

LASONG, n. a big hole.
   LASONG-LASONG, adj. full of big holes (as a road). Lasong-lasong diay dalan nga nagnaan mi. The road where we passed was full of big holes.

LASTOG, adj. /(NA-)/ being a humbug, sham, dishonest. v. /AG-/ to be a humbug; to be deceitful, dishonest; to lie.

LAS-UD, v. /AG-:-EN/ to hold, contain. Mano ti las-uden dayta lata? How much will that can contain? --syn. LAON.

LASUG, see KALASUGAN.

LASUT, v. /MAKA-:MA--AN/ to get rid of, to free oneself from. Saan nga makalasut ti adu nga ut-utang na. He cannot free himself from his many debts. /MAKAI-:MAI--AN/ to be able to clear (a debt), to discharge (a debt) by paying it. Mailasutan minto dagiti utang mi inton umay nga bulan. We will be able to clear our debts this coming month.

LATA [f. Sp.], n. can especially of tin. --syn. BALDE.

LATAK, adj. /NA-/ 1. clear, plain, evident. 2. popular, well-known. Isu ti nalatak nga artista nga taga-Manila. He is the popular actor from Manila.
v. /MANGI-:I-/ to publicize, make known.

LATEG, n. testicle, testis.   --syn. UKEL.

LATI, n. rust.
v. /AG-/ to rust (as iron).

LATIKO, n. whip.   --syn. PAGBAUT, SAPLIT.
v. /MANG-:-EN/ to hit with a whip.

LATLAT, v. /AG-/ to peel, come off: said of the skin. /MA--AN/ to be peeled, be skinned.

LATOK, n. 1. wooden plate. 2. aluminum or tin plate.

LAUD, n. west.

LAUK, v. /MANG-:-AN/ to mix, blend, adulterate (something) with. Laukan na dayta bagas ti mais. He will mix corn with that rice. /MANGI-:I-/ to mix, blend, adulterate with (something). Mais ti ilauk na dita bagas. He will mix corn with that rice. /MAKI-/ to mix, mingle with. /AG-/ [with pl. subject] to mix, mingle.

LAUREL [laurɛl; f. Sp.], n. bay leaf.

[1]LAUS, adj. /NA-/ excessive, overmuch. Nalaus ti ragsak na. His happiness was excessive.   --var. PALAUS. --syn. PALALO.

[2]LAUS, adj. out of fashion, out of date, antiquated, archaic, obsolete.

LAUYA [f. Sp.], n. stewed meat with spices.

LAWA, adj. /NA-/ wide, spacious, extensive, vast.
v. /-UM-/ to become this.

LAWAG, adj. /NA-/ 1. clear, bright. Nalawag ta silaw mo. Your light is bright. 2. clear, distinct, easily seen, heard, or understood. Nalawag ti imbaga na. What he said was clear.
PALAWAG, v. /AG-/ to explain, give an explanation.

/MANGI-:I-/ to explain, elucidate, elaborate on; to make clear.

LAWALAWA, n. spider. --var. LAWWALAWWA.

LAW-AN, v. /MANGI-:I-/ to fail, disappoint. /MAI-/ to do what one should not do unintentionally.

[1]LAWAS, n. week. --syn. DOMINGGO.

[2]LAWAS, n. one internode or segment (of sugar cane, bamboo, etc.).

LAWI, n. tail feathers of a cock, sickle feathers.

LAWIN, n. fish hook
v. /AG-, MANG-:-AN/ to catch (fish) with hook and line. Mapan kami aglawin ti sida. We will go catch fish with hook and line for our meal. /MA--AN/ to be caught with hook and line. Adu ti nalawinan. We caught many (fish) with hook and line. --see BANNIIT.

LAW-IT, adj. /NA-/ 1. sharp-pointed. 2. nimble-tongued.

LAWLAW, n. circumference, perimeter, surrounding area of another.
v. /AG-/ to go around, wander, roam. /MANG-:-EN/ to go around, surround, circle around. /MA-/ to be surrounded. Malawlaw ti dadakkel nga kaykayo diay balay mi. Our house is surrounded by big trees.

LAWWALAWWA, var. of LAWALAWA.

LAY; UMLAY, see under ELLAY.

LAYA, n. ginger (Zingiber officinale).

LAYAG, n. sail of a sea-going vessel.
v. /AG-/ to sail.

LAYÁK, adj. /NA-/ wide, loose (as garments). --syn. LAWA. --ant. KITING.

LAYAP, n. comet, shooting star, meteor.
v. /-UM-/ to flash, shine suddenly and briefly. Adda nakitak nga limmayap. I saw something flash.

LAYAS, see PALAYAS.

LAYAT, v. /MANGI-:I-/ to raise the hand or with the
hand to get ready to strike (someone); hence, to
threaten with. Saan mo nga ilayat kania dayta paltog
mo. Don't threaten me with that gun. /MANG-:-AN/ to
raise the hand or a weapon with the hand against;
hence, to threaten with something. Linayatan nak
diay kabsat mo. Your brother threatened me.

LAYAW, v. /-UM-/ to jump across (a place), to leap
over (a place). /MANG-:-EN/ to jump, leap over.
/MANGI-:I-/ to go across (a place) or to (someone)
by jumping. /AG- + -INN- + R2/ [with pl. subject] to
compete with each other in high jump. --syn. LAGTO.

LAYET, adj. /NA-/ withered, wilted: said of plants and
fruits.

LAYLAY, v. /MA-, AG-/ to become withered, to wilt.
Nalaylay diay immulam idi kalman. What you planted
yesterday wilted.

LAYOG, adj. /NA-/ very tall, high; towering: said
especially of persons and plants.

[1]LAYON, adj. /NA-/ straightforward, direct.
    v. /AG-/ 1. to continue moving, advancing, going
up to (a place). 2. to continue to be (in an office
or position). Sino ti naglayon nga presidente? Who
continued to be president? /MANGI-:I-/ to continue
carrying up to (a place), to take to (a place). 3.
to prolong, continue to do. Inlayon na ti naturog
inggana ti aldaw. He continued to sleep until
afternoon.

[2]LAYON; LAYON-LAYON, adj. stupid.

LAYOS, n. flood, deluge.
    v. /AG-/ to have a flood. /MANG-:-EN/ to flood,
inundate. --syn. DILAP.

LAYT [f. Eng.], n. light.

LEBBEK, v. /AG-, MANG-:-EN/ to pound, smash, crush in
the mortar with a pestle. Lebbeken tayo dayta bagas.
Let us pound that rice. /MA-/ to be pounded, smashed,
crushed.

LEBBUAK, v. /-UM-/ [= LUMBUAK] to boil. Lumbuak diay
danum. The water is boiling.

LEDDAANG, n. sorrow, sadness, grief.
adj. /NA-/ sorrowful, sad, mournful.
v. /AG-, -UM-/ [= LUMDAANG] to be sorrowful, sad.
Saan ka nga lumdaang. Don't be sad.   /MANG-:-EN/ to
be sorrowful or sad about, to grieve, mourn for.
Leddaangen na ti ipapatay ti kabsat na. He mourns for
the death of his brother.

LEGAL [ligal; f. Sp.], adj. legal, proper.

LEGGAK, v. /AG-, -UM-/ [= LUMGAK] 1. to rise: said of
the sun, moon, etc. 2. to come out, appear, be
revealed.

LEK; UMLEK, see under ELLEK.

LEKBA, v. /AG-/ to slide down, slip, fall. Naglekba
diay bado na. Her dress slid down.   /MANGI-:I-/ to
cause to slide down, slip, fall.

LEKKAB, v. /MANG-:-EN/ to remove, take apart, pry off,
tear off, detach.   /MA-/ to be taken apart, torn off,
detached.   --var. LEKSAB.

LEKSAB, var. of LEKKAB.

LEKSION [lɛksion; f. Sp.], n. lesson.
v. /AG-/ to have or take lessons.   /MANG-:-EN/ to
give lessons to, to teach (someone) a lesson.

LELANG [lɛlang; f. Sp.], n. grandmother.   --var. LILANG.

LELONG [lɛlong; f. Sp.], n. grandfather.   --var. LILONG.

LEMMENG, v. /AG-/ to hide, conceal oneself.   /MANGI-:I-/
to hide, conceal.   /AG- + -INN-/ to play hide and
seek.
adj. /NA-/ hidden, concealed.

LEMMES, v. /MA-/ [= MALMES], to be drowned, go under
water.   /MANG-:-EN/ to drown, put under water.

LENNED, v. /-UM-/ [= LUMNED] to sink, be submerged.
Limned diay bapor. The ship sank.   /MANGI-:I-/ to
cause to sink.

[1]LENNEK, adj. concave, hollow.

[2]LENNEK, v. /-UM-/ [= LUMNEK] to set (as the sun).
Lumnek ti initen. The sun is setting now.

LENGNGA, n. the sesame (Sesamum orientale).

LEP-AK, v. /MANG-:-EN/ to wrench off or separate at the
joint. Lep-aken na dayta payak ti manok. He will
wrench off the wing of the chicken.

LEPPAK, n. stalk of taro.

LEPPAS, v. /MANG-:-EN/ or /MANGI-:I-/ to finish, end,
conclude, terminate. Leppasen tayo daras ti mangan.
Let us finish eating hurriedly. /MA-/ [= MALPAS] to
be finished, concluded, terminated. --see KALPASAN.

LEPPAY, v. /AG-/ to droop, hang down. /MA-/ [= MALPAY]
to droop, be discouraged.

LEPPES, v. /MA-/ [= MALPES] to droop due to excess of
moisture: said of plants.

LETLET, v. /-EN/ to be unable to breathe due to
obstruction in the nasal passage.

LETRA [lɛtra; f. Sp.], n. letter of the alphabet.
v. /MANG-:-AN/ to put letters or lettering on.

LETSEPLAN [lɛtsɛplan; f. Sp.], n. custard.

LETTAT, v. /MANG-:-EN/ 1. to unfasten so as to close
(as an umbrella). 2. to release (the trigger of a
gun). 3. to break (a rib). /MA-/ [= MALTAT] to be
1. unfastened, 2. released, 3. broken.

LETTAW, v. /-UM-/ [= LUMTAW] to appear suddenly and
unexpectedly. Limtaw ti adu nga ikan. Many fish
appeared suddenly and unexpectedly.

LETTEG, n. boil, furuncle, abscess.
v. /-UM-/ [= LUMTEG] to swell, become inflamed.

LETTUAG, v. /-UM-/ to appear for the first time after
a period of absence, to be new: said of the moon.
Limtuad diay bulan. The moon appeared for the first
time.

LETTUNGAW, v. /-UM-/ [= LUMTUNGAW] to emerge on the

surface of the water, to come up to the surface of
the water, to float. Awan ti limtungaw nga kayo. No
wood came up to the surface of the water.

LIAD, v. /AG-/ to fall backward. /MANGI-:I-/ to cause
to fall backward. /MA-/ to be caused to fall
backward.

LIAS, v. /MANGI-:I-/ to cause to leave without being
noticed or inconspicuously. Ilias mo nga masapa ta
bagim. You leave early without being noticed.

LIBAK, v. /AG-/ to tell a lie, to conceal something,
to refuse to tell something. /MANGI-:I-/ to lie
about, conceal, refuse to divulge.

LIBAS, v. /AG-/ to leave surreptitiously, without being
noticed. /AG-, MANG-:-AN/ to leave (someone)
surreptitiously, without being noticed. Libasan tayo
ni nanang mo. Let us leave without being noticed by
your mother. /MANG-:-EN/ to take surreptitiously,
without being noticed, to filch, steal. Saan yo nga
libasen daytoy kuartak ditoy. Don't steal my money
here. /MANGI-:I-/ to do surreptitiously, without
being noticed, to do on the sly. Inlibas na ti
nangan idiay kusina. He ate in the kitchen on the
sly.

LIB-AT, v. /MANG-:-EN/ to strike treacherously.
Lib-aten yo dagiti kabusor tayo. Strike our enemies
treacherously.

LIBÁY, v. /MAI-/ to fall asleep unintentionally.
Nailibayak ti apagbiit. I fell asleep unintentionally
for a while.

LIBBI, v. /AG-/ to purse the lips, to pout.
/-UM-, MANG-:-AN/ to purse one's lips at (someone),
to pout at (someone).

LIBEG, adj. /NA-/ muddy, turbid; unclear.

LILIBEG, v. /MANG-:-EN/ to make turbid or murky.

LIBLIBRO, see LIBRO.

LIBNOS, adj. /NA-/ handsome, pretty, neat.

LIBOT, n. procession especially a religious one.
  v. /AG-/ to go around, to have a procession.
  /MANGI-:I-/ to take around.

LIBRAS [f. Sp.], n. pound.

LIBRE [librε; f. Sp.], adj. free.
  v. /MANGI-:I-/ to do something for (someone) free.

¹LIBRO [f. Sp.], n. book.

²LIBRO; LIBLIBRO, n. tripe.

LIBUKAY, v. /MA--AN/ to begin menstruating.

LIBUYONG, adj. /NA-/ overcast, cloudy, gloomy.

LIDAY, adj. /NA-/ sad, downcast, gloomy.

LIDDA, n. a coarse grass with harsh leaves (Saccharum
  spontaneum).

LIDDEG, n. a kind of small edible snail with pointed
  shell.

LIDEM, adj. /NA-/ dim. Nalidem la unay ta silaw mo.
  Your light is very dim.

LIDERATO [lidεrato; f. Sp.], n. leadership.

LIDING, n. string.

LIDLID, n. usually a rough and rounded stone used to
  rub off dirt from the body when taking a bath,
  anything used for this purpose.
    v. /AG-/ to rub off dirt from one's body
  especially when taking a bath. /MANG-:-EN/ to rub
  off, remove by scrubbing. /MANG-:-AN/ to rub off
  the body dirt of, to scrub (someone).

LIGASON [f. Sp.], n. block.

LIG-IS, v. /MANG-:-EN/ to crush especially with the
  nail. /MANGI-:I-/ to crush a louse on the head.

¹LIGSAY, v. /AG-/ to start declining or sinking to the
  west: said of the sun after midday. Nagligsay ti
  initen idi makadanom kami idiay. It was past midday
  when we reached there.

²LIGSAY, v. /MANG-:-EN/ to remove from a list.

³LIGSAY, v. /MANGI-:I-/ to get (a branch of a tree) out
   of the way.

LIKAW, v. /AG-/ to go around. /MANG-:-EN/ to go
   around, surround. /MA-/ to be surrounded.
   /MANGI-:I-/ to lead or take around. --syn. LIBOT,
   RIKOS.
      adj. /NA-/ roundabout, meandering, crooked,
   circuitous.

   PALIKAW, n. circumference, surrounding.

LIKÍG, v. /AG-/ to lean on one side, to sleep on one
   side.

LIKKAONG, n. hollow, hole.
      adj. /NA-/ full of hollows, holes.

LIKLIK, v. /MANG-:-AN/ to avoid, shun. Liklikam ti
   dakes nga dalan. Shun the evil ways. /MANGI-:I-/ to
   keep or protect (someone) (from danger or the evil
   ways). Iliklik na kami ti dakes nga dalan. Protect
   us from the evil ways.

LIKMOT, v. /MANG-:-EN/ to go around, surround,
   encircle. --syn. LIKAW, LIBOT, RIKOS.

   AGLIKMOT, n. surrounding, the area around another,
      the surrounding area. Pinidut na dagiti botelia
      nga agkarabaliktad iti aglikmot. He picked up the
      bottles that were scattered pell-mell in the
      surrounding area.

LIKTAD, v. /MANGI-:I-/ to push the top part of (a
   ladder) away from its resting place and hold
   suspended by a piece of rope, a strip of rattan, a
   piece of wire, etc.

   LILIKTADAN, n. the piece of rope, strip of rattan,
      or piece of wire that holds the top part of a
      ladder suspended when pushed away from its resting
      place.

LIKUD, n. 1. back part of body. 2. the area behind
   someone or something.
      v. /MANG-:-AN/ to turn one's back upon; hence, to
   forget.

   MALIKUDAN, n. those who are left behind in one's past.

LILANG, var. of LELANG.

LILI, v. /MANG-:-EN/ or /MANGI-:I-/ to rock in one's arms. Ililim dayta ubing tapno makaturog. Rock the child in your arms so that it will fall asleep.

LILIBEG, see under LIBEG.

LILIG, n. a section or division of an orange.

LILITSUNEN, see under LITSON.

LILONG, var. of LELONG.

LIMA, num. five; 5. --syn. SINKO.

LIMBONG, v. /AG-/ to clear up, to become settled, free from disturbance or uncertainty; to settle down. Inton aglimbong ti tiempo, mapan tay to idiay Manila. When the weather settles down, we will go to Manila.

LIMDO, v. /AG-/ to be peeved, dissatisfied, displeased, cross, impatient. Dika aglimdo. Don't be cross.

LIMED, v. /MANGI-:I-/ to hide, conceal, keep. Dika ilimed kaniak dayta ar-aramidem. Don't hide from me what you are doing. --syn. DULIN, LIMMENG.

LIMO, v. /MANG-/ to pretend, disguise oneself.

LIMOG, v. /MANG-:-EN/ to dissolve, melt. Limugem dayta tsokolate. Dissolve that chocolate bar.

LIMOS [f. Sp.], n. 1. alms. 2. fee for a church service or for having a religious object blessed.
    AGPALPALIMOS, MAKILIMLIMOS, or MAKILKILIMOS, n. beggar, pauper, indigent. --syn. AGPALPALAMA.

LIMTAW, pt. of LUMTAW.

LIMTEG, pt. of LUMTEG.

LINAB, adj. /NA-/ oily, greasy. --syn. LANIT.

LINABAG, see under LABAG.

LINAK, adj. /NA-/ calm, quiet, still: said especially of the sea or ocean.   --syn. KALMA.

LINAS, n. twine, string.
   v. /MANG-:-EN/ to twine.

LINAY, v. /MANG-:-EN/ to cook thoroughly by leaving it in the hot stove for a while after it has boiled: said of rice.   /MA-/ to be cooked thoroughly: said of rice.

LINIS, adj. /NA-/ smooth, even.

LINNAAW, n. dew, dew drop.
   v. /MA--AN/ to be exposed to the dew, to be in the open air at night.

   KALNAAWAN, n. outdoors, the open air at night.
      v. /AG-/ to be outdoors, in the open air at night.

LINONG, n. shade.
   adj. /NA-/ shady. Nalinong daytoy kayo yo. Your tree is shady.
   v. /-UM-/ to go under the shade, to shade oneself.
   /MANGI-:I-/ to put under the shade.

LINTEG, n. law.
   adj. /NA-/ straight.
   v. /MANG-:-EN/ to make straight, straighten.

   KALINTEGAN, n. privilege, right, prerogative.

LINYA [f. Sp.], n. line.   --syn. UGES.

[1]LINGALING, v. /AG-/ to shake one's head especially to indicate a negative answer.   /MANG-:-EN/ to disobey, go against. Dika nga lingalingen ti kayat ko. Don't go against my wish.

[2]LINGALING, v. /MAI-/ to be distracted, to have one's mind or attention wander away.

LINGAY; LINGLINGAY, n. joy, happiness, entertainment.
   v. /MANG-:-EN/ to entertain, amuse, cheer up, divert. Lininglingay na kami diay kasinsin mo. Your cousin entertained us.
   adj. /MAKA-/ amusing.

LINGED, n. a hidden or concealed place.

adj. /NA-/ hidden, concealed.
v. /AG-/ to hide or conceal oneself. /MANG-:-AN/
[= LINGDAN] to screen, obstruct the view of.
/MANGI-:I-/ to hide, conceal.

LING-ET, n. sweat, perspiration.
v. /AG-/ to perspire. Nalakaak nga agling-et. I
perspire easily. /MANGI-:I-/ to perspire. Adu ti
inling-et na. He perspired much.
BAGAS LING-ET, n. prickly heat.
v. /AG-/ to have prickly heat.

LING-I, v. /AG-/ to turn away one's head as in avoiding
a blow. /MANGI-:I-/ to turn away (the head) as in
avoiding a blow. Iling-im dayta ulom. Turn away your
head.

LINGSAT, adj. /NA-/ narrow.

LINGTA, v. /AG-, MANG-:-EN/ to boil (fish, eggs,
vegetables, etc.). /MA-/ to be boiled.

LION [f. Sp.], n. lion.

LIPAT, v. /-UM-, MANG-:-EN/ to forget (someone). Saan
nak nga liplipaten uran inton kaano man. Don't forget
me at any time. /MANG-:-AN/ often /MAKA-:MA--AN/ to
forget (something). Nalipatak ti mapan makimisa. I
forgot to go to church.
MANAGILLILIPAT, adj. forgetful.

¹LIPAY, n. 1. a coarse leguminous vine with large showy
flowers, compressed pods, and large dark-brown,
chestnut-like seed used by children to play with.
2. the seed of this. 3. the game using the seeds of
this.
v. /AG-/ to play the game using seeds of this.

²LIPAY; LIPAYLIPAY, n. kneecap, patella.

LIPISTIK, var. of LIPSTIK.

LIPIT, n. a narrow passage.
v. /MANG-:-EN/ to crush, press between two
opposing forces so as to break or injure, squeeze.
/MA-/ to be crushed. Nalipit diay tammudo na idiay
ridaw. His index finger was crushed at the door.

LIPPIAS, v. /AG-/ to overflow, flow over the brim.
Naglippias diay karayan kalpasan ti tudo. The river
overflowed its bank after the rain. --var. LUPPIAS.

LIPPIIT, v. /-UM-/ [= LUMPIIT] to snap. /AG- + -INN- + R2/
[with pl. subject] to strike each other.

LIPSTIK [f. Eng.], n. lipstick.
     v. /AG-/ to use lipstick. --var. LIPISTIK: used
by old people.

LIPUT, v. /MANG-:-AN/ to betray. Dina kam liputan.
Don't betray us.

LIS-A, n. nit, egg of a louse.

LISAY, v. /MA--AN/ to have some kind of indigestion
characterized by pain in the abdomen and evacuation
of undigested food.

LISDAK, n. heap, quantity obtained by. Adu ti lisdak
ti pisos. A peso buys much.
     adj. /NA-/ much in quantity. Nalisdak ti ginatang
na nga pisos. What he bought with one peso was much.

LISI, v. /AG-/ to get out of the way. /-UM-, MANG-:-AN/
to get out of the way of, to avoid, evade.
/MANGI-:I-/ to get out of the way, to keep away
from. Ilisim ta bagim ti ringgor. Keep yourself away
from trouble.

LISLIS, v. /AG-/ to roll up a sleeve or both sleeves,
a leg or both legs of one's pants, to pull up one's
dress or skirt. /MANG-:-EN/ to roll up (a sleeve,
a leg of pants), to pull up (a dress).
     n. the result of this. Nangato la unay ta lislis
mo. Your sleeves (or dress) are (or is) rolled up
(or pulled up) too high.

LISTA [f. Sp.], n. list. --var. LISTAAN.
     v. /MANGI-:I-/ to list down, to put in a list.

LISTAAN, var. of LISTA n.

LITEM, adj. /NA-/ livid, black and blue: usually due
to an injury.
     v. /-UM-/ to become livid, black and blue.

LITILIT, v. /MANG-:-AN/ to trim along the edges of.

Litilitan na inton bigat daytoy panyok. He will trim
my handkerchief along the edges tomorrow.
/MANGI-:I-/ to use to trim the edges of (a
handkerchief, doily, etc.), to trim the edges of
(a handkerchief, doily, etc.) with.

LITNAW, adj. /NA-/ clear, transparent as water, glass,
etc.

LITOK, v. /AG-/ to crack as a joint. Naglitok dagiti
tumtumeng ko. My knees cracked.

LITRO [f. Sp.], n. a unit of dry measure; three of
these make one SALOP.

LITSON [f. Sp.], n. roast pig.   --syn. INASAR.
    v. /AG-/ to roast a pig. /MANG-:-EN/ to roast (a
pig).   --syn. ASAR.
    LILITSUNEN, adj. suitable for roasting: said of a
    pig.

LITTAAK, v. /-UM-/ [= LUMTAAK] to produce a popping or
bursting sound. Lumtaak dagidiay kawayan. The
bamboo clumps are popping.   --see KANALTAAK.

LITTIIK, v. /-UM-/ [= LUMTIIK] to produce a snapping
or snipping sound.   --see KANALTIIK.

LITTIK, v. /MANG-:-AN/ to perforate, bore a hole
through.   /MA--AN/ to be perforated.

LITUP, v. /MANG-:-AN/ to finish doing (a piece of work),
paying (a debt), etc. Linitupan ni nanang na dagiti
ut-utang na. His mother finished paying all his
debts.

LIWAG; LIWLIWAG, v. /MANGI-:I-/ 1. to put out of one's
thought, to banish. Isuda ti nangiliwliwag ti
ladingit ko. They were the ones who banished by
sadness. 2. to distract, divert, amuse, cheer up.
Inliwliwag mi ni nanang ko. We cheered up my mother.

LIWAY, v. /MANG-:-AN/ to forget (something). Dika
liwayan ti makimisa. Don't forget to attend mass.
--syn. LIPAT.
    adj. /NA-/ forgetful, negligent, careless.

LIWENG; MANGLIWENGLIWENG, adj. deep, profound.

LIWES, v. /MANG-/ to go around. /MANGI-:I-/ to take
  around. Isu ti nangiliwes kadakami. It was he who
  took us around. --syn. RIKOS.

LIWLIW, v. /MANG-:-EN/ to do by a circuitous route, to
  do in a roundabout way. Mangliwliw kayo nga mapan
  idiay. Go there in a roundabout way.

LIWLIWA, n. consolation, solace, recompense.
    v. /MANG-:-EN/ to console, comfort, solace, raise
  the spirit of.
  PAGPALPALIWAAN, n. something that serves to console.

¹LOBO [f. Sp.], n. wolf.

²LOBO [f. Sp.], n. balloon.

LOKAL [f. Sp.], adj. local, made in or originating
  from the locality.

LOKO [f. Sp.], adj. /(NA-)/ foolish, mischievous.
    v. /MANG-:-EN/ to fool, dupe, deceive.

LOLA [f. Sp.], n. grandmother. --syn. LELANG. --ant.
  LOLO.

LOLO [f. Sp.], n. grandfather. --var. LOLONG. --syn.
  LELONG. --ant. LOLA.

LOLONG, var. of LOLO.

LOTE [lotɛ; f. Sp.], n. a subdivision of a block in a
  town or city, a lot.

LOTERIA [lotɛria; f. Sp.], n. lottery.

LUA, n. tear (of the eye).
    v. /AG-/ to shed, or fill with, tears. /MANGI-:I-/
  to shed as tears. Dara ti inlua na. He shed blood
  as tears.

LUAG, n. foam, bubble, froth.
    v. /AG-/ to bubble, foam.

LUALO, n. prayer, supplication.
    v. /AG-/ to pray. /MANG-:-EN/ to pray, recite as
  a prayer.

LUANG, adj. /NA-/ loose and shaking as a jar or can half full of water.

LUAS, v. /AG-, -UM-/ to leave on a trip, to travel. Agluas kaminto no bigat. We will leave on a trip tomorrow. /MANGI-:I-/ to take on a trip.

LUBBO, v. /MA-/ [= MALBO] to sink. Nalbo diay nagluganan da nga biray. The boat on which they were riding sank.

LUBBON, v. /MAKI-:KA-/ to pair with as in riding, sleeping, etc. /AG-/ [with pl. subject] to be paired with each other.

LUBBOT, v. /-UM-/ [= LUMBOT] to pass through (a hole, an opening, etc.). Saan nga lumbot daytoy ulok ti daytoy badok. My head won't pass through my dress. /MANGI-:I-/ to put or pass (something) through (a hole, an opening, etc.). Ilubbot mo dayta balotam ditoy. Pass your bundle through here.

LUBI, v. /AG-/ to make a kind of sticky sweet made of DIPPIG bananas, DIKET rice, grated coconut meat and sugar; or of cassava root, grated coconut meat and sugar. /MANG-:-EN/ to make into this kind of sweet.

LINUBIAN, n. this kind of sweet.

LUBID, n. string.

LUBNAK, n. puddle.
      v. /AG-/ to wallow or play in a puddle. /MANGI-:I-/ to throw into or make fall in a puddle. /MAI-/ to fall in a puddle.

LUBO, n. mud, mudhole, mire, slough.
      v. /MANGI-:I-/ to cause to get stuck (in mud, debt, etc.). /MAI-/ to get stuck (in mud, debt, etc.).

LUBONG, n. world, universe.

SANGALUBONGAN, n. the whole world or universe.

LUBOS, see PALUBOS.

LUDEK, v. /MA-/ to be partially or not fully cooked: said of rice.

LUDON, v. /MANG-:-EN/ to put together without any
   order, to throw into a heap.   /AG-/ [with pl.
   subject] to scramble.

LUDONG, n. a PURONG when more than a foot long.

LUGAD, v. /MANG-:-EN/ to loosen. Saan mo nga lugaden
   dayta poste. Don't loosen that post.

   LUGADLUGAD, v. /AG-/ to be loose. Aglugadlugad toy
      ngipen ko. My tooth is loose.   --syn. WALIWALI.

LUGAN, n. 1. vehicle, means of transportation. 2. load,
   passenger. 3. the taking of a vehicle.
      v. /AG-/ to ride in or on.   /MANGI-:I-/ to load
   in (a vehicle).

LUGAR [f. Sp.], n. 1. place, spot, situation. 2. chance,
   opportunity, time.
      v. /-UM-/ to stay, put oneself in (a place).
   Lumugar ka dita. Stay there.   /MANGI-:I-/ to put,
   place (someone or something) (in a place).
   /MAKA-:MA--AN/ to have the chance or time to do.

LUGAW, v. /AG-/ to make rice gruel or porridge.
   /MANG-:-EN/ to make into rice gruel or porridge.

   LINUGAW, n. rice gruel or porridge.

LUGAY, v. /MANG-:-AN/ to take off the hat to (someone).
   Dina kayat nga lugayan diay kapitan. He does not
   want to take his hat off to the captain.

LUGI, n. business loss.
      v. /MANG-:-EN/ to shortchange, cheat.   /MA-/ 1. to
   be shortchanged, to be cheated. 2. to suffer a loss,
   as in business, to lose in a business transaction.
   Malugiak no ited ko kenka dayta ti pisos. I will
   lose if I give that to you for one peso.

LUGLUG, v. /MANG-:-EN/ to make muddy or mushy by
   agitating with the hands or feet. Dika nga luglugen
   dayta pitak. Don't make that mud mushy.

LUGPI, adj. crippled, lame.
      v. /MANG-:-EN/ to cause to become crippled or lame,
   to cripple.   /MA-/ to become crippled.

LUGUB, v. to stay close to, huddle around. Saan mo nga
   luguban dayta apoy. Don't huddle around that fire.

LUGUD, see PALUGUD.

LUKAB, v. /MANG-:-EN/ to pry open, separate the two opposing sides of. Lukaben na dagita tirem. He will pry open those oysters.

LUKAG, v. /MA-/ to be awakened in one's sleep.

LUKAIS, var. of LUKAS.

LUKAS, v. /AG-/ to pull up the lower part of one's dress: said of women. --var. LUKAIS.

LUKAT, v. /AG-/ to open or be opened. /AG-, MANG-:-AN/ or /AGI-, MANGI-:I-/ to open. Lukatan ta daytoy ridaw. Let us open this door.

LUK-AT, v. /MANG-:-AN/ to free, release, liberate. Saan mo nga luk-atan dayta baboy. Don't release that pig. /MA--AN/ to be freed, released, liberated. Naluk-atan diay balud. The prisoner was released.

LUKAY, adj. /NA-/ loose, not tightly fastened.

LUKBAN, n. the pomelo (Citrus decumana).

LUKDIT, n. glans penis. --syn. (dial.) LUSI.
    adj. /NA-/ with the glans penis uncovered.

LUKIP, v. /MANG-:-EN/ to lift or raise slightly especially along the edge. Lukipen na dayta ikamen. He will lift that mat slightly along the edge. /MANGI-:I-/ to open lightly, set ajar (as a door, window, etc.). Ilukip mo dayta ridaw. Open that door ajar.

LUKKIAP, v. /MANG-:-EN/ to pry loose or off, to detach by prying. /MA-/ to be pried loose or off, to be detached.

LUKMEG, adj. /NA-/ fat, stout, obese. --ant. KUTTONG.
    v. /-UM-/ to become this.

LUKMO, n. a crustacean whose shell has been removed.
    adj. /NA-/ weak.

LUKNENG, adj. /NA-/ soft. --ant. TANGKEN.
    v. /-UM-/ to become this.

LUKOG, v. /MANG-:-EN/ to shuffle (the cards) such that one will eventually get the trump cards as the cards are dealt out: a form of cheating; to trump.

LUKONG, v. /MANGI-:I-/ to enclose (a note, check, money order, etc.) with (a letter). Ilukong mo daytoy dita surat mo. Enclose this with your letter. /MAI-/ to be enclosed with or inside. Adda kuarta nga nailukong ditoy surat na. There is money enclosed with his letter.

LUKOT, v. /AG-, MANG-:-EN/ to roll up. Lukuton tayo dagitoy ikamen nga nagturogan tayo. Let us roll up these mats on which we slept. /MANG-:I-/ to roll inside or with. /MAI-/ to be rolled inside or with.

LUKSAW, v. /MA-:KA-/ to be disgusted or irritated with.

KALUKSAW, n. that with whom one is disgusted.

LULEM, adj. /NA-/ overcast, cloudy. --syn. KUYEM.

LULO, v. /MANG-:-EN/ to cause (a fruit) to become soft by handling, dropping, beating, etc. /MA-/ to become soft through handling, dropping, beating, etc.

LULOD, n. shin of leg.

LULOK, v. /MANG-:-AN/ to loosen, slacken as a string. Lulukam dayta lubid ti ullaw mo. Slacken the string of your kite.
   adj. /NA-/ loose, slack. Nalulok daytoy pagbalaybayak. My clothesline is slack.

LULUKISEN, n. the mandarin orange (Citrus nobilis).

LULUNAN, n. fontanel, the soft, boneless area on top of the head of a baby.

LUMBA, n. race, running competition.
   v. /MAKI-:KA-/ to race with. /AG-/ [with pl. subject] to compete in a race, to race with each other.

LUMLOM, v. /MANGI-:I-/ to push through or under, to force to go under or in. /MAI-/ to be pushed through, under, or in.

LUMOT, n. moss.

LUMTAW, = -UM- + LETTAW.

LUMTEG, = -UM- + LETTEG.

LUMTIIK, see under LITIK.

LUNAG, v. /MANG-:-EN/ to melt, liquefy (a metal).
/MA-/ to be melted, liquefied.

LUNAS, v. /MA-/ to be worn out such that the surface
becomes smooth (as a coin).

[1]LUNES, v. /MANG-:-EN/ to crumple especially a dress.
Saan mo nga lunesen ta badom. Don't crumple your
dress. /MA-/ to be crumpled.

[2]LUNES [f. Sp.], n. Monday.

LUNLON, v. /MANG-:-AN/ to rinse as a bottle. Lunlonam
dayta botelya. Rinse that bottle. /MA--AN/ to be
rinsed.

LUNOD, n. curse.
v. /MANGI-:I-/ to curse, call or bring evil or
injury down on, damn. Saan mo nga ilunod dagiti
naganak kenka. Don't curse your parents. /MAI-/ to
be damned.

LUNG-AW, v. /-UM-/ to come out, rise out, emerge (as
when drowning). /MAKA-/ to be free from sickness,
danger, misfortune, hardships, etc.

LUNG-AY, n. way.

LUNGBOY, n. Java plum (Eugenia jambolana).
v. /-UM-/ to become livid, black-and-blue.
Limmungboy diay rupa ni Pedro. Peter's face became
black-and-blue.

LUNGGI; LUNGGI-LUNGGI, v. /AG-/ to rock, reel, totter,
sway. Aglunggi-lunggi diay lamisaan. The table is
tottering.

LUNGLONG; LUNGLONGAN, n.pl. kitchen utensils.

LUNGNGUOP, v. /MA--AN/ to be suffocated, stifled, or
smothered with heat, as in a dense crowd.

LUNGOG, n. hollow, a small valley, a depression.

LUNGON, n. coffin.

LUNGPO, adj. /NA-/ chubby, stout: implies good health.
   v. /-UM-/ to become this.

LUNGPOS, v. /MANG-:-EN/ to cover with, spread over.
   Saan mo nga lungposen dayta kusina ti danum. Don't
   spread water over that kitchen.   /MA-/ to be covered
   with.

LUNGSOT, adj. /NA-/ rotten, spoiled, decomposing,
   putrefying.
      v. /MANG-:-EN/ to cause to rot, putrefy, decompose.
   --var. LUNGTOT.

LUNGTOT, var. of LUNGSOT.

LUOB, v. /-UM-/ to stay or live (in somebody's house).
   /MAKI-:KA-/ 1. to stay or live with. 2. to stay or
   live with as common-law wife or husband.

   KALUOB, n. common-law wife or husband.
      v. /AG-/ [with pl. subject] to be or live
   together as common-law husband and wife.

LUOM, adj. /NA-/ ripe.
   v. /AG-, MA-/ to become ripe, ripen.

LUPAK, v. /MANGI-:I-/ to cause to sink or get stuck,
   to cause to submerge or go beneath the surface of
   (mud), to sink. Saan mo nga ilupak ta sapatos mo
   dita pitak. Don't sink your shoes in the mud.

LUPES, adj. sterile, barren, unable to have offspring.

LUPINAY, v. /AG-/ to sit down on one's breech with the
   legs folded and drawn close to the body; to crouch.

LUPING, adj. drooping, fallen (as the ears of a dog,
   the crest of a cock).

LUPISAK, adj. crippled, unable to stand or walk.
   v. /AG-/ to sit on the ground or floor.   --syn.
   DALUPISAK.

LUPOS, v. /AG-/ to cast off the slough, outer skin,
   or shell of.

NAGLUPOSAN, n. the cast off slough, skin, or shell.

LUPOT, n. 1. cloth, fabric. 2. dress, apparel; clothes.

LUPOY, adj. /(NA-)/ weak, feeble, as one who falls
down easily.

LUPPI, v. /MANG-:-EN/ to fold. --syn. KULPI.

LUPPIAD, v. /MANG-:-EN/ to bend back (a finger, etc.).
/MA-/ to be bent back.
   adj. bent back.

LUPPIAS, var. of LIPPIAS.

LUPPO, n. thigh.

LUPTAK, v. /AG-/ to chap, crack open, fissure: said of
the lips, tongue, skin, etc. Agluptak dagitoy bibig
ko. My lips are chapping.

LUSA, adj. /NA-/ soft: said of rice.

LUSDOY, v. /AG-/ to droop, sag.

LUSI [dial.], n. glans penis. --syn. LUKDIT.
     v. /MANG-:-EN/ to expose (the glans penis) by
pushing back the foreskin. /MA-/ to be exposed: said
of the glans penis.

LUSIAW, adj. /NA-/ pale, wan, pallid, ashen.

LUSIT, v. /MANG-:-EN/ to crush by putting a heavy
weight on. /MA-/ to be crushed by a heavy weight.

LUSLOS, v. /AG-/ to slip, slide off. Agluslos daytoy
singsing ko. My ring is slipping off (my finger).
/MANGI-:I-/ to slide down or off. Saan mo nga iluslos
toy paldak. Don't slide down my skirt.

LUSOB, n. the tubular, earthenware lining of a well,
well casing.
   adj. /NA-/ concave, hollow.

LUSONG, v. /MANGI-:I-/ to insert, put in or on, fit in.
Ilusong mo ta sapatos mo. Put on your shoes. /MAI-/.
to be inserted, thrust in, put in; to fall into.
Nailusong diay saka ni Rosa idiay abut. Rose's foot
fell into a hole.

LUSSOK, v. /MANG-:-EN/ to puncture, pierce, perforate,
bore a hole through.
   adj. perforated, having a hole.

LUSSOT, v. /-UM-/ [= LUMSOT] to go through, shoot or
break through, pierce. Limsot diay bala ditoy. The
bullet went through here.

LUSULUS, v. /AG-/ 1. to resign from one's position or
office. 2. to withdraw from one's candidacy for a
position or office. /MANGI-:I-/ to resign from,
withdraw from (a position, an office, etc.).
Ilusulos mo ti kinapresidentem. Resign from your
presidency.

LUTAB, n. foam, froth, spume.

LUTLUT, n. mud, mudhole, mire, slough.
   v. /AG-, MANG-:-EN/ to cause to become muddy.
/MANGI-:-EN/ to cause to sink or get stuck in mire,
to mire. /MAI-/ to be sunk or stuck in mud.
Mailutlut diay pilid ti karison yo ditoy. The wheels
of your cart will be sunk in mud here.

LUTO, v. /AG-/ to cook something. /AG-, MANG-:-EN/ to
cook.

LUTTOK, v. /MANG-:-AN/ to crack open as an egg.
Luttokan na dayta itlog. He will crack open that egg.
/MA-/ to be cracked open.

LUYA, v. /MA--AN/ to be induced to cry. Nalaka nga
maluyaan ni Rosa. Rose is easily induced to cry.

LUYAK, adj. /NA-/ gluey, sticky.

LUYLUY, v. /AG-/ to flow out, issue out. Agluyluy diay
buteg na. His nasal mucus is flowing out.

LUY-ONG, n. the pubic region.

-M, var. of MO after a vowel.

MAAG, n. idiot. Dika agbalin nga maag. Don't be an
idiot.

MAAY; MAMAAY, n. result, effect.

MABAGBAGI [cf. BAGI], n. genitals. --var. BAGI.

MABLO, = MA- + BULLO.

MABOLO, n. 1. a fruit-bearing tree (Diospyros discolor).
2. its fruit.

MABTAK, = MA- + BETTAK.

MADAMDAMA, see under DAMA.

MADI, v. 1. not to like or want (to do something), to
refuse (to do something). Madi mangan diay billit.
The bird refuses to eat. 2. not to like or want
(someone or something), to refuse (someone or
something). Madim dayta? Don't you like that? /AG-/
to refuse (to do something), to back out (from doing
something). --var. ADI. --see also INDIAK, MANDIAK.
  adj. not appropriate, not proper, not nice, not
good, not decent. Madi dayta nga aramid. That action
is not decent.

MADRE [madrɛ; f. Sp.], n. nun.
  v. /AG-/ to become a nun.

MAESTRA [maɛstra, mɛstra; f. Sp.], n. a female teacher.
  v. /AG-/ to become a female teacher. --ant. MAESTRO.

MAESTRO [maɛstro, mɛstro; f. Sp.], n. 1. a male teacher.
2. master.
  v. /AG-/ to become a male teacher. --ant. MAESTRA.

MAGA, adj. /NA-/ dry (as clothes, the ground, but not
leaves). --see GANGO.
  v. /MA--AN/ to become dry, to become waterless.
Namagaan diay bubon da. Their well became dry.

MAGASIN [f. Eng.], n. 1. magazine: a publication. 2.
magazine: a chamber attached to a pistol or rifle
from which the cartridges are fed.

MAGMAG, adj. /NA--AN/ very dry.

MAGNA, = M- + PAGNA.

MAHABLANKO [f. Sp.], n. a kind of sweet.

MAIKAMANO, inter. at what position in a sequence?

MAINGEL, see under INGEL.

MAIPANGGEP, see under PANGGEP.

MAIPUON [cf. PUON], prep. on account (of), because (of).

MAIS [f. Sp.], n. corn, maize.

MAKAN [cf. KAAN], n. anything that can be eaten, an eatable thing. Agbunga iti makan dagiti mula iti minuyongan da. The trees in their orchard bear fruits that can be eaten.
MAKAPUNO, n. 1. a variety of coconut. 2. its fruit.

MAKASTREK, = MAKA- + SERREK.

MAKINA [f. Sp.], n. 1. machine, engine. 2. a sewing machine.

MAKINARIA [f. Sp.], n. machinery.

MAKOY, v. /AG-/ to feel weak, feeble, languid.

MAKTANG, = MA- + KETTANG.

MAKUPA, n. the Malay apple (Eugenia javanica).

MALADAGA, n. infant, a baby under seven years of age.

MALAKSID, see under LAKSID.

MALAMAL, v. /MA--AN/ to be splattered all over with mud, food, etc.

MALANGA; MALMALANGA, v. /AG-/ to be dazed, stunned, stupefied.

MALARIA [f. Sp.], n. malaria.
   v. /AG-, -EN/ to have malaria.

MALAS, adj. /(NA-)/ 1. to be unlucky, to have bad luck. 2. causing bad luck, being the jinx. Namalas ta kaduam. Your companion causes bad luck.
   v. /-EN/ to become unlucky, to have bad luck.

MALASADO [f. Sp.], adj. soft-boiled, parboiled, half-cooked (as an egg).

MALDIT, v. /MANGI-:I-/ to print, imprint, impress,
mark, stamp on. Immaldit na ti nagan ko diay libro
na. He imprinted my name on his book.

MALETA [malɛta; f. Sp.], n. suitcase.

MALIKUDAN, see under LIKUD.

MALMES, = MA- + LEMMES.

MALO, n. a wooden mallet used especially for beating
clothes that are being washed.
v. /AG-, MANG-:-EN/ to beat, flog, club, pound
with a big and heavy piece of wood.

MALPAAN, = M-AN + PALPA.

MALPAS, = MA- + LEPPAS.

MALPAY, = MA- + LEPPAY.

MALPES, = MA- + LEPPES.

MALTAT, = MA- + LETTAT.

MALUKONG, n. bowl.

MAMA, n. a chewing preparation made of betel leaf,
lime and betel nut.
v. /AG-/ to chew this. /MANG-:-EN/ to chew (this
or something similar).

MAMAAY, see MAAY.

MAMADIGO, = MANG- + PADIGO.

MAMAGBAGA, = MANG- + BAGBAGA.

MAMAKIR, = MANG- + BAKIR.

MAMALON, = MANG- + BALON.

MAMAMATAY, see under PATAY.

MAMAYO, n. a general feeling of weakness of the body
with no apparent cause.
v. /AG-/ to have this.

MAMEG, v. /MANGI-:I-/ to press or crush down. /MAI-/ to be pressed or crushed down.

MAMELOKO [mamɛloko; f. Sp.], n. children's drawers.

MAMIN-ANO, = M- + PAMIN-ANO.

MAMISOS [cf. PISOS], adj. worth a peso.

MAMLES, = MANG- + PELLES.

MAMMADLES, see under PADLES.

MAMMALTOT, see under PALTOT.

MAMMARTEK, see under BARTEK.

MAMMIGAT, = M- + PAMMIGAT.

MAMMUKIS, = MANG- + PUKIS.

MAMMULLO, see under BULLO.

MAMON, n. a kind of soft bread.

MAN, adv. 1. please, I entreat you. Iyawat mo man ta lapis ko. Please hand me my pencil. 2. an emphatic word. Isu man ti nakitak. It was indeed he whom I saw.

SAAN MAN, an answer affirming a negative question, the positive answer to a negative question.

MANAGILLILIPAT, see under LIPAT.

MANALAPI [cf. SALAPI], n. worth fifty centavos or half a peso.

MANANG [f. Sp.], n. 1. an older sister. 2. any older woman. --ant. MANONG.

MANANGAASI [= MANANG- + KAASI], adj. merciful, compassionate, charitable, gracious. Manangaasi ni Apo Dios. God is merciful.

MANAS, n. beriberi.

MANDALA, n. a big heap of bundles of harvested rice.

MANDIAK, var. of INDIAK.

MANEHO [manɛho; f. Sp.], n. driver (of a car, a cart, etc.).
 v. /AG-/ to drive a car, a cart, etc. /MANG-:-EN/ to drive, be the driver of (a car, a cart, etc.). Isu ti nagmaneho iti kotse mi. It was he who drove our car.

MANEN, adv. again, once more.

MANI, n. peanut.

MANIPUD, adv. from (a place or time), since.

MANMANO, adj. 1. very few, very little. Manmano ti balasang nga immay. Very few unmarried girls came. 2. infrequent; very seldom. Manmano nga agdigos ta baro. That bachelor takes a bath very seldom.

MANNAIT [cf. DAIT], n. seamster, tailor, seamstress. --syn. SASTRE, MODISTA.

[1]MANO, v. /AG-/ in certain games, to throw one's flattened metal, stone, coin, etc. to determine one's place in the order of playing. /AG- + -INN- + R2/ [with pl. subject] in certain games, to throw flattened metals, stones, coins, etc. to determine the order in which the players are to play. --syn. KANO.
 adj. first in the order of playing.

[2]MANO, inter. how many, how much. Mano ti anak mon? How many children do you have now?

MANOK, n. chicken.

MANONG [f. Sp.], n. 1. an older brother. 2. an older man. --ant. MANANG.

MANSA [f. Sp.], n. stain.
 v. /MANG-:-AN/ to stain.

MANSANAS [f. Sp.], n. apple.

MANSANILYA, n. 1. a kind of plant of the aster family, with scented leaves and daisy-like flowers: the dried leaves, flowers and buds are used in medicine; camomile or chamomile. 2. its flower.

MANSO, v. /AG-, MANG-:-EN/ to beat, club, cudgel.
--syn. MALO.

MANTIKA [f. Sp.], n. lard, cooking oil.
v. /AG-/ to produce lard or cooking oil.

MANTIKILIA [f. Sp.], n. margarine.

MANTO [f. Sp.], n. mantle, cloak.

MANUBELA [f. Sp.], n. steering wheel.

MANUGANG, n. son-in-law, daughter-in-law, the spouse
of one's daughter or son.

MANGA; MANGAMANGA, v. /AG-/ to be uncertain,
undecided, hesitant, doubtful, unsure, perplexed.
Apay nga agmangamanga ka? Why are you hesitant?

MANGALDAW, = M- + PANGALDAW.

MANGAN, = M- + PANGAN, MANG- + KAAN.

MANGGA, n. 1. mango tree. 2. its fruit.

MANGGAGAMA, n. scorpion.

MANGGAS [f. Sp.], n. sleeve of a garment.

MANGGED; MANGMANGGED, n. laborer, worker.   --syn.
TRABAHADOR.

MANGLIWENGLIWENG, see under LIWENG.

MANGMANG, n. an inflammation at the corner of the lips.
v. /AG-/ to be afflicted with this.

MANGMANGGED, see MANGGED.

MANGNIBINIBI, adj. exceptional, extremely strong or
great.

MANGNGALAP [MANG- + KALAP], n. a fisherman.

MANGNGANUP, see under ANUP.

MANGNGEG, = MA- + DENGNGEG.

MANGNGILOT, see under ILOT.

MANGRABII, = M- + PANGRABII.

MANGUBOG, n. a kind of large bird with black plumage.

MANG-US, = M- + PANG-US.

MAPLENG, = MA- + PELLENG.

MARABUTIT, n. a newborn baby, a tiny mouse.

MARASABA, var. of MARSABA.

MARBA, = MA- + REBBA.

MARGAAY, = MA- + REGGAAY.

MARIGRIGAT [cf. RIGAT], adj. poor, destitute,
   impoverished. Marigrigat ti tao dagiti naganak
   kaniak. The parents of my parents were poor.

MARIS, n. color, hue. Berde ti maris ti kawes na. The
   color of her dress is green.   --syn. KOLOR.
   MARISMARIS, v. /AG-/ to be iridescent, to display a
      variety of colors. Agmarismaris diay bado na. Her
      dress is iridescent.

MARKA [f. Sp.], n. mark, brand, sign.
   v. /AG-, MANG-:-AN/ to put a mark or brand on, to
   mark, brand. /MANGI-:I-/ to imprint on as mark,
   brand, etc.

MARMOL [f. Sp.], n. marble.

MARSABA, adj. ripe and yellow: said of a tamarind
   fruit.   --var. MARASABA.

MARSO [f. Sp.], n. March.

MARTES [martɛs; f. Sp.], n. Tuesday.

MARTILIO [f. Sp.], n. hammer.
   v. /MANG-:-EN/ to hit with, or as if with, a hammer.
   /MANGI-:I-/ to use to hit with like a hammer.

MARTIR [f. Sp.], n. martyr.

MARUNGGAY, n. 1. the horse-radish tree (Moringa oleifera). 2. its fruit.

MASA [f. Sp.], v. /MANG-:-EN/ to knead (dough, clay, etc.).

MASAHE [masahɛ; f. Sp.], v. /MANG-:-EN/ to rub, massage. --syn. ILOT 1.

MASAKBAYAN [cf. SAKBAY], n. the future. Naraniag ti masakbayan ta asawam. The future of your husband is bright.

MASAKIT [cf. SAKIT], n. a sick person, a patient. Diak ammo ti nagan diay masakit. I don't know the name of the patient.

MASAKSAKIT [cf. SAKIT], adj. sickly, in poor health. Masaksakit ni nanang ko. My mother is sickly.

MASDAAW, = MA- + SEDDAAW.

MASETAS [masɛtas; f. Sp.], n. potted ornamental plant. Nadumaduma dagiti masetas. The potted ornamental plants were of different varieties.

MASETERA [masɛtɛra; f. Sp.], n. pot for ornamental plants.

MASINGGAN [f. Eng.], n. machine gun.
    v. /MANG-:-EN/ to shoot or kill with a machine gun.

MASNGAAD, v. /AG-/ to squat, sit down on one's hams and heels. Dika nga agmasngad. Don't squat.

MASO [f. Sp.], n. mallet.

MASPAK, = MA- + SEP-AK.

MATA, n. 1. eye: organ of sight. 2. pit on a pineapple, bamboo, timber, etc. 3. core of a boil.
    v. /AG-/ to open one's eyes. /MANGI-:I-/ to open (an eye). Imatam ta kattigid nga matam. Open your left eye.

MATAMATA, v. /MANG-:-EN/ to stare at. Apay nga matamataen nak? Why are you staring at me? --syn. MULAGAT.

MATAY, = M- + PATAY.

MATERIALES [materiales; f. Sp.], n.pl. materials.

MATIANAN, = ATIAN + MA--AN.

MATMAT, v. /MANG-:-AN/ to look closely at, examine
carefully. Matmatam dayta retrato. Examine carefully
that picture.   --see PAMATMAT.

MATRIKULA [f. Sp.], n. matriculation fee.
   v. /AG-/ to matriculate, to pay one's matriculation
fee.

MATRIS [f. Sp.], n. uterus, womb. --syn. AANAKAN.

MATTIT, adj. crazy, lunatic, insane.
   v. /AG-/ to become crazy, lunatic, insane.

   MATMATTIT, n. lunatic tendency. Adda matmattit dayta
   gayyem mo. Your friend has lunatic tendencies.

MATUON; AGMATUON, n. noon, midday.

MAYA, v. /AG-/ to be in heat, to be sexually aroused.

MAYAMAY, adj. /NA-/ gentle, quiet, placid, calm,
serene.

MAYANA, n. a kind of shrub with reddish leaves.

MAYAT, see under KAYAT.

MAYEKMEK, adj. /NA-/ fine, powdery.

MAYENG, v. /AG-/ to stare blankly. /MAI-/ to become
enraptured, engrossed, absorbed with something.

MAYENGMENG, adj. /NA-/ safe, secure, snug, cozy.

MAYO [f. Sp.], n. May.

MAYOR [f. Eng.], n. mayor.   --var. MEYOR.   --syn.
ALKALDE.

MAYSA, num. one; 1.   --var. -YSA, -SA, -SAN.   --syn.
UNO, UNA.

   MAYMAYSA, adj. one only.
      v. /AG-/ to stay or be alone.

MAYSA PAY, besides, in addition.

MAYSA UNAY, especially (since).

MAYYET, adj. /NA-/ slow, sluggish.

MEDIAS [mɛdias; f. Sp.], n. sock, stocking.
v. /AG-/ to wear a sock, stocking. /MANG-:-AN/ to
put a sock or stocking on (a foot or someone's foot).

MEDIKO [mɛdiko; f. Sp.], n. medical doctor. --syn.
DOKTOR.

MEDIO [mɛdio; f. Sp.], adv. somewhat, in a slight
degree. Ita, medio agnakem tayo ngem naladaw unayen.
Now we somewhat develop some sense but it is already
too late.

MEDIOR [mɛdior; f. Eng.], n. major in the army.

MEDMED, v. /MANG-:-AN/ to check, restrain, curb, hold
back.
adj. /NA-/ frugal, sparing, moderate, temperate.

MEHIKO [mɛhiko; f. Sp.], n. Mexico.

MEHIKANO [mɛhikano; f. Sp.], adj. Mexican.
n. a native or citizen of Mexico.

MEKMEK, v. /MANG-:-EN/ to grind or pound into powder.
Mekmekem dayta bagas. Pound that rice into powder.

MELMEL, v. /MANG-:-AN/ to fill the mouth of (with
food). /MANGI-:I-/ to use to fill (the mouth), to
cram with.

MELON [mɛlon; f. Eng.], n. melon, water melon. --syn.
SANDIA.

MEMORIA [mɛmoria; f. Sp.], v. /AG-/ to memorize something.
/MANGI-:I-/ to memorize.

MENSAHE [mɛnsahɛ; f. Sp.], n. message.

MENSAHERO [mɛnsahɛro; f. Sp.], n. messenger.

MERIENDA [mɛriɛnda; f. Sp.], n. snack, refreshments.
v. /AG-/ to take a snack or refreshments.

MERKADO [mɛrkado; f. Sp.], n. market.   --syn. TIANGGI, TIENDAAN.

MERKUROKROM [mɛrkurokrom; f. Eng.], n. mercurochrome.

MERMER, v. /MANG-:-AN/ to throw something at the eyes of.   /MA--AN/ to have something thrown into the eyes. /MANGI-:I-/ to throw into the eyes of.

MESMES, v. /MANG-:-AN/ to grasp firmly, to seize tightly. Saan nak nga mesmesan. Don't grasp me firmly.

MESTISA [mɛstisa; f. Sp.], n. the female child of a mixed or miscegenetic marriage, a female half-breed. --ant. MESTISO.

MESTISO [mɛstiso; f. Sp.], n. the male child of a mixed or miscegenetic marriage, a male half-breed.   --ant. MESTISA.

METRO [mɛtro; f. Sp.], n. meter.

MEYOR [mɛyor], var. of MAYOR.

[1]MI, pron. our (excl.): the enclitic possessive of DAKAMI.

[2]MI, pron. by us (excl.), we (actor): the agent of DAKAMI.

MIEMBRO, n. member of an organization, association, union, etc.   --syn. KAMENG.

MIERKOLES [miɛrkolɛs; f. Sp.], n. Wednesday.

MIKI, n. wheat noodle.

MIKKI, adj. /NA-/ fastidious, finicky.

MIKKIMIKKI, v. /AG-/ to be fastidious, finicky.

MIKROBIO [f. Sp.], n. microbe, germ, virus.

MIKROPONO [f. Sp.], n. microphone.

MILAGRO [f. Sp.], n. miracle, mystery, enigma. v. /AG-/ to perform a miracle.

MILAT, n. dirty spot usually on the face.
  MILATMILAT, adj. dirty, filthy, besmirched.

MILIA [f. Sp.], n. mile.

MILION; MILYON [f. Sp.], num. million. --syn. RIWRIW.

MILIONARIO [f. Sp.], n. millionaire.

MILMIL, adj. /(NA-)/ covered around the mouth with
  grease or food.

MINAS [f. Sp.], n. mine. Adda minas ti balitok da.
  They have a gold mine.

MINATAY [cf. PATAY], n. a dead person, corpse.
    v. /AG-/ to watch the dead.

MINUYONGAN, see under MUYONG.

MINGMING, v. /MANG-:-AN/ to look at or examine closely.
  Mingmingam nga nalaing ta rupa ni nanang mo. Look
  closely at your mother's face.

MIRAOT; MIRMIRAOT, v. /AG-/ to be tormented, to suffer
  (from hunger, etc.).

MIRMIRAOT, see MIRAOT.

MISA [f. Sp.], n. mass, church service.
    v. /AG-/ to celebrate a mass. /MAKI-/ to attend
  a mass or a church service. --see PAMISA.

MISMIS, adj. /NA-/ not being able to eat due to lack
  of appetite, shyness, etc.

MISMO [f. Sp.], adv. specifically, for sure. Idiay
  mismo uneg ti ili ti nakakitaan da kenka. It was
  specifically inside the town where they saw you.

MISTERIO [mistɛrio; f. Sp.], n. mystery, miracle,
  wonder, phenomenon. --syn. DATDATLAG.

MISUOT, v. /AG-/ to pout, look sullen, frown.
  /MANG-:-AN/ to pout at, frown at. Saan nak man nga
  misuotan ta napudot ti ulok. Don't pout at me for I
  am ill-tempered.

MITING [f. Eng.], n. meeting, conference.
v. /MAKI-/ to attend a meeting. /MANG-:-EN/ to
call to a meeting. /AG-/ [with pl. subject] to have
a meeting.

[1]MO, pron. your (sg.), of yours (sg.): the enclitic
possessive of SIKA. --var. -M (after a vowel).

[2]MO, pron. by you (sg.), you (as actor): the agent of
SIKA. --var. -M (after a vowel).

MODA [f. Sp.], n. fashion, style, mode. Kabaruanan nga
moda dagita kawes da. Their clothes are of the newest
style.

MODELO [modɛlo; f. Sp.], n. model, type.

MOHON [f. Sp.], n. a boundary post usually made of
concrete.

MONTURA [f. Sp.], n. saddle, especially horse saddle

MONUMENTO [monumɛnto; f. Sp.], n. monument.

MORADO [f. Sp.], adj. violet in color.

MORO [f. Sp.], n. Moor, a Moslem.

MOTORSIKLO [f. Sp.], n. motorcycle.

MUDIS, adj. /NA-/ placed near the edge or border of
something.

MUDMUD, v. /MANGI-:I-/ to press down on a surface with
the hands. Saan mo nga imudmud dayta ulo ti aso dita
datar. Don't press down with your hands on the floor.

MUDTOY, short for IYEG MO DITOY, bring it here, give
it to me.

MUGING, n. forehead.

MUGNA, n. deity especially of the pagans.

MUKAT, n. gum of the eyes.
v. /AG-/ to discharge gum: said of the eyes. /AGI-/
to remove gum from one's eyes.

MUKMOK, n. food crumb.

MUKOD, n. heel.

MULA, n. plant.
v. /AG-, AGI-, MANGI-:I-/ to plant. Agmula ka ti adu
nga saba. Plant plenty of bananas. /MANG-:-AN/ to
plant something on. Dika nga mulaan ti saba ta
inaladan mi. Don't plant bananas on our yard.

MULAGAT, v. /AG-/ to open the eyes widely; to stare,
glare. /MANG-:-AN/ to stare or glare at. /MANGI-:I-/
to open (the eyes) widely.

MULDOT, n. down; soft, fine feathers, as on young
birds; soft, fine hair or hairy growth.

MULENGLENG, v. /AG-/ to stare abstractly or absent-
mindedly. Dika nga agmulengleng tapno malpas mo ta
trabahom. Don't stare absent-mindedly so that you can
finish your work.

MULI, v. /MANG-:-EN/ to grind (wheat, coffee, cocoa
beans, etc.). Muliem dayta kakaw ta agaramid tayo
ti tsokolate. Grind those cacao beans and we will
make some chocolate.

MULIMOL, n. a feeble-minded person, an imbecile.
v. /AG-/ to be like a feeble-minded person, as to
stare vacantly.

MULIT, n. smirch, dirt.
v. /MANG-:-AN/ to smirch, soil, sully, make dirty.

MULMOL, v. /AG-/ to hold something in the mouth without
sucking. /MANG-:-AN/ to hold in the mouth without
sucking.

MULUMOG, v. /AG-/ to rinse the mouth, to gargle.

MUNAMON, n. a kind of small marine fish often used in
the preparation of BUGGOONG.

MUNAW, v. /AG-/ to decrease the effect of (wine or
liquor). Saan pay nga nagmunaw ta ininum ko nga tuba.
The effect of the fermented coconut juice which I
drank has not decreased. /MA--AN/ to become
relieved of one's drunkenness.

MUNO, adj. /NA-/ stupid.

MUNGAY, n. nipple, teat.

MURAY; MURMURAY, v. /AG-/ to stretch the body or limbs
   in order to shake off one's drowsiness: said of a
   person who just woke up.

MURDONG, n. tip, top, end (of a branch, a string, a
   finger, etc.).

MURENG, n. dirt, grime, filth.
   adj. /NA-/ dirty, grimy.
   NAGMURENGAN or MURENG, n. dirty clothes set aside
      for washing.

MURKAT, n. food crumb that falls out of the plate to
   the table or the floor.
   v. /AG-/ to allow food crumbs to fall out of
   one's plate.

MURMURAY, see MURAY.

MUSANG, n. wild cat.

MUSIIG, v. /AG-/ to grin by stretching out the lips
   open baring the teeth.

MUSIKERO [musikεro; f. Sp.], n. musician. --syn. MUSIKO.

MUSIKO [f. Sp.], n. musician. --syn. MUSIKERO.

MUSKITERO [muskitεro; f. Sp.], n. mosquito net. --syn.
   KULAMBO.

[1]MUSMOS, n. tobacco refuse.

[2]MUSMOS, adj. stupid.

MUTAL, v. /AG-/ to lisp.

MUTIA, n. an object with magical powers, an amulet, a
   charm.

MUTING, n. clitoris. --syn. TILDI.

MUTIT, n. the Philippine squirrel.

MUTON, n. pulley.

MUTTALAT, adj. wide-eyed.
v. /MAI-/ to meet or be exposed to one's gaze or view. Naimuttalat daydiay kuarta itay magmagnaak diay kalsada. The money met my gaze when I was walking along the street.

MUTTALENG, adj. agape.
v. /AG-/ to be agape.

MUYMUY, v. /MANG-:-EN/ to gather every bit of. Muymuyem ta inapoy mo. Gather every bit of your rice (in your plate).

MUYONG, n. garden plant, cultivated plant.
MINUYONGAN, n. garden, orchard.

N-, pt. of M-.

[1]NA, interj. an exclamation expressing surprise and wonder. --var. NAY. --syn. NI.

[2]NA, replaces MO by you (sg.) before enclitic nominative pron. -K me or KAMI us (excl.).

[3]NA, pron. by him or her, he or she (as actor): the agent of ISU.

[4]NA, pron. his, her: the enclitic possessive of ISU.

NA-, adjectivizing prefix; full of the quality or thing denoted by the stem.
NA- + R1, comparative form of NA-.

NA-, pt. of MA-.

NA- + R1, ptp. of MA-.

NA-AN, pt. of MA-AN.

NAAY, interj. an exclamation expressing sorrow; alas!

NABLO, pt. of MABLO.

NABTAK, pt. of MABTAK.

NADNAD, v. /AG-/ to be digested. Saan pay nga nagnadnad ti kinnan ko. What I ate has not yet been digested.

NAED, v. /AG-/ to reside, live, dwell. --syn. GIAN.

NAG-, pt. of AG-.

NAG-, superlative of NA-; very.

NAGAN, n. name, designation, appellation.
v. /AG-/ to have as name. Agnagan ti Perla diay balasang. My daughter has Pearl as her name. /MA--AN/ to be named as, to be designated or appointed as. /MANG-:-EN/ to name, mention by name. Naganem dagiti kimmamat kenka. Name those who ran after you.

NAG-AN, pt. of PAG-AN.

NAGANAK [cf. ANAK], n. parent, father, mother. --syn. DAKKEL.

NAGBAETAN [cf. BAET], n. the place between.

NAGISTAY; NAGISTAYAN, adv. almost, nearly. Nagistayan natay diay babai nga natnag idiay agdan. The woman who fell from the stairs almost died. --syn. DANDANI.

NAGLUPOSAN, see under LUPOS.

NAGMURENGAN, see under MURENG.

NAGNA, pt. of MAGNA.

NAGYAN [cf. YAN], n. content, substance.

NAKA-, pt. of MAKA-.

NAKA-AN, pt. of PAKA-AN.

NAKA- + R1, absolute superlative of NA-; so very.

NAKI-, pt. of MAKI-.

NAKI-AN, pt. of PAKI-AN.

NAKIN, pt. of AKIN- or MAKIN-.

NAKKONG, n. my child: an endearing term.

NAKTANG, pt. of MAKTANG.

NALMES, pt. of MALMES.

NALPAS, pt. of MALPAS.

NALPAY, pt. of MALPAY.

NALPES, pt. of MALPES.

NALTAT, pt. of MALTAT.

NAMA; NAMAK PAY NO, what if, suppose.

NAMAGBAGA, pt. of MAMAGBAGA.

NAMAN [= ANA + MAN ?] (rare), what is it? what is the matter? why? --syn. APAY MAN.

NAM-AY, adj. /NA-/ comfortable, full of ease.
    v. /AG-/ to become comfortable, to be full of ease.

NAMIN-, pt. of MAMIN-.

NAMIN-ADU, pt. of MAMIN-ADU.

NAMIN-ANO, pt. of MAMIN-ANO.

NAMINSAN, pt. of MAMINSAN.

NAMLES, pt. of MAMLES.

NAMMIGAT, pt. of MAMMIGAT.

NAMNAM, v. /MANG-:-EN/ to taste, savor.

NANAM, n. taste, savor, flavor.
    adj. /NA-/ tasty, savory, flavorful.
    v. /MANG-:-EN/ to enjoy or relish (eating, sleeping, dancing, etc.)

NANG-, pt. of MANG-.

NANGALDAW, pt. of MANGALDAW.

NANGAN, pt. of MANGAN.

NANG-AN, pt. of PANG-AN.

NANGKA, var. of LANGKA.

NANGRABII, pt. of MANGRABII.

NANG-US, pt. of MANG-US.

NAPLENG, pt. of MAPLENG.

NARBA, pt. of MARBA.

NARGAAY, pt. of MARGAAY.

NARKOTIKO [f. Sp.], n. narcotic.

NARNAR, v. /MANG-:-EN/ to separate the flesh (especially of small clams) from the shell by boiling.

NARRA, n. a tall leguminous tree (Pterocarpus sp.).

NARS [f. Eng.], n. nurse. --var. NERS.

NASAKIT [cf. SAKIT], n. sickness, illness, disease. Ania ti nasakit mo? What is your sickness?

NASANGER [cf. SANGER], n. strong wine.

NASION [f. Sp.], n. nation.

NASNAS, v. /MANG-:-AN/ to wipe or polish with a piece of cloth or rag. Ninasnasan na ti datar ti balay. He polished with a piece of cloth the floor of the house.

NASPAK, = NA- + SEP-AK.

NATAENGAN [cf. TAENG], n. an adult, a grown-up or mature person.

NATAY, 1. pt. of MATAY. 2. the dead.

NATENG, n. vegetable.
    v. /MANG-:-EN/ to gather or harvest (vegetables).

NATURAL [f. Sp.], adj. natural, not artificial; inborn.
n. nature, inborn character.

NAWNAW, v. /MANG-:-EN/ to dilute, prepare a liquid
formula. Mangnawnaw ka ti gatas diay ubing. Prepare
a milk formula for the child.

NAY, adv. an emphatic particle. Bumallasiw ka dita nay
alad. Cross over that fence there.

NAYAT, pt. of MAYAT.

NAYNAY, adv. repeatedly, continuously, again and again.

NE, interj. oh, but. Ne, apay ngay? Oh, but why?

NEBNEB, v. /MANGI-:I-/ to push or drive in deeply, to
cause to sink deeply. Saan mo nga inebneb dayta
lansa dita kayo. Don't drive that nail deeply in the
wood. /MAI-/ to be pushed or driven deeply.

NEGOSIANTE [nɛgosiantɛ; f. Sp.], n. merchant.

NEGOSIO [nɛgosio; f. Sp.], n. commerce, trade.

NEGRA [nɛgra; f. Sp.], n. a female Negro.

NEGRITO [nɛgrito; f. Sp.], n. a Negrito.

NEGRO [nɛgro; f. Sp.], n. a Negro.

-NEM, var. of INNEM, six: used only with certain
prefixes. MAIKANEM or MAYKANEM, sixth; SAGNENEM, six
each.

NENGNENG, adj. /NA-/ dull, stupid, dumb.

NEPNEP, n. a continuous fall of rain.
v. /AG-/ to rain steadily for days.

NERBIOSA [nɛrbiosa; f. Sp.], adj. becoming nervous
easily: used only for women.

NERBIOSO [nɛrbioso; f. Sp.], adj. becoming nervous
easily.

NERS, var. of NARS.

¹NI [pl. DA], art. nominative singular form of the proper article which occurs before a proper name.

²NI [pl. DA], possessive singular form of the proper article which occurs before a proper name.

³NI, interj. an exclamation expressing surprise and wonder. --syn. NA.

⁴NI, adv. used to call attention to a thing; look. Adda ditoy ni. It is here, look.

NI-, var. of -IN- before L.

NIBI, see MANGNIBINIBI.

NIKEL [f. Eng.?], n. five centavos.

NIOG, n. 1. coconut palm or tree. 2. its fruit. --var. INYOG.

NIPA, n. nipa.

NISNIS, n. a piece of cloth used principally for wiping or for holding hot pots and pans; rag.

NITSO [f. Sp.], n. tomb, niche. --syn. PANTEONG.

¹NO, v. /-UM-/ [prp. UM-UMNO] to be proper, correct, right.

²NO, conj. if.

NOBELA [nobɛla; f. Sp.], n. novel.

NOBELISTA [nobɛlista; f. Sp.], n. novelist.

NOBIA [f. Sp.], n. female sweetheart, fiancee. --ant. NOBIO.

NOBIEMBRE [nobiɛmbrɛ; f. Sp.], n. November.

NOBIO [f. Sp.], n. male sweetheart, fiance.
   AGNOBIO, n.pl. sweethearts.

NOMINASION [f. Sp.], n. nomination.

NOPAY, granted that, even if.

NOTARIO [f. Sp.], n. notary public.

NOWTBUK [f. Eng.], n. notebook.

-NSA, var. of SA after a vowel.

-NTO, var. of TO after a vowel.

NUANG, n. water buffalo, carabao.

NUEBE [nuɛbɛ; f. Sp.], num. nine; 9. --syn. SIAM.
ALAS NUEBE, nine o'clock.

NUGOT, v. /MANGI-:I-/ to apportion, distribute
proportionally, allocate. /MAI-/ to be distributed
proportionally.

NUKNOK, v. /MANG-:-EN/ to spool, wind into a ball.
Nuknokem dayta lubid. Wind that thread into a ball.

[1]NUMO, v. /AG-/ [with pl. subject] to enter into a
contract, to come to terms.

[2]NUMO, adj. /NA-/ poor, humble, lowly. Nanumo ti puon
na. He has a humble beginning.

NUNOG, v. /AG-/ to stay (in water) longer than
necessary, to soak (in water). Saan ka nga agnunog
dita danum. Don't soak in that water.

NUNONG, see KANUNONG.

NUNGNUNG, v. /MANG-:-AN/ to shower with favors. Diay
inauna nga anak na ti nunnungnungan na. She showers
favors on her eldest child.

NURNOR, v. /MANG-:-EN/ to do or follow unswervingly.
Nurnoren tayo daytoy dalan nga agpadaya. Let us
follow unswervingly this road that goes to the east.

NUTNOT, v. /AG-/ to suck one's thumb. /MANG-:-EN/ to
suck (the thumb).

NGABIT; NGANGABIT, v. /AG-/ to be on the verge of, close to. Agngangabit ken patay diay lakay. The old man is on the verge of death.

NGAD, var. of NGARUD.

NGADAL, v. /AG-/ to have difficulty in speaking or pronouncing.

NGADAS, n. 1. the palate. 2. the concave side of a pot, jar. etc.

NGALANGAL, v. /MA-/ to open again: said of wounds that have closed; to be dislocated again: said of dislocated bones that have been set.

NGALAY; AGNGALAY, n. middle (of). Agngalay manen ti Abril. It's the middle of April again.

NGALNGAL, v. /AG-, MANG-:-EN/ to chew, masticate. Ngalngalem nga nalaing dayta kanem. Chew well what you are eating.

NGAMAN (literary), inter. why. --syn. APAY.

NGAMIN, adv. a particle that expresses mild reproof or censure. Apay ngamin sumurot-surot ka. Why do you always tag along?

NGANNGANI, var. of DANDANI.

NGANGA, v. /AG-/ to open one's mouth. /MANGI-:I-/ to open (the mouth).
   NAKANGANGA, adj. with mouth open, agape.

NGANGABIT, see NGABIT.

NGARASNGAS, adj. /NA-/ brittle, crunchy.
   v. /-UM-/ to make a crunchy sound. Ngumarasngas diay kalding. The goat makes a crunchy sound.

NGARETNGET, v. /AG-/ to grit or gnash the teeth. Agngaretnget nga maturog ni Pedro. Peter gnashes his teeth as he sleeps.

NGARIET, v. /AG-/ to bite one's teeth.

NGARUD, adv. 1. expresses confirmation, affirmation, or acquiescence. Adda ngarud diay padi idiay balay.

The priest is indeed in our house. 2. expresses an alternative. Inka ngarud saludsuden diay padi no di nak nga patien. Go therefore as the priest if you don't believe me.

NGASANGAS, v. /AG-/ to wear out, to become worn off. Nagngasangas toy sapatos ko. My shoes became worn off.

NGASIB, v. /AG-/ the jaws to cease from action or motion. Uray la nga agngasib ni Rosa ti lam-ek na. It was so cold Rose's jaw ceased to move.

NGATA, adv. perhaps, maybe.

NGATANGATA, v. /AG-/ to be in doubt, to be doubtful, hesitant, undecided.

NGATINGAT, v. /AG-/ to ruminate, to chew something continuously for some time. /MANG-:-EN/ to ruminate, chew continuously for some time.

NGAWNGAW, v. /AG-/ to mew, to talk or make sounds like a cat.

NGAY, adv. an interrogative particle with the meaning: please tell me. Napanan na ngay? Where did he go, please tell me.

NGAYED, adj. /NA-/ grand, elegant. Nagayed diay parada da. Their parade was elegant.

NGEDNGED, v. /MANG-:-AN/ to make (a string, rope, etc.) shorter.

NGEG, see under DENGNGEG.

NGELNGEL, adj. blunt, not sharp. --syn. NGOLNGOL.

[1]NGEM, conj. but. Sadut ngem nabaknang. She is lazy but rich.

[2]NGEM, prep. than. Napinpintasak ngem sika. I am more beautiful than you.

NGENNGEN, v. /-UM-/ 1. to grow bigger, spread. Ngumenngen ti apoy diay dalikan. The fire in the stove will grow bigger. 2. to become worse.

Ngimmenngen ti sakit ni Ana. Ann's sickness became worse.

NGERNGER, v. /AG-/ to growl, snarl, gnarl. /MANG-:-AN/ to growl or snarl at.

NGETNGET, v. /MANG-:-EN/ to gnaw, tear off with the teeth.

NGIAW, n. mew.
    v. /AG-/ to mew.

NGILANGIL, v. /AG-/ to shake one's head. Nagngilangil diay maestra. The lady teacher shook her head.

NGILAW, n. house fly.
    v. /-EN/ to be stepped on by flies, to be eaten by flies.

NGINA, n. worth, price, value.
    adj. /NA-/ expensive, costly.
    v. /-UM-/ to become expensive, costly.

  DIOS TI AGNGINA, Thank you.

NGIPEN, n. tooth.

NGIRNGIR, adj. /NA-/ dirty, soiled.

NGISIT, adj. /NA-/ black, dark-colored.

NGIWAT, n. mouth.
    adj. /NA-/ noisy, talkative, loud.

NGIWNGIW, n. 1. border of the lip. 2. upper lip.

NGOBNGOB, adj. with sunken lips, especially the upper lip.

NGOLNGOL, adj. blunt, dull, not sharp. --syn. NGUDEL, NGELNGEL.

NGOTNGOT, v. /MANG-:-AN/ to gnaw.

NGUDEL, adj. /NA-/ blunt, dull, not sharp. --syn. NGOLNGOL.

NGUDO, n. tip (of anything).

NGURUNGOR, v. /AG-, MANG-:-EN/ to stab through the throat of, to cut at the throat of: done in slaughtering an animal or a chicken.

NGUSAB, v. /AG-/ to snap the jaws as when eating.

OBISPO [f. Sp.], n. bishop.

ONSE [onsɛ; f. Sp.], num. eleven; 11.   --syn. SANGAPULO KET MAYSA.
ALAS ONSE, eleven o'clock.

OPERA [opɛra; f. Sp.], v. /MANG-:-EN/ to operate on. Operaen diay doktor ta apendisitis mo. The doctor will operate on your appendix.

OPERASION [opɛrasion; f. Sp.], n. operation.

OPISIAL [f. Sp.], adj. & n. official.

OPORTUNIDAD [f. Sp.], n. opportunity, chance.

OPOSISION [f. Sp.], n. opposition.

ORASION [f. Sp.], n. Angelus.
v. /AG-/ to ring the bell to announce the time for the Angelus.

ORDINARIO [f. Sp.], adj. ordinary, common, usual.

OREGANO [origano; f. Sp.], n. an aromatic green herb cultivated for spice and medicine (Coleus amboinicus).

ORGANISASION [f. Sp.], n. organization.

OSO [f. Sp.], n. bear.

OSPITAL [f. Sp.], n. hospital.
v. /MANGI-:I-/ to confine in a hospital. /MAI-/ to be confined in a hospital.

OTEL [otɛl; f. Sp.], n. hotel.
v. /AG-/ to stay in a hotel. /MANGI-:I-/ to cause to stay in a hotel at one's expense.

OTO [f. Sp.], n. automobile, car. --syn. KOTSE.

OTOMOBIL [f. Sp.], var. of OTO.

OTSO [f. Sp.], num. eight; 8. --syn. WALO.
   ALAS OTSO, eight o'clock.

OY, interj. hey: an exclamation used to attract
   attention, express surprise, etc., or in asking a
   question.

PA-, v. /AG-/ to head toward, to go to. Agpabagatan ka.
   Head toward the south.
   PAANO, v. /AG-/ an interrogative verb asking
      direction of movement.

PAANO, see under PA-.

PAARUYOT, see under ARUYOT.

PAATIAN, var. of ATIAN.

PAAWAN [cf. AWAN], v. /MANG-:-EN/ to cause to vanish
   or disappear.

[1]PAAY, v. /AG-/ to go to, to be intended for, to be for
   the use or benefit of. Agpaay daytoy kadagiti
   agsursuro nga ubbing iti Kailokoan. This is intended
   for the children of the Ilocos region who are
   studying. /MANGI-:I-/ to give to, extend to, grant.
   Sino ti nangipaay ti tulong kenka? Who extended
   help to you?

[2]PAAY, v. /MANG-:-EN/ to refuse, reject, rebuff. Saan
   mo nga paayen ti dawat ko. Don't refuse my request.
   /MA-/ to be rebuffed, repulsed, thwarted. Napaay iti
   panagtarigagayna nga agbalin nga presidente. His
   desire to become president was rebuffed.
      adj. /NA-/ disappointed. Nagawid da amin nga
   napaay. They all went home disappointed.

PABANGLO, see under BANGLO.

PABARENG; PABPABARENG [cf. BARENG], v. /MANGI-:I-/ to
   try, make an effort to do. Impabpabareng ko nga
   tinawaran ket inted na metten. I tried to buy it at
   a lower price and he gave it to me for that price.

PABASOL [caus. of BASOL], v. /MANG-:-EN/ to blame for an error, accuse of making an error.

PABILO, n. wick of lamp.

PABLAAK, see under BELLAAK.

PABLAD, see under BELLAD.

PABOR [f. Sp.], n. favor, consideration.
v. /MANG-:-AN/ to favor, be considerate to.

PABORITO [f. Sp.], adj. favorite.

PABRIKA [f. Sp.], n. factory.

PABULOD [caus. of BULOD], v. /AG-:I-/ to lend. Agpabulod ka man ti suka yo? Will you lend me some of your vinegar?

PABULOG [caus. of BULOG], v. /AG-, MANG-:I-/ to cause to reproduce. Inka ipabulog dayta baboy mo. Go cause your pig to reproduce.

PABUREK [caus. of BUREK], v. /AG-, AGI-, MANGI-:I-/ to boil. Agpaburek ka ti danum nga pagdigos ko. Boil some water for my bath.

PABUYA [caus. of BUYA], n. live show for public entertainment. Adda pabuya idiay plasa. There's a live show in the plaza.
v. /AGI-, MANGI-:I-/ to show to the public.

PADA, n. equal, peer; one who is the same as or identical with another. --syn. KAPADA.
v. /AG-/ [with pl. subject] to be the same, similar, equivalent, or identical. /MANG-:-EN/ to equal, match, imitate.

PADALAN, v. /MANG-:-AN/ 1. to iron. 2. to sew.

PADALANAN TI PINTA, to paint.

PADANUM, see under DANUM.

PADAPAN, see under DAPAN.

PADARA [caus. of DARA], v. /AG-/ to hemorrhage; to vomit blood; to expectorate blood.

PADAS, v. /MANG-:-EN/ 1. to try to do. Padasen tayo
nga basaen ti surat na. Let us try to read his
letter. 2. to test. Padasen tayo ti kinatured dayta
lalaki. Let us test the courage of that man.
/MANGI-:I-/ to try to put on. Ipadas mo man daytoy
nangisit nga sapatos. Try to put on this black pair
of shoes.

PADATA, var. of DATA.

PADAYA [caus. of DAYA], n. feast, party, celebration.
Naar-arimbangaw ti padaya nga naisagut kaniak. The
party given for me was noisier.

PADDAK, n. sole of the foot of swine.

PAD-ENG; PADPAD-ENG, v. /MANGI-:I-/ to stop or put off
temporarily, suspend, delay, postpone. Ipadpad-eng
mo bassit dayta inggana ti isasangpet da. Stop that
for a while until their arrival.

PADER [padεr; f. Sp.], n. wall made of stone, brick,
or cement.

PADI [f. Sp.], n. priest.
    v. /AG-/ to become a priest.

PADIGO, see under DIGO.

PADING; PADINGPADING, n. hip bone.

PADINGALNGAL, n. 1. bridle. 2. bit.

PADIS, v. /AG-/ [with pl. subject] to overlap or
overlay each other completely.

PADLAW, see under DILLAW.

PADLES, v. /MANG-:-AN/ or /MANGI-:I-/ to foretell,
predict, prophesy. Narigat nga padlesan ti mapasamak
ti masakbayan. It is hard to predict what will happen
in the future.

    MAMMADLES, n. a person who predicts future events in
    any way, a prophet.

[1]PADRE [padrε; f. Sp.], n. a term of address for a
priest used with his family name.

[2]PADRE [padrɛ; f. Sp.], n. short for KUMPADRE.

PADRINA [f. Sp.], n. the female sponsor at a wedding.
--ant. PADRINO.

PADRINO [f. Sp.], n. the male sponsor at a wedding.
--ant. PADRINA.

PADSING, v. /MANG-:-EN/ to drive a person away from
where he is seated. /MA-/ to be fired from one's
position or job.

PADUYAKYAK, v. /MANGI-:I-/ to reveal, declare openly.
Ipaduyakyak mo ti panagdayaw mo ti Dios. Declare
openly reverence to God.

PAET, n. chisel.
   v. /MANG-:-AN/ to cut with a chisel, to chisel.

PAGA, adj. /NA-/ fastidious, squeamish, finicky.

PAGABLAN, see under ABEL.

PAGALSEM, see under ALSEM.

PAGAMMOAN; PAGAM-AMMOAN [cf. AMMO], adv. suddenly, all
of a sudden. Pagam-ammoan, natay ti silaw. All of a
sudden, the light went off.

PAGAN-ANAY, n.pl. wardrobe, clothes, garments. --syn.
BADBADO, KAWKAWES.

PAGANNAYASAN, n. situation, state of affairs, development,
progress. Kitaen tayonto ti pagannayasan ti tiempo.
Let's see how the situation develops.

PAGAPUGAN [cf. APUG], n. a small earthen jar or glass
jar used by chewers of betel nut for holding lime;
any receptacle for lime.

PAGARIGAN [cf. ARIG], n. example, model.

   KAS PAGARIGAN, for example.

PAGARUN [cf. ARUN], n. any inflammable material, e.g.
paper and shavings, used to start a fire. --var.
PANGARUN.

PAGARUP, n. guess, conjecture, supposition.
v. /MANGI-:I-/ to think, guess, conjecture,
suppose, assume.

PAGASIMBUYOKAN [cf. ASIMBUYOK], n. smoke flue, chimney.

PAGAW, n. a kind of turtledove.

PAGAY, n. 1. rice plant. 2. unhusked rice grain.

PAGAYATAN [cf. AYAT], n. wish, desire.

PAGBABASAAN [cf. BASA], n. the wet, muddy place under
the BANGSAL.

PAGBAGASAN [cf. BAGAS], n. any container for husked
rice, usually an earthen jar or a wooden box.

PAGBUNUBONAN [cf. BUNUBON], n. seedbed.

PAGDAKSAN [cf. DAKES], n. the bad thing (about it), the
evil (of it), the rub. Ti pagdaksan na, didak nga
piaren. The bad thing about it is that they won't
trust me.

[1]PAGEL, n. calamity, catastrophe. Nakaro nga pagel
dayta. That is a serious calamity.

[2]PAGEL, v. /MANGI-:I-/ to restrain, forbid, prohibit.

PAGGAAK, n. loud laughter. Matitileng payen dagiti
sairo iti paggaak da. Even the devils are deafened
by their laughter.
v. /AG-/ to laugh loudly.

PAGILIAN, see under ILI.

PAGINUMAN [cf. INUM], n. 1. drinking vessel, drinking
jar. 2. place where the drinking vessel is located.

PAGNA, v. /M-/ to walk. Agsursuro nga magna dayta anak
mon. Your child is now learning how to walk.
/M-, MANG-:-EN/ to walk, cover or reach by walking.
Magna ka ti maysa nga kilometro iti inaldaw. Walk
one kilometer every day. /MANGI-:I-/ 1. to walk
around with or for (something), to follow up. 2. to
manage, operate. Isu ti nangipagna ti negosio da.
It was he who managed their business.

PANNAGNA or PAGNA, n. manner or act of walking.

AGPAGNA, adj. current, present. Aganak ni baket ko ti daytoy agpagna nga bulan. My wife will deliver this current month.

PAGOD, v. /MANGI-:I-/ to tie (an animal, a vessel), to moor.

PAG-ONG, n. turtle.

PAGPAG, v. /MANG-:-EN/ to shake. Pagpagem ta ules mo. Shake your blanket. /MANGI-:I-/ to shake off. Ipagpag mo ta rugit ti ules mo. Shake off the dirt of your blanket.

PAGPALPALIWAAN, see under LIWLIWA.

PAGSALAPAYAN [cf. SALAPAY], n. clothesline, anything where clothes are hung to dry or air.

PAGSEP, v. /MANG-:-AN/ or /MANGI-:I-/ to soak in or saturate with (a liquid). Ipagsept mo ta lupot ti danum. Soak that cloth in water. /MAI-/ to be soaked in or saturated with (a liquid). Dalusam ta sugat mo ti kapas nga naipagsep ti alkohol. Clean your wound with cotton soaked in alcohol.

PAGSUGALAN [cf. SUGAL], n. gambling den, gambling place, gambling house.

PAGTAGTAGIAMMOAN [cf. TAGIAMMO], n. something not known for sure, something doubtful. Pagtagtagiammoan no agbiag daydiay ubing nga imminom ti gas. It is not known for sure if the child who drank kerosene will live.

PAGTENG, n. event, happening.
    v. /MA-/ to happen.

PAG-UT, v. /MANG-:-EN/ to uproot, pull out. Sino ti nangpag-ut kadagiti mula ditoy? Who uprooted the plants here?

PAGWADAN, n. model, example, prototype, paragon. --var. WADAN.

[1]PAID, n. fan.
    v. /AG-/ to fan oneself. /MANG-:-AN/ to fan (someone).

[2]PAID, v. /MANG-:-EN/ to refuse, reject. Paiden na ti
  tulong mo. He will refuse your help.

PAIDAM, adj. /(NA-)/ 1. stingy, selfish, being one who
  refuses to lend anything to anybody. 2. being one
  who refuses to go with anyone except his mother.
    v. /MANGI-:I-/ to refuse, deny, withhold, be
  stingy with. Saan mo nga ipaidam ta tulong mo kaniak.
  Don't withhold your help from me.

PAING, v. /AG-/ to run away from people, to isolate
  oneself. Saan ka nga agpaing. Don't run away from
  people.

PAIT, adj. /NA-/ bitter.

PAKA-, the form of MAKA- which is used with a
  verbalizing affix or as a nominalizer.

PAKAAMMO, see under AMMO.

PAKADA, n. good-by, farewell, adieu; leave-taking.
    v. /AG-/ to say good-by, to bid farewell.
  /MANGI-:I-/ to ask permission for (someone to leave
  or do something).

PAKAN, = PA- + KAAN: caus. of KAAN.

PAKARSO, n. a temporary residence in the country.

PAKASARITAAN [cf. SARITA], n. history, chronicle.

[1]PAKAT, v. /MANGI-:I-/ to set (a trap). Impakat na diay
  pasabing. He set the trap for fish.

[2]PAKAT, v. /MANGI-:I-/ to put into practice, to try to
  the utmost. Impakat ko amin nga kabaelak. I tried my
  best effort to the utmost.

PAKATAO [cf. TAO], v. /AG-/ to be impatient. Apay nga
  dika agpakatao? Why don't you not be impatient?

PAKAWAN, n. forgiveness.
    v. /AG-, MANG-:-EN/ to forgive.

PAKBO, v. /MANGI-:I-/ to pour out the contents of.
  /MAI-/ to have its contents poured out.

PAKDAAR, n. notice, announcement, warning.
  v. /MANGI-:I-/ to proclaim, announce, publish.
  /MAI-/ to be proclaimed, announced, published.

PAKI-, the form of MAKI- which is used with a
  verbalizing affix or as a nominalizer.

PAKIAW, see PAKKIAW.

PAKILO, v. /AG-/ to exacerbate, to fester and spread.
  Annadam ta sugat mo tapno di agpakilo. Be careful
  with your wound so that it won't fester and spread.

PAKIN-, the form of MAKIN- which forms stems which can
  be verbalized with I-.

PAKINAKEM [cf. NAKEM], n. mind, will, discretion,
  judgment, decision. Ania ti pakinakem mo? What is
  your decision?

PAKITA [cf. KITA], v. /MANGI-:I-/ to show, display,
  exhibit. Ipakitam man idiay balasang ti kinasayaat
  mo nga lalaki. Will you show to the young woman how
  good a man you are.

PAKKANG, v. /AG-/ to walk with the legs far apart, to
  straddle, to walk bowleggedly. Agpakpakkang diay
  koboy. The cowboy walks bowleggedly.

PAKKAW; PAKKAPAKKAW, v. /AG-/ to toddle.

PAKKIAW, v. /MANG-:-EN/ to do or buy wholesale.

PAKLEB, v. /AG-/ to lie prone or prostrate. Saan ka nga
  agpakleb dita daga. Don't lie prone on the ground.
  /MANGI-:I-/ to cause to lie prone or prostrate.
  /MAI-/ to fall prone accidentally.

PAKNI, v. /AG-/ to step aside, to withdraw, go out of
  one's way. /MANGI-:I-/ to put away.
    adj. /NA-/ orderly, neat.

[1]PAKO, v. /MANGI-:I-/ to hitch to a cart. /MAI-/ to be
  hitched to a cart.

[2]PAKO, n. a kind of edible fern (Athyrium esculentum).

PAKOL, adj. having a clubfoot or clubfeet; clubfooted.

v. /AG-/ to walk like a clubfooted person. /MA-/
to become clubfooted, to be like a clubfooted person.

PAKORTAR, v. /AG-/ to have a haircut. Mapanak agpakortar.
I am going to have a haircut. --syn. PAPUKIS.

[1]PAKPAK, v. /MANG-:-EN/ 1. to slap with the open hand.
2. to beat (clothes) with a wooden club when washing
them. --see PANAKPAK.

[2]PAKPAK, n. a kind of bamboo rattle.

PAKSET, = PA- + KESSET.

PAKSIW, n. a dish consisting of meat or fish seasoned
with vinegar.
v. /AG-/ to cook PAKSIW. /MANG-:-EN/ or /MANGI-:I-/
to cook into PAKSIW.

PAKSOY, adj. /MA--AN/ worn down, exhausted, weary,
tired.

PAKUBAS, v. /AG-/ to pretend to be poor, humble,
depressed, etc.

PAK-UL, v. /MANG-:-AN/ to knock on the head.

PAKULOT, v. /AG-/ to have one's hair curled.
/MANGI-:I-/ to cause to be curled: said of the hair.
Ipakulot ko ti book ko inton bigat. I will have my
hair curled tomorrow.

PAKUMBABA [cf. BABA], adj. /NA-/ humble, lowly.
v. /AG-/ to humble oneself.

PAKUTIBEG, v. /AG-/ to stand pat, to be immobile.
/MANGI-:I-/ to refuse (to move), to refuse to make
a motion (to do something). Apay nga ipakpakutibeg
mo ti aggunay? Why do you refuse to move?

PALA, n. spade, shovel.
v. /MANG-:-EN/ to shovel, to lift and move with a
spade or shovel, to dig out with a spade or shovel,
to hit with a spade or shovel.

PALAB-ONG, n. a camouflaged hole or pit used to trap
animals.
v. /MANG-:-AN/ 1. to trap in a hole or with a

lasso, to catch in or as in a trap. --var. LAB-ONG.
2. to entrap, ensnare; to deceive or trick into
difficulty.

PALAB-UG, n. a trap for birds.

PÁLAD, n. a line in the palm of the hand, the finger,
or the sole of the foot.

PALADPAD, n. window sill.

PALAIS, v. /MAI-/ to be carried away or swept away by
or as if by the wind.

PALAKOL, n. ax. --syn. WASAY.

PALALO, adj. /NA-/ excessive, overmuch. --syn. LAUS.

PALAMA; PALPALAMA, v. /MAKI-/ to beg, to ask for alms.
   AGPALPALAMA or MAKIPALPALAMA, n. beggar, pauper,
   indigent. --syn. AGPALPALIMOS, MAKILIMLIMOS,
   MAKILKILIMOS.

PALAMLAM, see under LAMLAM.

PALANAS, adj. /NA-/ smooth, level, even, polished.

PALANGGANA [f. Sp.], n. basin. --var. PLANGGANA.

PALANGGUAD, adj. /NA-/ boastful, proud, haughty.
   PALPALANGGUAD, v. /AG-/ to be boastful, proud, haughty;
   to boast.

PALANGKA, n. seat, chair. --syn. TUGAW.

PALAPALA, n. 1. scaffold, scaffolding. 2. a framework
to support a vine.

PALASIO [f. Sp.], n. palace.

PALATANG, n. a whole leaf of a palm tree.
   PALAT-ANGAN, form of PALATANG which occurs after a
   numeral.

PALATIPUT, n. a kind of soft candy made from sugar
cane juice.

PALATON [f. Sp.], var. of PLATO.

PALAUS, var. of LAUS.

PALAWAG, see under LAWAG.

PALAWAPAW, adj. fatuous, silly, foolish.

PALAY, v. /MAI-/ to be imbedded, to be set or fixed
    firmly in a surrounding mass. Naipalay ti lansa diay
    dapan. The nail was fixed firmly in his foot.

PALAYAS, n. irrigation. --syn. PADANUM.
    v. /MANG-:-AN/ to irrigate.

PALAYPALAY, n. malleolus.

PALBUAK, = PA- + LEBBUAK.

PALDA, n. skirt. --syn. PANDILING.

PALEK, v. /MANGI-:I-/ to hammer in or through, to
    drive by hammering, to cause to go through or
    penetrate by hammering. /MAI-/ to be driven by
    hammering.

PALET, adj. /NA-/ thick and sticky (as a liquid),
    gluey, syrupy, viscous.

PALGAK, v. /MANGI-:I-/ to reveal, predict, declare.
    Impalgak na ti yaay ti gubat. He predicted the
    coming of war.

PAL-ID, v. /MANG-:-AN/ to flap with a piece of cloth,
    as in dusting furniture. Pal-idan tayo dagiti tugaw
    nga natapok. Let us flap the dust off the dusty
    chairs.

PALIG, v. /MANGI-:I-/ to sweep off or away, to blow
    off or away. /MAI-/ to be swept off or away, to be
    blown off or away, to be carried off or away by the
    wind. Uray kami la nga naipalig ti kapigsa ti angin.
    We were blown off by the strength of the wind.

PALIGPALIG, n. anything that whirls or spins, as a
    propeller, a whirligig, a weather vane, etc.

PALIIW, v. /MANG-:-EN/ to observe, watch, notice, pay
    attention to. Paliiwen tayo ti gunay dagidiay nga
    tao. Let us observe the movement of those people.

PALIKAW, see under LIKAW.

PALIKPIK, n. fin of fish.   --syn. PIGAR.

PALILIT, v. /MANG-:-AN/ to look at from one side of the eyes, to glance at sideways.

PALINSUSOK, v. /MANG-:-AN/ to fill to the brim. Saan mo nga palinsusokan ta banga. Don't fill that pot to the brim.

PALLADAW, v. /MANG-:-AN/ to throw (something) to. Palladawan tayo dagidiay babbalasang ti mangga. Let us throw mangoes to the ladies.   /MANGI-:I-/ to throw to. Ipalladaw mo man kaniak dayta naluom nga bayyabas. Will you please throw to me that ripe guava.   /MAI-/ to be thrown away.

PALLANG, n. the asparagus bean (Psophocarpus tetragonolobus).

PALLANGATOK, v. /MANGI-:I-/ to toss, throw upwards. Ipallangatok mo dayta bola. Toss that ball.   /MAI-/ to be thrown upwards.   --var. PALLATOK.

PALLATIK, v. /AG-/ to swing, oscillate. Umadayo ka ta dinto agpallatik daytoy kenka. Go far away for this may swing to you.   /MANGI-:I-/ to make (something) swing or oscillate.   /MA--AN/ to be hit by something swinging or oscillating.

PALLATOK, var. of PALLANGATOK.

PALLAYAW, v. /MANGI-:I-/ to hint at, allude to, mention indirectly or subtly, make known indirectly. Impallayaw na ti ayat na ken ni Rosa. He made known indirectly his love for Rose.   /MAI-/ to be noticed accidentally.

PALLAYUG, v. /MANG-:-EN/ to rock or swing recklessly. Saan mo nga pallayugen ta indayon. Don't rock that cradle recklessly.
    adj. /NA-/ rocking or swinging recklessly.

PALLOT, v. /MAKI-:KA-/ to match one's gamecock with that of (another). Mapanak makipallot ken ni Berto. I am going to match my gamecock with that of Bert. /AG-/ [with pl. subject] to match the gamecocks of.

/MANGI-:I-/ to match (a gamecock) with (another).

PALLUKA, n. sandal.

PALNED, = PA- + LENNED.

PALOK, v. /MANGI-:I-/ to drive (a nail, stake, etc.) through. Ipalok mo daytoy lansa dita taleb. Drive this nail through that partition.

PALPA, v. /AG-/ to rest after eating. /M--AN/ [= MALPAAN] to be rested after eating.

PALPAL, v. /AG-, MANG-:-EN/ to break or reduce (the soil) to fine particles and level. Palpalem dayta daga nga pagmulaan ti tarong. Reduce the soil where the eggplants will be planted to fine particles and level it.

PALPALIWA [cf. LIWLIWA], v. /AG-/ to comfort oneself, entertain oneself, cool oneself off; to go somewhere for some entertainment.

PALSIIT, n. sling shot.
v. /AG-/ to hit someone with a sling shot. /MANG-:-AN/ to hit with a sling shot.

PALTAT, n. catfish.

PALTIK, n. homemade gun.

PALTING, v. /MANG-:-EN/ to tap, rap, or hit lightly with the fingers or with the tip of a cane. Saan mo nga paltingen dayta ngilaw dita rabaw ti lamisaan. Don't hit that fly with your fingers on top of the table.

PALTOG, n. gun.
v. /AG-/ to shoot someone or something. /AG-, MANG-:-AN/ to shoot. Apay nga paltugan nak? Why will you shoot me?

PALTOT, v. /MANG-:-EN/ to deliver (a child). /M--AN/ to be choked, as when food or water goes into the windpipe instead of the esophagus when swallowing.

MAMMALTOT, n. midwife. --syn. MANGNGILOT.

PALTUAD [PA- + LETTUAD], v. /MANG-:-EN/ to produce, invent, originate, create.

PALUBOS, n. permission.
v. /MANG-:-AN/ or /MANGI-:I-/ to allow, permit, grant. /MAI-/ to be allowed, granted.

PALUDIP, v. /AG-/ to look at fondly from one side of the eyes, to ogle at someone sideways. /MANG-:-AN/ to look at fondly from one side of the eyes, to ogle at sideways. Saan nak man nga paludipan. Don't ogle at me sideways.

PALUGUD, v. /MANG-:-AN/ to give in to the wishes of, to grant the wishes of. Narigat no palpalugudan yo dayta nga ubing. It is hard if you give in to the wishes of that child.

[1]PALUNAPIN, v. /MANGI-:I-/ to include, enclose, or insert in. Mangipalonapin ka man ti dua nga badok dita maletam. Will you please insert two dresses of mine in your suitcase.

[2]PALUNAPIN, var. of APIN.

PALUSPUS, v. /MANG-:-AN/ to permit, consent, grant permission to. Saan mo nga paluspusan nga mapan diay Manila ita rabii. Don't permit him to go to Manila tonight.

PALUTPUT, v. /MANG-:-EN/ to investigate, find out, inquire into the reason of. Palutputen da no apay nga saan nga immay nagbasa diay anak da idi kalman. They will investigate why their child did not come to school yesterday.

PAMASTREKAN [cf. SERREK], n. business, industry.

PAMATMAT [cf. MATMAT], v. /MANGI-:I-/ to show, exhibit, display. Ipamatmat mo kadakuada nga nasayaat ka nga tao. Show them that you are a good person.

PAMAYAN, v. /AG-/ to do something indifferently or without enthusiasm.

PAMBAR, n. alibi, excuse.
v. /AG-/ to give an excuse or alibi, to make use of pretext. /MANGI-:I-/ to use as an excuse. Ania man

ti impambar nan? What now did he use as an excuse?

PAMBORA, var. (dial.) of PAMBORAR.

PAMBORAR [cf. BORAR], n. eraser, eradicator. --var. PAMBORA.

PAMIENTA [pamiɛnta; f. Sp.], n. pepper, ground black pepper.

PAMILIA [f. Sp.], n. family. --syn. KAMAN.
  v. /AG-/ to have a family.

PAMIN-ANO, inter. v. /M-/ how many times? Mamin-ano ka nga mangan iti maysa nga aldaw? How many times do you eat a day? /-EN/ for how many times? Pamin-anoen da nga bay-oen dayta? For how many times will they pound that?

  SAGPAMIN-ANO, inter. adj. at how many times each? how often each?

PAMINSAN, v. /M-/ to do or be once or at one time. Maminsan ka la nga mangan. Eat only once. /-EN/ to do or be once or at one time. Paminsanen na nga labaan amin dagita. He will launder all those at one time.

  SAGPAMINSAN, adj. now and then, occasionally.

PAMISA [cf. MISA], n. a mass or a series of prayers recited in alternation by different persons for the dead.
  v. /AG-/ to have this.

PAMKUATAN, n. reason, motive, excuse.

PAMMABASOL [cf. BASOL], n. accusation, charge.

PAMMAGBAGA [cf. BAGA], n. advice, counsel.

PAMMIGAT [cf. BIGAT], n. breakfast. --syn. ALMUSAR.
  v. /M-/ [= MAMMIGAT] to eat breakfast. Nammigat kan? Have you eaten breakfast yet? /M-:-AN/ to eat or have for breakfast. Nammigatak ti kape laeng. I had coffee only for breakfast. Sika, ania ti pinammigatam? You, what did you have for breakfast.

PAMNIIT, n. slight fever, slight feverish feeling.

v. /-EN/ to be slightly feverish, to feel indisposed. Saanak nga makapan idiay sine ta pamniiten daytoy anak ko. I cannot go to the movie because my child is slightly feverish.

PAMPAG, v. /AG-, MANG-:-EN/ to beat or strike repeatedly with the hand or a stick.

PAMPAM, n. a prostitute.   --syn. PUTA.

PAMUGBUGAN [cf. BUGBOG], n. a receptacle or container for leftover food.

PAMUNPON, see under PUNPON.

PAMUSIAN, n. a hen that lays eggs, an egg-laying hen.

PAMUSPUSAN, n. remedy, ways and means.
v. /MANGI-:I-/ to find ways and means (to do something), to strive (to do something). Ipamuspusam ti yaay yo inton fiesta mi. Find ways and means to come during our feast.

PANA, n. bow and arrow; arrow.
v. /AG-, MANG-:-EN/ to hit with an arrow especially using a bow. /MA-/ to be hit with an arrow. /MANGI-:I-/ to send to attached to or like a propelled arrow.

PANAG, see KAPANAGAN.

PANAGKAYKAYSA [cf. MAYSA], n. cooperation, unity, oneness.

PANAIT [cf. DAIT], n. sewing thread.

PANAKKEL [cf. DAKKEL], v. /AG-/ to be boastful, proud, haughty, arrogant.   --var. PANNAKKEL.

PANAKPAK [cf. PAKPAK], v. /AG-/ to produce a succession of clapping or slapping sounds like that produced by a wooden club beating on wet clothes.

PANAL, n. a bird with bluish plumage.

PANATENG, n. cold: an acute inflammation of the mucous membranes of the respiratory passages.
v. /AG-, -EN/ to have this ailment.

PANAW, v. /-UM-/ to go away, leave, depart. Pumanaw ka
man ditoy ayan ko. Please go away from where I am.
/MANG-:-AN/ to leave, go away from, forsake, abandon.
No dinak kayat nga panawan siak ti pumanaw. If you
don't want to leave me I shall leave.

PAN-AW, n. the cogon (Imperata cylindrica).

PANAWEN [cf. TAWEN], n. opportune, designated, or
expected year, time, or season.

PANDA, var. of PINDA.

PANDAG, v. /MANG-:-AN/ to put a weight on, press down.
Saan mo nga pandagan ta imak. Don't press down on
my hand. /MANGI-:I-/ to put or place on something
as weight, to use to press down something.

PANDÁKA, adj. dwarfish. --syn. PANDEK.

PANDAN, n. the screw pine (Pandanus tectorius). --var.
PANGDAN.

PANDAY, n. blacksmith.
v. /AG-/ to make rings, earrings. /MANG-:-EN/ to
make (articles of metal, silver, or gold). Isu ti
nangpanday to singsing ko. It was he who made my
ring.

PANDEK, adj. /(NA-)/ short, low in stature, dwarfish.
--syn. PANDAKA.

PANDILING, n. skirt. --syn. PALDA.

PANDISAL [f. Sp.], n. a bread about the size of a fist
usually eaten for breakfast.

PANEKNEK, v. /AG-, MANG-:-AN/ to affirm, confirm; to
vouch for, guarantee. Paneknekan yo no adda opisina
inton bigat wenno awan. Confirm whether or not
offices are open tomorrow. /MANGI-:I-/ to confirm
or vouch for to (someone). Ipaneknek mo kenkuana nga
nagaget ni Perla. Confirm to him that Pearl is
industrious.

PANES, n. black dress used in mourning.
v. /AG-/ to wear a black dress in mourning.
/MANGI-:I-/ or /MANG-:-AN/ to wear a black dress in
mourning for (someone).

PANIANG, see PANNIANG.

PANID; SANGKAPANID, n. a unit of leaflike objects.

PANNAGNA, see under PAGNA.

PANNAKALEN, var. of PANNAKALENG.

PANNAKALENG, n. inflammatory swelling of the lymph
gland, usually at the groin.   --var. PANNAKALEN.
v. /AG-/ to have this.

PANNAKAYANAK [cf. ANAK], n. birthday.   --syn.
PANNAKASANGAY.

PANNAKKEL, var. of PANAKKEL.

PANNAYAG, adj. /NA-/ open, free of trees and other
plants to block the view. Napannayag ti ayan ti
balay da. The place where their house is is open.

PANNIKI, n. fruit bat.

PANSIT, n. rice noodle.

PANTALON [f. Sp.], n. long pants.
v. /AG-/ to wear this.

PANTEON, var. of PANTEONG.

PANTEONG, n. tomb.   --var. PANTEON.   --syn. NITSO.

PANTI [f. Eng.], n. lady's pants.

PANTOK, n. top, peak, tip.
adj. /NA-/ long and pointed: said of the nose.

PANUNOT, n. mind, thought, thinking.
v. /AG-/ to think, reflect on something.   /MANG-:-EN/
to think of, recall. Panunutem ti nagan diay immutang
kenka. Recall the name of the person who borrowed
money from you.

PANUOS, adj. /NA-/ smelling like that of slightly
burned substances, especially rice or food.

PANYO [f. Sp.], n. handkerchief, neckerchief.

PANYOLITO [f. Sp.], n. a small handkerchief.

PANGAG, v. /MANGI-:I-/ to heed, pay attention to.
Ipangag mo ti balakad ni tatang mo. Pay attention to
the advice of your father.

PANGALDAW [cf. ALDAW], n. lunch.
   v. /M-:-AN/ to eat or have for lunch. Mangaldawak
ita iti adobo. I will have ADOBO for lunch today.

PANGAMAEN [cf. AMA], n. uncle. --syn. ULITEG.

PANGAN, v. /M-/ to eat, to eat something. /MAKI-/
to eat with (someone at his house). Apay nga inaldaw
ka nga makipangpangan ditoy? Why do you eat with us
here every day? /MANGI-:I-/ to eat (an article of
food) with (another).

PANGANAN, n. dining room.

PANGARUN, var. of PAGARUN.

PANGAS, adj. /NA-/ presumptuous, conceited, vain,
boastful.

PANGASAAN [cf. ASA], n. whetstone.

PANGAT, v. /MANGI-:I-/ to cook fish seasoned with
vinegar or something sour.

PANGDAN, var. of PANDAN.

PANGEN, n. crowd, throng, multitude.

PANGET, v. /MAI-/ to be entangled in, to be closed in.
Nakpanget kami kadagiti siit ti kayo. We were
entangled in the thorns of the trees.

PANGGEP, n. aim, object, intention. Ania ti panggep
mo nga immay ditoy? What was your object in coming
here?
   v. /AG-:-EN/ to intend, plan. Panggepen tayo ti
mapan agkalap inton Sabado. Let us plan to go fishing
this Saturday.

   MAIPANGGEP, adv. 1. concerning, regarding, about.
   Maipanggep kenka daytoy damag. This news is about
   you. 2. on account of, on behalf of, in the interest
   of. Agrigrigatak maipanggep kenka. I suffer on
   behalf of you.

PANGGINGGI, n. a card game.

PANGINAEN [cf. INA], n. aunt. --syn. IKIT.

PANGIS, adj. 1. with its pair missing, as a shoe.
  2. odd, not even.
    v. /AG-/ to have its pair missing.

PANGKIS, adj. cross-eyed, strabismic.
    v. /AG-/ 1. to become cross-eyed. 2. to make one's
  eyes cross.

PANGLAKAYEN, see under LAKAY.

PANGLAW, adj. /NA-/ poor, indigent.
    v. /MANGI-:I-/ to be caused to become poor by (the
  loss of money or property). Saan mo nga ipanglaw
  dayta lugim ti negosio. Your loss in business will
  not cause you to become poor.

PANGMALEM [cf. MALEM], n. supper, early supper.
    v. /M-:-AN/ to eat or have for supper, especially
  early supper. Kaano tayo nga mangmalem? When do we
  eat supper?

PANGO, v. /MANGI-:I-/ to lead or coax into doing
  something. --SUNGSUNG.

PANG-OR, n. club, cudgel.
    v. /MANG-:-EN/ to beat with a club, to cudgel,
  club. /MANGI-:I-/ to use as or like a club to
  beat (someone).

PANGPANG, n. furrow.

PANGRABII [cf. RABII], n. supper, evening meal.
    v. /M-:-AN/ to eat or have for supper.

PANGRES, v. /AG-/ to blow the nose. /MANGI-:I-/ to
  blow (mucus) out of the nose.

PANGTA, n. 1. plot, conspiracy. 2. challenge.
  Impangruna na nga sinango ti pangta ti peggad. He
  especially faced the challenge of danger.
    v. /MANGI-:I-/ to plot or conspire against. Saan
  yo nga ipangta ti biag na. Don't plot against his
  life.

PANGUARTAAN, = PANG-AN + KUARTA.

PAO, n. a variety of mango whose fruits are small.

PAOS; PAPAOS, adj. /AG-/ desiring or envying (something
that belongs to another). Agpapaos ti bado. She
envies the dress of another person.

PAPAAWENG [cf. AWENG], n. a small bow made of bamboo
with a string made of a strip of buri palm leaf which
is attached to the back of a kite producing a sonorous
or shrill sound up in the air.

PAPAG, n. a bench or bed made entirely of bamboo.

¹PAPAIT, n. the thick, bitter juice of the intestines
of ruminants.

  PAPAITAN or PINAPAITAN, n. a meat dish consisting of
  beef or goat's meat and seasoned with PAPAIT.

²PAPAIT, n. an herb used to make salad (Mollugo
oppositifolia).

PAPAOS, see PAOS.

PAPARAW, see PARAW.

¹PAPAS, v. /AG-, MANGI-:I-/ to enjoy doing to the
utmost, to do to the limit of one's pleasure.
Ipapas mo ti agsigarilio. Smoke as much as you want.

²PAPAS, v. /MANG-:-AN/ to punish (someone) for a misdeed
or misfortune. Saan mo nga papasan dayta anak mo ta
awan ti basol na. Don't punish your child for he is
blameless.

PAPAYA [f. Sp.], n. papaya.

¹PAPEL [papɛl; f. Sp.], n. paper.

  PAPEL HAPON, thin but strong paper used for kites.

  PAPEL DE BANKO, check.

  PAPEL DE LIHA, sandpaper.

²PAPEL, v. /MANGI-:I-/ to drive or push into the mouth.
Saan mo nga ipapel nga maminpinsan ta kanem. Don't
push into your mouth all at once what you are eating.

PAPELES [papɛlɛs; f. Sp.], n. document, government or official paper or letter.

[1]PARA, n. the sprouting embryo of the coconut before or shortly after the cotyledon appears.

[2]PARA [f. Sp.?], prep. for, on behalf of. Daytoy ti para kenka. This is for you.

PARA-, a nominalizing affix denoting occupation or profession. Isu ti paraluto mi. He is our cook.

PARAANGAN, n. the entrance to the house, the area in front of the house especially where the ladder is, the front yard.

PARABUR, n. gift, present; favor.
    v. /MANG-:-AN/ to give something as a gift or favor. /MANGI-:I-/ to give (to someone) as a gift or favor.
    adj. /NA-/ generous.

PARADA [f. Sp.], n. parade.
    v. /MAKI-/ to join a parade. /AG-/ [with pl. subject] to hold a parade. /MANGI-:I-/ to show or display in or as in a parade, to parade.

PARADOR [f. Sp.], n. bureau, cabinet, cupboard. --var. APARADOR.

PARAGPAG, n. rib.

PARAGSIT, adj. /NA-/ agile, nimble, fast.

PARAGUPOG, v. /MANGI-:I-/ to drop or let fall abruptly and heavily. /MAI-/ to drop abruptly and suddenly.

PARAIS, n. shower.

PARANG, n. scene, appearance.
    v. /AG-/ to appear, show oneself; to become visible. /MANGI-:I-/ to show, display, make visible. Saan mo nga iparang kaniak dayta sugat mo. Don't make your wound visible to me.

PARANGARANG, v. /MANGI-:I-/ to make known to the public, publicize, reveal. Imparangarang na ti kinapanglaw na. He publicized his being poor.

PARANGET, see KAPARANGET.

PARAS, adj. /NA-/ open, exposed (to the wind).

PARASIPIS, v. /AG-/ to wriggle.

PARASPAS, v. /MANG-:-EN/ to cut, as grass. Paraspasen amin nga ruot dita paraangan. Cut all the grass in the front yard.

PARATO, adj. /NA-/ humorous, funny, amusing. v. /AG-/ to kid or tease someone.

PARATUPOT, v. /AG-/ to produce a series of sputtering sounds as during the evacuation of the bowels of a person having diarrhea.

PARAUT, v. /MANG-:-AN/ to tie, bind. /MANGI-:I-/ to use to tie or bind (something).

[1]PARAW; PAPARAW, n. hoarse voice. v. /AG-/ to have a hoarse voice.

[2]PARAW, n. a boat much larger than the BIRAY.

PARAWPAW, v. /AG-/ to exaggerate, to use exaggeration. adj. exaggerated. Parawpaw ti sao na. What he said is exaggerated.

PARBANGON, n. dawn.

PARBANGON NGA APAGSIPASIP, break of dawn.

PARBENG, adj. /NA-/ considerate, fair, judicious. v. /AG-/ to be considerate, fair, judicious. /MAI-/ to be suitable, appropriate.

PARDA, n. 1. a twining, leguminous vine with oblong, flattened pods. 2. its pod.

PARDAS, adj. /NA-/ quick, fast, swift. --syn. PARTAK.

PAREHO [parɛho; f. Sp.], adj. same, similar, equal, identical. v. /AG-/ [with pl. subject] to be the same, equal, similar, identical. /MANGI-:I-/ to make (something) the same as (another), to equate or compare with. --syn. PADA.

KAPAREHO, n. that to which the subject is similar, equivalent, identical. --syn. KAPADA.

PARI [short of KUMPARI], n. a term of address for the godfather of one's child, usually used with the first name of the person.

PARIIR, adj. /NA-/ breezy, well-ventilated.
v. /AG-/ to expose oneself to the breeze or to fresh air. /MANGI-:I-/ to expose (someone) to fresh air so as to cool. Ipariir mo dayta ubing idiay ruar. Expose that child to fresh air outside.

PARIKUT, n. problem, worry, anxiety.
v. /AG-/ to have a problem, to worry.

PARINTUMENG [cf. TUMENG], v. /AG-/ to kneel, to bend the knee. /MAI-/ to fall on the knees.

PARIOK, see PARYOK.

PARIT, v. /MANG-:-AN/ to forbid or prohibit (from doing something). /MANGI-:I-/ to forbid or prohibit (someone) from doing or having, to refuse to grant or give (to someone).

PARMATA [cf. MATA], v. /AG-/ to dream, have visions. /MAKA-:NA-/ to dream of, imagine, have visions of. Naparparmatak nga naragsak ti masakbayan na. I dreamed that his future will be happy.

PARMEK, v. /MANG-:-EN/ to subdue, overcome, conquer. Isuda ti nangparmek kadagiti kabusor. They were the ones who subdued the enemies. /MA-/ to be subdued, conquered.

PARMUON, v. /AG-/ to play the spy.

PARNUAY, n. invention, creation.
v. /AG-, MANG-:-EN/ to create, produce, invent, bring about, cause to appear or exist. Parnuayen ti dakes nga tiempo dayta nasakit na. That sickness of his is produced by bad weather.

PAROL [f. Sp.], n. lantern, especially a Christmas lantern.

PAROY, adj. /NA-/ being a haggler, being one who bargains for something at a very low price.

PARSIAK, v. /MANG-:-AN/ to sprinkle or splatter (with a liquid substance). /MANGI-:I-/ to sprinkle or splatter (on something), to cause to be sprinkled or splattered. /MA--AN/ to be sprinkled or splattered (with a liquid substance).

PARSUA, v. /MANG-:-EN/ to create. /MA-/ to be created.

MAMARSUA, n. the Creator, God.

PARTAAN, n. omen.
   v. /MANGI-:I-/ to convey or make known in a mysterious way, to show or reveal in a vision. /AG-, MAI-/ to be made known or revealed in a mysterious way. Naipartaan ken ni Pedro ti ipapatay ni tatang na. The death of Peter's father was made known to him in a mysterious way.

PARTAK, adj. /NA-/ alert, fast, agile.   --syn. PARDAS.

PARTE [partε; f. Sp.], n. share, portion.

PARTENG, n. a string, wire, piece of bamboo or wood used as guide when making a fence.

PARTI [f. Sp.?], v. /AG-/ to slaughter an animal. /MANG-:-EN/ to slaughter.

PARTIDISTA [f. Sp.], n. a partyman, a member of a political party.

PARTIDO [f. Sp.], n. party, especially a political party.

PARTISION [f. Sp.], n. partition.

PARUKMA, v. /MANG-:-EN/ to subjugate, subdue, overcome.

PARUKPOK, v. /-UM-/ to bubble: said of a liquid substance issuing from a spring, spout, wound, etc. Pumarukpok ti danum diay ubbog. The water in the spring is bubbling.

PARUSISI, v. /MANGI-:I-/ to scatter in all directions. /MAI-/ to be scattered in all directions. Naiparusisi amin nga ginatang na. All the things that she bought were scattered in all directions.

PARUT, v. /AG-/ to fall or be shed, as hair and feathers. Agparut ti dutdut dayta manok. The feathers of that

chicken are being shed. /MANG-:-EN/ to uproot,
extract, pull out. /MA-/ to be uprooted, extracted,
pulled out.

PARYA, n. bitter melon (Momordica charantia).

[1]PARYOK, v. /AG-/ to turn. /MANG-:-EN/ to spin,
rotate, turn around.

[2]PARYOK, n. frying pan, skillet.

PASABING, n. a trap for fish.

PASABLOG, n. trap.
v. /AG-, MANG-:-AN/ to trap, to catch with or as
if with a trap. Mapan kami agpasablog ti ikan. We
will go catch fish with a trap.

PASAG, v. /MA-, MAI-/ to fall unconscious suddenly, as
when fainting, shot or stabbed.

PASAGAD, n. sled, sledge. --see ULNAS.

PASAHERO [pasahɛro; f. Sp.], n. passenger.

PASAMAK, n. happening, event.
v. /MA-/ to happen, occur, take place.

[1]PASAMANO [f. Sp.], n. handshake. --syn. LAMANO.

[2]PASAMANO [f. Sp.], n. window sill.

PASARAY, adv. occasionally, now and then, once in a
while.

PASARUNSON, n. something that comes or is taken after
something else. Madadael it adobo no awan ti
pasarunson. The ADOBO won't be good unless something
is taken after it.

PASAS [f. Sp.], n. raisin.

PASAW, adj. /(NA-)/ presumptuous, vain, boastful.
PASPASAW, v. /AG-/ to boast, brag.

PASAYAK, n. irrigation. --syn. PADANUM, PALAYAS.

PASAYAN, n. a kind of shrimp about two inches long, prawn.

PASDEK, v. /MANGI-:I-/ to stick or fix in the ground, to implant; to establish. Impasdek da ti bandera idi makadanon da diay tuktok ti bantay. They stuck the flag in the ground when they reached the top of the mountain. /MAI-/ to be stuck or fixed in the ground.

PASET, n. division, section, part. Adda met paset ko iti pabuya. I also have a part in the show.

PASIAR, see PASYAR.

PASIENTE [f. Sp.], n. patient, a sick person. --syn. MASAKIT.

[1]PASIG, adj. /NA-/ importunate, obstinate.

PASPASIG, v. /AG-/ to be importunate, obstinate.

[2]PASIG, adj. all, purely, exclusively.

PASIKAL; ?ASPASIKAL [cf. SIKAL], v. /AG-/ to be in labor, in the process of childbirth.

PASIKING, n. knapsack.

PASILAW [cf. ᵕILAW], v. /AG-/ to ask (a sorceress) to find out whe.e a lost object, person, or animal is. /MANG-:-EN/ t᷄ cause (a lost object, person, or animal) to be ᵕocated (by a sorceress).

PASINDAYAG, adj. /NA-/ vain, conceited, pretentious.
    v. /AG-/ to be vain, conceited, pretentious.
/MANGI-:I-/ to show ostentatiously, to display with pride. Saan mo nga ipasindayag dayta baro nga badom. Don't show your new dress ostentatiously. --var. PASINDAYAW.

PASINDAYAW, var. of PASINDAYAG.

PASIPIKO [f. Sp.], n. the Pacific Ocean.

PASIROT [cf. SIROT], v. /MANG-:-AN/ to fasten, tie (a knot).

PASKUA [f. Sp.], n. Christmas.

PASLEP, n. steel.

PASNEK, adj. /NA-/ fervent, ardent, intense, passionate. Napasnek dagiti kararag na. Her prayers were passionate.
   v. /MANGI-:I-/ to do fervently, intensely, passionately, to do with all one's soul and heart.

PASNIIR, v. /MANGI-:I-/ to air.

PASNGAY, v. /MANGI-:I-/ to give birth to. /MAI-/ to be born.

PASO, n. a kind of large earthen jar.

PASOK, n. stake.
   v. /MANGI-:I-/ to drive in the ground.

PASPAS, adj. /NA-/ fast, quick. --syn. PARDAS, PARTAK.

PASPASIKAL, see PASIKAL.

PASTOR [f. Sp.], n. 1. shepherd. 2. Protestant minister.

PASTREK, = PA- + SERREK; see under SERREK.

PASUGNOD, v. /AG-/ to withdraw in disgust, to sulk.

PASUKSOK, n. bribe.
   v. /AG-/ to bribe someone. /MANG-:-AN/ to bribe. /MANGI-:I-/ to bribe with, to use to bribe (someone).

PASUNGAD, see under SUNGAD.

PASUROT [cf. SUROT], n. follower, disciple, supporter.

PASYAR [f. Sp.], v. /AG-/ to take a walk, promenade. /MANG-:-EN/ to visit, call on. /MANGI-:I-/ to take for a walk.

-PAT, var. of UPPAT, four: used only with certain prefixes.

   MAIKAPAT or MAYKAPAT, fourth.

   SAGGAPAT, four each.

PATÁ, n. bone marrow.

PATAD, see KAPATADAN.

PATAGGUAB, n. appendage, penthouse.

PATAK, adj. /NA-/ clear, evident, visible.

PATAKDER, see under TAKDER.

PATANI, n. lima bean (Phaseolus lunatus).

[1]PATANG, v. /MAKI-:KA-/ to talk or converse with. /AG-/
[with pl. subject] to talk or converse.

[2]PATANG, v. /MAI-/ to be coincident with, to happen at
the same time as. Maipatang ti bakasion ti piesta mi.
Vacation will be coincident with our feast. /MA--AN/
to be guessed, conjectured, supposed.

PATAS [f. Sp.], adj. same, equal, equivalent.
    v. /AG-/ [with pl. subject] to be the same, equal,
equivalent. --syn. PADA, PAREHO.

PATATAS [f. Sp.], n. potato.

PATAW, n. a buoy, float; a floating object.
    v. /AG-/ to float, especially by holding onto a
buoy.

[1]PATAY, n. support, stand.
    v. /MANG-:-AN/ to support (with something).
/MANGI-:I-/ to set on (a support).

[2]PATAY, v. /M-/ 1. to die; to be dead, be killed. 2. to
be extinguished, put off, as light. /MANG-:-EN/ 1.
to kill. Saan nak nga patayen ta adu ti anak ko.
Don't kill me for I have many children. 2. to
extinguish, put off. Saan mo nga patayen dayta
silaw ta mabutengak. Don't put off the light for I
am afraid. /AG-/ to kill oneself by doing something.

    MAMAMATAY, n. killer.

    NATAY, n. the dead.

PATEG, n. value, worth, price.
    adj. /NA-/ valuable, costly, precious, dear.
Napateg ka kaniak. You are dear to me.
    v. /AG-/ to be worth, to have the value of.
Agpateg ti sangaribo nga pisos daytoy diamantek.

My diamond is worth a thousand pesos. /MANG-:-AN/ [= PATGAN] to estimate the value of, to appraise. Patgem man daytoy singsing ko. Will you please estimate the value of my ring. /MANGI-:I-/ or /MANG-:-EN/ [= PATGEN] to value highly; to prize, esteem. Isu ti patpatgek nga asawak. She is my wife whom I value highly.

[1]PATI, v. /MANG-:-EN/ [= MAMATI] to believe. Dika ka nga patien. I don't believe you.

[2]PATI, v. /MANGI-:I-/ to do seriously.

[3]PATI, prep. including, together with, and also, as well as.

PATIAN, var. of ATIAN.

PATIKAWKAW, v. /AGI-/ to explain something in a roundabout way. /MANGI-:I-/ to lead (someone to a place) in a roundabout way.
    adj. /NA-/ circuitous, roundabout.

PATILAMBO, n. platter.

PATINAYON, adv. always, at all times; very often.
    --syn. KANAYON.

PATINUYNOY, v. /MANG-:-AN/ to yield to the wishes of. Saan mo nga patinuynoyan amin nga kayat na. Don't yield to all his wishes. /MA--AN/ to be given all the wishes of.

PATING, n. the young of a shark.

PATINGGA, n. end, conclusion, close.
    v. /AG-/ to end, terminate. Saan nga agpatingga ti panaglalais na kaniak. His mocking of me does not end.

PATIS, n. fish sauce.

PATIT, v. /AG-/ to strike, to make known the time and the like by sounding, to peal. /MANG-:-EN/ to strike, ring, as a bell.

PATNAG, v. /AG-/ all night long (doing something). /MANG-:-AN/ to do the whole night.

[1]PATO, v. /MANGI-:I-/ to suppose, think, assume.   /MAI-/
to announce a sentence, as by a judge.

[2]PATO, n. duck.

PATONG, n. hip.

PATPAT, v. /MANG-:-EN/ to cut down. Patpatem amin nga
kaykayo ditoy lapog mi. Cut down all the trees in
our vegetable garden.

PATRULIA [f. Sp.], n. patrol.
    v. /AG-/ to be on patrol.

PATTA; PATTAPATTA, n. calculation, estimation,
supposition.
    v. /MANG-:-EN/ to estimate, calculate.

PATTOG, v. /MANG-:-EN/ to overturn (a vessel or
container) so as to empty its contents. Saan mo nga
pattogen dayta balde ti danum. Don't overturn that
can of water.   /MANGI-:I-/ to spill out by overturning
its container, to pour out. Ipattog mo dayta danum
ditoy. Pour the water here.   /MA-/ to be overturned.
/MAI-/ to be spilled.

PATUDON, v. /AG-/ to shift the blame or responsibility
to another.   /MANGI-:I-/ to shift the blame or
responsibility to.

PATUPAT, n. a kind of soft pudding made of glutinous
rice; it is usually wrapped in plaited palm leaves.

PATUTOT, adj. vagrant, being a tramp; hence, being a
prostitute.
    v. /AG-/ to be a tramp; hence, to be a prostitute.

PAULO [cf. ULO], n. title, heading.
    v. /MANG-:-AN/ to entitle, to give a title to.
/MA--AN/ to be given the title, to be entitled.

PAUMAY, caus. of AY.

PAUT, adj. /NA-/ lasting, enduring, long-lasting.
    v. /AG-/ to stay or last long.

PAUYO, v. /AG-/ to sulk, to feel peeved.

PAWAD, adj. fingerless.

PAWIKAN, n. sea turtle, tortoise.

PAWIL, v. /MANG-:-AN/ or /MANGI-:I-/ to forbid, prohibit.

PAW-IT, v. /AG-, MANGI-:I-/ to send to through someone. Ipaw-itan ka ti kuarta intono Lunes. I will send you some money through someone on Monday.

PAWPAW, v. /AG-/ to wash oneself. Nagpawpaw diay ubing. The child washed himself. /MANG-:-AN/ to wash. Pawpawan diay nars diay ubing. The nurse will wash the child.

PAY, adv. a particle confirming an additional fact; still, yet, also.

PAYAK, n. wing. --var. PAYYAK.

PAYAKPAK, v. /AG-/ to produce a flapping or fluttering sound, as a bird flying.

PAYAPA, adj. /NA-/ tranquil, peaceful, quiet, calm.

PAYAPAY, v. /AG-/ to call or attract the attention of someone by waving the hand. /MANG-:-AN/ to summon or call the attention of by waving the hand.

PAYAT, v. /AG-/ to step on. /MANG-:-EN/ to tread on, trample on. Saan mo nga payaten dagiti mulak dita. Don't trample on my plants there. /MANGI-:I-/ to press or put (the foot) on.

PAYEGPEG, v. /AG-/ to shiver due to a chill or fever.

PAYONG, n. umbrella.
    v. /AG-/ to use an umbrella. /MANG-:-AN/ to shade or protect from the sun or rain with an umbrella. /MANGI-:I-/ to put over as or as if an umbrella.

PAYOS, adj. /NA-/ excellent, very good, perfect: not usually complimentary in connotation.

PAYPAY, n. fan.
    v. /AG-/ to fan, to use a fan; to fan oneself.
    /MANG-:-AN/ to fan (someone).

PAYSO, adj. /NA-, AG-/ true, exact. Agpayso diay
imbagam kaniak. What you told me is true. --syn.
PUDNO.
    v. /MANG-:-EN/ or /MANGI-:I-/ to do truly,
sincerely, faithfully, really. Paypasoen na ti
agadalen. He will really study now.

PAYUGPOG, v. /MANG-:-AN/ to spray with dust. /MANGI-:I-/
to blow, spray (dust, bits of paper, etc.): said of
the wind. Impayugpog ti napigsa nga angin amin nga
pappapel ditoy. The strong wind blew all the papers
here.

PAYYAK, var. of PAYAK.

PEBRERO [pɛbrɛro; f. Sp.], n. February.

PEDASO [pɛdaso; f. Sp.], n. piece (of cloth).

PEDPED, v. /MANG-:-EN/ to abate, lessen. Pedpedem ta
pungtot mo. Abate your anger. /MA-/ to be abated.

PEGGAD, n. peril, danger, turmoil.
    adj. /NA-/ dangerous, perilous, risky, hazardous.
    v. /AG-/ to be in danger, to be risky.

PEGGES, adj. /NA-/ strong, swift, violent, intense.
    v. /AG-/ to become violently strong and fast (as
current, wind, etc.).

PEGPEG, n. small particle of rice.

    MARAPEGPEG, adj. young, newly formed (as guava,
    rice, corn, etc.).

PEKAS [f. Sp.], n. freckle.

PEKKEL, v. /MANG-:-AN/ to squeeze or wring (clothes,
    fabrics, fibers) to force the water out of. /MA--AN/
    to be squeezed or wrung (as clothes, fabrics, fibers).
    /MANG-:-EN/ to squeeze, massage, press, knead.

[1]PEKPEK, v. /MANG-:-EN/ to cram, stuff or load fully
    and tightly. /MA-/ to be crammed, overstuffed.

[2]PEKPEK, v. /-UM-/ to produce a tapping sound as wood
    being beaten.

PELIKULA [pɛlikula; f. Sp.], n. film, movie. --syn.
  SINE.

PELLENG, v. /MA-/ [= MAPLENG] to be stunned, rendered
  senseless by a blow on the head.

PELLES, v. /AG-, MANG-/ [= MAMLES], to get dressed, to
  change one's clothes. Mamles ka ta mapan ta idiay ili.
  Get dressed and we will go to town. /MANG-:-AN/ to
  dress up (someone), to change the clothes of
  (someone). Sika ti mangpelles ti daydiay ubing. You
  dress up the child.
    adj. /NAKA-/ dressed.

PELPEL, v. /MANGI-:I-/ to press down or through (an
  opening). /MAI-/ to get stuck in an opening or
  hole.

PELTANG, v. /MANG-:-EN/ to dislocate the joints of.
  Saan mo nga peltangen ta ubing. Don't dislocate the
  joints of that child.

PENNÉD, n. dike, levee.

PENNEK, v. /AG-/ to satisfy oneself fully of something.
  /MANG-:-EN/ to satisfy fully of something. Penneken
  tayo dagiti babbalasang ti mangga. Let us satisfy
  the ladies with mangoes. /MA-/ [= MAPNEK] to be
  fully satisfied.

PENPEN, n. heap, pile.
    v. /MANG-:-EN/ or /MANGI-:I-/ 1. to pile (things)
  up in an orderly way. 2. to keep to oneself
  (heartaches, complaints, etc.).

PENSAR [f. Sp.], n. aim, purpose. --syn. PANGGEP.
    v. /MANG-:-EN/ to plan, aim, propose, intend.

PENSION [pɛnsion; f. Sp.], n. pension.
    v. /AG-/ to receive a pension. /MANG-:-AN/ to
  give a pension to, to pension (someone).

  PENSIONADO, n. male pensioner.

  PENSIONADA, n. female pensioner.

PENGED, v. /MANG-:-AN/ [= PENGDAN] to control, restrain,
  check, moderate. Pengdam ta panaginom mo. Moderate
  your drinking.

PENGNGET, v. /MAKI-:KA-/ to grapple with. /AG-/ [with
pl. subject] to grapple each other. /MANG-:-EN/ to
grapple, seize.

PEON [pɛon; f. Sp.], n. 1. peon, day laborer. 2. in
chess, a soldier.

PER-AK, v. /MANG-:-EN/ to break into pieces or bits,
to shatter. /MANGI-:-EN/ to throw so as to break
into pieces or to shatter. /MA-/ to be broken into
pieces, to be shattered.

PERDI [pɛrdi; f. Sp.], v. /AG-, MANG-:-EN/ to destroy,
ruin, damage. Agperdi dagiti walang nga baboy
kadagiti mulmula. The astray pigs will destroy some
of the plants. /MA-/ to be destroyed, ruined,
damaged. Madadael dayta relom no di mo nga an-annadan.
Your watch will be damaged if you are not careful
with it.

PERDIBLE [pɛrdiblɛ; f. Sp.], n. safety pin.

PERIODIKO [pɛriodiko; f. Sp.], n. newspaper. --syn.
DIARIO.

PERIODISTA [pɛriodista; f. Sp.], n. newspaperman. --syn.
AGIWARWARNAK.

PERMANENTE [pɛrmanɛntɛ; f. Sp.], adj. permanent.
   v. /AG-/ to stay (in a place) permanently, to
reside.

PERRENG, v. /MANG-:-EN/ to look at someone straight to
the eyes, to stare at. Saan mo nga perrengen dayta
asawa na. Don't stare at his wife. /MANGI-:I-/ to
focus or fix (the eyes) on.

PERRES, n. a general term for any sour citrus fruit.
   v. /MANG-:-EN/ to squeeze or press the juice or
sap out of (a lemon, orange, etc.). /MANG-:-AN/ to
press juice on (food and the like). Perresan tayo
ti kalamansi dayta ikan. Let us press lemon juice
on that fish.

PERSAY, v. /MANG-:-EN/ to tear, tear off. /MA-/ to be
torn, torn off.

   PERSAY-PERSAY, adj. ragged, torn (as cloth).

PERSIANO [pɛrsiano; f. Sp.], n. Persian.

PERSONALIDAD [pɛrsonalidad; f. Sp.], n. personality.

PERYODIKO; PERYODISTA, see PERIODIKO, PERIODISTA.

PES, see EPPES.

PES-AK, v. /MANG-:-AN/ or /MANGI-:I-/ to wet or soak in water (a piece of cloth) to allow to shrink, to preshrink. Pes-akam nga umuna dayta lupot sa monto daiten. Preshrink that cloth before sewing it.

PESETA [pɛsɛta; f. Sp.], n. twenty centavos, one-fifth of a peso.

PESPES, same as PERRES.

PESSA, v. /AG-/ to hatch: said of an egg. Saan pay nga nagpessa dagiti itlog ti manok ko. The eggs of my hen have not hatched yet. /MANG-:-AN/ to hatch (an egg).

PESSAT, n. a piece of cloth woven at one time, a certain length of cloth usually sufficient for making one garment.

PESTE [pɛstɛ; f. Sp.], n. pest, pestilence. --var. PISTI.
    v. /AG-, MA-/ to die due to a pest or pestilence, to be killed by a pest.

PETPET, v. /AG-/ to grasp or clutch something. /MANG-:-AN/ to hold tight, grasp, clutch.

PETROMAKS [pɛtromaks; f. Eng.], n. kerosene pressure lantern with the trade name "Petromax" or another like it.

PETSA [pɛtsa; f. Sp.], n. date.

PIA, n. health, well-being.
    adj. /NA-/ good, well, healthy.
    v. /-UM-/ to become well or healthy, to recover (as a sick person). --syn. SAYAAT.

PIANO [f. Sp.], n. piano.
    v. /AG-/ to play the piano. /MANG-:-EN/ to play (a musical piece) on a piano.

PIAPI [pi?api], v. /AG-/ sit on (a window, rail, etc.) with both legs dangling. Saan ka nga agpiapi dita tawa. Don't sit on the window sill with your legs dangling.

PIAR [f. Sp.], v. /MANG-:-EN/ to trust, have confidence in.

PIAS, n. 1. a tree that bears sour fruits. 2. its fruit.

PIDEG, v. /MANGI-:I-/ to push (an object) against (another), to put in contact with. Ipidas mo dayta lamisaan dita taleb. Push the table against the partition.

PIDIL, v. /MANG-:-EN/ to pinch lightly or gently. Saan mo nga pidilen ta pingping ta ubing. Don't pinch lightly the cheek of that child. --see KUDDOT, KEDDEL, KIDDIS.

PIDIPID, v. /MA-/ to be covered (with sores, wounds, etc.).

PIDIT; PIDITPIDIT, n. earlobe.

PIDOT, v. /AG-, -UM-, MANG-:-EN/ to pick up. Agpidot ka man ti bato. Will you please pick up some stones.

PIEK, n. chick, a young chicken.
  PIPIEK, v. /AG-/ to cry: said of a chick; to imitate the cry of a chick.

PIESTA, n. feast, festival, celebration. --var. of FIESTA.

PIGAD, v. /AG-/ to rub the dirt off the sole of one's feet or shoes. /MANGI-:I-/ to rub the dirt off (the sole of one's feet or shoes) on (a doormat or something else).

PIGAR, n. fin especially that of fish. --syn. SIGAR.

PIGERGER, v. /AG-/ to tremble, shiver, shudder.

PIGIS, v. /MANG-:-EN/ to tear, rend. /MA-/ to be torn, rent.
  adj. torn.

PIGIT, v. /MANG-:-EN/ to handle, touch or feel with the hand. Saan mo nga pigiten dagitoy lakok nga ikan. Don't handle the fish that I am selling.

PIGKET, n. paste, glue.   --syn. ALLID.
adj. /NA-/ sticky, gluey. Saan nak nga iggaman ta napigket dayta imam. Don't hold me for your hand is sticky.
v. /MANGI-:I-/ to paste or stick on.   /MANG-:-AN/ to stick or paste something on.   /MA--AN/ to have something pasted on.

PIGLAT, n. scar, cicatrix.

PIGSA, n. strength, power, force.
adj. /NA-/ strong, powerful, forceful.

PIGSOL, v. /AG-/ to walk with a slight hop or limp, to limp slightly.

PIGURA [f. Sp.], n. figure, form, appearance.   --syn. LANGA.

PIKA, n. spear, arrow.
v. /MANG-:-EN/ to spear.   /MA-/ to be speared.

PIKAPIK, v. /AG-/ to shake, tremble, palpitate due to anger, cold, hunger, etc. Agpikapik ti bibig ko iti lam-ek na. My lips were trembling due to the cold.

PIKEL; PIPIKEL, v. /AG-, MA-/ to become numb, to go to sleep (as the leg, hand, etc.).

PIKO [f. Sp.], n. pick, pickax.

PÍKON, v. /MANG-:-EN/ to wind around the arm, as a string.   /MA-/ to be wound around the arm.

PIKPIK, v. /MANG-:-EN/ to pat, tap lightly with the palm of the hand (as when making a child burp).

PILA, n. clay.

PILAT, syn. (dial.) of BAT-UG.

PILAY, adj. lame.
v. /MANG-:-EN/ to cause to be lame.   /MA-/ to become lame.

PILEGES, var. of PLEGES.

PILI, v. /AG-, MANG-:-EN/ to choose, select, pick.
Agpili ka ti kayat mo nga gatangen. Choose what you
want to buy.
adj. /NA-/ choosy, fastidious, finicky.

PILID, n. wheel.
v. /MANG-:-AN/ to run over with a vehicle or a
conveyance with wheels. /MA--AN/ to be run over
(by a vehicle or a conveyance with wheels).

PILIO [f. Sp.], adj. /NAG-/ naughty, mischievous,
roguish.

PILIPIG, n. young rice grains which are pounded and
husked after being toasted in a pan or an open fire.

PILKAT, n. blot, stain, smear. --var. PILTAK.
v. /MANG-:-AN/ to stain, blot, smear. /MANGI-:I-/
to use to stain, blot, smear (something). /MA--AN/
to be stained, smeared.

PILLAYOD, var. of PILLAYOS.

PILLAYOS, adj. having the legs paralyzed.

PILOT, v. /MANGI-:I-/ to cause to stick on by pressing.
Saan mo nga ipilot ta inapoy dita lamisaan. Don't
cause the rice to stick on the table. /MAI-/ to be
caused to stick on by pressing. Naipilot diay inapoy
dita lamisaan. The rice was caused to stick on that
table.

PILOTO [f. Sp.], n. pilot. --syn. ABIADOR.

PILPIL, v. /MANG-:-EN/ to crush, compress between two
hard bodies to make flat. Pilpilem ta laya. Crush
that ginger. /MA-/ to be crushed, flattened.
adj. crushed, flat.

PILTAK, var. of PILKAT.

PINABLAD, see under BELLAD.

PINAKBET, see under PAKBET.

PINANGABAKAN [cf. [1]ABAK], n. winnings; anything gained
or won in gambling, a contest, etc.

PINAS, v. /MANG-:-EN/ to level, make even or smooth. /MA-/ to be levelled, made even or smooth.

PINDA, v. /MANG-:-EN/ to do to or examine each one consecutively without exception. --var. PANDA.

PINDANG, n. dried or jerked meat or fish.
v. /MANG-:-EN/ to jerk or dry in the sun. /MA-/ to be dried by the heat of the sun.

PINIPIN, v. /MANGI-:I-/ to give or find room for. Ipinipin mo bassit daytoy badok dita maletam. Please find room for my dress in your suitcase.

PINO [f. Sp.], adj. /NA-/ refined, fine, polished.

PINTA [f. Sp.], n. paint.
v. /AG-, MANG-:-EN/ to paint. /MANGI-:I-/ to use to paint, to paint with. /MA--AN/ to be painted.

PINTAKASI, n. cockfighting feast.

PINTAS, adj. /NA-/ pretty, beautiful, attractive, charming.

PINTOR [f. Sp.], n. painter.

PINTURA [f. Sp.], n. 1. paint. --syn. PINTA. 2. painting.

PINYA [f. Sp.], n. 1. pineapple fruit. 2. pineapple plant.

PINGAS, v. /MANG-:-AN/ to cut off the ears or comb of. /MA--AN/ to have the ears or comb cut off.
adj. with ears or comb cut off.

PINGGAN, n. plate. --syn. PLATO.

PINGGI, v. /MANG-:-EN/ to shake. Saan mo nga pinggien toy tugaw ko. Don't shake my chair.
PINGGI-PINGGI, v. /AG-/ to shake continuously, to rock. /MANG-:-EN/ to shake repeatedly, to rock.

PINGGOL, n. chignon.
v. /AG-/ to knot one's hair. /MANG-:-EN/ to knot or coil (the hair). /MA-/ to be gathered into a knot: said of the hair.

PINGIL, n. corner, edge.

PINGKI, n. flint and steel used for striking a fire.

PING-O, v. /MANG-:-EN/ to twist (the arm or finger), to sprain. /MA-/ to be sprained.

PINGOD, adj. having but one or no ear.
    v. /MANG-:-AN/ to pinch or twist the ear of, to tweak the ear of.

PINGPING, n. cheek

   PINGPING TI UBET, buttock.

   PINGPING TI UKI, labia majora, the outer folds of skin of the vulva, the outer lip of the vulva.

   PINGPING TI SABANGAN, the sides of a bar at the mouth of a river or harbor.

PIPIIT, n. a very small bird.

PIPIKEL, see PIKEL.

PIPINO, n. cucumber.

PIRAK, n. money. --syn. KUARTA.
    adj. /MA-, NA-/ rich, wealthy.
    v. /MANG-:-AN/ 1. to bribe. 2. to finance.

PIR-AK, v. /MANG-:-EN/ or /MANGI-:I-/ to break into pieces. /MA-/ to be broken into pieces. --syn. BURAK.

PIRGIS, n. remnant of cloth.
    v. /MANG-:-EN/ to tear off. --cf. PIGIS.

PIRIT, v. /AG-, MANG-:-EN/ to roll between the tips of the finger so as to make smooth and slender.

PIRITO, var. of PRITO.

PIRMA [f. Sp.], n. signature.
    v. /MANG-:-AN/ to sign. /MANGI-:I-/ to affix (one's signature) on something.

PIRPIR; PIRPIR-PIRPIR, adj. ravelled, with threads separating. Pirpir-pirpir diay bado na. Her dress is ravelled.

PISANG, v. /MANG-:-EN/ to tear into pieces, to shred. /MA-/ to be torn into shreds.
   adj. torn.

PISARA [f. Sp.], n. blackboard.

PISAW; PISAWPISAW, v. /AG-/ to splash, as when a stone is thrown into the water or a fish jumps.

PISEL, v. /MANG-:-EN/ to squeeze, press. Saan mo nga piselen ta imak. Don't squeeze my hand.

PISGAR, n. neck feather of a fowl, hackle.

[1]PISI, n. half of, piece, part, portion.
   v. /MANG-:-EN/ to divide into two, split, halve. /MA-/ to be divided into two, split, halved.

[2]PISI [from P.C., Philippine Constabulary], n. 1. Philippine Constabulary. 2. a member of this. --syn. KONSTABULARIA.

PIS-IT, v. /MANG-:-EN/ to crush, squeeze between two opposing bodies. /MA-/ to be crushed. Napis-it diay kuton nga binaddekak. I crushed the ant that I stood on.

PISKAL [f. Sp.], n. fiscal.

PISKALIA [f. Sp.], n. fiscal's office.

PISKEL, n. large muscle of the arm or leg.
   v. /MA-/ to be sprained: said of a large muscle.

PISKIRIA [f. Sp.], n. fishpond.

PISOK, v. /MANGI-:I-/ to throw, drop, push or pour into a hole or a container. /MAI-/ to be thrown, dropped, pushed or poured into a hole or container.

PISON [f. Sp.], n. steam roller.
   v. /MANG-:-EN/ to compress and flatten with or as with a steam roller.

PISOS [f. Sp.], n. peso; one hundred centavos.

PISPIS, n. temple, either of the flat surfaces behind the forehead and in front of the ear.

PISSAT, v. /MANG-:-EN/ to cut (cloth).   /MA-/ to be cut: said of cloth.

PISTI, var. of PESTE.

PITAK, n. mud, mire.

PITAKA [f. Sp.], n. wallet.

[1]PITIK, v. /AG-/ to throb, pulsate, palpitate.

[2]PITIK, v. /MANG-:-EN/ to flip with the finger, to fillip.

PITING, v. /MANG-:-EN/ to flick with the fingers. Saan mo nga pitingen dayta sabong. Don't flick that flower with your fingers.

PIT-ING, v. /MANG-:-AN/ to break a piece from, to chip. Saan mo nga pit-ingan dayta tinipay. Don't break a piece from that sugar bar. /MANG-:-EN/ to break into pieces. Pit-ingem man dayta tinipay. Please break that sugar bar into several pieces.

PITIO, see PITTIO.

PITO, num. seven; 7.   --syn. SIETE.

PITPIT, v. /MANG-:-EN/ to forge, to compress or flatten by beating.   /MA-/ to be crushed, compressed, flattened.

PITSO, var. of PITTIO.

PITSON [f. Sp.?], n. squab, young of a pigeon or dove.

PITTIO, n. breast of chicken.   --var. PITSO.

PIUKOT, adj. hunchbacked.
    v. /AG-/ to stoop.

PIWIS, v. /AG-/ to have twisted lips.   --syn. DIWIG.

PIYESTA, var. of PIESTA.

PLAKA [f. Sp.], n. disc, record.

PLANO [f. Sp.], n. plan.   --syn. PANGGEP.
    v. /AG-, MANG-:-EN/ to plan.   /MA-/ to be planned.

PLANSA [f. Sp.], n. flat iron, pressing iron.
v. /AG-/ to iron something. /MANG-:-EN/ to iron,
press. /MA-/ to be ironed or pressed. --var.
PLANTYA.

PLANTA [f. Sp.], n. physical plant as buildings.

PLANTYA, var. of PLANSA.

PLANGGANA, var. of PALANGGANA.

PLASA [f. Sp.], n. plaza, town square.

PLASO [f. Sp.], n. 1. handicap; in a race or other
competition, an advantage given to the inferior
contestant(s); allowance, consideration. 2. limit,
deadline.

PLATERO [platɛro; f. Sp.], n. silversmith.

PLATITO [f. Sp.], n. small plate, saucer.

PLATO [f. Sp.], n. plate. --var. PALATON.

PLEGES [plɛgɛs; f. Sp.], n. pleat. --var. PILEGES.

PLEMAS [plɛmas; f. Sp.], n. phlegm. --syn. TURKAK.

PLETE [plɛtɛ; f. Sp.], n. fare, e.g. bus fare.
v. /AG-/ to pay one's fare. Dika ka pay nga
agplete. Don't pay your fare yet. /MANGI-:I-/ to
pay for the fare of.

PLUMA [f. Sp.], n. pen. --syn. PONTEMPEN.

PLUTA [f. Sp.], n. flute.

POBLASION [f. Sp.], n. the seat of a township, town
proper.

POBRE [pobrɛ; f. Sp.], adj. /(NA-)/ poor, indigent.
--syn. MARIGRIGAT, PANGLAW.

POLITIKO [f. Sp.], n. politics.

PONSION [f. Sp.?], n. party, banquet.
v. /AG-/ to give a party.

PONTEMPEN [pontɛmpɛn; f. Eng.], n. fountain pen, pen. --syn. PLUMA.

PORGADA [f. Sp.], n. inch.

PORMULA [f. Sp.], n. formula.

PORSELAS [porsɛlas; f. Sp.], n. bracelet, armlet.

PORSIENTO [porsiɛnto; f. Sp.], n. percent, percentage.

POSAS [f. Sp.], n. chain for binding hands or feet especially of prisoners.

POSIBILIDAD [f. Sp.], n. possibility.

POSISION [f. Sp.], n. position.

POSO [f. Sp.], n. pump, well.

POSPORO [f. Sp.], n. match, box of matches.   --syn. GURABIS, SAKAPUEGO.

PRAKTIS [f. Eng.], n. practice, training.
    v. /AG-/ to practice, to train oneself.   /MANG-:-EN/ 1. to practice, train oneself to doing. 2. to teach or train (someone) through practice.

PRASKO [f. Sp.?], n. bottle larger than a soft drink bottle (BOTE or BOTELIA); usually used as container for kerosene.

PRAYLE [fraịlɛ; f. Sp.], n. friar.

PREMIO [prɛmio; f. Sp.], n. prize, reward.   --syn. GUNGGUNA.
    v. /MANG-:-AN/ to give a prize to.   /MANGI-:I-/ to give as a prize or reward.   /MA--AN/ to be given a prize or reward.

PRENSA [prɛnsa; f. Sp.], n. press.

PRESERBATIBO [prɛsɛrbatibo; f. Sp.], n. preservative.

PRESIDENTE [prɛsidɛntɛ; f. Sp.], n. president.   --syn. PANGULO.

    PRESIDENTE ELEKTO, n. president-elect.

PRESIO [prɛsio; f. Sp.], n. price, cost.
  v. /MANG-:-AN/ to estimate the price of.
  adj. /NA-/ salable, in demand.

PRESKO [prɛsko; f. Sp.], adj. /(NA-)/ cool, fresh,
  breezy, well-ventilated.

PRESO [prɛso; f. Sp.], n. 1. jail, prison. --syn.
  KALABUS, PAGBALUDAN. 2. prisoner. --syn. BALUD,
  PRISONERO.
  v. /MANGI-:I-/ to imprison, confine. --syn.
  BALUD, KALABUS.

PRIBADA [f. Sp.], adj. private.

PRIMARIA [f. Sp.], adj. primary.
  n. primary grade.

PRINSESA [prinsɛsa; f. Sp.], n. princess.

PRINSIPAL [f. Sp.], adj. principal.
  n. principal, e.g. of a school.

PRINSIPE [prinsipɛ; f. Sp.], n. prince.

PRITO [f. Sp.], v. /AG-, MANG-:-EN/ or /MANGI-:I-/ to
  fry. /MA-/ to be fried.
  adj. fried. --var. PIRITO.

PROBINSIA [f. Sp.], n. province.

PROBINSIANA [f. Sp.], n. a girl or woman from the
  province. --ant. PROBINSIANO.

PROBINSIANO [f. Sp.], n. a boy or male, from the
  province. --ant. PROBINSIANA.

PROBLEMA [problɛma; f. Sp.], n. problem.

PRODUKTO [f. Sp.], n. product.

PROGRAMA [f. Sp.], n. program.

PROPESION [propɛsion; f. Sp.], n. profession.

PROPESOR [propɛsor; f. Sp.], n. professor.

PROTEKSION [protɛksion; f. Sp.], n. protection.

PROTESTANTE [prot\u025bstant\u025b; f. Sp.], n. a member of the
   Protestant Church.
      adj. Protestant. --var. PURTIS.

PROYEKTO [proy\u025bkto; f. Sp.], n. project.

PRUTAS [f. Sp.], n. fruit. --syn. BUNGA.

PUBLIKO [f. Sp.], n. & adj. public.

PUDAW, adj. /NA-/ white, light-complexioned, light-
   colored.
      v. /-UM-/ to become this.

PUDNO, n. truth.
      adj. true, genuine, real, correct, accurate. --syn.
   PAYSO. /NA-/ sincere, fervent. Napudno ti ayat ko
   kenka. My love for you is sincere.
      v. /AG-/ to tell the truth, confess. /MANGI-:I-/
   to tell (what is true), to confess. Impudno na nga
   isuda ti nagtakaw. He confessed that they were the
   ones who stole something. /-UM-/ to be realized, to
   materialize, to happen as indicated.

PUDON, v. /MANG-:-EN/ to crumple, to gather, throw or
   press together without order. Saan mo nga pudonen ta
   ules. Don't crumple that blanket.

PUDONAN, n. spool.

PUDOS, n. act of fortune telling. Pudno ti pudos na
   kaniak. His telling of my fortune is accurate.
      v. /MANG-:-AN/ or /MANGI-:I-/ to read or tell the
   fortune of. Impudosan nak ni Susana. Susan told my
   fortune.

PUDOT, n. heat, hotness, warmth.
      adj. /NA-/ hot, warm; feverish. Napudot ita. It is
   hot today.
      v. /-UM-/ to become hot, warm, feverish. /-EN/ to
   feel hot, warm. /AG-/ to be irritable, irascible,
   cranky.
   NAPUDOT TI ULO (NA). (He) is hot-tempered. or (He)
   is irritable.

PUDTO, v. /MANG-:-AN/ to guess. Saan na kayat nga
   pudtoan nu kaano ka nga nayyanak. He does not want
   to guess when you were born. --var. PUGTO.

PUEK, n. a kind of owl.

PUERSA [puɛrsa; f. Sp.], n. force, strength.
adj. /NA-/ strong. --syn. PIGSA. Napuersa ti angin idiay bantay. The wind in the mountain is strong.
v. /MANG-:-AN/ to force. /MANGI-:I-/ to enforce, insist. --syn. PILIT.

PUERTO [puɛrto; f. Sp.], n. port.

PUESTO [puɛsto; f. Sp.], n. 1. post, position. 2. stall, a booth, table, or counter, as at a market, at which goods are sold.
v. /AG-, -UM-/ to install or establish oneself (in a place). /MANGI-:I-/ 1. to install or establish (in a place). 2. to place (a person) in an office, rank, etc.

PUG-AW, v. /MANG-:-AN/ to breathe upon. /MANGI-:I-/ to breathe out to. /MA--AN/ to be breathed upon, to be hit by a breath, smoke, etc.

PUGIIT, adj. with protruding buttocks.
v. /AG-/ to put the head down and the buttocks up. /MANGI-:I-/ to cause (someone) to do this. /MANG-:-AN/ to do this toward (someone).

PUGLAY, v. /MA-/ to slide down, slip to the ground. Napuglay diay atep ti balay da. The roof of their house slipped to the ground.

PUGO, n. quail.

PUGON [f. Sp.], n. oven.

PUG-ONG, n. bundle.
v. /MANG-:-EN/ to bundle, tie in a bundle. /MA-/ to be bundled.

PUGOT, n. 1. a Negrito, a very dark or black person. 2. a black supernatural being that usually appears at night.

PUGPUG, v. /MANG-:-AN/ or /MANGI-:I-/ to broil. Ipugpog mo diay ikan. Broil the fish. /MA--AN/ to be broiled. --syn. TUNO.

PUGSAT, v. /MANG-:-EN/ to break, snap off, cut off.

/MA-/ to break, snap (as thread). Napugsat diay pagsalapayan. The clothesline snapped. --var. PUGSOT.

PUGSIT, v. /AG-, MANGI-:I-/ to squirt on. Saan ka nga agpugsit ti danum dita. Don't squirt water there. /-UM-/ to squirt, spurt, shoot out, as liquid, in a jet or thin stream. Pimmugsit ti dara ti sugat na. Blood spurted from his wound.

PUGSO, v. /MANG-:-AN/ to spew something to (someone). /MANGI-:I-/ to spew, to eject violently. /MA--AN/ to be spewed upon.

PUGSOT, var. of PUGSAT.

[1]PUGTIT, n. bit of excrement.
v. /MAKA-/ to excrete a bit of excrement usually involuntarily or unknowingly.

[2]PUGTIT, v. /AG-/ to produce a short hissing sound with the tongue to show contempt.

PUGTO, var. of PUDTO.

PUKAL, n. breast, udder. --syn. SUSO.

PUKAN, v. /AG-, MANG-:-EN/ to fell, cut down. Kayat ko nga pukanen dayta papaya. I want to cut down that papaya. /MA-/ to be felled or cut down.

PUKAW, v. /MANG-:-EN/ to lose. /MA-/ to be lost, to disappear, vanish. Napukaw ti sakit ti ulok. My headache disappeared.

PUKIS, v. /AG-/ 1. to give someone a haircut. 2. to have a haircut. --see PAPUKIS. /MANG-:-AN/ to give a haircut, cut the hair of. /MA--AN/ to have one's hair cut.

PAPUKIS, v. /AG-/ to have a haircut.

PUKKAW, n. shout, announcement, cry.
v. /AG-/ to shout or announce something in a loud voice, to call someone by shouting. /MANG-:-AN/ to call by shouting. /MANGI-:I-/ to say or tell by shouting. Impukkaw na ti nagan na. He told his name by shouting.

PUKOL, adj. having one hand or one leg.
v. /MANG-:-AN/ to cut off one hand or one leg of.

PUKPOK, v. /MANG-:-EN/ to hit, strike, hammer. Pukpukem
daytoy lansa. Strike this nail.

PUKRAY, adj. /NA-/ crumbly, friable.

PULAGID, v. /MANG-:-AN/ smear with something dirty.
/MANGI-:I-/ to wipe on something. Saan mo nga
ipulagid dayta narugit nga im-imam dita mantel.
Don't wipe your hands on that mantle. --var. PULIGAD.

PULANG, v. /AGI-, MANGI-:I-/ to return. /MA--AN/ to
recover one's good health, normal condition, money,
etc.

PULAPOL, v. /MAKI-/ to associate with, keep company
with, deal with. Ammo na ti makipulapol kadagiti
napanglaw. He knows how to associate with the poor.

PULBO, var. of PULBOS.

PULBOS [f. Sp.], n. powder. --var. PULBO.
v. /AG-/ to powder oneself. /MANG-:-AN/ to powder.
/MANGI-:I-/ to use to powder, to powder with.

PULIGAD, var. of PULAGID.

PULING, n. mote in the eye.
v. /MA-/ to catch or have a mote in the eye. Saan
ka nga tumangad ta mapulingan ka. Don't look up for
you will catch a mote in the eye. /MANGI--AN:I--AN/
to remove a mote from the eye.

PULINGLING, v. /MANG-:-EN/ to finger, toy with, tinker
with. Saan mo nga pulinglingen dayta ta dinto ket
madadael. Don't toy with that lest it gets destroyed.

PULIPOL, v. /AG-/ to wind yarn. /MANG-:-AN/ to wind
something around. /MANGI-:I-/ to wind, coil.

[1]PULIS, v. /MAKI-/ to test one's gamecock with that of
another. /MANGI-:I-/ to test (a gamecock).

[2]PULIS [f. Sp.], n. policeman.

PULISIA [f. Sp.], n. police.

PULKOK, v. /MA--AN/ to worry grievously, to be weighed
down by sadness, to feel great anxiety. Mapulkokan
kami maipanggep ti gubat. We feel great anxiety
because of the war.

PULLAT, v. /MANG-:-AN/ to plug, stuff. Pullatam dayta
botelya. Plug that bottle. /MANGI-:I-/ to use to
plug, to plug with. Daytoy ti ipullat mo dita botelya.
Use this to plug that bottle. --syn. SULLAT.

[1]PULLO, num. ten; 10: used especially in counting. WALO,
SIAM, PULLO, eight, nine, ten. --var. SANGAPULO.
--syn. DIES.

[2]PULLO, v. /AG-/ to reach the limit of another person's
patience, endurance, etc., to reach the breaking
point of another person.

PULO, num. tens, times ten. SANGAPULO, ten; DUAPULO,
twenty; TALLOPULO, thirty; UPPAT A PULO, forty;
LIMAPULO, fifty; INNEM A PULO, sixty; PITOPULO,
seventy; WALOPULO, eighty; SIAM A PULO, ninety.

PULONG, v. /AGI-, MANGI-:I-/ to report the wrongdoing
of, to denounce, inform against, tell on. Ipulong
kanto ken ni nanang mo. I will report your
wrongdoings to your mother.

PULOS, adv. 1. at all, entirely, completely: used
negatively. Saan nga nagdigos nga pulos dayta asawam
ti maysa nga tawen. Your husband did not take a bath
at all for one year. 2. completely, entirely, purely,
all of. Pulos nga babbai ti adda idiay bodaan. Those
who are at the dance are all girls.

PULOT, v. /MANG-:-AN/ to annoint, administer extreme
unction to, administer the last sacrament to.
Pinulotan diay padi daydiay agbugbugsot. The priest
administered the last sacrament to the dying person.

PUL-OY, n. breeze, a light gentle wind; a gentle blow
(of wind).
    v. /MA--AN/ to be hit by a breeze or a gentle blow
of wind.

PULPOG, v. /AG-/ to burn an animal in an open fire
until the hair or feathers are consumed and the skin
is partially cooked. /AG-, MANG-:-AN/ to burn (an

animal) in an open fire until the hair or feathers
are consumed and/or the skin is partially cooked.
/MA-/ to be burned in an open fire.

PULPOL, adj. dull, blunt, not sharp.

PULSO [f. Sp.], n. pulse.
  v. /MANGI--AN:I--AN/ to feel the pulse of.

PULSOT, v. /MANG-:-EN/ to cut off (thread or rope).
/MA-/ to be cut off.

PULTAK, v. /MANG-:-AN/ to cut the hair of unevenly.
/MA--AN/ to have one's hair cut unevenly.
  adj. having the hair unevenly cut or unevenly
shaved at the nape.

PULTING, v. /MANG-:-EN/ to cut, nip, pinch off.
Putingem dayta uggot ta mula. Pinch off the top of
that plant.

PULTIT, n. a bit of stool or feces, usually the first
or last to be expelled when defecating.   --cf.
PUGTIT.

PUNAS, v. /AG-/ to wipe one's hands, mouth, body, etc.
/AG-, MANG-:-AN/ to wipe, to clean by wiping.
Punasan yo ta lamisaan ta mangan tayon. Wipe the
table for we are going to eat now.   /MANG-:-EN/ to
wipe off. Punasen yo dayta buteg ti anak ko. Wipe
off the mucous of my child.   /MANGI-:I-/ to use to
wipe, to wipe with. Daytoy nadalus nga nisnis to
ipunas mo dita lamisaan. Use this clean rag to wipe
the table.   /MA--AN/ to be wiped clean or dry.

PUNER, adj. /NA-/ muscular, brawny.

PUNI, v. /AGI-/ to set the table.   /MANG-:-AN/ to set
(the table); to decorate, adorn (a house, etc.).

PUNIT, v. /MANGI-:I-/ to close, shut (a door, window,
etc.). Ipunit mo dayta ridaw. Close that door.
--syn. SERRA.

PUNNO, v. /AG-/ to supply or make up for what is
lacking.   /MANG-:-AN/ to supply what is lacking in
(a person or thing); hence, to overlook, be lenient
or excuse the fault of (a person).   /MANG-:-EN/ to

fill up. Punnoen na diay balay da ti tao. He will
fill up their house with people. /MA-/ [= MAPNO]
to be filled (with something). /MA--AN/ to reach
the limit of one's patience, tolerance or endurance,
to reach one's breaking point.

PUNO, see MAKAPUNO.

PÚNO, adj. /NA-/ worn out, dulled, blunted (e.g. a
knife).

PUNPON, n. burial, funeral, interment.
    v. /MANGI-:I-/ to inter, bury. /MA-/ [= MAMUNPON]
to conduct a funeral. --syn. TANEM.

    PAMUNPON, v. /MAKI-/ to assist at a funeral, to
    attend a funeral.

PUNYAL [f. Sp.], n. poniard, dagger.

PUNYOS [f. Sp.], n. cuff.

PUNGAN, n. pillow.
    v. /MAKI-/ to put one's head on the pillow of
(another).

PUNGANAY, n. beginning, start.

PUNGDOL, n. stump, stub of tree.

PUNGET, v. /MANGI-:I-/ to cut close to the bottom or
root. Saan mo nga ipunget dayta buok na. Don't cut
his hair close.

PUNGGOS, v. /MANG-:-EN/ to tie together into a bundle,
to draw together and tie (as the mouth of a sack).

PUNGO, n. bundle.
    v. /MANG-:-EN/ to tie together the four limbs of
an animal. /MA-/ to have the four limbs bound
together.

PUNGOPUNGOAN, n. wrist.

PUNGOT, v. /AG-, MANG-:-EN/ to pull the hair of.
/MA-/ to have one's hair pulled.

PUNGPONG, n. stub of bamboo. --syn. PUTEK.

PUNGSAY, v. /MANG-:-EN/ or /MANGI-:I-/ to remove by cutting, tearing, breaking, etc., to sever. Pungsayen na dayta sanga ti mangga nga nababa. He will sever that branch of the tree which is hanging low.

PUNGTIL, v. /MANG-:-EN/ or /MANGI-:I-/ to remove or sever top of. Saan mo nga puntilen dayta uggot ti saba. Don't cut off the top of the young leaf of the banana.

PUNGTO, see SIPUNGTO.

PUNGTOT, v. /AG-/ to get angry. /MAKA-/ to be angry. --syn. UNGET.

PUON, n. trunk, origin, beginning.

PUONAN [cf. PUON], n. capital in business.

PUOR, n. fire, conflagration.
      v. /AG-/ to make a fire. /MANG-:-AN/ to burn. /MA--AN/ to be burned.

PUPOK, v. /MANG-:-EN/ or /MANGI-:I-/ to shut in, confine, lock up.

PUPULAR [f. Eng.], adj. popular.

PURAR, v. /MA-/ to be dazzled. Saan mo nga ibatog dayta ubing dita silaw tapno saan nga mapurar. Don't put that child under the light so that he won't be dazzled.
      adj. /MAKA-/ dazzling.

PURAW, adj. white.
      v. /-UM-/ to be this.

PURGA [f. Sp.], n. purgative.
      v. /AG-/ to take a purgative. /MANG-:-EN/ to give a purgative to. /MA-/ to be purged.

PURGATORIO [f. Sp.], n. purgatory, hell.

PURI, v. /MANG-:-EN/ to cause to fall off or down, to drop from its base. /MA-/ to fall off or down, to drop from its base. Mano ti napuri nga ngipen mo? How many of your teeth fell off?

PURIKET, n. 1. sticktight, bur marigold, beggar's-ticks.
2. its fruit.

PURIS, n. sliver or thorn that pricks the skin especially
at the sole of the foot.
v. /MA--AN/ to be pricked by a sliver or thorn.

PUR-IS, n. excrement, feces.

PURNGI, v. /AG-/ to grin, to laugh showing the teeth.

[1]PURO [f. Sp.], adj. pure, genuine, real.

[2]PURO, n. island.

[1]PUROK, n. group, aggregation, cluster, gathering,
district. Adu ti balay ditoy purok mi. There are
many houses in our district.

[2]PUROK, v. /-UM-/ to attack, assault. Dika nga umasideg
ta manok ta pumurok. Don't go near that chicken for
it will attack (you).

PURONG, n. a kind of white, elongated fresh-water
fish.   --see SISIAW, LUDONG.

PUROS, v. /AG-, MANG-:-EN/ to pick (a fruit).   /MA-/
to be picked: said of fruits.

PURSILANA [f. Sp.], n. porcelain.

PURSING, v. /MA-/ to be broken off, to be severed.
Mapursing ta aputan ti payong ko. The handle of my
umbrella will be broken off.

PURTIS, var. of PROTESTANTE.

PURTOK, v. /MANG-:-AN/ to cut (the hair of someone).
Apay nga pinurtokan ta buok ti anak ko? Why did you
cut the hair of my child?

PURWAK, v. /MANGI-:I-/ to scatter, throw away, sow,
broadcast.   /MANG-:-AN/ to throw something to.   /MAI-/
to be scattered, thrown away, broadcast.   /MA--AN/
to be thrown something, to have something thrown to.

PUSA, n. cat.

PUSAKSAK, adj. /NA-/ pure white, dazzling white.

PUSASAW, v. /-UM-/ to become faded, discolored.
Pimmusasaw ti pintura ti balay da. The paint of their
house became faded.
    adj. /NAG-/ faded, discolored.

[1]PUSEG, n. navel.

[2]PUSEG, v. /MANG-:-AN/ [= PUSGAN] to designate, assign,
appoint. /MA--AN/ [= MAMUSEG:PUSGAN] to be
designated, appointed, assigned. Isu ti napusgan nga
presidente ti gimong mi. It was he who was designated
president of our association.

PUSEK, adj. /NA-/ compact, compressed, compacted,
fully packed or stuffed. /MANG-:-EN/ to pack or
stuff fully and tightly.

PUSGAN, adj. /NA-/ sincere, fervent, ardent,
passionate.

PUSI, v. /AG-, MANG-:-EN/ to shell (corn), to knock
off (a tooth). /MA-/ to be shelled: said of corn;
to be knocked off: said of a tooth.

PUSING, v. /MANGI-:I-/ to separate, sever, detach.
Narigat nga ipusing ti maymaysa nga inanak. It is
hard to separate an only child.

PUSIPOS, v. /MANG-:-EN/ or /MANGI-:I-/ to turn around,
rotate. --var. PUSPOS.

PUSISAK, v. /MANGI-:I-/ to dispose of, get rid of,
sell. /MAI-/ to dispose of, get rid of, sell.
Narigat nga maipusisak toy karne. It is hard to
dispose of this meat.

PUSISIT, v. /AG-/ to squirt, spurt water or other
liquid substance. Agpusisit diay gripo. The faucet
is squirting water.

PUSIT, n. squid.

PUSKOL, adj. /NA-/ thick, dense. Napuskol dayta libro
nga basbasaem. That book which you are reading is
thick.

PUSLIT, v. /MANGI-:I-/ to smuggle.
   adj. smuggled.

PUSO, n. heart.

PUS-ONG, n. abdomen.

PUSOT, v. /MANG-:-EN/ to wean.   /MA-/ to be weaned.

PUSPOS, var. of PUSIPOS.

PUSSUAK, v. /AG-, -UM-/ to bubble, gush out.

PUSTA, n. stake, wager, bet.
   v. /AG-/ to make a bet, place a bet.   /MANGI-:I-/
   to bet, wager.

PUTA, n. prostitute.   --syn. PAMPAM.

PUTAN, n. handle (of a knife, ax, etc.).

PUTAR, v. /MANG-:-EN/ 1. to construct, build.
   Mangputar ka ti pagyanan tayo. Construct something
   where we are going to stay. 2. to invent, create.
   Mangputar ka ti istorya. Invent a story.
      adj. not completely made, incompletely made (e.g.
   a window, door, house).

PUTED, n. a piece, a part of something.
   v. /MANG-:-EN/ [= PUTDEN] to cut off, sever.
   /MANG-:-AN/ [= PUTDAN] to cut a part off, to shorten.
   /MA-/ to be cut off.

PUTEK, n. stub of bamboo.   --syn. PUNGPONG.

PUTIPOT, v. /MANGI-:I-/ to wind around. Iputipot mo
   daytoy tali dita adigi. Wind this string around that
   post.   /MANG-:-AN/ to wind something around.
   Putiputam daytoy adigi ti tali. Wind a string around
   this post.

PUTO, n. a kind of soft rice cake.

PUTOL, v. /MANG-:-AN/ to cut something from.

PUTONG, adj. solitary, alone, sole.
   v. /MANGI-:I-/ to isolate, separate from the rest.

[1]PUTOT, n. descendant, progeny, child, offspring.

   KAPUTOTAN, n. generation.

   SANGAPUTOTAN, n. one generation, one family.

[2]PUTOT, v. /MANG-:-AN/ to shorten (sleeves, trousers, skirts, etc.).
   n. shorts.

[1]PUTPUT, v. /MANG-:-EN/ to do completely or thoroughly, to finish. Putputem daytoy trabahom. Finish your work.

[2]PUTPUT, v. /AG-/ to make a sound like that of a horn.

PUTTOT, n. fishpond.

PUYAT, v. /AG-/ to stay awake late in the night or the whole night. /MANG-:-AN, -EN/ to cause (someone) to stay awake, to prevent someone from having his sleep. /MA--AN/ or /MA-/ to lack enough sleep; hence, to be sleepy.

PUYO, v. /-UM-/ to swell, puff up. Pimmuyo diay kankanen nga lutlutoek. The cake which I was baking puffed up.

PUYOT, v. /MANG-:-AN, -EN/ to blow. Puyutam ta apoy. Blow the fire.

PUYUPUY, n. breeze, a gentle blow of the wind.
   adj. /NA-/ breezy.

RAAY, n. a cluster (of fruits or rice).

RABA, v. /-UM-/ to increase, worsen. Rimmaba ti sakit ni Rosa. Rose's sickness worsened.

RABAK, n. joke, jest, banter.
   v. /MANG-:-EN/ to joke with, banter, make fun of.

RABANOS [f. Sp.], n. radish.

RABARAB, v. /MANG-:-AN/ to trim at the ends. Rabarabam dayta buok ti ubing. Trim the hair of that child.

RABAW, n. top (of).
v. /-UM-:-AN/ to go on top of. Rumabaw ka dita
lamisaan. Go on top of that table.

PARABAW, v. /AG-/ to go on top of. /MANGI-:I-/ to
put on top of. Iparabaw mo daytoy dita lamisaan.
Put this on top of that table.

RABER, adj. /NA-/ thick, lush.

RABII, n. night, evening. Rabiin. It is already night.
v. /-UM-/ to turn to night. /MA--AN/ to be caught
by darkness or night.

RABNIS, v. /MANG-:-EN/ to snatch away, grab away.
Saan mo nga rabnisen dayta buneng nga igiggaman ta
ubing. Don't snatch away the big knife that the
child is holding. --syn. RABNOTA.

RABNOT, v. /MANG-:-EN/ to snatch away, grab away.
--syn. RABNIS.

RABNGIS, v. /MANG-:-EN/ to address familiarly, to
treat with disrespect. Apay nga rabrabngisen nak?
Why are you treating me with disrespect?

RABOK, v. /MAI-/ to come upon by chance, to stumble at,
to join or be invited to join by chance. Nairabok
kami ti ponsion da. We joined their party by chance.

RABONG, n. bamboo shoot.

RABOY, adj. /NA-/ frail, delicate, easily injured.

[1]RABRAB, adj. /NAG-/ talkative.

[2]RABRAB, adj. /NAG-/ greedy, voracious, avaricious.
--syn. RAWET.

RADIO [f. Eng.], n. radio.

RADRAD, v. /MANGI-:I-/ to rub vigorously on something.
Iradrad mo ta asin dita karne. Rub the salt
vigorously on that meat. /MANG-:-AN/ to rub
vigorously with something. Radradam ti asin dayta
karne. Rub that meat vigorously with salt.

RAEB, v. /-UM-/ to go deep inside, to go to the
interior of. Saan kay nga rumaeb dita kabakbakiran.
Don't go deep inside the forest.

RAEM, v. /AG-/ to treat with respect, to show deference to, to be polite or courteous to, to honor. Raemem daigit naganak kenka. Treat your parents with respect.

RAEP, v. /AG-/ to transplant rice seedlings. /MANGI-:I-/ to transplant (rice seedlings). /MAKI-/ to transplant rice seedlings for someone.

RAGADI, n. carpenter's saw.
     v. /AG-, MANG-:-EN/ to saw, to cut or wound with a saw. /MANGI-:I-/ to use to saw something, to saw with.

RAGAS, v. /MANG-:-EN/ to cut (a garment).

RAG-O, n. joy, happiness, delight, exultation.
     v. /AG-/ to rejoice, exult. Agrag-o dagiti tattao ta nangabak ti kandidato da. The people are rejoicing for their candidate won.

RAGPAT, v. /MANG-:-EN/ to obtain, attain, achieve. Masapul nga ragpatem ti kangatoan nga adal. It is necessary that you attain the highest level of learning. /MANGI-:I-/ to elevate, raise, advance, lead. Iragpat na kami iti nasayaat nga biag. Lead us to a good life.

RAGSAK, n. joy, happiness, merriment.
     adj. /NA-/ joyful, happy, merry.

RAGUP, n. assembly, gathering.
     v. /MANGI-:I-/ to join, connect, put together. /AG- + R2/ to be together, stay together, unite. Agraragup kayo nga mapan idiay ili. You go to town together.

RAGUT, v. /AG-/ crave, desire strongly, yearn for. Agragut nga mapan diay Amerika ni Rosa. Rose yearns to go to America (i.e. the United States).

RAGUTOK, v. /AG-/ to make a cracking sound as burning reeds.

RAHA, n. rajah.

RAIT, v. /MANGI-:I-/ to put alongside of. --syn. DINNA.

RAKAB, v. /MANGI-:I-/ to fasten, tie. Irakab mo dayta

manok dita adigi. Tie the chicken to that post.
--syn. RAKED.

RAKED, v. /MANGI-:I-/ to fasten, tie. Iraked mo dayta
pusa dita poste. Tie the cat to that post. --syn.
RAKAB.

[1]RAKEM, n. a reaper's knife used to cut rice below the
ear.

[2]RAKEM, n. fistful; SANGARAKEM, one fistful.
   v. /MANG-:-EN/ to scoop a handful of.

RAKEP, v. /AG-, MANG-:-EN/ to embrace, hug, clasp to
the body.

RAKIT, n. raft.

RAKRAK, v. /MANG-:-EN/ to demolish, tear down, tear
apart, destroy. /MA-/ to be demolished.

RAKURAK, v. /MAI-/ to spread, disseminate, broadcast.
Nadaras nga mairakurak ti dakes nga damag. Bad news
easily spreads.

RÁMAN, v. /MANGI-:I-/ to include, take in, allow to
participate. /-UM-/ to participate with in an
activity.

AGRAMAN, adv. with, including, in addition. --syn.
   PATI.

RAMÁN, n. taste, flavor.
     v. /-UM-:-AN/ 1. to taste, flavor. Kayat mo nga
ramanan daytoy lutlutoek? Do you want to taste what
I am cooking? 2. usually with /MAKA-:MA--AN/ to be
able to experience or undergo. Naramanan na ti di
nga mangan ti maysa nga aldaw. He experienced not
eating for one day.

RAMARAM, v. /MANG-:-EN/ to spread to, extend to,
affect. Iyadayom dayta lupot dita apoy ta dinanto
ket ramaramen. Take that cloth far from the fire
lest it spreads to it.

RAMAS, v. /MANG-:-EN/ to squeeze, crush, or knead with
the hand while turning over. --syn. GAMAY.

RAMAY, n. finger, toe.

RAMBAK, n. feast, festival, festivity, celebration.
   adj. /NA-/ joyous, pompous, gala.
   v. /AG-/ to celebrate, rejoice, be happy. Agrambak
tayo ta nangabak ti kandidato tayo. Let's celebrate
for our candidate won.

RAMIT, n. implement, tool, appliance.

RAMOK, adj. /NA-/ abundant, copious, plentiful.

RAMOT, n. root.
   v. /AG-/ to develop or grow roots.

RAM-OY, v. /MANG-:-EN/ to buy at less than the real
value.

RANA, v. /MANG-:-EN/ or /MANGI-:I-/ to do (an action)
at approximately the same time as another. /MAI-/
to happen or occur at approximately the same time as
another action or event. /AG-/ [with pl. subject]
to meet or see each other by pre-arrangement.

RANSO [f. Sp.], n. ranch.

RANUD, v. /AG- + R2:PAG- + R2/ [with pl. subject] to
share.

RANYAG, adj. /NA-/ very bright, brilliant, lustrous.

RANG-AY, adj. /NA-/ prosperous, affluent, well-off,
   wealthy.
   v. /-UM-/ to become this. Rimmang-ay ti ili mi.
Our town became prosperous.

RANGEN, v. /-UM-/ to flare up, blaze up; to be aroused,
   inflamed. Rimmangen ti apoy. The fire blazed up.

RANGET, n. fight, battle, combat.
   v. /AG-/ [with pl. subject] to fight, to engage in
a combat or battle. Nagrangep dagiti soldado ti
Amerika ken Hapon. The soldiers of America and
Japan engaged in a combat.

RANGGAS, adj. /NA-/ cruel, injurious, destructive,
   harmful.
   v. /MANG-:-AN/ to harm, injure, hurt. Saan mo nga
ranggasan dayta ubing. Don't harm that child.
/MA--AN/ to be harmed or injured by someone through
black magic.

RANGKAP, v. /AG-:-EN/ to gain, profit. Adu ti rangkapen ti tao nga nagaget. An industrious person will gain many things.

RANGKAY; RANGRANGKAY, v. /MANG-:-EN/ to cut up, to cut into pieces, to chop or carve. Rangrangkayem dayta manok. Cut that chicken into several pieces.

RANGPAYA, adj. /NA-/ branchy, full of branches.

RANGRANG, adj. /NA-/ blazing, flaring, glaring, dazzling.
   v. /-UM-/ to become this.

RANGTAY, n. bridge.   --syn. KALANTAY.

RAOT, v. /MANG-:-EN/ to attack, invade. Mapan mi raoten dagiti tulisan. We go attack the robbers.

RAPAS, adj. being a person whose palm is traversed by a straight and continuous line.
   v. /MANG-:-EN/ to cut at one stroke.

RAPIN, v. /AG-/ [with pl. subject] to be stuck together, to be side by side each other. Nagrapin toy kuarta nga inted mo kaniak. The money you gave me is stuck together. /MANGI-:I-/ to insert, put between, enclose. Inrapin ko tay pisos idiay surat ko. I inserted the one peso in my letter.

RAPIS, adj. /NA-/ slender, slim, thin.
   v. /-UM-/ to become this.

RAPIT, v. /MANG-:-EN/ to take two or more with one hand.

RAPOK, n. commotion.
   v. /MAKI-:KA-/ to do something with another or others, to join another or others in an activity. /AG-/ [with pl. subject] to do something jointly or together.

RARASA, see RASA.

RAREK, n. rhonchus, rattle, rale.
   v. /AG-/ to have rhonchus, rale, or rattle.

RAREM, v. /MANGI-:I-/ to immerse, dip (into water). Irarem mo dayta ulom dita danum. Dip your head into the water.

RARIT, v. /MANG-:-EN/ to devastate, ravage, destroy, ruin.

[1]RASA, n. a kind of large edible crab.

[2]RASA; RARASA, n. a cutaneous eruption caused by sitting on a carabao or constant walking through tall grasses and rice plants.
   v. /AG-/ to be afflicted with this.

RASAY, adj. 1. scarce, very few. 2. rare, infrequent. 3. sparse, thin.
   v. /-UM-/ to become any of these.

RASI, adj. /NA-/ delicate, fragile, frangible.

RASOK, v. /-UM-/ to flare up, blaze. Rimmasok ti apoy gapo ti kinaangin na. The fire flared up due to the much wind. /AG-/ to produce steam, steam up.

RASYON [f. Sp.], n. ration.
   v. /AG-, MANG-:-AN/ to ration to.   /AGI-, MANGI-:I-/ to distribute as ration, to ration.

RATA, n. chink, crack; a small cleft or fissure. --syn. RIKKI.

RATIW, adj. /NA-/ very slim or slender, very thin.

RAWAY; RAWAYRAWAYAN, adj. branchy, full of branches. --syn. RANGPAYA.

RAWET, adj. /(NA-)/ voracious, gluttonous, ravenous.

RAY-AW, v. /MANG-:-AN/ to make laugh, to amuse, entertain.

RAYO, v. /AG-:PAG--AN/ to be attracted to, to be pleased with, to like, be fond of. Adu to agrayo kenkuana. Many are attracted to her.

RAYOS [f. Sp.], n. spoke of a wheel.

RAYRAY, v. /-UM-/ to light up brightly, to flash, flare up. Rimmayray diay silaw da. Their lamp lit up brightly.

RAYUMA [f. Sp.], n. rheumatism.
   v. /AG-/ to be afflicted with this.

REBBA, v. /MANG-:-EN/ to tear down, demolish, destroy.
Saan mo nga rebbaen dayta balay mi. Don't demolish
our house. /MA-/ [= MARBA] to collapse, to be
wrecked. Narba diay alad da. Their fence collapsed.

REBBEK, v. /MANG-:-EN/ to raze, ravage, devastate,
ruin.

REBBENG, n. duty, obligation, responsibility.
     v. /-UM-/ [= RUMBENG] to be proper, just,
reasonable, fit, becoming. Saan nga rumbeng dayta
nga aramid mo. That act of yours is not becoming.

KARBENGAN, n. duty, privilege, prerogative, right.

REBOLBER [rɛbolbɛr; f. Eng.], n. revolver (a pistol).

REBOLUSION [f. Sp.], n. revolution.

REBOLUSIONARIO [rɛbolusionario; f. Sp.], adj.
revolutionary.

REBREB, v. /MANGI-:I-/ to plunge into, immerse, sink
in. Saan mo nga irebreb ta bagim ti kinadakes. Don't
plunge yourself into evil.

REBULTO [rɛbulto], var. of BULTO.

REDDEK, n. sparerib.
     v. /MANG-:-EN/ to cut into (smaller) parts or
pieces, to cut up. Reddekem dagita tultulang. Cut
those bones into smaller pieces.

REELEKSIONISTA [rɛɛlɛksionista; f. Sp.], n. reelectionist.

REGGAAY, v. /MANG-:-EN/ to cause to collapse, crumble
down. /MA-/ [= MARGAAY] to collapse, crumble down.
Nargaay ti rangtay idiay ili mi. The bridge in our
town collapsed.

REGGES, v. /MANG-:-EN/ to tear off or detach by
twisting or pulling.

REGGET, adj. /NA-/ diligent, earnest, assiduous (in
doing something). Naregget nga agsapul ni Pedro.
Peter is diligent in searching for something.

REGKANG, n. interstice, crevice, crack. Simmirip diay
baro iti regkang ti diding. The young man peeped
through the crack in the wall.

REGREG, v. /MANG-:-EN/ to drop, cause to fall down.
/MA-/ to drop down, fall down. Naregreg diay bunga ti
kayo. The fruit of the tree dropped down. /MAKA-/ to
become sick due according to folk belief to having
"dropped" or lost part of his soul or spirit.

REGTA, adj. /NÁ-/ upright, virtuous, just.

REHION [f. Sp.], n. region.

REHISTRADO [f. Sp.], adj. registered.

REKADO [rɛkado; f. Sp.], n. spice, condiment, seasoning.
v. /MANG-:-AN/ to add spice, condiment or seasoning
to.

REKKET, v. /AG-/ [with pl. subject] to stick together.
Nagrekket dagiti papel ko. My papers stuck together.

REKOMENDA [rɛkomɛnda; f. Sp.], v. /MANGI-:I-/ to
recommend.

REKOMENDASION [rɛkomɛndasion; f. Sp.], n. recommendation.

REKORD [rɛkord; f. Eng.], n. record.
v. /MANGI-:I-/ to record. /MAI-/ to be recorded.

RUM [f. Sp.?], n. rum.

[1]SA, adv. probably, very likely.

[2]SA, conj. then, after which: introduces a clause that
refers to an action subsequent to the previous one.

[3]SA, var. of MAYSA, one: used only with a following NGA
interchangeably with MAYSA. MAYSA NGA BULAN or SANGA
BULAN, one month.

[4]SA, interj. an expression used to call or drive away a
cat.

SAAD, v. /MANGI-:I-/ to put, lay, place, set or fix
(in a place or position).

KASASAAD, n. status, condition, situation.

SAAN, adv. no. --var. HAAN.

SAANMAN, adv. of course I will (in answer to a negative question).

SAANG, v. /MANGI-:I-/ to put on the stove over a fire in order to cook or heat.

SABA, n. banana.

SABADO [f. Sp.], n. Saturday.
SABADO DE GLORIA, the Saturday before Easter Sunday.

SABALI, adj. another; different.
v. /AG-/ to become different; to change. /MANG-:-AN/ 1. to change. 2. to do again.

SABANGAN, n. mouth of a river.
v. /-UM-/ to go to the mouth of a river.

SABBUAG, v. /MANGI-:I-/ 1. to cast, throw. 2. to cast a gamecock at its opponent. /MANG-:-AN/ 1. to cast or throw (something) at (a person or animal). 2. to cast (a gamecock) at (another gamecock).

SABENG, n. the stench of some fruits.
adj. /NA-/ stenchy.

SABET, v. /-UM-, MANG-:-EN/ to meet someone. /AG-/ [with plural subject] to meet each other. /MANGI-:I-/ to present (something to someone) upon arrival.

SABIDONG, n. poison. --cf. GAMUT.
v. /MANG-:-AN/ to poison.

SABIKEL, v. /MANGI-:I-/ to insert inside one's waistband.

SAB-IT, n. hook on which to hang things.
v. /MANGI-:I-/ to hang, suspend on a hook.

SABLE [f. Sp.], n. sword, saber.

SABLUG, see PASABLUG.

SABSAB, v. /AG-, MANG-:-EN/ 1. to eat or chew noisily and voraciously. 2. to bite by snapping the jaw, as a pig.

SAB-UK, v. /AG-, MANG-:-EN/ to carry in one's lap, skirt, apron, etc. /MANGI-:I-/ to put in one's lap, skirt, apron, etc.

SABUN [f. Sp.], n. soap.
v. /AG-, MANG-:-EN/ to wash with soap, to soap. /MANGI-:I-/ to wash with soap in a place.

SABUNG, n. flower, blossom.
v. /AG-, MANGI-:I-/ to bear flowers, to blossom. Agsabungen ta mangga yon. Your mango tree is now blossoming.

SABUNG TI KUKO, lunule of the nail.

SAB-UNG, v. /MANGI-:I-/ to give a dowry. /MANG-:-AN/ to give (someone a dowry). --see PANAB-UNG.

SABUNGANAY, n. the unopened flower cluster of the banana.
v. /AG-/ to have this (said of a banana).

SABUT, n. coconut shell.

SADAG, v. /AG-, -UM-:-AN/ to lean on. /MANGI-:I-/ to cause to lean on.

SADAR, see KASADAR.

SADI, prep. in, at, to (a geographical place).

SADIAY, dem. there: far from both speaker and hearer. --var. of IDIAY.

SADIN, var. of SADINU.

SADINU, inter. where?

SADIWA, adj. /(NA-)/ fresh: said of fish, vegetable or meat. ·
v. /-UM-/.

SADSAD, v. /-UM-/ to get stuck to the ground. /MANGI-:I-/ to cause to get stuck to the ground. /MAI-/ to be caused to get stuck to the ground.

SADUT, adj. /(NA-)/ lazy. /MA-/ to feel sluggish, have no appetite to eat or do anything.
   v. /-EN/ to feel lazy about doing something.

AGSASADUT, adj. spiritless, listless, sluggish.

SADYA, adj. /NA-/ gentle, kind, tender, gracious.

SAED, v. /AG-, MANG-:-EN/ to ambush.

SAEM, adj. /NA-/ sharp, acute; intense, as pain.

SAG-, a numerical prefix used to form distributive numerals. sagdudua, two each.

SAGA, v. /MANG-:-EN/ to throw into disorder.

SAGABA, n. suffering.
   v. /AG-, MANG-:-EN/ to experience, undergo, go through (a suffering).

SAGABASAB, v. /AG-/ to have a fever.

[1]SAGAD, n. harrow.

[2]SAGAD, n. broom made of grass, or flowers of grass.
   v. /AG-, MANG-:-EN/ to sweep away (dirt). /AG-, MANG-:-AN/ to sweep away the dirt from.

SAGANA, v. /AG-, -UM-/ to prepare oneself, make oneself ready. /MANGI-:I-/ to prepare or make ready (something).

SAGANAD, v. /-UM-/ to follow a sequence or order. /AG-/ [with pl. subject] to follow one after the other. /MANGI-:I-/ to cause to follow in a sequence.

SAGANG, v. /MAKA-/ to meet, encounter.

SAGANGASANG, adj. /NA-/ pungent, piquant, biting.
   v. /-UM-/.

SAGAP, n. a large net.

SAGAPA, n. a ring made of braided strips of rattan or bamboo on which a pot is placed.

SAGAT, v. /AG-, MANG-:-EN/ to filter, strain.

SAGAT, n. a tree with very hard wood.

SAGAWISIW, n. whistle.
v. /AG-/ to whistle. /MANG-:-AN/ to whistle at.

SAGAYSAY, n. comb.
v. /AG-/ to comb one's hair. /MANG-:-EN/ to comb.

SAGEPSEP, v. /MANG-:-EN/ to seep.

SAGGAYSA, num. one each.
v. /AG-/ [with pl. subject] to have one each. /-EN/
to separate one by one.

SAGIBAR, adj. /NA-/ biting, cutting, stinging.

SAGIBSIB, n. shoot of sugar cane, taro, banana, etc.
v. /AG-/ to have or develop this. --syn. SUBBUAL.

SAGIBU, n. aftergrowth of rice plant or any similar
plant.

SAGID, v. /AG-, MANG-:-EN/ to touch esp. with the hand.
/-UM-/ to brush against, touch.

SAGIKSIK, adj. /NA-/ brisk, lively, active.
v. /-UM-/.

SAGIRAD, v. /AG-/ to trail, touch the bottom or surface.
/MANGI-:I-/ to cause to trail or touch the bottom or
surface.

SAGKING, adj. unstable, unbalanced, tilted on one side.
v. /AG-/ to be like this.

SAGMAK, v. /MANGI-:I-/ to endanger, put in jeopardy,
imperil.

SAGMAMANO, see under MANO.

SAGPAT, v. /-UM-/ to ascend, climb up on, go up to,
mount. /MANGI-:I-/ to put up, take up, carry up.

SAGPAW, n. meat, fish or shrimp mixed with vegetables
in cooking a dish.
v. /MANGI-:I-/ to use as this.

SAGRADO [f. Sp.], adj. pious, religious, devout.

SAGSAG, v. /MANG-:-EN/ to wear out, destroy by beating or shaking.

SAGO, n. watery secretion in wounds.

SAGU, n. the arrowroot.

SAGUBANIT, n. indisposition, lassitude, temporary illness.
    v. /AG-, -EN/ to have this.

SAGUD, v. /AGI-, MANGI-:I-/ to cause to get caught on a hook.

SAGUDAY, n. prerogative, privilege, distinction.

SAGUMBI, n. annex, side-room.

SAGURSUR, adj. /NA-/ coarse, full of loose fibers or knots, burly.
    v. /AG-/ to be like this.

SAGUT, n. gift, present, offering.
    v. /MANG-:-AN/ to give (someone) a present, to give an offering to.

SAG-UT, n. thread, cotton yarn used in weaving.

SAIBBEK, v. /AG-/ to sob, cry fitfully.

SAIDDEK, v. /AG-/ to hiccup, have a hiccup.

SAINNEK, v. /AG-/ to cry breathily.

SAIR, v. /MANG-:-EN/ to irritate, needle.

SAIRO, n. devil, tempter.
    v. /MANG-:-EN/ to tempt, lead to evil.

SAIS, var. of SEIS, six.

SAKA, n. foot, leg.
  SAKAANAN, n. the part of the bed where the feet are placed when sleeping.

SAKA, n. ransom.
    v. /MANG-:-EN/ to ransom, redeem a pledge.

SAKAB, v. /-UM-/ to stretch oneself full length on a bench, board, etc. /MANGI-:I-/ to stretch (someone or something) on a bench, board, etc.

SAKAL, v. /MANG-:-EN/ to stir the contents of.

SAKANG, adj. bow-legged.

SAKAPUEGO [f. Sp.], n. box of matches. --var. KASAPUEGO. --syn. GURABIS.

SAKASAK, v. /-UM-/ to force one's way through roughly.

SAKAT, adj. with glans of penis completely uncovered. --syn. PUNGAT.

SAKAY, v. /AG-, -UM-/ to ride on. /MANGI-:-I-/ to load on or in. --syn. LUGAN.

SAKBAT, v. /MANG-:-EN/ to carry on the shoulder.

SAKBAY, v. /-UM-/ to obstruct the way.
     adj. /MA--AN/ (this) coming, future.

SAKDU, v. /AG-, MANG-:-EN/ to fetch (water).

SAKIT, n. sickness, illness, malady.
     adj. /NA-/ painful, sore, aching. /MA-/ sick, ill.
     v. /AG-/ to be sick or ill.

SAKLANG, adv. front of, before.
     v. /MANGI-:I-/ to bring in front of or in presence of; to bring to court.

SAKLUT, n. lap.
     v. /MANG-:-EN/ to carry in one's lap.

SAKMAL, v. /MANG⁺ :-EN/ to catch with the mouth; to run away with.

SAKMUL, v. /MANG-:-EN/ or /MANGI-:I-/ to take or put into the mouth esp. food.

SAKRAB, v. /MANG-:-EN/ to seize with the teeth, grab with the mouth, bite.

SAKRIPISYO [f. Sp.], n. sacrifice, hardship.
     v. /AG-/ to suffer hardships.

SAKRISTAN [f. Sp.], n. sacristan, acolyte.
 v. /AG-/ to become this.

SAKRUY, v. /MANG-:-EN/ to carry in the arms.

SAKSAK, v. /AG-/ to clear one's throat.

SAKSI, n. witness.
 v. /AG-/ to be a witness, appear as witness.
 /MANG-:-AN/ to testify for, be a witness of, attest
 for.

SAKSUPUN [f. Eng.], n. saxophone.   --var. SUKSUPON.
 v. /AG-/ to play this.

SAKU [f. Sp.], n. sack.   --cf. MANTALUNA.
 v. /MANGI-:I-/ to put in a sack.

SAKUL, v. /AG-/ to limp, the sole of the foot being
 turned inward and its edge resting on the ground.

SAKUNTAP, n. the noise made by the hogs when eating.
 v. /AG-/ to smack.   --cf. SANUNTIP.

SAKUP, v. /-UM-, MANG-:-EN/ to include, put under one's
 jurisdiction.

SALA, n. dance.
 v. /AG-/ to dance.   /MANG-:-EN/ to dance.   /MANGI-:
 I-/ to dance with (someone).

SALABAT, n. ginger drink.

SALABUG, v. /MA--AN/ to get wet through leaks, to
 suffer from leakage, e.g. houses.

SALABUSAB, adj. /(NA-)/ inconsiderate, thoughtless.

SALAKAN, n. protector, saviour.
 v. /MANGI-:I-/ to save, protect, assist.

SALAKDAY, v. /MANGI-:I-/ to hang as to dry or air.

SALAKI [f. Sp.?], interj. an expression used to drive
 away dogs.

SALAKNIB, n. protection.
 v. /MANG-:-AN/ to protect, guard.

SALAKSAK, n. a kind of kingfisher.
v. /AG-/ to cry like this.

SALAMA, v. /MAKA-:MA--AN/ to catch in the act of doing something.

SALAMAGI, n. 1. the tamarind tree. 2. its fruit.

SALAMANGKA, v. /AG-/ to do some juggling tricks. /MANG-:-EN/ to trick.

SALAMBAW, n. a kind of large fishing net.

SALANGAD, v. /-UM-, MANG-:-EN/ to disagree with, argue with.

SALAPANG, n. trident for sling shot.

SALAPASAP, v. /MANGI-:I-/ to spread, disseminate.

SALAPAY, v. /AG-, MANGI-:I-/ to hang or suspend on a clothesline, wire, rope, fence, etc. in order to dry or air.

SALAPI, n. fifty centavos, half a peso.

SALAPSAP, v. /MANG-:-EN/ to pick, pluck, gather esp. bulky fruits.

SALAPUN, v. /-UM-, MANG-:-EN/ to collide with.

SALAS [f. Sp.], n. living room, receiving room, hall.

SAL-AT, interj. an expression used to express displeasure, impatience, anger, etc.

SALAWASAW, adj. talkative, tattler; gossip; unreliable.
v. /AG-/ to talk loosely; hence to lie, blaspheme.
/MANG-:-EN/ to talk loosely to, lie to, blaspheme.

SALAYSAY, n. story, narration.
v. /AG-, MANG-:-EN/ or /MANGI-:I-/ to tell, relate, narrate (to someone). /MANG-:-EN/ to investigate, find out, inquire about.

SALBAG, interj. an expression used to express displeasure, impatience, irritation, etc.

SALBAT, v. /MANG-:-EN/ to intercept, stop on the way.

SALDA, v. /AG-, MANGI-:I-/ to mortgage.

SALEMSEM, adj. /NA-/ fresh, cool, invigorating.
v. /-UM-/.

SALENG, n. a kind of pine tree.

SALI, v. /-UM-/ to place oneself in the way. /MANGI-:
I-/ to place (oneself) in the way.

SALIKAD, n. waistband.
v. /MANGI-:I-/ to insert in one's waistband.

SALIKAWKAW, v. /MANG-:-AN/ to surround.

SALIKBAW, v. /-UM-, MANG-:-AN/ to overtake by taking a
shorter route.

SALINDRU [f. Sp.], n. harmonica. --var. SILINDRU.
v. /AG-/ to play this.

SALINGED, v. /AG-/ to hide, take cover. /MANGI-:I-/ to
hide, keep away from danger.

SALINGSING, v. /AG-, MANG-:-AN/ to trim esp. felled
branches of trees.

SALIP, n. contest, competition.
v. /-UM-/ to compete with, join in a competition.

SALISAL, v. /AG-/ [with pl. subject] to compete with
one another.

SAL-IT, n. lightning, flash of lightning. --cf. KIMAT.
interj. expresses displeasure, disappointment,
irritation, etc.

SALIWANWAN, adj. /NA-/ free, without any obstruction.
v. /-UM-/.

SALIWASIW, v. /-UM-/ to transgress, go astray, sin.
/AG-/ to separate and meet again as in country dances.

SALLABAY, v. /AG-/ to ride on the back of someone.
/MANG-:-EN/ to carry on one's back.

SALLADAY, n. something to lean on as when lying down, e.g. a pillow.
v. /AG-/ to rest one's legs on someone or something like a pillow. /MANGI-:I-/ to rest (one's legs) on someone or a pillow.

SALLAKUNG, adj. knock-kneed.
v. /AG-/ to be like this.

SALLAPID, n. tresses of hair; braid.
v. /MANG-:-EN/ to braid. /MANGI-:I-/ to insert in a braid. /AG-/ [with pl. subject] to fling into each other.

SALLAPIDING, n. mole. --syn. SIDING.

SALLAWID, n. a ring used to keep a gate closed.
v. /MANGI-:I-/ to close (a gate) with this.

SALMUN [f. Sp.?], n. salmon.

SALPUT, v. /-UM-/ to go through. /MANG-:-EN/ to pierce through.

SALSAL, v. /AG-/ to masturbate. /AG-, MANG-:-EN/ 1. to beat repeatedly. 2. to masturbate.

SALSALAMAGI, n. tonsil.

SALTA, v. /-UM-, MANG-:-EN/ to invade.

[1]SALTEK, n. house lizard.
v. /AG-/ to cry like this.

[2]SALTEK, v. /MANGI-:I-/ to drop abruptly so as to hit the ground, floor, etc. with force.

SALUDSUD, n. question, query, inquiry.
v. /AG-, MANG-:-EN/ to ask, inquire about, question.

[1]SALUG, v. /-UM-/ to descend, go down a slope, go to a lower place.

[2]SALUG, n. slip of sugar cane, upper part of sugar cane stalk used for propagation.

SALUGSUG, n. a thorn or the like which gets embedded under the nail or the surface of the skin.
v. /MA--AN/ to be pricked by a thorn, needle or the like.

SALUKAG, adj. /NA-/ diligent, attentive.
v. /MANGI-:I-/ to call to one's attention, to make (someone) aware of.

SALUKET, v. /MANGI-:I-/ to insert or stick in the wall.

SALUKSUK, v. /MANGI-:I-/ to insert between. /MANG-:-AN/ to put something on a surface underneath someone or something.

SALUKUB, v. /MANG-:-AN/ to cover, shield; hence to protect, guard, conceal. /MANGI-:I-/ to use to cover, shield, protect, guard, conceal.

SALUMINA, v. /-UM-/ to differ from. /AG-/ [with pl. subject] to be different from each other. /MAI-/ to be different, to stand apart.

SALUMPAYAK, v. /AG-/ to bend due to weight of fruits or leaves.

SALUN-AT, n. health.
adj. /NA-/ healthy.
v. /-UM-/.

SALUNSUN, v. /MANG-:-EN/ to put one over the other, to stack up.

SALUNGASING, v. /MANG-:-EN/ to disobey, differ with. /AG-/ [with pl. subject] to stand apart from others.

SALUNGAYNGAY, adj. lame, paralyzed.
v. /AG-/ to become lame or paralyzed.

SALUNGKIT, v. /AG-, MANG-:-EN/ to pick with a pole provided with a hook.

SALUNGSUNG, v. /MANG-:-EN/ to prepare a betel nut chew.

SALUP, n. dry measure equivalent to three liters.
v. /-UM-, MANG-:-EN/ to measure with this.

SALUPINGPING, v. /MANGI-:I-/ to tuck up one's skirt.

SALUTATORIAN [f. Eng.], n. salutatorian.

SALUYOT, n. the jute or Jew's mallow whose leaves are eaten.

SAMAK, n. bitter leaves added to BASI.

SAMBUT, v. /MANGI-:I-/ to finish doing in between jobs.

SAMEK, adj. /NA-/ dense, thick, full of undergrowth, weeds, etc.

SAMIRA, v. /MANGI-:I-/ to insert, add another job to one's job.

SAM-IT, adj. /NA-/ sweet.
    v. /-UM-/.

SAMPA, n. top, summit, peak of a mountain.
    v. /-UM-/ to reach the top. /MANGI-:I-/ to carry to the top.

SAMPAGA, n. the Arabian jasmine flower.

SAMPION, var. of KAMPEON.

SAMPITAW, v. /-UM-/ to meddle, interfere.

SAMRID, n. a kind of small, black, hairy caterpillar.

SAMSAM, v. /AG-, MANG-:-EN/ to confiscate, seize forcibly, loot.

SAMUKOL, adj. /NA-/ clumsy, awkward.

SAMUTSAMUT, n. floss on stems, fruits, etc.

SAMUT-SAMUT, n. cobweb. --syn. SAPUT.

SAMYENTO [f. Sp.], n. cement. --var. SIMYENTO, SEMENTO.
    v. /AG-/ to make cement. /MANG-:-EN/ to cement.

-SAN, var. of MAYSA, one: used with MAMIN- or NAMIN-.
    MAMINSAN, once.

SANAANG, adj. /NA-/ acutely painful, stinging, biting.
v. /-UM-/.

SANAY, v. /AG-/ to practice doing something. /MANG-:
-EN/ to train, practice (someone) in doing something.

SANDIA, n. water-melon.

SANIATA, n. jewel, precious stone, gem.

SANIGKI, v. /-UM-/ to start up from sleep breathing
deeply and laboriously.

SANIKUA, n. properties, possessions, assets.
adj. /NA-/ rich, wealthy, affluent.
v. /AG-/ to have or own properties. /MANG-:-EN/ to
claim as one's property.

SANSAN, adj. /MA-/ often, frequently, many times.
v. /-EN/ to do frequently.

SANTANG, n. a kind of shrub with terminal cymes of
pink, reddish or whitish flowers.

SANTO [f. Sp.], n. saint.

SANTOL, n. 1. a kind of fruit-bearing tree. 2. its
fruit.

SANUD, v. /AG-, -UM-/ to move backwards. /MAKA-:MA--AN/
to hit while walking backwards.

SANUT, v. /MANG-:-AN/ to whip, flog, thrash.

SANYATA, n. muse. --syn. IMNAS.

SANGA-, = (MAY)SA NGA.

SANGA, n. branch.
v. /AG-/ to have or develop this. /MANG-:-EN/ to
break off (a branch).

SANGAILI, n. guest, visitor.
v. /MANG-:-EN/ to entertain as guest. /AG-/ to
entertain guests.

SANGAILI, n. menses.
v. /AG-/ to menstruate.

SANGALUBONGAN, see under LUBONG.

SANGAT, v. /AG-, MANG-:-EN/ to inspect a trap, snare, the like.

SANG-AT, v. /-UM-/ to climb up to, ascend; to land, disembark. /MANG-:-EN/ to reach by climbing. /MANGI-:I-/ to carry up to a place.

SANG-AW, n. breath.
    v. /-UM-/ to breathe, exhale. /MANG-:-AN/ to breathe upon.

SANGBAY, v. /-UM-/ to lodge.

SANGDU, v. /-UM-, MANG-:-EN/ to hit with the horns, butt. /MANGI-:I-/ to bump, knock against.

SANGER, adj. /NA-/ 1. strong-smelling as wine. 2. brave.

[1]SANGGA, v. /MANG-:-EN/ to block, ward off, parry, deflect.

[2]SANGGA, v. /MAKI-:KA-/ to be the partner of in a table game.

SANGGIR, v. /AG-/ to lean on, rest on for support. /MANGI-:I-/ to lean (something) on.

SANGGUL, v. /MANG-:-EN/ to put the arm around the neck or back of.

SANGI, n. molar tooth.

SANG-IL, v. /-UM-, MANG-:-EN/ to strike with the horn sideways, butt sideways. /AG-/ [with pl. subject] to strike each other with the horns sideways.

SANGIT, v. /AG-/ to cry, weep.

SANGKA-, a prefix added to verbal stems indicating frequent or continuous doing of the action expressed by the stem.

SANGKAI-, var. of SANGKA-.

SANGKAP, n. chip of wood separated by an ax, an adz, etc.

SANGLAD, v. /-UM-/ to anchor.   /MANGI-:I-/ to anchor (a
boat or ship).

SANGLAY, n. Chinese.

SANGO, n. front.   --cf. SANGWANAN.
    v. /-UM-/ to face toward.   /AG-/ [with pl. subject]
to face each other.   /MANG-:-EN/ to attend to,
confront.   /MANGI-:I-/ to cause to face toward
(someone or something).

SANGPET, v. /-UM-/ to arrive at one's house.   /MANGI-:
I-/ to bring to one's house.   /MAKA-:MA--AN/ to find
upon arriving at one's house.

SANGSANGAYAN, v. /MAI-/ to be exceptional, extraordinary,
remarkable.

SANGUL, n. yoke.
    v. /MANGI-:I-/ to hitch, harness.

SANGWANAN, n. front.   --cf. SANGO.

¹SAPA, adj. /NA-/ early.   --see AGSAPA.
    v. /-EN/ to do something early.

²SAPA, n. residue, leavings of chewed betel.

SAPAD, n. one hand of bananas.

SAPAL, n. fork of a tree, streets, etc.

SAPASAP, adj. universal, common, general.
    n. the multitude, masses; the people as a whole.

SAPATA, n. vow, oath.
    v. /AG-/ to swear.   /MANG-:-AN/ to swear for.
/MANGI-:I-/ to promise or swear to do something.

SAPATUS [f. Sp.], n. shoe.
    v. /AG-/ to wear shoes, to put on one's shoes.
/MANG-:-AN/ to put shoes on someone's feet, to shoe.
/MANGI-:I-/ to put on someone's feet as shoes.

SAPAW, n. shade, shelter.
    v. /MANG-:-AN/ to shade, screen, shelter.   /AG-/ to
make a shelter or shade.

[1]SAPAY, conj. indicates the optative. SAPAY KUMA, I hope it happens so.

[2]SAPAY, var. of APAY.

SAPIDENG, v. /-UM-/ to take shelter, seek protection. /MANG-:-AN/ to protect.

SAPIN, n. undergarments; trousers, panties, drawers. --see KARSUNSILYO.
v. /AG-/ to put one's trousers or panties on. /MANG-:-AN/ to put trousers, panties or drawers on someone. /MANGI-:I-/ to put on someone as trousers, panties or drawers.

SAPIT, v. /MANGI-:I-/ to insert or enclose inside.

SAPLID, v. /MANG-:-AN/ to shake or beat away dust, to dust. /MANG-:-EN/ to beat away as dust.

SAPLIT, v. /AG-, MANG-:-AN/ to whip. /MANGI-:I-/ to use to whip someone or something.

SAPPUYUT, v. /MANG-:-EN/ to hold close to one's body, to cuddle as a baby.

SAPRI, v. /AG-/ to get sprinkled toward. /MA--AN/ to become sprinkled with water as by the rain when blown by the wind.

SAPU, v. /MANG-:-AN/ to daub, rub with oil, grease or the like. /MANGI-:I-/ to use to rub (something) with.

SAPUL, v. /AG-, MANG-:-EN/ to look for, find; to need. /AG-/ to earn a living.

SAPUT, n. membrane, cobweb.
v. /MANG-:-AN/ to envelope or wrap with cobwebs or the like.

SARA, n. horn, antler.

SARAAW, v. /AG-, -UM-/ to feel loose as when hungry: said of the stomach.

SARAB, v. /MANG-:-AN/ or /MANGI-:I-/ to singe, scorch.

SARABASAB, v. /MANG-:-EN/ or /MANGI-:I-/ to roast or cook by putting near a fire.

SARABU, n. gift, present given by someone upon arrival. v. /-UM-/ to visit a person who has just arrived so as to be given a gift. /-UM-:-EN/ to visit (a person) so as to be given a gift.

SARABUSAB, var. of SALABUSAB.

SARAGASANG, adj. /NA-/ thin and transparent, sheer, gauzy. v. /AG-/.

SARAIT, v. /AG-, MANG-:-EN/ to sew. /MANGI-:I-/ to sew on (something). --see DAIT.

SARAK, v. /MANG-:-EN/ to go out for the purpose of meeting (someone). /AG-/ [with pl. subject] to meet each other.

SARAKUY, v. /-UM-/ to mix with. /AG-/ [with pl. subject] to get mixed together.

SARAMSAM, v. /AG-/ to eat not as part of a meal.

SARAMULYO, syn. of SARABUSAB.

SARANAY, n. aid, help, protection. v. /MANG-:-EN/ to help, protect, defend. /MANGI-:I-/ to give as aid, protection, support.

SARANTA, adj. /NA-/ often, many times. v. /-UM-/.

SARANG, v. /MANGI-:I-/ to turn toward the sun or any other source of light so as to reflect light.

SARANGSANG, adj. /NA-/ crispy, brittle, crunchy. v. /-UM-/.

SARANGUSUNG, n. coconut shell.

SARAPA, v. /MANG-:-EN/ to support at the bottom.

SARDAM, n. evening.

SARDENG, v. /AG-/ to stop. /MANGI-:I-/ to stop, end, suspend. /-AN/ to stop from doing.

SARDINAS, n. sardine.

SAREBSEB, v. /-UM-/ to produce a hissing sound. --syn. SARETSET.

SARETSET, syn. of SAREBSEB.

SARHENTO [f. Sp.], n. sergeant.

SARI, v. /-UM-/ to break through, pass through, trespass.

SARIDAT, v. /-UM-/ to follow, succeed.

SARIGSIG, v. /-UM-, MANG-:-AN/ to move in a half circle, as a cock courting a hen, to sidle around.

SARIMADENG, v. /AG-/ to hesitate or be undecided, to be doubtful.

SARINGGAYAD, v. /AG-/ to hang down reaching the ground, to trail. /MANGI-:I-/ to cause to trail or drag.

SARINGIT, n. bud, shoot.
    v. /AG-/ to develop this.

SARIPATPAT, v. /MANG-:-EN/ to catch a glimpse of.

SARIPIT; SARSARIPIT, v. /-EN/ to discharge urine a few drops at a time intermittently or irregularly.

SARIRIT, adj. /NA-/ keen, bright, intelligent, shrewd.
    v. /-UM-/.

SARITA, n. tale, story, narration.
    v. /MAKI-:KA-/ to talk or converse with (someone).
/AG-/ to talk or converse with one another. /MANG-:-EN/ to tell, relate, narrate, report.

SARIWAGWAG, v. /MANGI-:I-/ or /MANG-:-EN/ to shake with force so as to dislodge dirt or extraneous matter. /AG-/ to shake oneself so as to remove dirt, water or the like.

SARMING, n. 1. glass, mirror. 2. eyeglass.
v. /AG-/ 1. to look at oneself before a mirror. 2. to use a pair of eyeglasses. /MANG-:-AN/ to put eye-glasses on (someone). /MANGI-:I-/ to put on someone as eyeglasses.

SARSA, n. sauce, esp. for roast pig.

SARSARDAM, n. twilight or early evening.

SARSUELA, n. native drama; a native stage presentation.

SARTIN [f. Sp.], n. enamel-coated cup.

SARUAG, v. /MANGI-:I-/ to cast.

SARUKAG, v. /MANG-:-EN/ to beat repeatedly in order to make soft and spongy.

SARUKANG, n. a pole with a basket-like contraption at its end used to pick mangoes.
v. /AG-, MANG-:-EN/ to pick (mangoes) using this.

SARUKUD, n. cane, prop.
v. /AG-/ to use a cane. /MANGI-:I-/ to put as prop or support. /MANG-:-AN/ to prop, support with a prop.

SARUNU, v. /-UM-/ to follow. /MANG-:-EN/ to follow. /MANGI-:I-/ to do next.

SARUNGKAR, v. /-UM-, MANG-:-AN/ to call upon, visit.

SARUSAR, n. granary, warehouse. --syn. KAMARIN, KAMALIG.

[1]SARUT, adj. /NA-/ intelligent, bright. --syn. SARIRIT.

[2]SARUT, n. tuberculosis.
v. /AG-/ to be afflicted by this.

SARWA, v. /AG-/ to vomit. /MANGI-:I-/ to vomit (some-thing).

SASTRE, n. tailor.

SATANAS [f. Sp.], n. satan, the devil. --syn. SAIRU, DEMONYO.

SATSAT, v. /MANG-:-EN/ to rip as garments.

SAU, n. word, language, speech, talk.
   v. /AG-/ to talk, speak, say something. /MAKI-:KA-/
to talk or converse with. /MANG-:-EN/ to say, tell.
/MANGI-:I-/ to tell to someone.

SAUNG, n. tusk, canine tooth; ivory.

SAUR, adj. liar, deceitful.
   v. /AG-/ to deceive, cheat; to tell a lie. /MANG-:
-EN/ to deceive, cheat (someone); to tell a lie to
(someone).

SAWALI, n. interwoven splits of bamboo used esp. for
   walling.

¹SAWANG, v. /MANGI-:I-/ to reveal, disclose, declare.

²SAWANG, n. breach, opening as on a dike.
   v. /MANG-:-EN/ to make a breach or opening on.

SAWI, n. a kind of hawk.

SAW-ING, n. the tusk of the wild boar.
   v. /MANG-:-EN/ to gore, to wound with the tusk or
   horn.

SAWIT, n. barb of an arrow, a fishhook, harpoon, spear,
   etc.

SAWSAW, v. /MANGI-:I-/ to dip, dunk in.

SAYA [f. Sp.], n. skirt.

SAY-A, v. /AG-/ to clear one's throat.

SAYAAT, adj. /NA-/ good, nice, appropriate, suitable;
   well, recuperated.
   v. /-UM-/ to become good; to become well. /-EN/ to
   do well.

SAYAD, adj. /NA-/ shallow, e.g. a plate.
   v. /-UM-/.

SAYAG, v. /-UM-/ [SUMYAG] to deviate as when carried by
   the wind, to be deflected, to drift along.

SAYAK, see PASAYAK.

SAYAKSAK, adj. /NA-/ cheerful, merry.
v. /-UM-/.

SAYANG, interj. what a waste!

SAYANGGUSENG, v. /AG-, -UM-/ to produce a buzzing
sound like mosquitoes, bees, etc. /MANG-:-EN/ to
importune.

SAYAW, adj. /NA-/ thin, watery as chocolate, gruel, etc.

SAYU, v. /AG-, MANG-:-AN/ to splash or dash water on.

SAYUD, adj. /NA-/ adroit, quick, skillful.

SAY-UP, v. /MANG-:-EN/ to smell, sniff at.

SEBBA, v. /MANGI-:I-/ to throw into the fire.

SEBBAAL, v. /MA--AN/ [MASBAALAN] to be able to endure
or suffer or bear.

SEBBANG, n. track, trail.
v. /MANGI-:I-/ to lead (to sin, danger and the
like).

SEBSEB, v. /AG-, MANG-:-AN/ to douse (fire) with
water, extinguish with water.

SEDA, n. silk.

SEDDU, v. /MA-/ [MASDU] to feel faint or light-headed.

SEDSED, v. /MANG-:-EN/ to compress, make compact. /MA-/
to be compressed.

SEGGAR, v. /-UM-/ [SUMGAR] to stand on end: said of the
hair; to bristle.

SEGGED, v. /-UM-/ [SUMGED] to kindle, burn.

SEGGET, n. water in which rice has been boiled.

SEGURADO [f. Sp.], adj. sure, surely, certain,
certainly.

SEGURIDAD [f. Sp.], n. security.

SEGURO [f. Sp.], adv. probably, maybe, perhaps, very
likely.
v. /MANG-:-EN/ often /MAKA-:MA-/ to make sure or
certain (that something is done or happens). --var.
SIGURU.

SEIS [f. Sp.], num. six, 6. --syn. INNEM. --var. SAIS.

SEKKA, v. /AG-/ to uproot rice seedlings for replanting.
/MANG-:-EN/ to uproot (rice seedlings).

SEKKAD, v. /-UM-/ to push the feet firmly against the
ground; hence, to resist.

SEKRETA [f. Sp.], n. detective, secret agent, private
investigator.

SEKRETARIO [f. Sp.], n. secretary.

[1]SEKSEK, v. /AG-, MANG-:-EN/ to shuffle (cards).

[2]SEKSEK, v. /-UM-/ to penetrate into the interior of.
/MANGI-:-AN/ to cram into, thrust into.

SEKSI [f. Eng.], adj. /NAG-/ sexy, sexually provocative.

SEKTOR [f. Eng.], n. sector.

SEKUNDARIA [f. Sp.], n. secondary school, high school.
--syn. HAISKUL.

SELLAG, adj. /NA-/ [NASLAG] bright, luminous, shining;
hence, lovely, fair, comely.

SELLANG, n. groin, inguen.

SELLEP, v. /-UM-/ [SUMLEP] to absorb moisture. /MA-/
[MASLEP] to be drenched, soaked.

SELSEL, v. /-UM-/ to push oneself through a crowd or
the like. /MANGI-:I-/ to push in, stuff in, cram in.

SELYO [f. Sp.], n. stamp. --var. SILYU.
v. /MANG-:-AN/ to put a stamp on.

SEMENTO, var. of SAMIENTO.

SENADOR [f. Sp.], n. senator.

SENNAAY, n. sigh.
    v. /AG-/ to sigh.

SENGNGAW, n. vapor, steam, fume, breath.
    v. /-UM-/ [SUMNGAW] to rise out as steam, emit
vapor; hence, to appear unexpectedly. '/MANGI-:I-/
[:IYISNGAW] to reveal, disclose, confess.

SENGNGAY, v. /-UM-/ [SUMNGAY] to be born.

SENTIMOS [f. Sp.], n. centavo, one-hundredth of a peso.

SENTIMU, var. of SENTIMOS.

SENTO [f. Sp.], n. center.

SENYAS [f. Sp.], n. sign, signal.
    v. /MANG-:-AN/ to make a sign or signal to.   /MANGI-
:I-/ to signal (something) to.

SEP-AK, v. /MA-/ [MASPAK] to break, snap.   /MANG-:-EN/
to break, snap.

SEP-ANG, n. the upper part of the thigh at the inside.

SEPPEG, v. /-UM-, MANG-:-EN/ [SUMPEG] to swoop down
upon, to pounce on: said of birds of prey.

SEPSEP, v. /-UM-, MANG-:-EN/ to sip, suck.

SEPTIEMBRE [f. Sp.], n. September.   --var. SETIEMBRE.

SERBESA [f. Sp.], n. beer.   --syn. BIR.

SERBI [f. Sp.], n. use, avail.
    v. /AG-/ 1. to be used as, to serve. 2. to be a
servant to.   /MANG-:-AN/ to serve, to be of service
to.   /MANGI-:I-/ to serve to someone.

SERBISIO [f. Sp.], n. service, toilet seat.
    SERBISIO SIBIL, civil service.

SEREMONIA [f. Sp.], n. ceremony, rites.

SERIOSO [f. Sp.], adj. serious, grave, solemn.

SERMON [f. Sp.], n. sermon.
v. /AG-/ to deliver a sermon. /MANG-:-AN/ to preach
to. /MANGI-:I-/ to preach (something) to someone.

SERRA, v. /-UM-/ to close like a door. /MANGI-:I-/ to
close, shut, obstruct, block.

SERREK, v. /-UM-/ [SUMREK] 1. to go in, enter. 2. to go
to school. /MANG-:-EN/ to go in to (someone).
/MANGI-:I-/ to take in, bring in, carry inside.

SESSION [f. Eng.], n. session.

SETIEMBRE, var. of SEPTIEMBRE.

SI, art. singular of the proper article.

[1]SI-, a pronoun prefix used to form some of the full
nominative pronouns.

[2]SI-, a prefix used with verbal stems whose first
consonant and vowel are reduplicated; the resultant
form means: being in the state of the action expressed
by the stem.

SIAG, var. of SAYAG.

SIAK, pron. [pl. DAKAMI] I, me: the person speaking or
writing.

SIALAK [f. Eng.], n. shellac, varnish. --syn. BARNIS.

SIAM, num. nine; 9. --syn. NUEBE.

SIASI, v. /-UM-/ to stray, wander off.

SIASINU, pron. who?

SIBBARUT, v. /AG-, MANG-:-EN/ to snatch, to grab
suddenly. --syn. RABNUT.

SIBBU, v. /MANGI-:I-/ to do or use for the first time.

[1]SIBET, n. waist. --cf. SIKET.

[2]SIBET, v. /MA-/ to go intending to come back after a
short while, to be away for a short while.

SIBU, v. /AG-/ to bubble as water.

SIBUG, v. /AG-/ to sprinkle water on plants and the
   like. /MANG-:-AN/ to water, sprinkle water on.

SIBUYAS [f. Sp.], n. onion. --cf. LASUNA.
   SIBUYAS BUMBAY, a kind of big onion.

SIDA, n. side-dish, viand; any article of food that is
   eaten with rice or sometimes corn, yam, cassava or
   bread.
   v. /AG-, MANG-:-EN/ to have as this.

SIDDAAW, v. /MA-/ [MASDAAW] to be amazed or astonished,
   to be struck with admiration, wonder or fear.

   NAKASKASDAAW, adj. amazing, astonishing, marvelous.

SIDDUKER, v. /AG-/ to be obstructed, clogged.

SIDING, n. mole. --cf. SALLAPIDING.

SIDUK, n. spoon.
   v. /-UM-, MANG-:-EN/ to scoop with a spoon.

SIDUNGET, adj. /NA-/ serious, grave, solemn.
   v. /AG-/ to show a grave or solemn face.

SIENSIA [f. Sp.], n. science.

SIETE [f. Sp.], num. seven, 7. --syn. PITU.

SIGAR, n. fish fin. --cf. PIGAR.
   v. /MANG-:-AN/ to hurt with the fin: said of a fish.

SIGARGAR, v. /AG-/ to stand on end: said of hair,
   feathers, and the like.

SIGARILIO [f. Sp.], n. cigarette.
   v. /AG-/ to smoke a cigarette. /MANG-:-EN/ to
   smoke as a cigarette.

SIGGAWAT, v. /MANG-:-EN/ to take away suddenly, snatch
   off.

SIGIT, v. /AG-, MANG-:-EN/ to cut into small pieces.

SIGKAT, v. /MANG-:-EN/ to raise with a prop, to prop up.

SIGKING, var. of SAGKING.

SIGLO [f. Sp.], n. century.

SIGLUT, v. /AG-, MANG-:-EN/ to tie into a knot.

SIGPAT, v. /AG-, MANG-:-EN/ to cut with a slantwise stroke.

SIGPET, n. clip, clasp.
    v. /MANG-:-EN/ to pinch, clip. /MANGI-:I-/ to insert. /MANG-:-AN/ to put a clip or clasp on.

SIGU, v. /MANGI-:I-/ to fit or join to another, to unite with another by a joint.

SIGUD, adv. at once, right away, immediately. --syn. DARAS.
    v. /MANG-:-EN/ to do right away.

SIGUIDA [f. Sp.], adv. at once, immediately. --var. INSIGUIDA. --syn. DARAS.

SIIM, v. /AG-, MANG-:-EN/ to spy on, to watch secretly.

SIIT, n. 1. thorn. 2. fish bone.
    v. /AG-/ to remove fish bones. /I--AN/ to remove the bones of (a fish). /MA--AN/ to be pricked by a thorn, fish bone, or the like.

[1]SIKA, n. dysentery.
    v. /AG-/ to have this, to be afflicted with this.

[2]SIKA, pron. [pl. DAKAYU] you singular: the person to whom one is speaking or writing. SIKA is the full nominative case form, KA the enclitic nominative, KUKUAM the full possessive, MO the enclitic possessive and the agent, and KANYAM or KENKA the oblique.

SIKSIKA, you (singular) only, you (singular) alone.

SIKAL, v. /AG-/ to feel pain in the abdomen.

PASIKAL, v. /AG-/ to have labor pains.

SIKAM, var. of SIKAMI.

SIKAMI, var. of DAKAMI.   --var. SIKAM.

SIKSIKAMI, var. of DAKDAKAMI.

SIKAP, adj. /NA-/ sly, crafty, wily, shrewd, clever.
v. /AG-/ to be shrewd, clever, cunning.

SIKAPAT, num. a unit of money worth twelve and one-half
centavos or half of twenty-five centavos.

SIKAWALU, num. half of a SIKAPAT and one-fourth of a
BINTING, six and one-fourth centavos.

SIKAYU, var. of DAKAYU.   --var. SIKAY.

SIKSIKAYU, var. of DAKDAKAYU.

SIKET, n. waist, waistband.
v. /-EN/ to be afflicted with pain in the waist.

SIKIG, n. side.
v. /AG-/ to lie or turn on one's side.

SIKIGAN, n. 1. side of (a mountain, hill, etc.). 2.
side of the body from shoulder to foot.

[1]SIKIL, n. barbel of fish.
v. /-UM-, MANG-:-EN/ to attack with its barbel:
said of fishes.

[2]SIKIL, v. /-UM-, MANG-:-EN/ to push or hit with the
elbow.

SIKKARUD, var. of SIKKAYUD.

SIKKAWIL, v. /AG-/ to cross the legs.

SIKKAYUD, v. /AG-/ to drag the legs.   /MANG-:-EN/ to
trip up, to cause to stumble.

SIKKI, n. a game played by tossing pebbles aloft and
catching as many of.them as possible on the back of
the hand; those that fall on the ground are made to
hit each other.
v. /MAKI-:KA-/ to play this game with someone.
/AG-/ [with pl. subject] to play this game together.

SIKKIL, adj. /NA-/ stiff, rigid, tense.
    v. /-UM-/.

SIKKU, v. /-UM-/ to turn a corner.

SIKMAW, v. /-UM-, MANG-:-EN/ to catch or snap at with
    the mouth.   --syn. SAKRAB.

SIKSIK, n. scale of fish, legs of birds and the like.
    v. /AG-, MANG-:-AN/ to remove the scales of.

SIKUG, adj. /MA-/ pregnant, heavy with child.
    v. /AG-/ to become pregnant. /MANG-:-EN/ to make
    pregnant, to cause to become pregnant.

SILAG, n. buri palm.

SILAMUT, v. /AG-, MANG-:-AN/ to lick clean.

SILAP, adj. /NA-/ shining, dazzling.
    v. /-UM-/.

SILAW, n. lamp, light, illumination.
    v. /AG-/ to use a lamp, to provide oneself with
    light. /MANG-:-AN/ to focus the light on, to
    illumine.

SILBATO, n. whistle.
    v. /-UM-, MANG-:-AN/ to whistle at with a whistle.

SILED, n. room.   --syn. KUARTO.

SILENG, adj. /NA-/ bright, shining, brilliant, dazzling.
    v. /-UM-/. /MA-/ to be dazzled.

SILET, n. small intestine.

SILI, n. pepper.

SILIASI, n. a big iron kettle or vat.   --var. TILIASI.

SILINDRU, var. of SALINDRU.

SILLENG, v. /-UM-/ [SUMLENG] to have a paroxysm, to
    have a fit.

SILMUT, v. /MANG-:-AN/ to set fire to; to kindle,
    ignite.

SILO, n. noose, snare.
v. /AG-, MANG-:-AN/ to catch with a loop or noose;
to snare or trap.

SILPO, v. /MANGI-:I-/ to join, link, connect; to fit
together. /AG-/ [with pl. subject] to be linked
together. /MANG-:-AN/ to join to in order to make
longer.

SILUD, n. sting of bees, wasps, etc.
v. /AG-, MANG-:-EN/ to sting: said of bees, wasps,
etc.

SIM, n. galvanized iron.   --syn. GALBA, YERO.

SIMA, n. barb of a spear, an arrow, a fishhook, etc.

SIMBAAN, n. church, chapel, oratory, temple.

SIMBALUD, v. /MA-/ to have the feet entangled.

SIMBAYUG, n. sling.
v. /AG-, MANG-:-EN/ to hit with a sling

SIMBULO [f. Sp.], n. symbol.

SIMPA, adj. /NA-/ level, even; hence, stable.
v. /AG-/ to stand level, steady, firm. /MANG-:-EN/
or /MANGI-:I-/ to cause to stand level, steady or
firm; to make stable.

SIMUT, v. /MANG-:-EN/ to take all.

SIMUT-SIMUT, n. moth.

SINA, v. /-UM-/ to separate from. /MAKI-:KA-/ to
separate from, part with. /AG-/ [with pl. subject]
to separate or part from each other. /MANGI-:I-/
to separate (someone or something) from.

SINAMAR, n. ray of light.

SINAMAY, n. a coarse cloth woven from abaca fiber.

SINAM-IT [rt. SAM-IT], n. sweets, candy.

SINDAYAG, see PASINDAYAG.

SINDIKATO [f. Eng.], n. syndicate.

SINE [f. Sp.], n. 1. cinema, movie, film. 2. cinema house, moviehouse.
v. /AG-/ to see a movie, to go to a moviehouse to see a show. /MANGI-:I-/ to take to a show or movie.

SINELAS [f. Sp.], n. slipper.
v. /AG-/ to use this. /AG-, MANG-:-EN/ to hit with a slipper.

SINIGUELAS [f. Sp.], n. plum. --var. SARGUELAS, SIRGUELAS.

SINIT, v. /AG-, MANG-:-EN/ to scorch, singe, burn.

SINNU, var. of SINU.

SINSILYU, n. small change of money.

SINTAS [f. Sp.], n. leather strap, tassel.

SINTUK, v. /-UM-, MANG-:-EN/ to hit with the fist, to knock on the head.

SINTURUN [f. Sp.], n. belt.
v. /AG-/ to use this. /-UM-, MANG-:-EN/ to hit or whip with a belt.

SINU, inter. who? --var. SINNU, SIASINU.

SINUBLAN, n. a very large kettel or pot, bigger than the SILIASI.

SINULID, n. thread, esp. sewing thread.

SINYAS [f. Sp.], n. signal, sign.
v. /AG-/ to make a sign or signal. /-UM-, MANG-:-AN/ to make a sign to, to signal.

SINGASING, n. suggestion, recommendation.
v. /MANGI-:I-/ to suggest, recommend.

SINGAT, v. /-UM-, MANG-:-EN/ to pry open, to open forcibly.

SINGAY, n. a bunch of palay.

SINGDAN, n. string used to tie something.
  v. /MANG-:-AN/ to attach a string or the like for
  tying purposes.

SINGED, adj. /NA-/ close, intimate.
  v. /-UM-/

SINGGAPUNG, n. a net used to catch birds, frogs, fish,
  etc.

SINGGIT, adj. /NA-/ high in pitch, shrill.

SINGIL, n. fish fin esp. that of catfish, barbel.
  v. /-UM-, MANG-:-EN/ to hit with the fin or barbel:
  said of certain fishes.

SINGIN, n. twins. --syn. KAMBAL.

SINGIR, v. /AG-, MANG-:-EN/ to collect as debts.

SINGKAMAS, n. turnip bean.

SINGKU [f. Sp.], num. five, 5. --syn. LIMA.

SINGKUL, adj. paralyzed in one or both hands, having
  one or both arms twisted.

SINGLAG, v. /AG-/ to extract oil from coconut milk by
  boiling it. /MANG-:-EN/ to boil (coconut milk)
  until only oil and scum are left.

SINGLUT, v. /AG-/ to suck up nasal mucus. /MANG-:-EN/
  to suck up as nasal mucus.

SINGPET, adj. /NA-/ good, virtuous, righteous, well-
  behaved.
  v. /-UM-/. /AG-/ to behave well, righteously,
  virtuously.

SINGSING, n. ring.

SIPA, n. a game played with a very light ball which is
  kicked from one person to another.
  v. /AG-/ to play this game. /-UM-, MANG-:-EN/ to
  kick.

SIP-AK, v. /-UM-, MANG-:-EN/ to break as a branch of a
  tree. /MA-/ to be broken, esp. a branch of a tree.

SIPAT, v. /AG-, MANG-:-EN/ to slap, spank.

SIPET, n. cockroach.

SIPILYO [f. Sp.], n. toothbrush. --syn. GISIGIS.
   v. /AG-/ to brush one's teeth. /MANG-:-EN/ to
brush (the teeth).

[1]SIPING, n. two fruits, fingers, bodies, etc. grown
   together.

[2]SIPING, n. one centavo. --syn. SENTIMOS.

SIPIT, n. forceps, tongs.
   v. /-UM-, MANG-:-EN/ to pinch, hold or seize with
tongs or forceps.

SIPLAG, v. /AG-, MANG-:-EN/ to chase and peck on: said
of a hen.

SIPNGET, adj. /NA-/ dark, obscure.
   v. /-UM-/

   SUMIPNGET, n. twilight, dusk, sunset. --syn.
   SARSARDAM.

SIPPADUNG, v. /MANG-:-EN/ to trip up, cause to stumble.

SIPPAW, v. /-UM-, MANG-:-EN/ to catch with the hand a
falling object.

SIPPAYUT, v. /-UM-, MANG-:-EN/ to catch, hit or buzz at
(an object) while flying or aloft.

SIPPIT, n. bill (of fowls), beak.
   v. /-UM-, MANG-:-EN/ to peck at.

SIPU, v. /AG-, MANG-:-AN/ to hold the genitals of.

SIPUD, see AGSIPUD.

SIPUK, n. small heap of harvested rice.

SIPUT, v. /AG-, MANG-:-AN/ to watch, keep an eye on,
observe.

SIRAP; SISIRAP, v. /MA-/ to be dazzled by the light.

SIRENA [f. Sp.], n. mermaid.

SIRIB, adj. /NA-/ wise, shrewd, sagacious, erudite.
   v. /-UM-/.

SIRIG, v. /MANG-:-EN/ to aim at, to look at so as to
   ascertain its straightness or alignment.

SIRIP, v. /-UM-/ to peep in, look in. /AG-, MANG-:-EN/
   to peep on (someone) like a peeping-tom.

SIRKERO [f. Sp.], n. stuntman, circus man, tumbler.

SIRKO [f. Sp.], n. circus, vaudeville.
   v. /AG-/ to somersault, roll over.

SIRKULAR [f. Eng.], n. circular.

SIRO [f. Eng.], n. zero, nil, nothing.
   v. /-UM-, MANG-:-EN/ to cause to get zero or
   nothing.

SIRUHANO [f. Sp.], n. surgeon.

SIRPAT, v. /MAKA-:MA-/ to be able to see from afar, to
   see accidentally from afar.

SIRUK, n. the space or area under a house, any space or
   area under something.
   v. /-UM-/ to go under. /MANGI-:I-/ to put under
   the house, the tree, etc.

SIRUT, v. /MANG-:-EN/ to fasten into a knot.

SISI, v. /AG-, MANG-:-EN/ to fry in order to extract
   the lard of.

SISILENG, v. /MA-/ to be deafened or annoyed by the
   loud sound.

SISIP, v. /AG-, MANG-:-EN/ to sip through closed teeth.

SITA, var. of DATA.

   SITSITA, var. of DATDATA.

SITAY, var. of SITAYU.

SITAYU, var. of DATAYU. --var. SITAY.
  SITSITAYU, var. of DATDATAYU.

SITIO [f. Sp.], n. sitio, hamlet.

SITSARUN, n. bacon rind.

SITSITBUNG, n. hide and seek game. --syn. GIRIT,
  KIRIKIT.
    v. /AG-/ [with pl. subject] to play this game.

SITUASION [f. Eng.], n. situation.

SIU, interj. an exclamation used to drive away chickens,
  pigs, birds, goats, etc.

SIUDAD [f. Sp.], n. city.

SIUMAN, n. stepchild.

SIWAK, v. /MANG-:-EN/ to tear wide apart.

SUA, n. pomelo.

SUAKO, n. pipe for smoking. --var. KUAKO.

SUALIT, v. /MA-/ to drop, fall down to the ground.
  /MANGI-:I-/ to cause to fall to the ground.

SUAT, v. /MANG-:-EN/ to prick, to take out by pricking.

SUBA, v. /-UM-/ to go against the current, wind or the
  like; to go upstream.

SUBALIT, v. /-UM-, MANG-:-AN/ to answer, reciprocate.
  /MANGI-:I-/ to be the response or reply to.

SUBBUAL, n. shoot of the banana, sugar cane, etc.

SUBBUT, v. /-UM-, MANG-:-EN/ to redeem, ransom.

SUBEG, adj. /NA-/ disobedient, rebellious.
    v. /AG-/.

SUBLAT, v. /-UM-, MANG-:-AN/ to substitute for, to take
  the place of, to do the task of, to relieve.

SUBLI, v. /AG-/ to return. /MANGI-:I-/ to return, give
back. /MANG-:-EN/ to return in order to do or get.

SUBRA [f. Sp.], n. excess, surplus.
v. /AG-/ to be in excess, to be more. /MANG-:-AN/
to put more than necessary, to add some more to.

SUBRI, var. of SOBRE.

SUBSUB, n. snout as of pigs.
v. /AG-, MANG-:-EN/ to turn up the earth with the
snout.

SUBU, v. /AG-/ to take food to the mouth. /MANG-:-AN/
to take food to the mouth of, to feed. /MANGI-:I-/
to put to the mouth of, to feed to.

SUDI, adj. /NA-/ illustrious renowned, celebrated,
famous.
v. /-UM-/.

SUEKUS, n. wooden shoe. --syn. KAMMADANG.
v. /AG-/ to wear or use this.

SUELDO [f. Sp.], n. salary, wages, pay.
v. /AG-/ to earn as salary. /MANG-:-AN/ to give
salary to. /MANGI-:I-/ to give to someone as salary.

SUELO [f. Sp.], n. floor, usually made of wood. --syn.
DATAR.

[1]SUER, n. bronze, brass.

[2]SUER, adj. /(NA-)/ obstinate.

SUGAL [f. Sp.], n. game of chance, gamble.
v. /MAKI-/ to gamble with someone. /MANGI-:I-/ to
use for gambling, to gamble with.

SUGAT, n. wound, cut.
v. /-UM-, MANG-:-AN/ to wound, cut. /MA--AN/ to be
wounded.

SUGIGI, v. /AG-/ to brush one's teeth. --syn. GISIGIS,
SIPILYO.

SUGNUD, see PASUGNUD.

SUGPET, adj. /NA-/ tart, sour.
v. /-UM-/.

SUGPUN, v. /MAKI-/ to associate with, join. /AG-/ [with pl. subject] to associate with each other, to join together.

KASUGPON, n. a junior partner as in farming.

SUGUD, n. lice comb.
v. /AG-/ to use this. /MANG-:-EN/ to comb with this.

SUIKI, n. fish basket.

SUITIK, adj. /(NA)/ cheater, deceitful, unfair.
v. /AG-/ to cheat, deceive, be unfair. /MANG-:-EN/ to cheat, swindle, deceive; to be unfair to.

SUKA, n. vinegar.
v. /MANG-:-AN/ to add this to.

SUKAIN, v. /AG-, MANG-:-AN/ to search through, inspect thoroughly, explore. /MA--AN/ to discover.

SUKAL, v. /MANG-:-AN/ often /MAKA-:-AN/ to detect, discover.

[1]SUKAT, n. measure.
v. /MANG-:-EN/ to measure.

[2]SUKAT, v. /-UM-:-AN/ to change, take the place of, replace. /AG-/ [with pl. subject] to exchange something with each other. /MANGI-:I-/ to exchange for something else. /AG-/ 1. to change, become different. 2. to change one's clothes.

SUKI, n. customer of long standing.

SUKIMAT, v. /MANG-:-AN/ to discern, perceive, fathom.

SUKIR, adj. /NA-/ disobedient, perverse.
v. /AG-/.

SUKISUK, v. /AG-, MANG-:-EN/ to examine or search diligently, scrutinize, go through carefully.

SUKIT, n. a pole used to pick fruits and the like.
v. /AG-, MANG-:-EN/ to pick or poke with this.

[1]SUKSUK, adj. /(NA)/ hidden or unfrequented, remote.
v. /-UM-/ to hide, to stay away from people, to
isolate oneself.

[2]SUKSUK, see PASUKSUK.

SUKSUPON, var. of SAKSUPON.

SUKTO, v. /MANG-:-EN/ to disconnect, detach, separate.
/MA-/ to be disconnected, detached or separated.

SUKUB, v. /-UM-/ to take shelter, to screen oneself.
/MANG-:-AN/ to shelter or screen.

SUKUNG, adj. /NA-/ concave.

SULAR, n. yard, lot. Nalawa ti sularda. They have a
spacious yard.

SULBATANA, n. blowgun.

SULDADO [f. Sp.], n. soldier.
v. /AG-/ to be a soldier.

SULEK, v. /AG-, MANG-:-EN/ to poke the eyes of with a
pointed object. /MA-/ to be poked or pricked in the
eyes with a pointed object.

SULENG, adj. /NA-/ half-blind.
v. /MA-/ to be half-blind.

SULI, n. corner.

SULISUG, v. /MANG-:-EN/ to entice, lure, seduce,
persuade.

SULLAT, n. plug.
v. /MANG-:-AN/ to plug, obstruct, close.

SULPENG, adj. /NA-/ slothful, sluggard, slow,
procrastinating.
v. /-UM-/.

SULTIP, v. /AG-/ to whistle. /MANG-:-AN/ to whistle
at, to call by whistling.

SULTUP, v. /AG-, MANG-:-EN/ to suck from its shell.

SUMA, v. /AG-, MANG-:-EN/ to obstruct, impede, stop.

SUMAG-, a complex prefix used to form indefinite
  numbers. sumagdudua a lakay, some two old men.

SUMAGMAMANO, adj. several, a few. sumagmamano a lukban,
  some pomelos.

SUMAN, n. a native cake made of glutinous rice, sugar
  and coconut milk.
      v. /AG-/ to make this cake. /MANG-:-EN/ to make
  into this cake.

SUMANG, v. /AG-, MANG-:-EN/ to cure (someone who is
  believed to have been made sick by an evil spirit)
  by performing a certain rite.

SUMBAT, var. of SUNGBAT.

SUMPIT, n. blowgun.
      v. /AG-, MANG-:-EN/ to hit with a blowgun.

SUNATA [f. Sp.], n. sonata.

SUNAY, n. top (a toy).
      v. /AG-/ to spin a top.

SUNI, n. breech baby, a child born with the legs
  coming out first.
      adj. contrary, going the opposite direction.

SUNO, n. representative, substitute.
      v. /-UM-:-EN/ to come after, follow. /MANGI- :I-/
  to substitute for, to put in place of.

SUNSUN, v. /MANG-:-EN/ to gather close to each other.

SUNU, see KASUNO.

SUNUT, v. /MANG-:-AN/ to do again, repeat.

SUNGAD, v. /-UM-/ to approach, draw near.
      adj. /MA-/ coming, succeeding.

SUNGANI, adj. contrary, contradictory, diametrically
  different.

SUNGBAT, n. answer, reply, response.
   v. /-UM-:-AN/ to answer to, reply to, respond to.
   /MANGI-:I-/ to give as one's answer to.

SUNGDU, adj. /NA-/ kind, gracious, considerate.

SUNGGO, n. monkey, ape.   --syn. BAKES.

SUNGKA, n. a native game.
   v. /MAKI-:KA-/ to play this game with someone.
   /AG-/ [with pl. subject] to play this game together.

SUNGO, n. upper lip, snout.

SUNGRUD, n. fuel, specifically firewood.
   v. /MANG-:-AN/ to add fuel, i.e. firewood, to.

SUNGSUNG, v. /MANGI-:I-/ to lead on, goad, incite.

SUPA, n. a unit of dry measure equivalent to the eighth
   part of a GANTA.

SUPA [f. Sp.], n. sofa.

SUPADI, v. /MAI-/ to be distinctive, to be different
   from the others.

SUPAPAK, n. prize, reward.
   v. /MANG-:-AN/ to give a reward to, to repay.
   /MANGI-:I-/ to give as a reward or recompense.

SUPERINTENDENTE [f. Sp.], n. superintendent.

SUPERVISOR [f. Eng.], n. supervisor, overseer.

SUPLA, v. /AG-, MANG-:-EN/ to insult, belittle, degrade,
   mock, ridicule.

SUPLI, n. change in money.
   v. /MANG-:-AN/ to change one's money.   /MANGI-:I-/
   to give as change.

SUPNET, adj. /NA-/ sticky, cohesive.
   v. /-UM-/.

SUPPIAT, v. /-UM-, MANG-:-EN/ to contradict, oppose.
/AG-/ [with pl. subject] to be opposed, to take
opposite or contrary views; hence, to argue.

SUPRING, adj. rebellious, intractable.
v. /-UM-, MANG-:-EN/ to disobey, oppose.

[1]SUPUT, n. a small bag, pouch or purse; a pillow case.
v. /MANGI-:I-/ to put in a small bag, pouch or
purse. /MANG-:-AN/ to cover (a pillow) with a pillow
case.

[2]SUPUT, adj. uncircumcised.

SUPUT-SUPUT, n. urticaria, hives, nettle rash.
v. /AG-/ to be afflicted with this.

SURAT, n. 1. writing, inscription. 2. letter, note.
v. /AG-/ to write a letter or note to. /MANGI-:I-/
to write, inscribe, put into writing. /-UM-:-AN/ to
write to.

SURBETES [f. Sp.], n. ice-cream.

SURIAB, adj. having deformed upper lip.

SURO, v. /AG-, MANG-:-EN/ to study, learn, know.
/MANGI-:I-/ to teach, point at. /MANG-:-AN/ to teach
to do something.

SURPRESA [f. Sp.], n. surprise.
v. /MANG-:-EN/ to surprise.

SURRU, v. /-UM-/ [SUMRU] to recur: said of sickness,
madness, anger, etc.

SURUK, n. excess, surplus.
adj. /NA-/ over, in excess of.
v. /AG-/ to be in excess of. /MANG-:-AN/ to cause
to have an excess of.

SURUN, v. /AG-, MANG-:-EN/ to tease, torment, irritate.

SURUT, v. /-UM-, MANG-:-EN/ 1. to follow, go with. 2.
to obey. /MAKA-:MA--AN/ to be able to understand.

SUS, short for SUSMARYOSEP.

SUSIK, v. /MAKI-:KA-/ to quarrel or argue with. /AG-/ [with pl. subject] to quarrel, to argue.

SUSKRIPSION [f. Eng.], n. subscription.

SUSMARYOSEP [f. Sp.], interj. an exclamation expressing surprise or wonder.

SUSPITSA [f. Sp.], n. suspicion. --syn. DUDA. v. /AG-/ to have a suspicion, to suspect.

SUSTANSIA [f. Sp.], n. substance, nutritional contents.

[1]SUSU, n. breast, mammary gland, udder. v. /-UM-/ to suck milk from the breast, to nurse. /MANG-:-EN/ to suck as milk.

[2]SUSU, n. snail in general.

SUSUON, v. /AG-, MANG-:-EN/ to carry on the head.

SUSUP, v. /-UM-, MANG-:-EN/ to suck, sip, inhale.

SUUB, v. /AG-, MANG-:-AN/ to smoke, fumigate.

SUUR, see KASUURAN.

SUWENG, adj. /NAG-/ stubborn, hard-headed.

SUYA, v. /MA-/ to be tired of, to be cloyed. adj. /MAKA-/ causing one to feel nauseated or cloyed.

SUYAAB, v. /AG-/ to yawn.

SUYAT, v. /-UM-/ to spill out as liquid. /MANGI-:I-/ to cause to spill out. /MANG-:-AN/ to spill out liquid on (someone).

SUYSUY, v. /AG-/ to ravel, fray.

SUYUT, v. /-UM-/ to spout, squirt out.

[1]TA, conj. because, lest, that, so that, etc.; a ligature.

IBAGAM TA UMAY, tell him to come.

ANANSA TA IBAGAK KADAKAYU, therefore I tell you.

AGSIPUD TA IMMAY, because he came.

SAPAY KUMA TA MAYAT, I wish he were willing.

[2]TA, pron. by the two of us, by you (sg.) and me, the two of us (as actor): the agent of DATA.

[3]TA, var. of DITA or DAYTA; abbreviation of the demonstrative adjective DAYTA and of the adverb of place DITA.

TAAW, n. ocean, sea.   --cf. BAYBAY

TABA, n. fat of an animal; adipose tissue; bacon; suet; grease; cream; substance of food.
    adj. fat, fatty oily, unctuous, greasy; fertile, rich (soil).

TABAKU, n. tobacco.
    v. /AG-, MANG-:-EN/ to smoke tobacco, esp. a cigar.

TABAN, adj. select, choice, exquisite, superior, of the best quality; applied to coconuts, betel nuts, fruits of the red pepper or chili, etc.

[1]TABAS, n. form of a dress, a face, etc.; fit, style, fashion, shape, pattern, outline, type; figure, look, aspect, countenance, air, appearance, semblance.
    v. /AG-, MANG-:-EN/ to cut (a cloth or dress) according to a pattern. /MA-/ to be cut, as of a dress.

[2]TABAS, v. /AG-, MANG-:-EN/ to cut grass.

TABATAB, v. /AG-, MANG-:-EN/ to trim the brim of a hollow receptacle.

TABBAAW, v. /AG-/ [AGTABTABBAAW] to curse, utter imprecations, swear; to blaspheme. /MANG-:-AN/ to curse someone. /MA--AN/ to be cursed.

TABBED, adj. /NA-/ dull, slow, stupid, heavy, rude

(used of one's understanding.).
  v. /AG-/ to be dull, etc.

TABBEL, n. hard evacuation from the intestines.
  v. /AG-/ to excrete hard waste from the intestines
with difficulty.

TABBI, v. /AG-/ to fall together, both of them, e.g.
wrestlers, gamecocks.

TABBIRAW, v. /-UM-/. /AG-, MANG-:-EN/ to intrude,
intermeddle, meddle, interpose officiously; to look
from behind, over the shoulder.

TABBUGA, v. /AG-/ to stamp heavily with the feet.

TABID, v. /MANG-:-EN/ to twist yarn or thread.

TABLA, n. wooden board.
  v. /AG-/ [with pl. subject], /MAKI- KA-/ in a game
or contest, to have a draw; to end in a tie.
  adj. being a draw, a tie.

TABNAW, v. /-UM-, AG-/ to plunge, thrust or cast oneself into water, submerge, dive, immerse oneself,
immerge; to interpose, intervene, step in, interfere
so as to defend somebody. /MANGI-:I-/ to thrust or
cast into water, to plunge into water, immerse,
submerge.

TABTAB, v. /MANG-:-EN/ to hollow out the side pieces
of a ladder or stairs for the rungs or steps that
fit in them.

TABU, n. can scooper; a kind of dipper consisting of a
section of a thick bamboo, about half a yard long,
attached to a long pole and used to dip water; used
in some districts.
  v. /-UM-, MANG-:-EN/ to scoop. /MAI-/ to be used
as a scoop.

TABUKUL, n. a casting net; a round casting net used in
rivers and at sea, and occasionally to catch birds.
  v. /AG-, MANG-:-AN/ to cast a net. /MA--AN/ to
be caught by a net, said of fish.

TABUN, n. burial.
v. /MANGI-:I-/ to inter, bury, inhume. /-AN/ to
embank; to throw up a bank, an embankment. /MAKI-/
to attend a funeral.

TABUNU, v. /-UM-/ to join a large party, assembly,
concourse, etc. /-EN/ to accumulate, pile up, heap
up, amass, agglomerate. /AG-/ [AGTATABUNU] to
accumulate, crowd, e.g. duties, work, etc.

TABUNGAW, n. gourd; the bottle gourd. Lagenaria
leucantha (Lam.) Rusby.

TABUY, v. /MANGI-:I-/ to incite, stimulate, excite,
encourage, spur, urge on, stir up, animate, prompt.
/MAI-/ to be stimulated.

TADEM, n. edge; the cutting side of the blade of a
knife, an axe, a saw, etc.
adj. /NA-/ sharp, keen, penetrating; clever, shrewd,
acute, quick; cutting, trenchant, incisive, crisp;
mordant, stinging, biting; piercing, burning,
excessively hot; said of knives, etc.; the sight,
the intellect, expressions, the tongue, the sun, etc.
v. /-UM-/ to become sharp, keen, etc.

TADI, n. gaff, metal spur for gamecocks.
v. /MAKI-/ to go to a cockfight. /MANGI-:I-/ to
match a gamecock with another. /I-/ to put a metal
spur for gamecocks.

TADTAD, adj. /NA-/ cut into pieces, etc.; covered with
wounds, wounded all over.
v. /AG-, MANG-:-EN/ to cut or chop into pieces,
to mince, hash. /MA-/ to be cut into pieces.

TAEB, v. /AGKA-/ to be contemporaries, of the same
age, coetaneous.

TAENG, n. residence, domicile, dwelling place, place
of habitation.
v. /AG-/ to reside, abide, dwell, stay, tarry; to
come from; to refrain, abstain, forbear, hold back.
adj. /NA--AN/ adult, mature.

TAEP, n. chaff, husk (of rice); glume, husk, hull of
grains.
v. /AG-, I-:-AN/ to winnow.

TAER, adj. /NA-/ graceful, elegant, well-shaped, high-minded, spirited.

TAGA-, a prefix indicating place of origin.

TAGA, v. /AG-, MANG-:-EN/ to trim, work, shape by cutting, e.g. wood, stone, etc.

TAGAANU, interj. from where?

TAGAANG, n. a kind of underground furnace similar to the ANAWANG.

TAGABU, n. servant.
   v. /AG-/ to make someone a servant.   /MANG-:-EN/ to cause to be a servant, to enslave.

TAGAINEP, n. dream.
   v. /AG-/ to dream.   /MANG-:-EN/ to dream of.

TAGAPULUT, n. sugar.

TAGARI, v. /AG-, -UM-/ to make a noise, to talk, say something.
   adj. /NA-/ talkative, noisy, chatterer.

TAGBAT, v. /-UM-, MANG-:-EN/ to cut or hack with a big knife.

TAGENTENG, adj. /NA-/ hard, firm, compact: said of the soil.

TAGGUAB, see PATAGGUAB.

TAGIBALAY, v. /AG-/ to keep house.   --cf. BALAY.

TAGIBI, n. infant, nursing child, baby.
   v. /AG-/ to nurse a baby.   /MANG-:-EN/ to nurse, take care of as a baby.

TAGIKUA, n. property, possessions.
   v. /AG-, MANG-:-EN/ to own, possess, be the owner of.

TAGIRGIR, v. /AG-/ to tremble, shake, shiver.

TAGIRUUT, n. love charm.   --cf. GAYUMA.

TAGNAWA, v. /MAKI-/ to help, cooperate in doing a task.

TAGTAG, v. /MANG-:-EN/ to cause to be shaken, jerked, jolted or addled. /MA-/ to be shaken, jerked or jolted.

TAGUUB, n. howl (of dogs).
   v. /AG-/ to howl.

TAHAR [f. Sp.], v. /AG-, MANG-:-AN/ to sharpen as a pencil. --var. TASA.

TAHU, n. a kind of delicatessen.

TAKAW, v. /AG-, MANG-:-EN/ to steal, pilfer, filch.
   MANNANAKAW, n. robber, thief, pilferer.

TAKBA, v. /-UM-, MANG-:-AN/ to embrace from behind, to go piggy-back on.

TAKDANG, v. /-UM-/ to go ashore or on land from the water. /MANGI-:I-/ to take to land out from the water.

TAKDER, n. form posture, appearance.
   v. /AG-, -UM-/ to stand up, to rise. /MANGI-:I-/ to set upright, to cause to stand up.
   PATAKDER, v. /MANGI-:I-/ to construct, build.

TAKEM, n. position, office.
   v. /AG-, -UM-/ to hold an office or position.

TAKKAB, n. cover, lid. --syn. KALUB.
   v. /AG-, MANG-:-AN/ to cover. /MANGI-:I-/ to use as cover on.

TAKKI, n. excreta, stool, feces, dung.
   v. /-UM-/ to defecate, evacuate. /MANGI-:I-/ to excrete as excreta. /AG-/ to have loose bowel movement, to have diarrhea.

TAKKIAG, n. arm of body.

TAKKIAS, v. /AG-, -UM-/ to escape, slip off, run away.

TAKKUAP, v. /AG-, MANG-:-AN/ to patch up, to repatch as the roof of a house.

TAKKUAT, v. /MAKA-:MA--AN/ to discover unexpectedly, to find out by chance.

TAKKUB, n. lid or cover.   --cf. AKKUB.

TAKKUN, adj. /NA-/ seldom, scarce, few.

TAKNENG, adj. /NA-/ courteous, amiable, suave, affable.

TAKRUT, adj. /(NA-)/ cowardly, timid, fainthearted.
   v. /-UM-/.

TAKTAK, v. /AG-, MANG-:-EN/ to delay from leaving, to hold back longer.

TAKTIKA [f. Sp.], n. tactics, strategy.
   TAKTIKA MILITAR, military tactic.

TAKU, n. scoop, dipper.
   v. /AG-, MANG-:-EN/ to scoop.

[1]TAKUNG, n. sow; the female hog.

[2]TAKUNG, n. sole (of shoe).

TAKUP, n. patch.
   v. /AG-, MANG-:-AN/ to patch (clothes).

TAKYAG, see TAKKIAG.

TALAGA, adj. true, in fact.

TALATAL, v. /AG-/ to roll or turn over and over.
   /MANGI-:I-/ to cause to roll over and over.

TALAW, v. /AG-/ to go away, run away, flee. /MANGI-:
   I-/ to go or run away with.

TAL-AY, v. /AG-/ to walk, travel, to journey by land.

TALAYTAY, n. bridge.
   v. /AG-/ to walk on a bridge. /MANG-:-EN/ to walk on as a bridge.

TALDENG, n. hole in the nasal septum of a carabao or other mammals.
v. /MANG-:-AN/ to put a hole in the nasal septum of.

TALDIAP, v. /-UM-, MANG-:-AN/ to take a glimpse of, to glance at.

TALEB, n. wooden partition inside a house.

TALEK, adj. /NA-/ trusted, trustworthy; close, intimate.
v. /MANGI-:I-/ to pay attention to, take care of.

TALI, n. rope, cord, cable.
v. /AG-, MANG-:-EN/ to twist into a rope or cord.
/MANG-:-AN/ to attach a rope, string or cord to.
/MANGI- :I-/ to tie, bind, attach to something with a string or rope.

TALIAW, v. /-UM-/ to look back by turning the head.
/MANG-:-EN/ to look back at.

TALIBAGUK, n. luck-bringing talisman.

TALIMUDAW, v. /AG-/ to feel faint, dizzy.

TALINAAY, adj. /NA-/ peaceful, calm, serene.

TALINAED, v. /AG-/ to reside, live, stay, remain.

TALIWAYWAY, v. /MANG-:-AN/ to set free, let go.

TALLAKEB, n. a basket-like contraption used in catching fish in shallow waters.
v. /AG-, MANG-:-AN/ to catch (fish) using this.

TALLAUNG, n. crowd.

TALLIKUD, v. /AG-, -UM-/ to turn one's back, to turn around. /MANG-:-AN/ to turn one's back to.

TALLU, num. three, 3.   --var. -TLU. --syn. TRES.

TALMEG, v. /MANGI- :I-/ to press down, to put pressure on.

TALNA, adj. /NA-/ calm, peaceful, quiet, tranquil, still.
v. /-UM-/. /AG-/ to keep calm, still, quiet.

TALTAG, v. /AG-, MANG-:-EN/ to pound (rice) in order to remove only the husk.

TALTAL, v. /-UM-/, MANG-:-EN/ to beat into a pulp, to crush.

[1]TALUKAB, n. eyelid. --cf. KALUB TI MATA.

[2]TALUKAB, n. carapace of crabs.

TALUKATIK, v. /AG-/ to play a tune with the finger; to tap with the fingers.

TALUN, n. field, esp. rice field.
  v. /AG-, MANG-:-EN/ to farm, cultivate; to plant with rice.

TALUNTUN, v. /MANG-:-EN/ to investigate, examine, trace.

TAMA, v. /-UM-:-AN/ to hit as with a missile.

TAMALES [f. Sp.], n. a dish of small fish seasoned with vinegar, salt and ginger, wrapped in banana leaves and steamed in a small amount of water.
  v. /AG-/ to cook this dish. /MANG-:-EN/ to cook into this dish.

TAMBAK, n. dike, levee, embankment.
  v. /AG-/ to build a dike or levee. /MANG-:-AN/ to build a dike across or around.

TAMBUR, n. drum.
  v. /AG-/ to beat a drum. /MANG-:-EN/ to beat like a drum.

TAMMI, adj. with protruding underlip.
  v. /AG-/.

TAMMUDU, n. forefinger, index finger.

TAMNAY, adj. /NA-/ lacking salt, tasteless, insipid, flat.
  v. /-UM-/.

TAMPIPI, n. chest or trunk made of split bamboo or the like.

TANABUTUB, v. /AG-, -UM-/ to mumble, grumble, growl.

TANAP, n. plain, level land; plateau.
v. /AG-, MANG- :-EN/ to level.

TAN-AW, v. /-UM-/ to look out from a window or an
elevated place. /MANG-:-EN/ to look out or down at.

TANDA, n. sign, mark, indication; signal.
v. /MANG-:-AN/ to put a mark or sign on. /AG-/ to
make the sign of the cross.

TANEM, n. graveyard, tomb, grave, mound.
v. /MANGI-:I-/ to bury, inter.

TANTAN, v. /MANGI-:I-/ to defer, postpone, delay.

TAN-UK, adj. /NA-/ exalted, eminent, famous, illustrious,
celebrated.
v. /MANGI-:I-/ to exalt, extol, praise, commend.

TANGA, adj. /NAG-/ stupid, ignorant, dumb.

TANGAN, n. thumb.

TANGATANG, n. sky, firmament.
v. /AG-/ to fallow, to remain uncultivated for one
or more years: said of rice fields. /MANGI-:I-/ to
hang, suspend.

TANGAY, var. of YANTANGAY.

TANGBAW, n. beam or shaft of a plow or sugar mill.

TANGDAN, n. salary, pay, wages, hire; salary, stipend,
fee. --cf. SUILDU.
v. /AG-, MANG-:-AN/ to pay for work done, to give
salary to.

TANG-ED, n. /AG-, -UM-/ to nod usually as a sign of
assent. /-UM-:-AN/ to nod at.

TANGGA, v. /MAKI-:KA-/ to pitch pennies against. /AG-/
[with pl. subject] to pitch pennies against one
another.

TANGGAD, v. /AG-/ to be in a period of confinement after
childbirth.

TANGGUYUB, n. bugle made of carabao horn.
v. /AG-/ to blow this horn.

TANGIG, adj. /NA-/ haughty, proud, arrogant. --syn.
TANGSIT.

TANGKAL, n. cage or basket for chicken, birds, etc.
v. /MANGI-:I-/ to confine in a cage or basket.

TANGKAY, n. stem of plant.

TANGKEN, adj. /NA-/ hard, solid, firm. /NA--AN/
hardened; mature.
v. /-UM-/.

TANGKUY, n. 1. a kind of vine with oval edible fruits.
2. the fruit of this.

TANGSIT, adj. /(NA-)/ haughty, proud, arrogant, vain,
conceited. --syn. TANGIG.
v. /-UM-/.

TAPA, n. dried salted meat.
v. /AG-/ to make this. /MANG-:-EN/ to make into
this.

TAPAL, n. plaster, patch.
v. /MANG-:-AN/ to put a plaster on, to patch.
/MANGI-:I-/ to patch on, to put on as plaster.

TAPAT, v. /AG-, MANG-:-EN/ to serenade.

TAPAW, v. /-UM-/ [TUMPAW] to float.

TAPAYA, v. /AG-/ to support one's head with the hands.
/MANG-:-EN/ to support with the palm of the hand,
to hold up, support.

TAPINGAR, n. comb of a fowl.

TAPKAL, v. /MANG-:-AN/ to stick something on, to put
a plaster on, to smear.

TAPLIAK, v. /MANG-:-AN/ to spill or splash hot water
on. /MANGI-:I-/ to spill or splash on as hot water.

TAPNO, conj. so that, in order that, lest.

TAPPUAK, v. /AG-, -UM-/ to jump down.   --var. TAPWAK.

TAPUG, v. /-UM-/ to jump into the water.   /MANGI-:I-/
to jump with someone or something into the water.

TAPUK, n. dust.
    v. /MANG-:-AN/ to make dusty.

TAPUN, n. cork for plugging a bottle, hole, etc.   --cf.
SULLAT.

TAPUS, n. end, termination, close.
    v. /AG-, MA-/ to end, terminate, finish.   /MANG-:
-EN/ to end, finish, terminate.

TAPWAK, var. of TAPPUAK.

TARABIT, adj. /NA-/ rapid, fast, quick.
    v. /-UM-/.

TARABITAB, adj. talkative, chatterer, babbler, tattler.
    v. /AG-/ to gossip, tattle, chatter.   /MANG-:-EN/
to gossip about, chatter about.

TARABUTAB, n. foam, froth, spume, scum.

TARADDEK, v. /AG-/ to move with light quick steps.

TARAIGID, n. the edge, border or rim of.
    v. /AG-/ to walk on the edge, border or rim of.

TARAKATAK, v. /AG-/ to produce intermittent sounds,
like the sounds produced by a heavy rain.

TARAKEN, n. pet, ward.
    v. /AG-, MANG-:-EN/ [:TARAKNEN] to take care of,
raise, rear.

TARIKITIK, v. /AG-/ to produce intermittent light
sounds like those produced by a drizzle.

TARAMPO, n. top (a toy).   --syn. SUNAY.
    v. /AG-/ to spin a top.

TARAUDI; TARTARAUDI, n. last part, ending.

TARAUK, n. crow of rooster.
    v. /AG-/ to crow like a rooster.

TARAUN, n. food, nourishment.

TARAWITAW, adj. /(NA-)/ talkative.

TARAY, v. /AG-, -UM-/ to run, run away. /MANG-:-EN/ to
run to.   /MANGI-:I-/ to run away with.   /MAKI-:KA-/
to run away with, to elope with.

TARIGAGAY, n. desire, wish, aspiration.
v. /AG-, MANG-:-EN/ to wish, desire, hope, aspire
for.

TARIKAYU, n. timber.   --cf. KAYU.

TARIMAAN, v. /AG-, MANG-:-EN/ [:TARIMNEN] to put in
proper order, to do properly; to fix.

TARINDANUM, n. a skin infection affecting the hands and
feet caused by prolonged and repeated soaking and
characterized by itchiness.
v. /AG-, -EN/ to be affected by this.

TARIPNUNG, n. meeting, assembly, congregation.
v. /-UM-/ to attend a meeting or assembly. /MANG-:
-EN/ to convene, gather together for a meeting.

TARMIDUNG, n. pimple.   --syn. KAMURO.
v. /AG-, -EN/ to have pimples.

TARUNG, n. eggplant.

TARUS, adj. /NA-/ keen, sharp.
v. /AG-, -UM-/ to go directly or straight. /MAKA-:
MA--AN/ to be able to understand or grasp.

[1]TASA [f. Sp.], n. cup.   --syn. KAP.

[2]TASA, var. of TAHAR.

TASTAS, v. /AG-, MANG-:-EN/ to rip, tear up.

TATANG, n. 1. father, godfather. 2. any old man.
TATANG ITI BUNYAG, godfather.

TAU, n. person, human being.

TAUD, v. /AG-/ to come from, originate.

TAUL, v. /AG-/ to bark.   /MANG-:-AN/ to bark at.

TAWA, n. window.

TAWAG, v. /MANGI-:-I-/ to publish, proclaim, cry.

TAWAR, v. /-UM-/ to haggle, bargain.   /MANG-:-AN/ to
   lower the price of, to offer a lower price for.

TAWATAW, v. /AG-/ to roam, wander.

TAWEN, n. year, age.
      v. /AG-/ to have as age, to be as old as.

TAWID, n. inheritance, heritage.
      v. /AG-, MANG-:-EN/ to inherit.

TAWWATAWWA, n. the castor-oil plant.

TAY, 1. var. of TAYU. 2. short form of DAYTAY.

TAYA, v. /AG-, MANG-:-EN/ to catch, collect.

[1]TAYAB, n. pot with wide mouth used for cooking
   vegetables, meat, fish, etc. but not rice.

[2]TAYAB, v. /AG-, -UM-/ to fly.   /MANG-:-EN/ to fly to.
   /MANGI-:I-/ to fly away with.

   TUMATAYAB, n. bird, anything that flies.   --syn.
      BILLIT.

TAYAG, adj. /NA-/ tall, high.
      v. /-UM-/.

[1]TAYU, pron. you (plural) and I, we (inclusive): the
   enclitic nominative of DATAYU.   --var. TAY.

[2]TAYU, pron. 1. our (inclusive), of you (plural) and me,
   your (plural) and my. 2. by you (plural) and me,
   by us (inclusive): the enclitic oblique of DATAYU.
   --var. TAY.

TAYYEK, v. /AG-, -UM-/ to spin, whirl, rotate.

TEATRU [f. Sp.], n. theater.

TEBBA, v. /AG-, MANG-:-EN/ to cut down (a banana plant).

TEBBAG, v. /AG-, MANG-:-EN/ to cause to crumble down.
/MA-/ [MATBAG] to crumble down.

TEBBENG, n. a hole in the earlobe for earrings.
v. /AG-/ to make a hole in the earlobe. /MANG-:-AN/
to put a hole in the earlobe of.

TED, see ITED.

TEDDEK, n. post. --syn. ADIGI, POSTE.

TEDTED, v. /AG-/ to fall in droplets, to drip, trickle.

TEKKA, n. a kind of gecko.

TEKKEN, n. a pole for pushing a boat.
v. /AG-/ to use this.

TEKNIKO [f. Sp.], n. technician.

TEKTEK, v. /AG-/ to cry like a house lizard.

TELEBISION [f. Eng.], n. television.
v. /AG-/ to watch television.

TELEPONO [f. Sp.], n. telephone.
v. /AG-/ to use a telephone. /AG-, MANG-:-AN/ to
call by telephone, to telephone. /MANGI-:I-/ to tell
or send by telephone.

TELON [f. Sp.], n. stage curtains, screen on which
movie is projected.

TELTEL, n. nape, back of neck.

TEMPORARIO [f. Sp.], adj. temporary.

TEMTEM, n. bonfire.
v. /MANGI-:I-/ to bake in hot ashes. /AG-/ to make
a bonfire.

TENIDOR [f. Sp.], n. fork used for eating.

TENIENTE [f. Sp.], n. lieutenant.

TENGNGA, n. middle, center.

  TENGNGA TI ALDAW, midday, noon.

TENGNGEL, v. /MANG-:-EN/ to subdue, restrain, check, hold back.

TEPPANG, n. precipice, cliff.

TERITORIO [f. Sp.], n. territory.

TESURERO [f. Sp.], n. treasurer.

[1]TI, art. the.

[2]TI, var. of ITI.

TIA [f. Sp.], n. aunt. --syn. IKIT.

TIAN, n. belly, stomach.

TIANI, n. tweezers, pliers.

TIBAB, v. /MANG-:-EN/ to knock under the chin.

TIBBAYU, v. /AG-/ to heave due to alarm, fear, surprise, etc.: said of the chest.

TIBBENG, v. /AG-, MANG-:-AN/ to pierce a hole through the lobes of the ear where earrings are hooked.

TIBKUL, v. /MAI-/ to stumble, trip.

TIBNUK, v. /MANG-:-AN/ to throw cold water into hot liquid to make it cooler. /MANGI-:I-/ to throw into hot liquid so as to make it cooler.

TIDDA, n. remainder, leftover, residue.
   v. /MANGI-:I-/ to leave as remainder or leftover.
/MA-/ [MATDA] to be left.

TIEMPO [f. Sp.], n. time; condition, situation.
   v. /MANG-:-AN/ often /MAKA-:-AN/ to come upon by chance.

TIENDA [f. Sp.], n. store, market.
   v. /MAKI-/ to buy something at a store or market.
   TIENDAAN, n. market. --syn. TIANGGI, MERKADO.

TIG-AB, v. /AG-/ to eructate.

TIGERGER, v. /AG-/ to tremble, shiver, shake.

TIGNAY, v. /AG-/ to move, stir.   /MANG-:-EN/ to stir, move.

TIKAG, adj. /NA-/ arid, dry, parched: said of land.
   v. /-UM-/.

TIKET [f. Eng.], n. ticket.
   v. /AG-/ to get a ticket.   /AG-, MANG-:-AN/ to give a ticket to.

TIKLEB, v. /MAI-/ to fall down on one's face.

TIKTIK, n. spy.   --syn. ISPIA.
   v. /MANG-:-AN/ often /MAKA-:MA--AN/ to spy on.

TIK-UL, v. /MANG-:-AN/ to knock (someone) on the head.
   /MANGI-:I-/ to knock on something.   /AG-/ [with pl. subject] to collide, knock against each other.

TIL-AY, v. /AG-/ to tiptoe.

TILDE [f. Sp.], n. period, dot (punctuation mark).

TILDI, n. clitoris.

TILLAYON, v. /AG-/ to dangle, swing.

TILMUN, n. swallow of food or water.
   v. /MANG- :-EN/ to swallow.

TIMAM, v. /MANG-:-EN/ to knock on the point of the chin or lower jaw.

TIMBA [f. Sp.], n. pail, bucket.
   v. /AG-, MANG-:-EN/ to use a pail or bucket in fetching or getting.

TIMBENG, adj. /NA-/ calm, prudent.
   v. /MANG-:-EN/ to weigh.

   TIMBENGAN, n. scales.

TIMBUKEL, adj. /(NA-)/ round, globular, spherical.
   v. /AG-, MANG-:-EN/ to make round or spherical.

TIMEK, n. voice.
v. /AG-/ to speak, to make a sound.

TIMID, n. chin.

TIMMUTIL, n. Adam's apple.

TIM-UG, v. /AG-/ [with pl. subject] to collide, to hit each other on the head. /MANGI-:I-/ to hit or knock against. /MAI-/ to knock one's head against something accidentally.

TINA, n. dye, indigo. --syn. TAYUM.
v. /AG-, MANG-:-EN/ to dye.

TINABI, n. sewing thread.

TINAPA, n. salted fish, smoked fish.

TINAPAY, n. bread, biscuit.

TINING, adj. /NA-/ calm and clear like water in a pond.

TINNAG, v. /AG-/ to fall down, drop unintentionally. /MANG-:-EN/ or /MANGI-:I-/ to cause to fall down, to drop. /MA-/ [MATNAG] to fall down, drop.

TINTA [f. Sp.], n. writing ink.

TINTURA DE YODO [f. Sp.], n. tincture of iodine.

TINUKEL, n. bit, particle.

TINGAL, n. prop, wedge.
v. /MANG-:-AN/ to put a wedge under, to prop or support. /MANGI-:I-/ to use as wedge or prop.

TINGGA, see PATINGGA.

TINGI, v. /AG-/ to retail, to sell by piece not by lot.

TING-IAN, n. a native of the province of Abra.

TINGIG, adj. leaning or inclined sideways.
v. /AG-/ to lean or incline sideways.

TIPED, v. /AG-/ to economize, be frugal, economical. /MANG-:-EN/ [:TIPDEN] to use economically, to conserve.

TIPKEL, n. mass, lump, clod.
   v. /MANG-:-EN/ to form into a lump, clod, etc.

TIPO [f. Sp.], n. type.

TIPPAY, v. /-UM-, MANG-:-EN/ to knock out of someone's hand, to cause to fall down from someone's grasp.

TIPPING, n. chip, notch, break
   v. /-UM-, MANG-:-AN/ to cause to have a chip, to chip or break off a part of. /MA--AN/ to be chipped.

TIPUN, v. /MANG-:-EN/ to gather, assemble, put together, collect. /MANGI-:I-/ to add to a collection, gathering, assembly or the like. /AG-/ [with pl. subject] to gather, assemble; to come together; hence, to live as man and wife.

TIRAD, adj. /NA-/ pointed, sharp.
   v. /-UM-/. /-AN/ to make pointed, furnish with a sharp point.

TIRAYUK, v. /-UM-/ to gush out, spout, jet, spurt.

TIREM, n. oyster.

TIRITIR, adj. twisted.
   v. /AG-/ to become twisted. /MANG-:-EN/ to wring, twist.

TIRTIRIS, n. doll.   --syn. MUMUNYIKA, TUTUNIKA.

TISA [f. Sp.], n. chalk.

TITSER [f. Eng.], n. teacher.   --syn. MAESTRO, MAESTRA.

TITULO [f. Sp.], n. title.

TIWATIW, v. /AG-/ to dangle, hang.   --var. TIWWATIW.

TIWENG, adj. /NA-/ moving from one side of the bed to the other when sleeping.

TIWWATIW, var. of TIWATIW.

-TLU, var. of TALLU, three: used only with certain prefixes.

TO, an enclitic particle used to indicate future time. --see INTO, INTONO.

TONO [f. Sp.], n. tone.

TORO [f. Sp.], n. bull.

TOY, short for DAYTOY or DITOY.

TRABAHADOR [f. Sp.], n. laborer.
    adj. hard-working.

TRABAHO [f. Sp.], n. work, job, task.
    v. /AG-/ to work. /MANG-:-EN/ to do.

TRAHEDIA [f. Sp.], n. tragedy.

TRAIDOR [f. Sp.], n. traitor.

TRAK [f. Eng.], n. truck.

TRAMBIA [f. Sp.], n. tramcar, streetcar that runs on rails.

TRANSIT [f. Eng.], n. bus. --syn. BUS.

TRAPO [f. Sp.], n. rag, a piece of cloth used in wiping.
    v. /AG-, MANG-:-AN/ to wipe with a wiping cloth.

TREN [f. Sp.], n. railway train.

TRES [f. Sp.], num. three, 3. --syn. TALLO.

TRIBO [f. Sp.], n. tribe.

TROPEO [f. Sp.], n. trophy.

TROSO [f. Sp.], n. log.

TRUMBUN [f. Eng.], n. trombone. --syn. ISLAID.

TRUMPETA [f. Sp.], n. trumpet.

TSAMPION [f. Eng.], n. champion. --var. KAMPEON.

TSANI [f. Sp.], n. tweezers.

TSESA, n. a kind of fruit-bearing tree.

TSIKO, n. 1. a kind of fruit-bearing tree. 2. its
  fruit.

TSINELAS [f. Sp.], n. slipper.
    v. /AG-/ to wear slippers. /MANG-:-EN/ to beat
  with a slipper.

TSIP [f. Eng.], n. chief; chief of police; chief of an
  office.

TSUKULATE [f. Sp.], n. chocolate.

TUANG, v. /AG-, MANG-:-EN/ to cause to fall down from
  an upright position, to tumble down. /MA-/ to fall
  down, tumble down.

TUBA, n. sap of palm trees.
    v. /AG-/ to get juice from a palm tree.

TUBBU, v. /AG-/ to harvest sugar cane by cutting it
  down. /MANG-:-EN/ to harvest (sugar cane) by cutting
  it down.

TUBBUG, n. juice, sap; any liquid secretion.
    v. /AG-/ to secrete juice, sap, milk, etc.

TUBEG, v. /MA-/ to become rotten due to too much
  moisture or water.

TUBLAK, v. /MAI-/ to slide down, tumble down, fall
  down. /MANGI-:I-/ to cause to tumble down, fall
  down.

[1]TUBO, n. sprout, shoot, bud.
    v. /AG-, -UM-/ to sprout, shoot; to germinate.

[2]TUBO, n. gain, profit.
    v. /AG-:-EN/ to gain, profit; to get as profit.

TUBONG, n. a tube consisting of an internode of bamboo.

TUDING, v. /MANGI-:I-/ to designate, appoint, specify.
  /MA--AN/ to be designated, appointed.

TUDIO, adj. /NA-/ meek, docile, obedient, submissive.
v. /AG-/.

TUDO, n. rain.
v. /AG-:-EN/ to rain. /MA--AN/ to be caught in the
rain, to be wet by the rain.

TUDU, v. /MANGI-:I-/ to point at, show, indicate.

TUGAW, n. seat, chair, bench.
v. /AG-/ to sit down. /MANGI-:I-/ to cause to sit
down, to sit; to put on a seat. /-UM-:-AN/ to sit on.

TUGI, n. a kind of yam with brown skin and white meat.

TUGKEL, v. /-UM-/ to stick; to be driven into something.
/MANGI-:I-/ to plant or drive into something.

TUGLEP, v. /AG-/ to have one's eyes closed and head
nodding due to drowsiness.

TUGUT, v. /AGI-, MANGI-:I-/ to bring, take along, carry
along.

TUKAD, n. step of a ladder, rung.

TUKAK, n. frog.

TUKAKTUKAK, n. wart.

TUKAR [f. Sp.], v. /AG-, MANG-:-EN/ to play as a
musical instrument.

TUKAY, v. /MANG-:-EN/ to disrupt the sleep of, to
disturb (someone) while asleep.

TUKKUL, v. /-UM-, MANG-:-EN/ to break off, snap. /MA-/
to be broken.

TUKMA, v. /-UM-, MANG-:-AN/ to seize, grab, catch with
the hand.

TUKNO, v. /MANG-:-EN/ to hit or reach with the head.

TUKTUK, n. top; crown of head, summit of mountain or
hill, top of tree, etc.

TUKUD, v. /MANG-:-EN/ to measure the depth of, to
fathom.

TULAG, n. contract, agreement, bargain.
   v. /MAKI-:KA-/ to make a contract or agreement with.
/AG-/ [with pl. subject] to enter into an agreement,
to make a contract.

TULATID, v. /AG-/ to roll, turn over.   /MANG-:-EN/ or
/MANGI-:I-/ to cause to roll or turn over.

TULBEK, n. key.   --syn. KANDADO, SUSI.
   v. /MANG-:-AN/ to lock or open with a key.

¹TULENG, v. /MA-/ to be blinded by light.

²TULENG, adj. /NAG-/ deaf.

TULID, v. /AG-/ to roll, turn over.   /MANG-:-EN/ to
cause to roll or turn over.   --syn. TULATID.

TULISAN, n. robber, thief.

TULNUG, adj. /NA-/ obedient, dutiful, submissive.

TULONG, n. help, aid.
   v. /-UM-, MANG-:-AN/ to help, aid, assist, support.
/MANGI-:I-/ to give as help, aid, or assistance.

¹TULUD, v. /MANGI-:I-/ to accompany, escort to a place:
usually home.

²TULUD, v. /MANGI-:I-/ to rock (the cradle).

TULUY, v. /-UM-, AG-/ to continue, proceed, go on.
   /MANGI-:I-/ to continue to do.

TUMA, n. body louse.

TUMEG, v. /MANGI-:I-/ to knock someone's head against
something.

TUMEK, v. /MANG-:-EN/ to crush, pulverize, reduce to
fine particles.   /MA-/ to be crushed, pulverized or
reduced to fine particles.

TUMENG, n. knee.

TUMPUNG, v. /AG-/ [with pl. subject] to agree, concur.
/MA--AN/ to come upon accidentally.

TUMUK, n. 1. a variety of banana with thick-skinned
greenish fruit. 2. its fruit.

TUNANO, short for INTON ANO?, when?

TUNAW, v. /MANG-:-EN/ to melt, dissolve, liquify.
/MA-/ to be melted or dissolved.

TUNDAL, n. 1. a variety of banana with thin-skinned
yellow fruits. 2. its fruit.

TUNTUN, v. /AG-, MANG-:-EN/ to seek to know, to claim,
inquire about.

TUNTUNIKA, n. doll. --syn. MUMMUNYIKA, TIRTIRIS.

TUNU, v. /AG-/ to broil, roast, toast. /MANGI-:I-/ to
broil, roast, toast.

TUNGAW, n. mite. --cf. AYAM, TUMA.

TUNGGAL, adj. each, every.
conj. whenever, each time, every time.

TUNGLAB, v. /AG-/ to gasp for air, to pant.

TUNGNGANG, adj. stupid, half-crazed, simpleton.

TUNGO, n. fuel, firewood.
v. /MANGI-:I-/ to use as fuel or firewood.

TUNGPA, v. /-UM-, MANG-:-EN/ to slap, cuff.

TUNGPAL, v. /AG-/ to be fulfilled, to come true.
/MANG-:-EN/ to fulfill, comply with, effect.

TUNGTUNG, v. /MAKI-:KA-/ to talk or converse with.

TUPAK, v. /MANGI-:I-/ to throw down, to drop heavily.
/MAI-/ to drop heavily by chance.

TUPI, n. hem, fold.
v. /MANG-:-EN/ to hem, fold.

TUPIG, n. a kind of sweet made of rice and brown sugar
formed like a hotdog.
   v. /AG-/ to make this.   /MANG-:-EN/ to make into
this.

TUPPUL, adj. with one or two front teeth missing.

TUPRA, n. sputum, spit, saliva.
   v. /AG-, MANGI-:I-/ to spit.   /-UM-:-AN/ to spit on.

TURAY, adj. /NA-/ authoritative, supreme.
   v. /AG-/ to rule, govern.

TURED, adj. /NA-/ brave, bold, daring.
   v. /MANGI-:I-/ to endure, suffer bravely.

TURISTA [f. Sp.], n. tourist.

TURKAK, n. phlegm.   --syn. PLIMAS.
   v. /AG-/ to spit phlegm.

TURNILYO [f. Sp.], n. screw.

TURPE [f. Sp.], adj. /NAG-/ stupid, idiotic, imbecile.

TURPUS, v. /AG-/ to finish a course or degree, to
   graduate.   /MANG-:-EN/ to finish (a degree or course).

TURRE [f. Sp.], n. steeple.

TURUD, n. hill, hillock.
   adj. /NA-/ on a high place.

TURUG, v. /MA-/ to sleep.

TURUKUTUK, v. /AG-/ to coo, e.g. pigeons.

TURUNG, v. /AG-/ to go toward (a place).   /MANGI-:I-/
   to lead, guide or direct (to a place).

TURUTUT, n. 1. trumpet. 2. the sound of this.
   v. /AG-/ to produce the sound of a trumpet.

TUTAL [f. Sp.], n. total, sum.
   v. /MANG-:-EN/ to sum, total.   --syn. SUMA.
   adv. after all.

TUTTUTERA, n. gossiper.

TUTUT, v. /AG-/ to secrete a milky or thick sap.

TUUN, v. /-UM-/ to go on top of. /MANGI-:I-/ to put
on top of. /AG-/ [with pl. subject] to have one on
top of the other; hence, to copulate. /-UM-:-AN/ to
put oneself on top of another; hence, to copulate
with someone.

TUWATU, n. dragon fly.   --var. TUWWATU.

TUWWATU, var. of TUWATU.

TUYU, n. rice bran.

TUYUT, n. a period when the harvest is poor due to
drought.

UBAN, n. gray hair.
     v. /AG-/ to have gray hair.

UBAS [f. Sp.], n. grape.

UBBA, v. /AG-, MANG-:-EN/ to carry as a baby.

UBBAK, n. sheath of the banana leaf.

UBBAW, adj. /NAG-/ inane, empty.

UBBUG, n. spring of water, fountain.
     v. /AG-/ to gush out water.

UBBUUB, v. /AG-/ to take vapor bath.

UBET, n. anus, buttocks; bottom.

UBI, n. yam with purple meat.

UBING, n. child, boy, girl.
     adj. /NAG-/ young, immature.
     v. /-UM-/ to become younger.

UBO, v. /AG-:I-/ to leak.

UBOG, n. soft pith of palm trees.
     v. /AG-, MANG-:-EN/ to get the pith of (a palm
   tree).

UBON, n. a string of beads or the like.
   v. /AG-, MANG-:-EN/ to thread on a string.

UBONG, n. pigpen, sty.

UBOR, v. /AG-, MANG-:-EN/ to pelt with stones continuously.

UDANG, n. lobster, crayfish.

UDAUD, n. the bow of a violin.
   v. /MANG-:-EN/ to pull to and fro like the bow of
   a violin.

UDI, n. rear.
   v. /MA-/ to be late or last.

UDONG, v. /-UM-/ to go to the town proper (POBLASION)
   from the BARRIO or SITIO. /MANGI-:I-/ to take to
   the town proper.

UD-UD, v. /-UM-:-AN/ to ask for repeatedly, beg for.

UGA, v. /AG-/ to low, moo.

UGALI, n. custom, habit, tradition, way.

UGAOG, v. /AG-/ to bawl, cry loudly.

[1]UGAS, n. a shrub whose leaves are used for scouring
   purposes.

[2]UGAS, v. /AG-, MANG-:-AN/ to wash (dishes, plates, etc.)

UGAW, adj. /NA-/ wasteful, lavish.

UGED, n. line.
   v. /-UM-:-AN/ to put a line on.

UGGOT, n. young leaves of a plant.
   v. /-UM-:-AN/ to take some of the young leaves of.

UGING, n. charcoal, soot. --var. URING.
   v. /AG-/ to make charcoal. /MANG-:-EN/ to make
   into charcoal. /-UM-:-AN/ to smear with charcoal
   or soot.

[1]UGIS, v. /AG-/ to make the sign of the cross.

²UGIS, n. line. --syn. UGED.
    v. /-UM-:-AN/ to put or make a line on.

UGMA, n. remote time in the past; the beginning; long
    time ago.

UGMOK, v. /-UM-:-AN/ to do something on something
    persistently or tenaciously.

UGSA, n. 1. deer. 2. venison.

UG-UG, v. /AG-/ to weep with closed mouth.

UGUT, v. /MA--AN/ to be drained of blood, sweat or tears.

UHAL, n. buttonhole. --var. UHALIS.
    v. /MANG-:-AN/ to provide with buttonholes.

UHALIS, var. of UHAL.

UKAG, v. /MANG-:-EN/ to open, spread out.

UKAP, v. -AG-/ to open by itself, e.g. clams. /MANG-:
    -EN/ to pry open.

UKARKAR, v. /AG-/ to open, e.g. a flower. /MANG-:-EN/
    to open, unwrap, unroll.

UKAS, v. /MANG-:-EN/ to loosen, untie, unfasten. /MA-/
    to be untied or unfastened.

UKBOS, v. /MAI-/ to be spilled.

UKEL, n. testicle. --cf. LATEG.

UKEN, n. puppy.

UKI, n. vulva, vagina.

UKIS, n. peeling, bark, rind, husk.
    v. /AG-, MANG-:-AN/ to remove the peeling, bark,
    rind, or husk of.

UKKON, v. /MANG-:-EN/ to join, gather together. /MA-/
    to be gathered together.

UKKOR, n. a piece of cloth or handkerchief tied around
    the neck.

UKLOT, n. covering of the head, cap.

UKNOG, v. /MANG-:-EN/ to knock out, e.g. the marrow of the bone.

UKOM, n. judge.
    v. /MANG-:-EN/ to judge, try.

UKOP, v. /MANG-:-AN/ to sit on (eggs) in order to hatch (them).

UKRAD, v. /AG-/ to unfurl, spread out, unfold, unroll. /MANG-:-EN/ to unfurl, unfold, unroll.

UKRIT, v. /MANG-:-EN/ to cut open with a single line using a scalpel or a sharp object. /MA-/ to be cut open.

UKSUB, v. /MANG-:-EN/ to remove, pull off.

UKSUT, v. /AG-, MANG-:-EN/ to pull out, unsheathe, e.g. a sword.

UKTUBRE [f. Sp.], n. October.

UKUUK, v. /-UM-/ to smolder.

ULA, v. /MANGI-:I-/ to spit out, eject from the mouth.

ULAW, n. dizziness.
    v. /MA-/ to be dizzy. /MANG-:-EN/ to cause to become dizzy.

ULAY, n. neckerchief.
    v. /AG-/ to use a neckerchief. /MANG-:-AN/ to put a neckerchief on someone.

ULBOD, adj. /NAG-/ liar, deceitful.
    v. /AG-/ to tell a lie, to deceive. /MANG-:-EN/ to deceive, to tell a lie to.

ULEG, n. snake.

ULEP, n. cloud.
    adj. /NA-/ cloudy, overcast.

ULES, n. blanket.
      v. /AG-/ to use a blanket, to cover oneself with a
   blanket.   /MANG-:-AN/ to cover someone with a blanket.

ULI, v. /-UM-/ to climb up, go up, ascend, rise.
   /MANG-:-EN/ to climb.   /MANGI-:I-/ to climb up in
   order to give something to someone.

ULIDAN, n. model, example, paragon.

ULIKBA, n. a fowl with black meat.

ULILA, n. orphan, one whose mother or father or both
   are dead.
      v. /MA-/ to become an orphan.   /MANG-:-EN/ to make
   someone an orphan.

ULIMEK, adj. /NA-/ quiet, calm, peaceful, tranquil,
   serene.
      v. /AG-/ to keep quiet.

ULIT, v. /MANG-:-EN/ to repeat, say again, do again.

ULITEG, n. uncle.   --syn. TIO.

ULLAW, n. kite.
      v. /AG-/ to fly a kite.

ULLAYAT, adj. /NA-/ slow.
      v. /MANG-:-EN/ to do slowly.

ULLUM, v. /AG-/ to stay indoors.   /MANG-:-EN/ to wrap
   well in order to improve the quality of or to ripen.

ULMOG, n. chicken tick.

ULNAS, n. sled.

ULO, n. head, roof.
      adj. /NA-/ 1. with a large head. 2. intelligent,
   bright, smart.
      v. /MANG-:-EN/ to behead, decapitate.

ULPIT, adj. /NA-/ cruel, merciless, ruthless, brutal.

ULTIMATUM [f. Eng.], n. ultimatum.

ULUD, v. /MANG-:-EN/ to pull, drag.   /MA-/ to be pulled or dragged.

ULUG, v. /-UM-/ to go down, come down.   /MANG-:-EN/ to go down for, to come down for.   /MANGI-:I-/ to bring down, take down; to translate.

ULUY, v. /MANG-:-AN/ to give the death blow to.   /MA-/ to expire.

-UM-, a verbalizing affix placed immediately before the first vowel of the stem with meanings: (a) to do the action expressed by the stem. (b) to assume the state or condition described by the stem.

[1]UMA, v. /AG-/ to satiate oneself with.   /MA-/ to be satiated with.   /MANG-:-EN/ to satiate someone with.

[2]UMA, n. tract of land cleared for cultivation, kaingin. v. /AG-/ to clear a tract of land for cultivation. /MANG-:-EN/ to clear for cultivation.

UMAN, v. /MAKI-/ to consult, seek the opinion or advice of.

UMANG, n. hermit crab; hence, a person who continually changes his residence.

UMBAL, = -UM- + EBBAL.

UMDAS, v. to be sufficient, to be enough.

UMEL, adj. /NAG-/ dumb, mute.

UMILI, see under ILI.

UMIT, v. /MANG-:-EN/ to pilfer, steal, filch.   --syn. TAKAW.

UMLAY, = -UM- + ELLAY.

UMLEK, = -UM- + ELLEK.

UMMONG, v. /MANG-:-EN/ to gather, assemble.
   UMMONGAN, n. meeting, assembly.

UMNO, = -UM- + NO.

UMOK, n. nest.
    v. /AG-/ to build a nest; to stay put in a place.

UMPES, = -UM- + EPPES.

UMRES, = -UM- + ERRES.

UMSI, v. /MANG-:-EN/ to scorn, despise, mock.

UNA [f. Sp.], num. one; 1: used only with ALA, o'clock.
    ALA UNA, one o'clock. --syn. UNO, MAYSA.

UNA; UMUNA, adv. first.

    INAUNA, n. eldest child.

    KAMAUNA, n. foreleg, forefoot.

    PAKAUNA, n. presage.

[1]UNAS, n. sugar cane.

[2]UNAS, v. /-UM-/ to become hard.

UNAY, adv. very much.
    v. /MANGI-:I-/ to recommend to be done urgently.
    adj. excessive, very insistent: usually in
    exclamations.

[1]UNDA, n. interval between the steps of a ladder.

[2]UNDA, v. /MANG-:-EN/ to do intermittently.

UNDAY, adj. /NA-/ long, lengthy.

UNEG, n. inside, within.
    adj. /NA-/ deep inside, remote.
    v. /-UM-/ to go inside; to become deep. /MANGI-:I-/
    to take inside; to make (it) deep.

UNI, n. sound, noise.
    v. /AG-/ to make a sound or noise, to speak.

UNIBERSIDAD [f. Sp.], n. university.

UNIPORME [f. Sp.], n. uniform.
    v. /AG-/ to wear a uniform.

UNMONG, n. heap, pile.   --syn. PENPEN, BUNTON.
   v. /MANG-:-EN/ to heap, pile.

UNNAT, v. /AG-/ to stretch oneself.   /MANG-:-EN/ to
   stretch, extend.

UNNOY, v. /AG-/ to sigh, moan; hence, to complain.

UNO [f. Sp.], num. one; 1.   --syn. MAYSA, UNA.

UNOR, v. /MANG-:-EN/ to give something to all.

UNOS, v. /MANG-:-EN/ to hoist, raise with a tackle.

UNSUY, v. /MA-/ to suffer pain due to dangling.

UNUNG, v. /MANGI-:I-/ to report.

UNUUN, v. /AG-/ to produce a sound like that produced
   by the contents of a coconut, an egg, etc. when
   shaken.

UNGAB, v. /MANG-:-AN/ to notch, dent, chip.   /MA--AN/
   to be dented, notched, chipped.

UNGAR, v. /AG-/ to revive, recover, recuperate; to get
   better.

UNGAT, v. /MANG-:-EN/ to open by prying.

UNGET, adj. /NA-/ hot-tempered, quick-tempered, strict,
   severe, irritable; fierce, ferocious.
   v. /AG-/ to get angry, to scold.

UNGIB, v. /MANG-:-AN/ to bite a part of in order to
   taste.

UNGIK, n. grunt of a pig.
   v. /AG-/ to produce this sound.

UNGKAY, n. stem or stalk of flowers, fruits, etc.;
   handle.

UNGNGO, v. /-UM-, MANG-:-EN, -AN/ to kiss, buss.

UNGNGOB, adj. having cleft palate.

UNGOR, n. roaring sound.
   v. /AG-/ to roar, growl.

UNGOT, n. coconut shell used as scoop.   --cf. BUYUBUY.

UNGTO, n. end; tip, apex.

UNG-UNG, adj. /NAG-/ foolish, crazy.

[1]UPA, n. hen esp. mother hen.

[2]UPA, n. pay, salary, hire, rent.
   v. /MAKI-/ to work by the day for daily wages.
   /MANG-:-AN/ to rent, hire.   /MANGI-:I-/ to use as
   payment, rent or hire.

UPAW, n. a small leather bag.

UPAY, v. /MANG-:-EN/ to discourage.

UPER, v. /AG-/ to stay immersed in water for some time.
   /MANGI-:I-/ to soak, immerse in water.   /MANG-:-AN/
   to make soggy by soaking in water.

UPISINA [f. Sp.], n. office.
   v. /AG-/ to hold office, to work in an office.

UPLAS, n. a tree whose leaves are used for scouring
   purposes.

UPPAT, num. four; 4.   --var. -PAT.   --syn. KUATRO.

UPPOK, v. /MANG-:-AN/ to live with someone.

URAGA, v. /MANGI-:I-/ to retail meat.   /-UM-/ to buy
   meat at retail.

URAM, n. fire, conflagration.
   v. /MA-/ to be burned.   /MANG-:-EN/ to burn.

URAT, n. vein, root.
   v. /AG-/ to develop roots.

URAUR, adj. /NA-/ slender.

[1]URAY, v. /AG-/ to wait.   /MANG-:-EN/ to wait for.
   /MANGI-:I-/ to keep for someone expected to come or
   arrive.

²URAY, adv. no matter, even so.
    conj. though, although.

URBUN, n. the young of horse or carabao.

URDEN, n. priest's crown.
    v. /MANG-:-AN/ to put this on someone's head.   /AG-/
    to have this on one's head.

URDON, v. /MANG-:-EN/ to gather, bring together,
    assemble.

URIAG, v. /AG-/ to shout as when scolding someone.
    /MANG-:-AN/ to shout at angrily.

URING, var. of UGING.

URIRIS, n. the sound made by a hungry pig.
    v. /AG-/ to make this sound.

URISAY, interj. an expression used to call pigs to eat.
    v. /AG-/ to call pigs to eat.

URMOT, n. pubic hair.

URNONG, v. /AG-/ [with pl. subject] to gather together,
    assemble.   /AG-, MANG-:-EN/ to collect, gather,
    assemble.

URNOS, adj. /NA-/ orderly, well-arranged, neat.
    v. /AG-, MANG-:-EN/ to put in order, arrange, fix;
    to make neat.

UROK, v. /AG-/ to snore.

UROT, v. /AG-/ to drop, fall, e.g. flowers, hair, seeds,
    etc.   /MANG-:-EN/ to pull (the hair) when delousing.

URO-URO, v. /MANG-:-AN/ to cleanse with water.

-US, see under PANG-US.

USANG, n. bagasse.

USAOS, v. /MANG-:-AN/ to polish by rubbing with a piece
    of cloth.

USAT, v. /MANG-/ to open a road, clear a path.

USAW, v. /AG-/ to fade, discolor. /MA--AN/ to be colored or stained due to contact with a piece of cloth that fades.

USIG, v. /MANG-:-EN/ to investigate, probe, examine.

USO, [f. Sp.], adj. in vogue, in style.
v. /MA-/ to be in vogue, in style, in fashion. /MANG-:-EN/ to cause to be in vogue, in style, in fashion.

USONG, v. /AG-/ to put on one's clothes. /MANGI-:I-/ to put on (one's clothes) over the head.

USSOG, adj. without clothes, esp. the upper garment.
v. /AG-/ to remove one's clothes. /MANG-:-EN/ to remove (one's clothes). /MANG-:-AN/ to remove the clothes of.

USTISIA, var. of HUSTISIA.

USUK, v. /-UM-/ to pass under or through a narrow opening.

UTANG, n. debt, obligation.
v. /-UM-, MANG-:-EN/ to borrow.

PAUTANG, v. /AG-:-EN/ to lend, loan.

UTEK, n. brain.
adj. /NA-/ brainy, intelligent, bright.

UTENG, n. tang, tongue of knife, bell, etc.

UTOB, v. /MANG-:-EN/ to consider, reflect upon, ponder on.

UTOL, n. sibling, brother, sister. --syn. KABSAT, KABAGIS.

UTONG, n. bean.

UTOT, n. mouse. --syn. BAO.

UTOY, v. /MA--AN/ to tire out from waiting.

UTTOG, adj. /NA-/ lustful, sexually excitable.
v. /MAKA-/ to feel sexually excited.

UTTOT, n. fart, a release of air from the anus.
   v. /-UM-/ to fart, to release air from the anus.

UT-UT, adj. /NA-/ sore, painful, aching.
   v. /AG-/ to ache, feel sore, feel painful.

UUNG, n. mushroom.

UWWAK, var. of WAK.

UYAS, v. /AG-/ to slither, creep, crawl like a snake.

UYAUY, v. /AG-/ to dangle, hang and swing loosely.
   --var. UYYAUY.

UYAW, v. /AG-, MANG-:-EN/ to mock, criticize, deride,
   ridicule.

UYEK, n. cough.
   v. /AG-/ to cough.

UYON, n. a measure of palay; ten BAAR of palay.

UYONG, adj. /NA-/ cruel, sadistic, fierce, ferocious.

UYUKAN, n. honeybee.

UYUS, v./MANG-:-EN/ to pull out as a fiber or thread.

UYUT, v. /MANG-:-AN/ to persuade, induce.

UYYAUY, var. of UYAUY.

WAB, v. /AG-/ to yawn.   --syn. SUYAAB.

WADAG, v. /MANGI-:I-/ to fling aside with the extended
   arm, to push or throw aside.

WADAN, var. of PAGWADAN.

WADAWAD, v. /AG-/ to fling one's arms left and right.
   /MANGI-:I-/ to strike with the arms flinging left
   and right.

WADWAD, adj. /NA-/ abundant, much, many, plentiful, ample. Masapul ti nawadwad nga anus. Ample patience is needed.

WAGAS, n. method, way. Diyo kadi mapampanunot no ania dagiti nanamnam-ay nga wagas ti panagkalap? Don't you think of the more convenient method of fishing?

WAGAT, v. /MAKAI-:MAI-/ to mislay or misplace.

WAGAYWAY, n. flag, banner, streamer.   --syn. BANDERA.

WAGSAK, v. /AGI-, MANGI-:I-/ to shake strongly, as a heavy piece of cloth, by holding it at two corners.

[1]WAGWAG, n. a variety of awned early rice with light-colored hull, few awns and white kernel.

[2]WAGWAG, v. /AG-/ to shake someone or something. /MANG-:-EN/ to shake.

WAIG, n. brook, creek, rivulet.

WAK, n. crow.   --var. (dial.) UWWAK.

WAKAS, v. /MANGI-:I-/ or /MANG-:-EN/ to get rid of, free oneself of, finish off satisfactorily. Kayat ko kuma nga iwakas amin nga utang ko sakbay ti ipapanaw mi. I would like if possible to get rid of all my debts before our departure. /MANG-/ to clear up as the weather after a storm. Nangwakas met laeng ti langit. The sky finally cleared up.

WAKAWAK, v. /MANG-:-AN/ to sprinkle with dust or powder. /MANGI-:I-/ to sprinkle (dust or powder) on something.

WAKRAY, v. /MANG-:-EN/ to let loose, dishevel (hair). adj. loose, disheveled: said of hair.

WAKSI, v. /AG-/ to stop wearing one's clothes for mourning. /MANGI-:I-/ to rid oneself of (sorrow, worries, etc.).

WALANG, adj. loose, astray. Adu ti walang nga baboy ken aso dagiti karruba da. Their neighbors have many loose pigs and dogs.

v. /AG-/ to wander, be wayward, be loose.   /MAI-/
to be abandoned, forsaken.

WALANGWALANG, adj. wandering.

WALAWAL, n. a kind of dibble used to make holes in the
ground especially for fences.
   v. /MANGI-:I-/ to use to make a hole in the ground.

WALI; WALIWALI, v. /AG-/ to wobble: said of a tooth or
a post.   /MANG-:-EN/ to cause (a tooth or a post) to
wobble.

WALIN, v. /MANGI-:I-/ to push aside or out of one's
way.

WALLAGES, v. /MANGI-:I-/ to throw aside.

WALO, num. eight; 8.   --syn. OTSO.

WANAS, v. /MANG-:-EN/ to do from the beginning to the
end.   /MA-/ to finish doing from the beginning to
the end.

WANAWAN, v. /MANG-:-AN/ to watch for, focus one's
attention upon.

WANGAWANGAN, n. mouth of a river, a cave, a hole, etc.

WANG-IL, v. /AG-/ to shake one's head: said of animals.

WANGWANG, n. abyss, chasm, gulf.

WARA, v. /AGI-, MANGI-:I-/ to scatter, strew. Sino ti
nangiwawa kadagitoy luplupot ditoy? Who strewed these
clothes here?   /MANG-:-EN/ 1. to loosen, untie. Saan
mo nga waraen dayta buok mo. Don't loosen your hair.
2. to disassemble, dismantle, take apart.

   WARAWARA, adj. /NA-/ dishevelled, tousled: said of
   the hair.

WARAGWAG, v. /MANG-:-AN/ to sprinkle with salt, powder,
etc.   /MANGI-:I-/ to sprinkle on.

WARAKIWAK, v. /AGI-, MANGI-:I-/ to strew (on something).
/MANG-:-AN/ to strew (something) on.

WARAKWAK, adj. /NA-/ spongy, elastic and porous.

WARAS, v. /MANGI-:I-/ to distribute, spread out, allot (some things, one's eyes, mind, etc.).

WARASIWIS, v. /MANGI-:I-/ to sprinkle as water.

WARIS, v. /AG-/ to be scattered around. /AGI-, MANGI-: I-/ to scatter around, strew.

WARNAK, v. /AGI-, MANGI-:I-/ to publish, divulge, make known.

WARNAKAN, n. newspaper. --syn. DIARYO.

AGIWARWARNAK, n. newspaperman, newspaper reporter. --syn. PERIODISTA.

WARRAGAWAG, v. /MANGI-:I-/ to disseminate, proclaim, publish. /MAI-/ to be disseminated, proclaimed, published.

WARSI, v. /AG-:-AN/ to sprinkle (with water or any other liquid). /MANGI-:I-/ to shake off with force.

WARWAR, v. /MANG-:-EN/ to unbind, untie, unfasten. /MA-/ to be unbound, untied, unfastened. Nawarwar ti tali ti sapatos ko. The lace of my shoes was unfastened.

WAS, v. /MA-/ to withdraw from, back out of, retract.

WASANG, v. /AG-/ to writhe as when in pain, to squirm as when uneasy, worried, impatient, etc.

WASAWAS, v. /MANGI-:I-/ to brandish, to wave or shake around, as a sword.

WASAY, n. ax.
    v. /AG-/ to hit someone with an ax. /MANG-:-EN/ to hit (someone) with an ax.

WASAYWASAY, n. praying mantis.

WASNAY, adj. /NA-/ straight-grained.

WASWAS, v. /MANG-:-EN/ to undo what has been done, to terminate or nullify an agreement. /MA-/ to be undone, to be terminated or discontinued as an agreement.

WATIWAT, adj. /NA-/ extended, prolonged, very long.

WATWAT, v. /MANG-:-EN/ to exercise, train, practice, teach.

WAW, v. /MA-/ to be thirsty, to thirst.

[1]WAWA, v. /MANG-:I-/ to lead someone astray. /MAI-/ to be led astray.

[2]WAWA, v. /AG-/ to blow a rice culm or stem that has been crushed slightly to have a few small slits so as to produce a shrill sound. --see UWAO.

WAWAK, n. supernatural used to frighten children (bogeyman).

WAY, n. rattan.

WAYA, n. time, chance, opportunity. Awan ti wayak nga mapan idiay kasar yo. I have no time to go to your wedding.
adj. /NA-/ wide, spacious, roomy.
v. /MAKA-:MA--AN/ to be able to have the time, chance or opportunity (for doing something): usually used in the negative. Indiak nga mawayaan ti makiay-ayam kenka. I cannot have the time to play with you.

WAYAWAYA, n. freedom, independence, liberty.

SIWAWAYAWYA, adj. free.

WAYANG, adj. /NA-/ spacious, roomy. --syn. LAWA.

WAYAS, v. /AG-/ to stay alone. /MAKA-:MA-/ to be able to do alone or by one's self. Makawayas ka met las nga mapan idiay Manilan? Can you go to Manila by yourself now?

WAYAT, v. /MANGI-:I-/ to begin, set about.

WAYWAY, n. a long rope usually fastened to a stake at one end and to whose other end an animal may be tied. This rope is normally used to pasture animals.
v. /AGI-, MANGI-:I-/ to pasture (as an animal) by tying to a long rope (WAYWAY) which is tied to a stake, a tree, etc. /MANG-:-AN/ to slacken, let out, give more (rope).

WEGWEG, v. /MANG-:-EN/ to jolt.   /MA-/ to be jolted.

WELWEL, v. /MANGI-:I-/ to drive (a stake) into the ground and wriggle (it) in order to make a hole.

WEN, adv. 1. yes. Wen, mapanak. Yes, I'm going. 2. indeed. Nangina wen daytoy. This is indeed expensive.

WENNO, conj. or.

WENGWENG, v. /AG-/ to have a buzzing sound: said of the ear.

WERWER, v. /AG-/ to produce a sound like that of a sewing machine.

WESWES, v. /-UM-/ to produce a sound like that of bats flying around, or of people passing or running along.

WETWET, adj. /NA-/ tight as a door, drawer, etc.

WIDAWID, v. /AG-/ to swing the arms as when walking. /MANGI-:I-/ to swing (the arms).

SIWIWIDAWID, adj. empty-handed.

WINGIWING, v. /AG-/ to shake one's head as a sign of dissent.

WITIWIT, n. the handle of a plow.

[1]Y-, var. of [1,2]I- before a vowel.   --see [1]IY-.

[2]Y- (+ R2), var. of [3]I- (+ R2) before a vowel.   --see [2]IY- (+ R2).

YAAY, var. of IYAAY.

YABYAB, v. /MANG-:-AN/ to fan (a fire, wheat, rice, etc.).

YADI, adj. /NA-/ 1. grown (as rice). 2. seasoned (as BUGGOONG).

YAGYAG, v. /MANG-:-AN/ to shout at, yell at.   --syn. BUGKAW.

YAKAYAK, n. a shallow basket with meshes through which rice bran and small particles of rice are passed to separate them from the polished rice; a basket used as a seive. --var. YUKUYOK.
   v. /MANG-:-EN/ to seive, sift.

YAMAN, v. /AG-/ to be thankful, grateful; to give thanks. Agyamanak. I am thankful.

   YAMAN PAY, thanks. Yaman pay ta adda ka nga tumulong kanyak. Thanks that you are here to help me.

YAMYAM, v. /-UM-/ to spread: said of fire.

YAN, n. place, location, position.
   v. /AG-/ [= prp. AGGIGYAN, ptp. NAGGIGYAN] 1. to stay or remain (in a place). Agyan ka dita. Stay there. /-UM-/ to spend the night or lodge temporarily (in a place). Umyan ka idiay balay mi intono piesta. You spend the night at our house during the feast.

   NAGYAN, n. content, substance.

YANTA, var. of YANTANGAY.

YANTANGAY, conj. whereas, while. --var. YANTA, ANTA.

YANGYANG, adj. /NA-/ clear, bright.

YARDA [f. Sp.], n. yard.

YAWYAW, v. /MA-/ 1. to be frustrated. 2. to be lost due to constant borrowing by many people.

YEG, v. /MANGI-:I-/ [= MANGIYEG or MANGYEG:IYEG or YEG] to take or bring to, to give to (someone).

YEGYEG, v. /AG-/ to tremble, shiver, shudder. /MANG: -EN/ to shake.

YEKYEK, v. /-EN/ to cough constantly.

YELO [yɛlo; f. Sp.], n. ice.

YENGYENG, v. /MA-/ to be troubled, disturbed, bothered, confused.

YERO [yɛro; f. Sp.], n. galvanized iron sheet.   --syn. SIM. Yero ti atep ti balay da. The roof of their house is made of galvanized iron sheets.

[1]YO, pron. by you (pl.), you (pl.) (as actor): the agent of DAKAYO.

[2]YO, pron. your (pl.): the enclitic possessive of DAKAYO.

[3]YO, n. shark.

YOT, var. of IYOT.

YOYO [f. Sp.], n. yoyo.
    v. /AG-/ to play with a yoyo.

-YSA, var. of MAYSA, one: used only with certain prefixes. SAGGAYSA, one each; KAYKAYSA, only one, sole.

YUBYUB, v. /-UM-/ to produce a sound like that of the bellows.

YUDYUD, v. /AG-/ to sag, droop.

YUGYUG, v. /MANG-:-EN/ to beat (an egg or any mixture).

YUKUYOK, var. of YAKAYAK.

YUNGAYONG, v. /AG-/ to jut out, protrude.

YUYEM, adj. /NA-/ overcast, cloudy, gloomy.   --syn. KUYEMYEM.

YUYENG, n. abyss, chasm, gulf.